1989

Samuel Richardson

Samuel Richardson

TERCENTENARY ESSAYS

Edited by

Margaret Anne Doody
Professor of English, Princeton University

and

Peter Sabor
Professor of English, Queen's University, Ontario

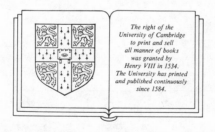

The right of the University of Cambridge to print and sell all manner of books was granted by Henry VIII in 1534. The University has printed and published continuously since 1584.

CAMBRIDGE UNIVERSITY PRESS

Cambridge

New York   New Rochelle

Melbourne   Sydney

Published by the Press Syndicate of the University of Cambridge
The Pitt Building, Trumpington Street, Cambridge CB2 1RP
32 East 57th Street, New York, NY 10022, USA
10 Stamford Road, Oakleigh, Melbourne 3166, Australia

First published 1989

Printed in Great Britain at
the University Press, Cambridge

British Library cataloguing in publication data

Samuel Richardson: tercentenary essays.
1. Fiction in English. Richardson, Samuel
Critical studies
I. Doody, Margaret
II. Sabor, Peter
823'.6

Library of Congress cataloguing in publication data

Samuel Richardson: tercentenary essays/edited by
Margaret Anne Doody and Peter Sabor.
p.   cm.
ISBN 0-521-35383-1
1. Richardson, Samuel, 1689–1761 – Criticism and interpretation.
I. Doody, Margaret Anne.
II. Sabor, Peter.
PR3667.S27   1989
823'.6 – dc19   88-37621   CIP

ISBN 0 521 35383 1

Contents

Illustrations

Contributors

JANET E. AIKINS, Associate Professor of English at the University of New Hampshire, has published several articles on Richardson, as well as on Swift, Defoe, and Rowe, and has edited Samuel Derrick's *The Dramatic Censor*.

GILLIAN BEER, Reader in Literature and Narrative at the University of Cambridge, is author of *Darwin's Plots*, of numerous studies of eighteenth- and nineteenth-century writers, and of a much-cited essay on Richardson and Milton.

EDWARD COPELAND, Professor of English at Pomona College, California, has written on Richardson, Jane Austen, and the eighteenth-century novel.

MARGARET ANNE DOODY, Professor of English at Princeton University, is author of *A Natural Passion: A Study of the Novels of Samuel Richardson* and of several essays on Richardson, as well as books on Augustan poetry and on Frances Burney. She has also published two novels.

JOHN A. DUSSINGER, Professor of English at the University of Illinois, is author of *The Discourse of the Mind in Eighteenth-Century Fiction*, articles on Richardson and other eighteenth-century writers, and a forthcoming book on Jane Austen.

CAROL HOULIHAN FLYNN, Associate Professor of English at Tufts University, Boston, is author of *Samuel Richardson: A Man of Letters* and of a forthcoming book on the body in literature, as well as of a detective novel.

ISOBEL GRUNDY, Reader in English at Queen Mary College, London, is author of *Samuel Johnson and the Scale of Greatness*, and has written on Pope, Fielding, Lady Mary Wortley Montagu, and other women writers. She has been working on *A Feminist Companion to Literature in English*, a jointly compiled reference book on women's writing.

JOCELYN HARRIS, Associate Professor of English at the University of Otago, New Zealand, has edited *Sir Charles Grandison*. Her monograph on Richardson is among the most recent books on the novelist, and her *Jane Austen's Art of Memory* is in press.

TOM KEYMER, Research Fellow at Emmanuel College, Cambridge, has recently completed a doctoral dissertation on letter-narration, casuistry, and the reader's role in Richardson's novels.

SIOBHÁN KILFEATHER, Assistant Professor of English at Columbia University, has recently completed a doctoral dissertation on Irish women writers from the late seventeenth to the early nineteenth century.

DAVID ROBINSON is a graduate student in dance at the Tisch School of the Arts in New York. He has a particular interest in gender roles and sexuality in literature.

PAT ROGERS, DeBartolo Professor in the Liberal Arts at the University of South Florida, is author of some dozen books on and editions of eighteenth-century writers, including Pope, Swift, Defoe, Fielding, and Johnson, as well as several articles on Richardson.

PETER SABOR, Professor of English at Queen's University, Ontario, has written extensively on Richardson, edited *Pamela* and other eighteenth-century novels, and is author of two books on Horace Walpole.

FLORIAN STUBER, Assistant Professor of English at the Fashion Institute of Technology, New York, is author of several articles and a forthcoming book on Richardson. With Margaret Doody he is working on a dramatization of *Clarissa*, part one of which was produced in New York in 1984.

JAMES GRANTHAM TURNER, Associate Professor of English at the University of Michigan, is author of *The Politics of Landscape: Rural Scenery and Society in English Poetry 1630–1660*, of *One Flesh: Paradisal Marriage and Sexual Relations in the Age of Milton*, and of numerous articles on seventeenth- and eighteenth-century topics. He is currently completing a study of libertinism and the representation of sexuality.

Acknowledgements

In a work so celebratory in nature it is pleasant to have the opportunity to celebrate those who have helped to make it happen. We are of course extremely grateful to all the contributors, without whom this book would not exist; we have enjoyed the insights and ideas we have received in reading their essays. We are both very glad to take this opportunity to thank our two Cambridge editors, Andrew Brown and Kevin Taylor. Andrew Brown encouraged the work in its planning stages, and Kevin Taylor has seen it through with devoted attention. We appreciate both the cool eye he has been able to cast upon work in progress and the warm enthusiasm which helped us through rough spots. We are also most grateful to our meticulous subeditor at Cambridge, Caroline Drake.

Special thanks should be offered to Mark Kinkead-Weekes, for encouragement in the early stages and for putting us in touch with Tom Keymer. Tom has not only contributed an outstanding essay but has also been of immense help in assisting us to realize the design of the book; we very much appreciate his allowing us to use photographs of printer's ornaments taken from works printed by Richardson in his possession.

Both of us wish to express appreciation of our own universities (Princeton University and Queen's University) and of our separate English Departments for various forms of assistance, material and psychological. Margaret Anne Doody wishes to express particular thanks to Princeton University for the grant that allowed her to come to England in the summer of 1987, not only to complete her research for her own essay in the Victoria and Albert Museum but also to get in touch with contributors in Britain. We are also indebted to the librarians of the Bodleian Library, the British Library, the Victoria and Albert Museum Library, the Firestone Library of Princeton University, and Queen's University Library, for their assistance.

We should like to offer our personal thanks to the following individuals for their interest in and help with the project: Paula Backscheider, Lindy Jordan, Richard Kroll, Marie Legroulx, F. P. Lock, Robert Mack, Thomas P. Roche Jr, and Emmi Sabor.

MARGARET ANNE DOODY

PETER SABOR

Chronology

Note on texts

In the absence of a standard modern edition of Richardson's works, references in this volume are to the best available text in each case, as follows:

Pamela, the Riverside edition, ed. T. C. Duncan Eaves and Ben D. Kimpel (Boston: Houghton Mifflin, 1971), based on the first edition text.

Pamela, Part II, the Shakespeare Head edition, 2 vols. (Oxford: Basil Blackwell, 1929).

Clarissa, the third edition of 1751, 8 vols. For convenience, the corresponding volume and page of the inaccurate but widely available Everyman edition, 4 vols. (London: Dent, 1962) are also cited, in italics.

Sir Charles Grandison, ed. Jocelyn Harris, 3 vols. (London: Oxford University Press, 1972), based on the first edition text.

Selected Letters of Samuel Richardson, ed. John Carroll (Oxford: Clarendon Press, 1964).

The Correspondence of Samuel Richardson, ed. Anna Laetitia Barbauld, 6 vols. (London: R. Phillips, 1804). This inaccurate edition is cited only when a letter is not in *Selected Letters*.

Secondary works

The following frequently cited works will be referred to throughout the text by their short titles:

Castle, *Clarissa's Ciphers*
Terry Castle, *Clarissa's Ciphers: Meaning and Disruption in Richardson's 'Clarissa'* (Ithaca, NY: Cornell University Press, 1982)

Doody, *A Natural Passion*
Margaret Anne Doody, *A Natural Passion: A Study of the Novels of Samuel Richardson* (Oxford: Clarendon Press, 1974)

Eagleton, *The Rape of Clarissa*
Terry Eagleton, *The Rape of Clarissa: Writing, Sexuality and Class Struggle in Samuel Richardson* (Oxford: Basil Blackwell, 1982)

Eaves and Kimpel, *Biography*
T. C. Duncan Eaves and Ben D. Kimpel, *Samuel Richardson: A Biography* (Oxford: Clarendon Press, 1971)

Flynn, *Man of Letters*
Carol Houlihan Flynn, *Samuel Richardson: A Man of Letters* (Princeton: Princeton University Press, 1982)

Kinkead-Weekes, *Dramatic Novelist*
Mark Kinkead-Weekes, *Samuel Richardson: Dramatic Novelist* (Ithaca, NY: Cornell University Press, 1973)

Myer, ed., *Passion and Prudence*
Valerie Grosvenor Myer, ed., *Samuel Richardson: Passion and Prudence* (London: Vision Press, 1986)

Sale, *Master Printer*

William Merritt Sale, Jr, *Samuel Richardson: Master Printer* (Ithaca: Cornell University Press, 1950)

Warner, *Reading Clarissa*

William Beatty Warner, *Reading Clarissa: The Struggles of Interpretation* (New Haven: Yale University Press, 1979)

Watt, *The Rise of the Novel*

Ian Watt, *The Rise of the Novel: Studies in Defoe, Richardson and Fielding* (Berkeley: University of California Press, 1957)

Introduction

MARGARET ANNE DOODY AND PETER SABOR

This volume of essays commemorates the tercentenary of Samuel Richardson's birth in 1689. Richardson was born in Mackworth, Derbyshire, where he was baptized in August 1689; biographers have surmised that he was born on 31 July, but his birthday may well have been the one he gave to his heroine Clarissa: 24 July. Richardson was to die in the same month, on 4 July 1761, in the London which was always his true home. To be born in 1689 was to be born in a decade of revolutions and into a Revolution in progress. Richardson connected his father's removal to Derbyshire with the fate of the Duke of Monmouth after the failure of the Monmouth Rebellion of 1685, and the novelist was born just after the 'Glorious Revolution' of 1688. In 1689 a new Revolution settlement was being drawn up, a somewhat precarious new constitution. The new Whig England was involved in wars of colonial expansion throughout Richardson's life; the decade in which he entered his apprenticeship and the last decade of his life were alike marked by great wars against France. Throughout Richardson's mature life there were constant dangers of internal political convulsions, including two Jacobite rebellions. The triumph of the Whigs after the death of Queen Anne in 1714 meant unremitting suspicion of Tory opposition, and occasional aggressive moves on the part of the government, which wanted to keep political comment and protest well in check. Old barbarity had not yet yielded to new gentility, as was shown in ugly events such as the brutal execution of the Jacobite Archibald Cameron in June 1753. The world in which Richardson lived was expanding and prosperous but neither peaceful nor peaceable, and in his profession he was well aware of the currents of opinion and action. Despite his father's assumed sympathies with Monmouth, the mature Richardson seems to have been a Tory, like his close friend Samuel Johnson.

The year 1689 marks Richardson's birth, making him a child of the seventeenth century, and of revolution. The year 1740 marks Richardson's birth as a novelist. There is another date of almost equal significance in his life. In 1721 Richardson became an independent printer. Previously he had completed his printing apprenticeship and become a freeman of the Stationers' Company; the Company's high opinion of him can be seen by his subsequent election to various offices. A small legacy from Elizabeth Leake, widow of a printer with whose family he was closely associated, allowed him to set up his own business. In the same year he married Martha Wilde, daughter of his former employer.[1]

In the 1720s Richardson established a reputation as an outstanding printer, one who could be entrusted with large projects, who could understand argument, information and reference, and could supply editorial material. Most important of all, he printed what he chose and could not be intimidated.

In 1722 people whom Richardson knew, including the Duke of Wharton, were arrested and tried for treason. Samuel Richardson, a beginner in business, a young man with his way to make and no rich or influential family to pick him up if he fell down, had reason to bow to the rich and the powerful and keep out of trouble. It should, however, be recognized that Richardson, in his early thirties, with a new family and a great deal to lose, did not take the prudent course. He bravely printed works by a number of Tory authors during the 1720s, and was named to the Secretary of State as one of the 'High Flyers'. Richardson printed the Duke of Wharton's opposition paper, *The True Briton*; it has even been alleged since that he wrote one of the numbers. Thomas Payne, the bookseller associated with this venture, was arrested in June 1723. Richardson was one of those who offered bail for Payne, as he did again in 1724 when Payne was arrested and tried for seditious libel. Payne was sentenced to a fine and a year's imprisonment. Richardson saw then how those in power could treat those who dared to speak out. Yet he still went on working for the Tories; he was one of the printers of the Tory journal *Mist's Weekly Journal*, which got into trouble in 1728; Edmund Curll curried favour with the government by naming Richardson as one of the printers. Richardson escaped arrest, and did not have his press broken as Mist did. Yet he cannot have been at all certain during the 1720s that he would escape serious trouble. He courted danger. If Richardson had been the prudent and placid person that his later antagonists have wished to represent, then he would not have set himself and his new livelihood and his hopes so much at risk for a cause.

There is no reason to believe that Richardson ever went back on the beliefs he had held when he was a 'High Flyer' and something of a Tory firebrand. He refers in his later works to Tory writers he had published earlier. His friend Arthur Onslow, Speaker of the House of Commons, said that he could have obtained for Richardson some 'station at court' had the printer desired it. But Richardson did not. He never manifested any interest in fostering the affections and begging the favour of the Hanoverian monarch or any of the great Whig lords.

Richardson's political attitudes – political in the largest sense – seem closely related to the views and feelings of the central characters in his novels. These characters, most of them women, rebel in some way, and it is when they rebel that they are most interesting and most complex. The author has very little patience with toadies and time-servers, and is particularly severe upon time-serving clergymen such as Brand in *Clarissa*, who care only for their own advancement and will not respond to the needs of human beings who are powerless, without gifts to give. Such clergymen have betrayed a sacred trust; they have misunderstood and perverted and betrayed the Word. Richardson values the Word of God, and also all words truly uttered that try to explore and define human reality. His characters are on a quest for the Word through words. Evil in Richardson's novels is felt in the choking-off of words; it is evil to endeavour to suppress another's utterance, or to control or censor it. To have one's words cut off, suppressed, forged or otherwise meddled with is a terible injury.

Richardson is thus at some very deep level the same as printer and as novelist. He had known the fear of censorship and brutal suppression in watching the unjust power wielded by Walpole against the printing press. And Richardson at the time would not countenance that or stand tamely by, even though he was a young man who stood to lose all he had in the world. Richardson's work as a printer meant that he was on an important crossroads of communication, the Enlightenment's network of exchange of information and ideas. He believed – as writers and printers both must do – that words have the power to make change. History is always being rewritten, as Enlightenment scholars knew – rewritten, amplified, reconsidered, interpreted, and annotated. Richardson's characters are all authors, all engaged in the never-ending business of publishing the word. Richardson's life as a printer was not a sideline of his existence, but something important at the core of his life.

As a reminder of the subject's other complementary profession, this volume is itself embellished with some of the printer's ornaments used by Richardson at his press.[2] We have brought into our volume the glowing sun that illuminates *Clarissa*, and the little 'Rape of Europa' that appears at the end of Volume IV (3rd edition) of that novel, and thus visibly unites old myth with his new myth. We also include the graceful basket of fruit, signifying the abundance, the plenitude, Richardson has to offer.

During the last two decades critics have done justice to this plenitude, yet only twenty years ago Richardson's reputation was still much less secure. In 1969, two collections of essays on Richardson were published: John Carroll's *Samuel Richardson: A Collection of Critical Essays* and Rosemary Cowler's *Twentieth-Century Interpretations of Pamela*. Each reprinted articles and excerpts from books on Richardson of the 1950s and 1960s, prefaced by an introductory essay. But in both introductory essays there were signs of editorial disquiet. Carroll concluded that 'despite the increasing number of books and articles on Richardson in the past several years, he is still in need of "candid reexamination"'. Cowler, more urgently, regretted that *Pamela* 'has been as badly abused in reading and study as its heroine in her adventures'; 'critical guidance' was needed to direct readers 'to a better understanding and appreciation of a flawed but valuable work'.[3]

In the twenty years since these collections were published, such 'critical guidance' to Richardson has appeared in abundance: some thirty full-length studies, together with hundreds of articles, chapters in books, doctoral dissertations and master's theses. Panels on Richardson have become an established, and often highly animated, feature of conferences on the eighteenth century. In her essay on 'The rise of Richardson criticism' at the conclusion of this volume, Siobhán Kilfeather examines the major concerns and methodologies of recent Richardson criticism, while acknowledging that any such survey can take account of only a fraction of the whole. Kilfeather writes of the 'revolution in attitudes to the representation of women' that has transformed the nature of Richardson criticism. Her response to Dorothy Van Ghent's disdain for the 'singularly thin and unrewarding plot' of *Clarissa*, the 'deflowering of a young lady', is one of several examples of feminist revisionism in this volume. Florian Stuber counters Ian Watt's characterization of *Pamela* as a 'mixture of sermon and striptease'; David Robinson considers the subversive potential of male, as well as female, friendship in Richardson's novels; and Isobel Grundy reassesses the achievement of women writers influenced by and reacting against Richardson's example. A dissenting voice is that of Carol Houlihan Flynn, for whom Richardson's exaltation of women is suspect, exacting female restraint and submissiveness as the price of male applause. That Richardson's role as a 'champion and protector' (Margaret Collier's phrase)[4] of women is now coming into question is itself a sign of the growing maturity of Richardson criticism: both Flynn and Grundy pose cogent objections to Richardson's ideology, without feeling impelled to belittle his art.

There is, as yet, no standard scholarly edition of Richardson's writings, but accurate editions of Richardson's three novels are now available in annotated, inexpensive paperback editions. In the case of *Pamela* readers have access to the text of both the first edition of 1740 and the entirely rewritten final version first published only in 1801.[5] Thanks to the recent publication of the first edition text of *Clarissa*, edited by Angus Ross, George Sherburn's appalling abridgement, which traduces almost everything *Clarissa* has to offer, will surely at last be laid to rest.[6] And now that Jocelyn Harris's edition of *Sir Charles Grandison* has appeared in paperback, making Richardson's final novel widely available for the first time, students can begin to explore this long-neglected but astonishingly rich and influential work.[7]

As Florian Stuber notes in the essay on *Pamela* that opens this volume, some of the old critical condescension towards Richardson lingers on. But such condescension, with its patronizing, class-bound distrust of the 'bourgeois printer', the 'self-righteous moralist', the 'unconscious genius', has come to seem distinctly dated. Stuber's students at a New York City technical college, in contrast, bring an engagingly fresh and open approach to Richardson. As our concept of the literary canon expands to include previously neglected kinds of writing, Richardson begins to stand out as a central figure. Pat Rogers concludes his essay here on the dynamics of the mid-eighteenth-century world of letters by placing Richardson at its centre, contending that 'the age of Johnson had its roots in the age of Richardson'.

The contributors to this volume are united not only in their admiration for Richardson's art but also in their desire to relate his achievement to that of other writers. Many of the essays range widely in English and other literatures, seeking points of comparison to explicate Richardson's novels. Gillian Beer studies *Pamela* as a response to and a reappraisal of Sidney's depiction of the social order in *Arcadia*. James Grantham Turner, who places *Clarissa* in the European as well as the English libertine tradition, begins with a quotation from Molière's *Dom Juan* and ends with Mozart's *Don Giovanni*. Tom Keymer shows that the Bible is as important for *Clarissa* as for Clarissa: just as Clarissa's Meditations provide 'patterns of authority, conduct and language' for her life, these biblical texts furnish exemplary patterns for Richardson's novel. Margaret Anne Doody discusses Richardson's exploration of identity and character in *Sir Charles Grandison* in the light of seventeenth- and eighteenth-century psychological treatises, such as those of Locke, Hume, and Adam Smith. Carol Houlihan Flynn sets Richardson's demands in *Sir Charles Grandison* for female compliance against those of Defoe in his *Family Instructor*. Isobel Grundy examines Richardson's twofold influence on late eighteenth-century women novelists, as a 'teacher to be imitated and a father to be challenged', and Jocelyn Harris, demonstrating the remarkable breadth and depth of Richardson's own reading, argues that he, like all great artists, needed other works to create his works. Harris's apt concluding quotation from Hester Lynch Piozzi, who remarked that Richardson's memory 'fermented all that fell into it, and made a new creation from the fertility of its own rich mind', shows that intertextuality was appreciated by eighteenth-century readers, as well as practised by its authors.

In addition to exploring Richardson's links with other writers, many of the essays in this volume trace connections among his own works. David Robinson throws new light on Sir Charles Grandison's fervent friendship with Jeronymo della Porretta through a contrast with Lovelace's more conventional rake's companionship with Belford and Mr B.'s negligible male friendships in *Pamela*. John Dussinger draws on Richardson's *Collection of . . . Moral and Instructive Sentiments* in his analysis of *Clarissa*, noting its capacity for broadening the novel's significance 'and even changing its direction altogether'. In his essay on *Clarissa*, Tom Keymer turns to Richardson's *Meditations Collected from the Sacred Books* (printed in 1749 but never published). Ostensibly the heroine's own compilation, and hence Clarissa's *Clarissa*, this remarkable piece has an intriguing relationship with the parent text, and should be better known to readers of Richardson's novel. Keymer is also one of several contributors to this volume to make substantial use of Richardson's published and unpublished correspondence. Margaret Anne Doody examines letters written shortly before the publication of *Sir Charles Grandison* which reveal Richardson's preoccupations in composing the novel, while Carol Houlihan Flynn compares the fictive exchanges of letters in *Grandison* with Richardson's correspondence with Sarah Westcomb. Pat Rogers draws on Richardson's correspondence with Edward Young and others, and on Young's letters to a variety of correspondents. In his essay on the publishing history of Richardson's correspondence, Peter Sabor observes that hundreds of letters are still unpublished, despite their obvious importance; a collected edition is needed to make this virtually inaccessible material more widely available.

Two of the essays in this volume are concerned with the relationship between Richardson and the art world of his day. Edward Copeland writes on *Clarissa* in the context of depictions of eighteenth-century London by artists such as Hogarth and Samuel Scott, showing that the novel is filled with the teeming city life that fascinated and horrified contemporary painters. Janet Aikins explores the strongly visual elements in each of Richardson's novels, comparing his 'speaking pictures' with the engravings and paintings by Hubert Gravelot, Francis Hayman, and Joseph Highmore that illustrated his works.

The three-hundredth birthday of an author is a festive, solemn, and absurd occasion. Absurd, because the subject is beyond any of our happy returns. Solemn, because there is a certain sublimity in the long endurance of one person's words, and we participate in the grandeur that we contemplate. Human dignity is reaffirmed in our articulated consciousness of contact with the precious life-blood of a master spirit, bound up to a life beyond life. The vampirish element in Milton's image – as well as the pomposity that lurks within the solemnity – can be subsumed in festivity, as we recognize the pleasure that our author has afforded us. This tercentenary volume of essays is offered with festive appreciation for Samuel Richardson.

Teaching *Pamela*

FLORIAN STUBER

'This book is far ahead of its time. Here I am in the 1980s reading the same book they read 200 years ago. It's funny that the book still holds an audience's interest after all that time. That is definitely a sign of a true classic.' 'It amazes me how contemporary this book seems, the plot and the morals. I always thought the people of the 1700s to be extremely backward. I never realized how times back then are similar to the times now.' 'The book was written centuries ago and yet you find in it problems in our society, actual problems that are caused by money and poverty, by differences in color and so many other things.' 'It's funny, but morals these days really haven't changed all that much. A woman's value of herself gains respect from others. It still holds true today.' 'This book is such an up – I wish it were a movie!'

These comments, some may be surprised to learn, were written in 1985 by young women who had been reading Samuel Richardson's *Pamela*, a novel many find hard to teach because they say it is dated, too serious, so morally fatuous. For my students, *Pamela* was, on the contrary, fresh, vital, morally relevant, and, in its essence, a very happy book. At any rate, for five years it afforded me the happiest experiences of my teaching career. Semester after semester, students formed groups to read the book aloud, recommended it to friends, and told me that *Pamela* was the best book they had ever read. No other work of literature I have taught has infected students with such enthusiasm, even to the celebration of fictional events.[1]

This re-created *Pamela*-mania took place in the heart of Manhattan, at the Fashion Institute of Technology, a college for business and design, where I have been teaching English for over ten years. FIT is part of the State University of New York, the only branch which offers no major in any of the liberal arts. While some students continue into the upper division to earn a BS or BFA degree, most graduate after two years with an AAS. Of the graduates, ninety-seven per cent are placed in entry-level jobs within the fashion and

related industries. Yet to avoid an overly specialized and narrow professional-
ism among its students, FIT has a strong commitment to the liberal arts,
twenty-four credits of which are required before the AAS can be granted.

The great majority of FIT students are women; fewer than a fifth are men.
In their first year, they tend to be slightly older than most college students –
between the ages of nineteen and twenty-two. Only one of every five
applicants is accepted, and for eighty-nine per cent of them, FIT is their first
choice of college. These highly motivated students have concrete goals and
specific vocations. They wish to become, they *do* become, buyers for stores,
creators of textiles, fashion designers, and illustrators. They are visually
rather than verbally gifted; indeed, for one whose training leads him to equate
verbal facility with intelligence, it has been humbling to work with them. It has
been challenging and satisfying to try to teach students so imaginatively
sophisticated about line and colour to be equally playful and imaginative with
words.

Gifted as these FIT students are, English is not their favourite subject, and
few are enthusiastic about EN 121, the Composition course, which is
required. The English Department at FIT believes that writing and reading
go together, and each instructor of Composition must assign a novel of his or
her choice to be read in the course. It was in this course on Composition that I
decided some years ago to teach *Pamela*.

I thought then, and I am more sure now, that *Pamela* was in many ways a
perfect choice for FIT students and the purposes of the course. Since they
were students with vocations, many living away from home for the first time, I
thought they might recognize themselves in Pamela, a working woman away
from her parents, a woman who had become 'a little expert at [her] Needle'
(p. 25), and who, like many of them, both designed and made her own clothes.
I thought that Pamela's situation at the opening of the novel would immediately interest women who planned to enter the business world, who would
have to face the possibility of sexual harassment on the job; I thought, too, that
they would appreciate the chance to discuss seriously the issues of love,
marriage, and family raised in the rest of the book since their professional
goals did not preclude these more personal hopes. Finally, since this was a
course in Composition, I thought it good to present my students with a model
of a woman who was a writer, who took pleasure and pride in writing, who
wrote at length and who wrote well, and whose writing had real effects on
people in her world and outside it.[2]

And I must admit that, as a Richardsonian, I had an ulterior purpose in
mind. The first time I taught *Pamela* at FIT, I did so as an experiment. I
wanted to find out how truly innocent readers, coming to the novel with no
preconceptions, would really react to the book. I wanted to test our prevailing

critical assumptions about the novel and its appeal. I wanted to see whether these readers would raise the objections that have been voiced since the publication of *Shamela*, objections which have now solidified into a body of critical doctrine officially promoted in reference works and literary handbooks. I wondered whether my students' experience of *Pamela* would force me to agree with the assessment of R. F. Brissenden in an essay meant to be a standard introduction to Richardson for many years to come: 'In recent years the critical estimate of his novels has begun to rise again, but there are still many who would claim that Richardson's importance is mainly historical. It is understandable that this is so, for his faults, both as a novelist and as a man, are obvious and unpleasant.'[3] Would my students find *Pamela* 'insupportably prolix'? Would they be offended by 'the vein of prurience, hypocrisy, and sheer vulgarity that in varying degrees runs through everything he wrote' and determine that 'in *Pamela* ... its effect is extremely damaging'?[4] I wondered how young women would react to the 'mixture of sermon and striptease' Ian Watt had declared *Pamela* to be,[5] the 'puritan striptease' as Maximillian Novak more recently called it.[6]

For a long time, I had been bothered by the condescending and denigrating language used in so much that has been written about Richardson and, particularly, *Pamela*. In teaching the novel at FIT, I hoped to discover how necessary the apologetic, defensive, and even hysterical tone of such criticism was. In her Introduction to *Twentieth-Century Interpretations of Pamela*, for example, Rosemary Cowler says: 'The new critical perspectives that are so essential for Richardson studies in general are nowhere more desperately needed than for *Pamela*, which has always proved a "provoking" problem novel.'[7] The essays included in her book have had, indeed, a life beyond their time; the widely available and convenient paperback collection seems to establish a critical consensus with which teachers and students of *Pamela* must come to terms. It is not especially helpful for a new reader to learn that the essays are written, as Cowler says, 'by a rather select group of sympathizers who respond with enthusiasm to what is admirable in the novel, but who are also aware of crudities, limitations, and problems', that *Pamela*'s 'psychological and artistic significance is being recognized by discerning readers, but ... the discovery is not an easy one'.[8] If enjoyment must be so hard wrung, even by 'sympathizers', reading *Pamela* seems hardly worth the effort or the energy. In Cowler's collection, as in other essays written since, critics certainly stress what they see as the novel's moral crudities ('Virtue Rewarded'), its technical limitations (first-person narrative), and its thematic and other problems (for example, the conflict between Richardson's imaginative realization of Pamela and his didactic concerns). Amidst faults and flaws apparently so manifest to everyone, whatever is admirable is hard to see, and any appreciation, thus carefully qualified and grudgingly admitted, must seem the result of special pleading. If *Pamela* truly stands in need of all this argument to be enjoyed, perhaps F. R. Leavis was right when he pronounced so many years ago that 'it's no use pretending that Richardson can ever be made a current classic again'.[9] At the end of his book on Richardson, Mark Kinkead-Weekes admits that Richardson will always find 'fit audience though few' – adding in his final sequence, 'But only by the form ...' [sic], as if the content has no appeal.[10] Presumably the foolish little trials of a virginity-mad but 'calculating'[11] servant girl could be of no interest to energetic young men and women. Surely modern young people not aspiring to be part of 'a rather select group' of 'discerning readers' would reject this crude and moralistic novel with contemptuous laughter or blank dismissive boredom. Yet when I first taught *Pamela* at FIT, I was surprised at the result, so surprised that I continued to teach *Pamela* for many years.

Careful scheduling was needed if I were to test these critical assumptions while working to achieve the other goals of a Composition course. I met students twice a week, and the first two classes of the fourteen-week term had to be introductory. Since Pamela herself divides her book into twelve sections – six parts in Volume I and six in Volume II[12] – I decided to give weekly readings to accord with this inherent structure. Reading *Pamela* thus became a semester project, similar to the long-term projects the students pursued in their studio courses; it provided time for the detailed study I hoped for and time to attend to the other requirements of the course. Twelve sections gave me an extra week, so I decided to end the term with a reading of *Shamela*.

To help my students get into a habit of writing, I asked them to keep a journal, in which they were to write freely for twenty minutes each week about their reactions to that week's reading. These journals, I suppose, turned my students into imitation Pamelas, as they then responded at the moment to her writing 'to the moment'. The journals let me spot problems and questions which I could then clarify and answer, and from them, I discerned patterns of reaction, patterns which recurred with surprising consistency semester after semester. It is from journals written during 1985, the last year I taught the course, that I quote my students' reactions to *Pamela*, and I have tried not to quote the same student twice.

In the third class of the semester, the reading of *Pamela* began. I told the students that *Pamela* was the first English novel, the first bestseller, the *Star Wars* of the eighteenth century. Using the Riverside text of the first edition, we looked at Eaves and Kimpel's table of 'The *Pamela* Vogue' (pp. xvii–xxii), and then, impressed by the cultural phenomenon which was *Pamela*, we turned to the first letter. I had asked them beforehand not to even open the book until this class. I did not want them to face the language or the odd look of the words on the page without a guide. Nor did I want them to read any of the introductory material – I wanted them to have no preconceptions about *Pamela* before they read it themselves, nor did I want them prejudiced by the attitudes of any critics.

I read the first letter aloud, up to the Postscript. *Pamela*, after all, had been read aloud when it came out, and I wanted them to hear the modern rhythms of the language, the talkiness of the prose. It was an important example to set, for students later commented in their journals that if they came upon a confusing paragraph, they would read it aloud, and then it suddenly made sense. I believe it was because of this first class that each semester, some students got together to read the book aloud, and in some years had their whole dormitory floor reading *Pamela*. Through question and answer, we discussed the opening situation. We talked of the hierarchy in the household and Pamela's place as the Lady's personal maid. I showed them pictures of an eighteenth-century 'Great House', with its rooms and furniture, its grounds and gardens. Then we analysed the novel's thesis sentence, 'I have great Trouble, and some Comfort, to acquaint you with' (p. 25). If the 'Trouble' was that with the death of the Lady, Pamela was out of a job, the 'Comfort' was that she had been given another place, could stay at the luxurious Great House and not return to poverty, 'to be a Clog upon [her] dear Parents' (p. 25). Like Pamela, my students were very aware of the importance of employment and the chances for social mobility. My students' first impressions of Mr B. were continually unsuspicious. Even after reading the Postscript, while they could understand Pamela's embarrassment at being discovered writing a letter when she should have been working, they generally felt the new Master was, if not 'the best of Gentlemen', as Pamela wrote (p. 26), 'a nice guy'.

The first letter provided information; the second, written by her parents '*In Answer to the preceding*' (p. 27), provoked uproarious laughter. As one student later wrote, 'It's so true that parents take everything that you think is fantastic and twist it around to find all the faults about it, and it really disheartens you. She was so excited in the beginning that he had held her hand twice, and her parents twisted it around to make it seem like it was the worst thing he could ever do.' The students could see immediately that Pamela's parents had read her letter very differently from the way they had, that details they had accepted at face value have been interpreted, and that they were forced to reread Pamela's letter to see what her parents are reacting to. Reading from the parents' point of view, they could see how Pamela's 'Letter was indeed a great Trouble' and little 'Comfort' to Mr and Mrs Andrews (p. 27): 'The parents remind me of my own when it comes to their concern for her with males, so I am pretty much amused by them and their responses to Pamela.

They're just plain ordinary folks who love their kid, so with that realization I can understand them.'

My students enjoy Pamela's answer to her parents' warning letter. They appreciate the fact that she is hurt by her parents' lack of trust in her; but when she asks, 'what could he get by ruining such a poor young Creature as me?' (p. 28), they fear for her naiveté (and then they guess that Pamela must be younger than themselves, reckoning her age, rightly, at fifteen or six-teen).[13] They also enjoy the first example of a characteristic in Pamela they come to like very much – her sauciness, as revealed in her talking back to her parents: 'Sure they can't *all* have Designs against me because they are civil' (p. 28). They leave the class eager to read the next ten letters on their own, hoping to discover whether her parents' suspicions are realized.

Dividing the book into weekly reading assignments emphasized in ways I did not at first anticipate (but later came to depend on) various aspects of Richardson's technique of 'writing to the moment'. Even at the end of just thirteen letters, students felt some major effects: 'So far, I'm really enjoying this book. It's better than expected. I thought it would be a dud because most books that are assigned in English classes are duds.' 'I thought it was going to be very boring . . . It wasn't at all boring . . . Richardson sort of throws you into this maiden's problems.' As they read on, suspense builds: 'I can't wait to sit down and read it. I find it hard not to continue ahead.' 'The more I read, the more I want to read.' *Pamela* involves them, and they become involved because 'you get the feeling you're really reading someone's letters and it is written in a way where it seems everything is happening at that time.' 'It is almost as intimate as letters one hides in the dark recesses of a dresser or closet.' 'I've never read anything similar except for *The Diary of Anne Frank* which I loved. These two books really get the reader into them and under-stand day by day the activities of the characters, their thoughts, and their reactions.' 'Pamela describes things in such detail that I felt I really got to know her. Richardson does a fantastic job of making everything as clear and defined as possible so you can understand and feel exactly what is going on.'

Problems I had expected from the language barrier, the time barrier, simply did not materialize for these twenty-year-old technical students: 'I see Pamela, not only as a character in the eighteenth century, but as a girl today, growing up and having to face problems with sexuality, puberty, love, trust and family loyalty.' 'It's almost as if you, the reader, are going through the action. It's not as if the author is explaining a story that has happened already.' 'It's hard to believe that it's all made up. I feel like they are people I know and that I'm seeing each one of their views on all the problems that have arisen. The funny thing is that once you really feel like you know the characters' next move, they do something entirely different.'

This quality of unpredictability and surprise, characters changing, plotting and scheming, delighted them and kept them in suspense: 'There are so many surprises that it keeps you on edge all the time.' '*Pamela* is a page turner. The characters bounce you around with the change of feelings that they go through.' 'I am beginning to feel as if I am watching a tennis match rather than reading a novel. My support and pity have gone back and forth so many times that for me there is no villain and no victim. I'm almost dizzy deciding whether to side with Pamela's position or her Master's.'

Even students who did not enjoy the confusions and ambiguities, the sudden twists of the opening sections of the novel, revealed in their journals how much they were affected by the technique. The immediacy and openness of the epistolary form led them to address the characters as if they were real people and offer suggestions as to how to behave: 'Pamela, you immature brat, get the hell out of that house or you are just asking for trouble. Brightness is obviously a virtue of hers, but please, Mr Richardson let her use her brain to learn about life!' 'In a way, Pamela's dilemma could be turned into a blessing if only she wasn't so honest. She should blackmail him, continue to receive the gifts and stick close to Mrs Jervis so that he could not seek revenge.' 'When they talked by the pond, she should've suckered him into marrying her. Instead she played her sweet self. To understand my feeling toward her – you would have to be a girl.' 'Mr B., what is his problem? Now he's getting more open – or is it that he's more exasperated? If he loves her so much, why can't he marry? Is he saying he's not ready for marriage, or is he saying he cannot marry Pamela because she is just a servant? I don't understand him.' And from two men: 'He tells her that he cares so much about her but just can't marry her since she is from a lower class. I think this is quite insulting. He wants it both ways. He can fulfill his lust or passion or whatever for her, yet no one will find out about it. What a slob he is. He then asks her opinion. Which, by the way, is pretty damn nervy considering he doesn't even respect her because of her social status, yet he values her opinion. Come on!' 'If I were him and a woman turned me down, I'd say fine, I'll see you later. I'd never pursue the issue. Forget it. It's her loss anyway.'

I came to look forward to and enjoy these explosive judgements. They were proof that the book was affecting my students, almost in spite of themselves. They led me to understand more clearly other aspects of 'writing to the moment', a technique which constantly calls for judgement, and as the action works out, constantly calls those judgements into question. As one of my students pointed out at the end of her journal: 'They have changed and we have changed, and we know we have since all our impressions are written down.' As Richardson himself once said, 'Ye World is not enough used to this way of writing, to the moment ... & judges of an action undecided, as if it were absolutely decided.'[14] Just as no teacher would expect students to be as competent or skilled in the first week of a course as they will be (we hope) at its end, just as we monitor the development of skills and confidence through assignments that come in at different moments of time, seeing a gradual progress even with slips and backtreadings, so the action of *Pamela* takes place, so the relationship between Mr B. and Pamela develops. Through the confusions, the ambiguities, the indeterminacies of situation and character in Volume I, we ultimately reach the clarifications of culminating events in Volume II, climactic moments which make us reread the incidents of the first volume as a progressive development which has made these events both possible and probable.

Pamela's personal progress is a forward movement, in which, through trying situations, aspects of her character are tested and found genuine. Mr B.'s character is both presented and developed differently. I used to think, as many of my students did and as critics such as William M. Sale still do, that B. is 'less clear' than he could be 'since Richardson wrote the novel from Pamela's point of view';[15] we are so much in her mind that B. seems shadowy, his motivations difficult to discern. But the limited point of view did not prevent some male students from reading *Pamela* as B.'s story: 'This excellent novel (which I've told quite a few people they should read) is the most trial and error story of love I've ever read. Having to deal with pride of self and pride of class and love for a lowly servant girl tears the hero apart.' 'Volume I is a very exciting story of a man's love for a woman but not knowing how to handle it the right way.'

I now believe that this putative weakness of Pamela's first-person narrative has a corresponding strength in that it records how one person's character gradually comes to be perceived and understood through another person's eyes. That is, Mr B. becomes a person we understand only as Pamela comes herself to understand him. If Mr B. seems shadowy in Volume I, this cannot be said about him in Volume II, where he is a central presence. As we see more of his behaviour and his words recorded by Pamela in the present, his character achieves fullness and coherence because we also learn more about his past. His affair with Sally Godfrey and his solicitous concern for their illegitimate daughter are facts which force us to reread him. We then see him at the beginning as a character divided; coming into his inheritance, his independence reinforced with the great power of wealth, B., like Pamela, could develop in different ways: he could make Pamela another Sally Godfrey, or he could remember his daughter and treat Pamela more humanely. As one of my students said, 'Throughout Volume I, one thing is very notable and that is the implication of a mutual feeling of Pamela toward the master and the master toward Pamela. This is indicated very often by the trusting and the hoping that he would or indeed had changed. I think it is this hope that has kept the story going – maybe it is not Pamela's hope; rather it is the reader's hope.' That there has been reason for this hope, based on a potentiality of character with roots in B.'s past, is revealed only in the last pages of the novel.

But the narrative does place Pamela in the spotlight, and her character receives the most attention from the students. They respond first to her adolescence: 'It seems as if Pamela is caught in the impossible, insecure, uncertain time of life – somewhere between dolls and diaphragms – so much a little girl and so much a woman.' Many found it 'difficult to believe that a man of fifty has so accurately characterized a girl of sixteen!' 'Even though Pamela is out on her own, and taking care of herself, the girl *is* only fifteen or sixteen. She has not yet learned to think on her own, and her mind is just basically a teenage mess.' 'Pamela is lucky, at least, to have her writing as an outlet – when I was her age, I often wrote poems and stories that sometimes let me live out my dreams, other times served as trial solutions to problems.' Early on, they expect that Pamela's maturing will be a major part of the action.

Some of the most moving passages in my students' journals were meditations on sex and maturity, revealing a profound identification with the heroine's experience which was almost embarrassing for me to read. They made me, frankly, ashamed of what I came to realize was a superficiality in my own self-consciously 'liberal' – and male – attitude towards sex. Those who speak lightheartedly about Pamela's 'trials', who call the book a 'striptease', know less about the book's impact on young women than they may realize. 'Pamela is a type of the young, naive innocent that we all should be. She is the character that is also abused by her innocence and naiveté. She is someone I can relate to when I was about fourteen and having the big dirty seniors in high school taking advantage of me ... It is with malice that I look forward to the day when Pamela is abused so she will be on the same level of all of us who have been abused. I respect her convictions toward virtue – yet I want her to be tampered with and become a weak human being. I feel if Pamela holds to her convictions she will be a much stronger, better person than myself.' 'I thought it impossible not to yield to temptation and I don't want her to prove that it is possible. I wish her strength to herself, yet if she remains strong I will feel awful about how weak I have been.' 'Pamela portrays a character that is timeless. A majority of women have lived what Pamela is experiencing. Pamela is the character of the innocence I have lost. I hope that Pamela can remain strong, and I wish for her to maintain the little girl that once survived in myself.' 'With sorrow I see what Pamela is going to experience and I wish to tell her that the world is cruel and perhaps giving in is easier and less traumatic than holding on. When she lets go, my heart will ache for her. Poor

Pamela is headed for the destruction of her innocence. I wish I could be with her to tell her that it sucks.'

Many of the women were disturbed by Pamela's hope to preserve her virginity. 'Nobody who has given up values wants to read about a person who hasn't.' 'After reading about how virtuous Pamela is, the book could easily make one feel very guilty about one's life style.' Yet a great change in attitude occurs once she is abducted to Lincolnshire. 'At first I found this novel funny but now I see Pamela is suffering – as anyone would in her situation. I can understand her fear and wish I could help her in some way. She has nowhere to turn and is lost.' 'I feel bad for poor Pamela. At this point I can really say I do. If I were in her shoes (thank God I'm not), I wouldn't be able to cope with this. It's like you are alone and everyone is out to get you.'

The idea that Pamela's virginity, besides its physical reality, comes to represent character and strength of character can be seen in the students' journals – sometimes in negative ways. When Mr B. offers Pamela proposals to be his mistress, one woman wrote: 'Why doesn't Pamela accept them? I guess she feels her pride at stake. But hasn't her pride been chewed on and spit out already? I don't think Pamela has a pride to worry about anymore.' Others put it more positively: 'It must have been hard to refuse his proposals, especially the financial security for her parents. I'm proud of Pamela for not accepting and let's see how far she holds on.' 'This section was filled with many plans and plots against Pamela, and her rebellion against them and their control over her life. I admire her and her ability to try to stand up against them, and wish her much hope through the remainder of the book. I think she'll need it.' 'There are few people in the world with such strength. Most people have good intentions, but give in after being pushed to a certain point. I really admire her for this.' Far from seeing Pamela as an example of feminine delicacy and weakness, these students are struck by the character's toughness, her grit and determination. 'I have to give Pamela a lot of credit. She has so much strength in her character. The average person would not be able to handle all the troubles she has withstood.' 'I admire her courage in trying to escape but more than that, her courage to keep living even though she knows things are bad and may get worse after her attempt to escape.' At the end of Volume I, one student seemed to state the consensus: 'As I flip through the pages of *Pamela*, I find myself stopping and re-reading some of my favourite parts – such as her description of Mrs Jewkes, her opinions of everyone including herself, and her remarks about being virtuous. No matter how much I laughed at or scorned her, I really admire her stubbornness in retaining her innocence. She was tempted by money, power, and love. Many people would have been "bought" a long time ago. I have to admire her for believing in herself and never giving up what she believes in.'

I myself am uncomfortable, however, with seeing Pamela's virginity merely as a symbol – as it seems Terry Eagleton wishes to do in *The Rape of Clarissa*.[16] For Richardson, Pamela's virginity can be symbolic only because it is a physical fact. When my students compared themselves to Pamela, they could question the contemporaneity of her virtue. But when asked to write an essay about the advice they would give their fourteen-year-old daughter, who asked if she should have sexual relations with her boyfriend for the first time, all said to *wait*. Why does our judgement about chastity change when reading a character's struggle in fiction and when faced with the problem in our lives, in our families, in our homes? As students eventually perceived, the real point in *Pamela* has less to do with chastity *per se* than with the right a woman has over her own body. It is one thing to give; it is another to be taken. Even Mr B. cannot bring himself to take Pamela. When Pamela faints in the Lincolnshire bedroom scene, few students were surprised: 'Being a young woman, I'm not sure I would have reacted too differently to such a situation. She's lying next to an ugly lesbian whom she abhors and a man (her master) who she thinks is her friend, the maid. I'm not sure what the Master and Mrs Jewkes had planned to result from the scheme. Obviously they assumed Pamela would retaliate and Mrs Jewkes would be there to assist her Master in the rape. If Mr B. desired Pamela so much, could he really be satisfied by this scene? How could Pamela have enjoyed it, even if she wanted to? It seems totally absurd with Mrs Jewkes present and Mr B. in drag.' 'When Pamela discovered it was him instead of Nan in bed with her, and Mrs Jewkes telling him to "stop dilly-dallying and get on with it" [p. 176], it's no wonder she passed out.'

The first time I taught *Pamela* at FIT, I came to the reading of the novel's second volume with some trepidation. The very fact of a happy ending has distressed some critics; as John J. Richetti says, 'To the disgust of many modern readers, "virtue" is rewarded' at the end of this 'crude moral melodrama.'[17] And the conduct of the story in the second volume has been strongly deprecated; the introductions to widely read editions of *Pamela* tell the new reader that 'this spinning out of the novel is ... tedious',[18] that 'when Mr B. accepts the marriage chain, the story is really over.'[19] My students' experience challenges such assertions. Semester after semester, I was surprised to discover that these young readers found Volume II better than Volume I. '*Pamela* becomes more interesting as you go on.' '*Pamela* has gone from a poor servant girl to a rich mistress. The whole wedding is brought out in this volume. The major points in the story occur in this volume.'

Far from thinking that Richardson is 'spinning out' materials, students still feel suspense in Volume II. They wonder about the possibility of a sham marriage and are surprised at the risk Pamela took to return. Opinions divide: 'How, after she has been tricked, kidnapped, and tortured, could she go back?

Can being in love make someone take such a turn?' 'I have to agree with her on her uneasiness, but I would go back too. How can anyone help going to someone they love when she hears he's sick and he needs her?' 'She is following her heart now; before she followed her head, and it paid off. I hope it will now.' Mr B.'s character comes under severe scrutiny; his sincerity becomes as problematic as Pamela's was in Volume I: 'Mr B. definitely seems to be treating Pamela much more nicely, and I can see an effort on his part to make up for all the bad he's done. Maybe he is sincere. Maybe he's tired of letting the difference in classes bother him, and the town ladies and the gossip. He doesn't like being threatened by Lady Davers, and I really wonder what he's going to do.' They wonder whether Pamela will be accepted by society, they are deeply moved by the reunion of Pamela and her father, and the confrontations between Lady Davers, Pamela, and Mr B. are consistently their favourite parts of this novel. Particularly they wonder whether Pamela's character will change in her new position: 'I am eager to see how her virtue stays in her heart.'

In later years I knew that after the seventh week, students would be so enthusiastic about readings that the book seemed virtually to teach itself. Speaking of *Grandison*, Richardson said, 'Many things are thrown out in the several Characters, on purpose to provoke friendly Debate',[20] but it seems that this had always been part of his artistic intention. At least, I have rarely had such earnest class debates as those raised by events in the second part of *Pamela*. The rambling talk about marriage B. and Pamela have in bed together (from which talk Pamela later abstracts her forty-eight Marriage Rules) provoked not only sharp attacks on his 'male chauvinism' but also arguments over how many of the rules, especially the ones concerning the way children should be brought up (8–18, p. 370), are essentially valid today; as one student observed, 'The point is he's trying to talk to her. Most men today just don't take the time to communicate. Nor do the women.' Pamela's acceptance of Mr B.'s past and her wish to adopt Sally Goodwin are both criticized and admired. The scene raised at least one criticism of Pamela I had never read before: 'I don't think she should have so quickly suggested that Miss Goodwin live with her and Mr B. She should have discussed it with Mr B. when Miss Goodwin was not standing right there. If I was Mr B., I would have been a little annoyed with her for putting them both on the spot like that. I am not saying that she should not have thought of it but that she should have given herself some more time to think about it.'

Reading the novel in weekly sections may partly account for my students' real involvement with the second volume. Events in Volume I cover a year and two months and then forty days of Pamela's imprisonment; time slows down in Volume II, where events take place in forty days. A weekly reading in

Volume II covered a week in Pamela's life, and each semester, some students told me they would end their day by reading what happened in Pamela's day. The reading pace, concurrent with novelistic time, as well as the technique of 'writing to the moment', encouraged them to experience and enjoy Pamela's detailed daily accounts – so much so that when the end came, most of them wished for more.[21] 'I understand why the first readers demanded a sequel. They were such a happy couple I was waiting for the son to be born and to have a picture of a happy little family. It was an ending that needed following up on.' 'I feel kind of sad because the story has now completed a full circle. We are now at the end of the story.' 'I wonder what is going to happen next. There should have been more.' 'I feel as though Pamela was now writing to *me*, as a friend, and telling me her adventures. I feel that in her own way, she brought the twenty people in our class together as one. We shared stories and lives with each other, and I loved it. I'm sorry it's over. I feel as though I'm losing a good friend.'

But essentially, I think, their pleasure in reading the second volume derives from the fact that it is about the happiness of someone they have come to care for, a happiness that Pamela deserves to enjoy. For them, Virtue is Rewarded – and should be. 'It is good to read how a little peasant girl but a very deserving person of all the riches and goodness in the world, finally got all of that. She didn't even want it but got it anyway. That made her all the more deserving.' 'I remember reading somewhere a line that went something like "*Pamela*: The story of a lucky maid". I don't think "lucky" is a good word for her present situation. I think she more than deserved it after all she went through.' 'I really enjoyed reading *Pamela*, especially Volume II. So much bad happened to Pamela in Volume I that I'm surprised she never gave up or really didn't commit suicide. I think I would have. I liked Volume II best because it was full of happiness most of the time.'

The possibility of deserving happiness and attaining it – this is the hope the book holds out to us. The elements of happiness Pamela and Mr B. enjoy are those we ourselves most wish to have – love, social acceptance and recognition, and more than that, social esteem.[22] *Pamela* says that a good life may be attained by living honestly, by being true to oneself, by having respect for others. The novel shows that living by such standards is not easy, that it demands struggle and may bring pain. Yet *Pamela* can actually reactivate the sense of good within oneself and make one realize the possibilities for good in others.

At least, I believe it can, for I have no other way to account for my students' unconventional reactions to Fielding's *Shamela*. When I assigned the book, I thought they would enjoy the parody as we in universities are told we should do, as they themselves enjoyed satirical sketches on *Saturday Night Live*. Very few did. Rather than sharing Martin Battestin's gleeful pleasure in a burlesque that exposed 'the absurdities and pretensions of *Pamela* ... once and for all',[23] these students read *Shamela* with extraordinary revulsion. They certainly did not feel that 'there [was] something essentially healthier in *Shamela*'s lusty good humour than in the prurient sobriety of *Pamela*'.[24] Quite the contrary: 'I don't like *Shamela* very much. It destroys everything good that made *Pamela* so entertaining.' 'I guess my greatest difficulty with *Shamela* is that I truly try to see the world as possessing at least some good – no, a lot of good! Reading 70-odd pages of lies, deceptions and evil really makes a person feel disgusted and sick.' '*Shamela* is a perversion of the book *Pamela*. All the goodness, virtue, and modesty inspired in us in the original book is vulgarized in the second.' 'I hated seeing Pamela in this way. I myself looked up to her.' 'The book *Shamela* was not in the least bit funny to me and I'm sorry I read it. The character Shamela is an insult to Pamela and I really felt bad about it. I saw Shamela as a contemporary street girl from Brooklyn.' 'The whole story is a disgrace; it let women down to the lowest level, and I hated the book.' 'If it is not his dislike for women, it's the disgrace he desires for people of no estate background to have. *Shamela* shows how equality is hard to accept both today and in the 1700s.' 'Fielding made *Pamela* sound like a lie. Shamela was as low as her class stereotype was supposed to be. She saw no interest in bettering herself intellectually. She was only out for material goods. Richardson's *Pamela*, on the other hand, showed how a poor girl could educate herself to become something better.' '*Shamela* I sold back to the bookstore, whereas *Pamela* I will keep.'

'I think of Pamela as an example. Now when I have to make an important decision about myself or others, I ask myself, "What would Pamela do?"' *Pamela*'s optimism, its idealism and romance, are meant to be inspiring, are meant to inspire young people. This is true from the beginning. As Lady B. dies, the old generation passes away, making way for the new. One might call this the generative Richardsonian moment, for it is that moment of generational change that provides the opportunity for action in *Clarissa* and *Sir Charles Grandison* as well as in *Pamela*. Here, the new generation is represented by the poor Pamela Andrews and the rich Mr B., whose interaction and discovery of one another ultimately provide a vision of love and community and hope. It is to challenge the young to realize that vision that Richardson writes, addressing deliberately, as he proclaims on his title-page, 'the Minds of the YOUTH of BOTH SEXES'. He believes in the mind, the mind's ability to perceive character, to be character, to make character. He believes, too, in the possibility of change.

The fact is that *Pamela* still does inspire young people. 'I've enjoyed this book, because it helped me learn about myself. Pamela has her own character.

Money does not make her what she is, nor does her love for Mr B. She is her own person.' 'Pamela is a novel about the good in people, even though that might be hard to see in the beginning. It shows how people can work together to help each other overcome their own weak natures.' 'It may sound a bit strange, but as I read this book, I began to draw lessons for my own life from it. I found myself trying to follow Pamela's example of being forgiving and trying to find good in everyone, and let me tell you, it's not easy.' 'It has been able to reshape my character and my morals, I feel – I have never sent so much money to my parish! Until the end of this novel, I did not remember what my duties and responsibilities towards others were any more.'

Lionel Trilling once observed that 'time has the effect of seeming to quiet the work of art, domesticating it and making it into a classic, which is often another way of saying that it is an object of merely habitual regard. University study of the right sort can reverse this process and restore to the old work its freshness and force – can, indeed, disclose unguessed-at power.'[25] Our habitual regard of Pamela presents the novel as a dead book, of historical importance certainly, but too firmly rooted in its own time to have much to say to ours. Its story and its themes are held to be quaint, if not downright embarrassing, and its literary techniques, despite occasional signs of talent, too crude to be continually engaging. The twentieth-century critic's tone of aloof detachment and condescension contrasts sharply with the enthusiasm of the book's first readers, whose letters printed as an Introduction to the second edition of Pamela testify to the original freshness and force of Richardson's work and to its inspirational power. In this tercentenary year of the novelist's birth, it seems appropriate to record reactions of readers today. In this essay, I have tried to let these readers speak for themselves, these young men and women whose vocational goals at the Fashion Institute of Technology demand they be attuned to the tempo of the moment if they are to succeed in that most sophisticated, most competitive art and business of fashion. Teaching Pamela to them, I have myself been taught. I have learned primarily that it is time our habitual regard was reversed, that it's no use pretending Pamela is not a current classic. These students tell us that the book is alive and stands in need of no apology. Recovering in their reading the novel's original freshness and force, they also reveal Pamela's continuing vitality and disclose indeed unguessed-at power.

2

Pamela: rethinking *Arcadia*

GILLIAN BEER

We know that Richardson had read Sidney's *Arcadia*, or read *in* it (since it is not a work that demands total word-by-word reading to declare its characteristic excellences). We need not assume that he read it for the first time when in 1724–5 his firm printed the fourteenth edition of Sidney's *Works*,[1] though that activity would bring the work close to his eye and his thoughts. That edition would, moreover, particularly have drawn to Richardson's attention the possibility of extending and rethinking Sidney's great work.

The first two volumes of the edition that Richardson printed comprise the five books of 'The Countess of Pembroke's *Arcadia*': the third volume opens with 'A sixth book to the Countess of Pembroke's *Arcadia*, written by R.B. of Lincolns Inn, Esq'. This sixth book, first added in 1627, takes up Sidney's hint in the last sentence of *Arcadia* that if you want any more you must sing it yourself or, as he more graciously puts it, the next generation of his characters 'may awake some other spirit to exercise his pen in that wherewith mine is already dulled'. R.B. takes up the invitation humbly and with a will, opening his book with the marriage of Pamela. The third paragraph begins 'And now was the marriage-day come, when *Pamela*, attired in the stately ornament of beauteous majesty, led by the constant forwardness of a virtuous mind, waited on by the many thoughts of his fore-past crosses in her love, which now made up a perfect harmony in the pleasing discord of indeared affection, was brought to church.'[2] 'The constant forwardness of a virtuous mind' provides a pithy characterization of what some readers have found hard to accept in Richardson's Pamela. The princess Pamela and the serving-maid Pamela share a grounded sense of their own worth and a willingness often wittily to voice their own claims. That is one of the radical congruities that Richardson asserts by means of the name he gives his heroine. If, like R.B., he was provoked into rethinking the after-world of Sidney's *Arcadia*, his rethinking – unlike R.B.'s – was no slight continuation. Instead it was a new (if finally

23

hedged) appraisal of the social order as manifested in relationships between men and women, masters and servants, town and country people.

By the time Richardson wrote *Pamela* Sidney's heroic narrative had been famous for a hundred and fifty years and had been succeeded by a host of French and English writers of romance. The work that Richardson knew was what we now call the *New Arcadia*, which incorporates Sidney's 1580s revisions, along with those of his sister the Countess of Pembroke in the 1593 folio, and a bridging passage by Sir William Alexander which appeared in the fifth edition of 1621.[3] Like *Pamela*, *Arcadia* is an accumulating text which incorporates the writer's and his readers' responses to the first version in the later revisions and continuations. Recent work on intertextuality and re-writing has, I hope, made it possible to reach a juster and more complex assessment of Richardson's response to *Arcadia*, among other kinds of writing.

My argument does not propose Sidney as simple or single discursive progenitor of Richardson. The emphasis is on response, not influence, and beyond that, on congruity and resistance. By the naming of his heroine Richardson implied *de facto* for his early readers, in a way that is now largely invisible since *Arcadia* is no longer wide-spread pleasure reading, a riddling accord between the works.

In a brief but substantial article Jacob Leed[4] has noted a number of correspondences between Richardson's Pamela and the princess Pamela in Sidney's *Arcadia*. These correspondences he finds both in personality and in situation: Sidney's Pamela is 'vivacious, striking, and independent-minded … in heavily emphasized contrast to her sister, Philoclea, who is an equally important heroine of the book'. Pamela in both *Arcadia* and *Pamela* is properly conscious of her own merits, Leed observes. He notes the parallels between their situations: both are imprisoned, both are threatened with forced marriages, both are 'involved in a problem of love between persons placed high and low in society'. Richardson, Leed argues, is less hostile to romance while writing *Pamela* than his later comments might lead us to believe. Leed's observations are sound – and the similarities could be multiplied; see, for example, the great meditations on suicide in each book, or observe the figures of Cecropia and her low counterpart, Mrs Jewkes. But on their own such similarities do not take us far enough into the issues raised by Richardson's extension and revision of Sidney's text. A clue to differences between the works is given already in that question of cross-class matches: as so often in pastoral (for example, in *The Winter's Tale*) one partner in a love match *appears to be* of a lower class; but Perdita proves to be the lost daughter of a king despite her shepherdess upbringing; Musidorus is a prince, only opportunis-tically disguised as a shepherd Dorus in order to get access to Pamela.

Richardson's Pamela, in contrast, has risen to being a lady's maid. Leed concentrates on the apparent similarity between the situations in the two books. There is more to be discovered, however, by analysing the divergences in Richardson's revisionary reading and rewriting of *Arcadia*.

In the figure of his Pamela, Richardson goes far beyond allusion to a single character, though that allusion is the reader's referential starting-point from which to observe difference as well as likeness. Richardson gathers within his single isolated figure, Pamela, aspects of both of Sidney's princesses, Pamela and Philoclea. Sidney's Pamela displays 'the majesty of virtue'; her sister Philoclea its playfulness and responsiveness. In Richardson, the two are mingled in his ordinary girl, who is seen by others as 'pert', 'a baggage', 'a creature' – yet as an adamant soul. Richardson goes further: he abrades the distinctions so hierarchically observed in the language and events of *Arcadia* between princess and serving girl, Pamela and Mopsa. Richardson's writing raises questions of genre, moving away from romance and pastoral towards Christian epic in *Pamela II*, where Pamela is likened to the alternative possible state of an unfallen world imaged in 'old *Du Bartas*' (III, 54).

Richardson responds to the immense discursive range of Sidney's work, endowing Pamela herself with a linguistic register which can move freely between the specificities of the servant's world she inhabits and the geographical region she comes from, and the high styles of Bible and epic. Whereas in Sidney the panoply of discourses emanates from a single conversational aristocratic voice, in *Pamela* the letter form attributes the linguistic excellence specifically and predominantly to the servant-heroine Pamela. Both Sidney and Richardson are composing their works for a precisely imagined readership of women. Questions of cross-dressing and of voyeurism are, however, very differently treated by each of them. These then, in summary, are some of the ways in which Richardson responded to his great predecessor. I shall here concentrate on the ways in which Richardson's naming of his heroine works to unsteady assumed correspondences between social class and authoritative writing.

The naming of Pamela was not an allusion simply to a single character. It summoned up and made available for translation the achievement of *Arcadia*, as well as the symbolic repertoire of later romances. *Arcadia* offered, for re-appraisal, a mood of endless possibility chastened by peremptory trials; perspicuous analysis often realized as conceit; enquiry into the interest groups within a social order; and a pleasure-giving process in which page-by-page reading provokes and allays anxieties within each sentence that are more immediate than the anxieties of the plot. The invocation of *Arcadia* would set a narrative tempo and would recall for the reader the reasoned leisure of the older work, a leisure which is employed at once erotically and ethically.

Richardson was looking back to a work which was a great aristocratic classic and one which, with all its comedy, combined religious and erotic dignity. The alliance with *Arcadia* enhanced his heroine's authority. He called on some of the same themes as Sidney, in particular that of the heroine's imprisonment and the moral implications of disguise. Both works moreover invoke an extraordinary variety of styles. Sidney shifts dextrously to and fro among discourses with a single sentence. His linguistic register is finely calibrated and yet capable of violent ricochets. For its full realization, it demands the speaking voice – the voice, first, of himself and his sister. In Richardson, the writing is largely occupied by Pamela's variable voice: and its silenced state as letter is the condition both of her predicament and of Richardson's concealment.

Letters in Sidney's work are usually the result of long cogitation, but he excels at complex analysis of the psychological processes of composition and reception. In *Pamela*, the writing or receipt of letters is further refracted through these activities being themselves described in letters. The princess Pamela in Sidney's *Arcadia* finds herself, towards the end of the work's immense length, imprisoned with her sister Philoclea, unable to get news either of the outcome of the civil disturbances in the land or of the fate of their lovers, Musidorus and Pyrocles. Each of the women writes a letter to 'the general assembly of the *Arcadian* nobility' and these letters show their differing though equally perfect characters. The 'humble hearted *Philoclea*' (II, 855) passionately beseeches the life of her lover. Pamela, always majestically articulate, casts the desperation of her position in the terms of writing itself. The letter form requires that the writer have an identity and that the letter be addressed to knowable persons. But for Sidney's Pamela here, the letter is a form of locked-up speech, a silenced voice. It demands reception and has none.

In such a state, my Lord, you have placed me, as I can neither write nor be silent; for how can I be silent, since you have left me nothing but my solitary words to testify my misery? and how should I write, for as [for] speech I have none but my jailor, that can hear me who neither can resolve what to write, nor to whom to write? What to write is hard for me to say, as what I may not write, so little hope have I of any success, and so much hath no injury been left undone to me-wards. To whom to write, where may I learn, since yet I wot not how to entitle you? Shall I call you my sovereigns? set down your laws that I may do you homage. Shall I fall lower, and name you my fellows? shew me I beseech you the lord and master over us. But shall Basilius's *heir name her self your princess? alas I am your prisoner.*   (II, 857)

Pamela's dilemma, like that of her later namesake is such that she 'can neither write nor be silent'. She *cannot* write because she no longer knows who she is, in terms of the body politic. Is she any more a princess? She *must* write because her words alone can testify to her emotions, which endure beyond her civil state. The letter is the only evidence that she still exists. It is her bodying forth, the last expression of her power, and written in the expectation that her enemies will 'prevent my power with slaughter' (II, 857). Her lines 'signify', in repeating and extending utterance, her ineluctable sense of herself as a princess. She is beset, isolated. She grates the word 'princess' against the word 'prisoner' and strikes some frail sardonic sparks with them. But above all the activity of expression sustains her as a presence to whoever reads her, and to herself. Richardson seized that same connection between writing, imprisonment, and the self in his Pamela's continued writing when there seems no hope of delivery, for herself or her letters.

When Richardson's Pamela claims that her *soul* is of equal importance with the soul of a princess, it turns out that she necessarily means that her body is so too. Soul and body, in the letter, take on the form of writing. Letters become the wafer of the body, the promise of the person. They become, during her trials, the one form for Richardson's Pamela of self survival. By writing, and by reading her writing, she assures herself that she endures. Later she thickens and scrutinizes her self-understanding by rereading; in *Pamela II* she comes to perceive that the lines she quotes from Dryden have even to some degree been true of herself also:

> *And yet the Soul, shut up in her dark Room,*
> *Viewing so clear abroad, at home sees nothing:*
> *But like a Mole in Earth, busy and blind,*
> *Works all her Folly up, and casts it outward*
> *To the World's open View ...* (IV, 319)

Though held within the greater range of narrative approaches, letters are important to *Arcadia*; they forward the plot, as challenges and chivalric exchanges; they announce upheaval in the state and in personal life, as in the tragic story of Parthenia and Argalus where the coming of the fatal challenge by letter is described with all the finicky desperation of anxiety. At the opening of the third book, Dorus (Musidorus disguised as a shepherd) declares his desire for Pamela. She repels him and in despair he writes her a letter. The description of the writing and the reception of the letter moves tenderly between intense feeling and comedy, as Dorus attempts to cram all his emotions into a verse letter: 'he thought best to counterfeit his hand ... and put it in verse, hoping that would draw her on to read the more, chusing the *Elegiac* as fittest for mourning'.

But never pen did more quakingly perform his office; never was pen more double-moistened with ink and tears; never words more slowly married together, and never Muses more tired than now with changes and re-changes of his devices: fearing how to end, before he had resolved how to begin, mistrusting each word, condemning each

sentence. This word was not significant; that word was too plain: this would not be
conceived, the other would be illconceived: here sorrow was not enough expressed,
there he seemed too much for his own sake to be sorry: this sentence rather shewed
art than passion, that sentence rather foolishly passionate, than forcibly moving.

(II, 404)

(We may recall here Richardson's description of his experience as a scribe
composing a letter for the young women of his acquaintance to send to their
lovers, and their trembling at the fear of being misconstrued.) Pamela in
Arcadia, like Richardson's Pamela, has helplessly mixed feelings about her
would-be seducer, here represented by the delicate comedy of her rationalization.

But when she saw the letter, her heart gave her from whence it came; and therefore
clapping it to again she went away from it, as if it had been a contagious garment of an
infected person: and yet was not long away, but that she wished she had read it, though
she were loath to read it. Shall I, said she, second his boldness so far, as to read his
presumptuous Letters? And yet (saith she) he sees me not now to grow the bolder
thereby: and how can I tell whether they be presumptuous? The paper came from him,
and therefore not worthy to be received; and yet the paper she thought was not guilty.
At last she concluded, it were not much amiss to look it over, that she might out of his
words pick some farther quarrel against him. Then she opened it, and threw it away,
and took it up again, till (e're she were aware) her eyes would needs read it.

(II, 404–5)

In Richardson's *Pamela* the threat to the heroine is far more oppressive and
the reader must construe without a guiding commentary the charged
incongruities of Pamela's feelings.

The comedy and subtlety of Sidney's work comes not only from the
controlled vacillation between discourses but also from the mimicking by
means of syntax of the actions of mind and body, moment by moment as they
occur. It is to this freedom and multiplicity of language 'to the moment' that
Richardson so notably responds in the writing of *Pamela*. But at the same time
Richardson breaks apart the assumed connection in Sidney's writing between
social status and lingustic control. The language of *Arcadia*'s characters is
stratified: poised, refined, and allusive for the aristocrats; punchy and verbose
for the servants. Sensibility likewise is controlled by class. Nobility is the
moral perquisite of princesses (though by no means all of them); racy
pragmatism typifies the lower classes. Richardson's Pamela cuts right across
these classifications. The sinuous discursive play of authorial narrative in
Sidney is now occupied by Pamela's own writing in her letters.

It is suggestive to find both that Richardson selected for his heroine a name
which allied her with the world of romances rather than that of humdrum
representation, and that he transgressed the social class-categories of

romance in his naming. His choice of the name Pamela for his heroine was allusive, not naturalistic. Though to us it may seem an ordinary enough name, to his first readers it would have been highly surprising. Indeed Fielding jokes about it in *Joseph Andrews*: ' "She told me ... that they had a Daughter of a very strange Name, *Paměla* or *Paméla*; some pronounced it one way, and some the other." '[5] It was a literary name, apparently invented by Philip Sidney himself, and strongly associated with the romance tradition from then on. As an ordinary Christian name it had some vogue only *after* the appearance of Richardson's Pamela. We do not need to invent aspiring motives for Pamela's parents to explain its provenance: the name sets up disturbances in the hierarchies represented in the older text: hierarchies of class and of language, of social and material power.[6]

The hierarchies of naming had already been mocked in a comedy which Pamela discusses in *Pamela II* (IV, letter XII), Steele's *The Tender Husband* (1705), where the heroine is called Biddy Tipkin. Under the influence of the romances, Steele's heroine repines at her name and renames herself Parthenissa, for, as she observes, there are strict class-rules for names in romance: 'the Heroine has always something soft and engaging in Her Name.... 'Tis strange Rudeness those Familiar Names they give us, when there is *Aurelia*, *Sacharissa*, *Gloriana*, for People of Condition; and *Celia*, *Chloris*, *Corinna*, *Mopsa*, for their Maids, and those of Lower Rank.' A little later, Biddy is assured that she is not too young for love by the hero's direct allusion to *Arcadia*: 'Do you believe *Pamela* was One and Twenty before she knew *Musidorus*?'[7]

So Richardson's act of naming his servant-heroine Pamela *challenged* Arcadian doctrine as well. Richardson counter-proposed a working world, cluttered with a servant's duties. The naming proves, though, that within this world there is, as in Arcadia, time for speculation and desire, for anxious analysis of affairs of state – here expressed as affairs of the estate. Pamela clings to the law; Mr B. asserts the cavalier virtues of honour, trust, and magnanimity: virtues in the possession of those with power. The battles that range across the whole Arcadian landscape are here held within the house and garden. All the land within sight belongs to Mr B. The pond, the field with the cows in it, are as far as Pamela can venture. So rooms become condensed body-images, and the body – in a rewriting of Renaissance imagery – becomes a landscape moralisé. Moreover, the loft, the summer-house, the closet, the dressing-room: these are Pamela's body-spaces. We hear little about the public spaces of the house because, in her time as servant, she has little access to them. When, after marriage in *Pamela II*, she seeks an image for her new estate she lights on a counter-metaphor. She does not want to be a great estate like Chatsworth where they levelled 'a Mountain at a monstrous

Expence' and so produced a place where the destruction of all the natural contours of the landscape has left the house unconnected with its origins or wider setting (IV, 39).

A further point: in calling his heroine Pamela, Richardson draws attention to a romance dimension of his tale. With the same stroke, he resists the romance tradition in which the scions of noble houses are inevitably the heroes and heroines of the work, and servants have at best comic roles. The name raises questions of descent, and class. Will Pamela prove to be of high rank like her namesake? How can a serving girl justify her aristocratic name? Is the name a secret promise of higher things proffered by author to reader? Does it mark her out as an exception to everyday possibilities?

In Sidney's *Arcadia* the social equivalent of the servant Pamela is the servant Mopsa (a name for romance-servants ratified by Biddy Tipkin's list). Mopsa (in *Arcadia*) has a certain earthy energy; she is a good but prolix story-teller: her version of Cupid and Psyche is cut short when she reaches the sentence: 'And so she went, and she went, and never rested the evening, where she went in the morning; till she came to a second aunt, and she gave her another nut' (I, 275). She is used as a catspaw by Dorus (Musidorus) in his pursuit of Pamela. Dressed as a shepherd Dorus must woo the maid, and this he does only too effectively: 'with that he imprisoned his look for a while upon *Mopsa*, who thereupon fell into a very wide smiling' (I, 207). Mopsa is 'as glad as of sweet-meat' to go on an errand to fetch Dorus (I, 206). She is a figure of fun, driven by her body and not fully in control of it. Dorus takes the chance of Mopsa being asleep to woo Pamela: 'He looked, and saw that Mopsa indeed sat swallowing of sleep with open mouth, making such a noise withal, as no body could lay the stealing of a nap to her charge' (I, 244). The humorous pressure on the word *stealing* reminds us of assumptions about thieving servants – and of the requirements that servants be constantly attentive – even while it counters the image of Mopsa's noisy sleeping.

Pamela wakes her as a defence against Dorus:

> He would have said farther, but *Pamela* calling aloud *Mopsa*, she suddenly started up, staggering, and rubbing her eyes, ran first out of the door, and then back to them, before she knew how she went out, or why she came in again: till at length, being fully come to her little self, she asked *Pamela*, why she had called her. For nothing said *Pamela*, but that ye might hear some tales of your servants telling: and therefore now, said she, *Dorus*, go on.   (I, 244)

The mechanistically exaggerated response is clownlike as Mopsa is galvanized out of sleep and into hyperactivity by her name being called, running out of the door and then back to them, 'before she knew how she went out, or why she came in again'. Dorus is Mopsa's servant because he is purportedly paying court to her but, of course, in this work and its tradition the aristocracy can only truly woo the aristocracy. Mopsa is Pamela's servant in another sense and so, in the hierarchy of this book, has no full life of her own. If she is deluded in love, that is the matter of comedy.

Richardson's challenge to older styles of romance involves the compression not only of Pamela and Philoclea, two princesses into one, but of Pamela and Mopsa, princess and serving-maid. Richardson takes entirely seriously the dynamics of the household. He places at the centre of attention, not princes and princesses in disguise, but the serving girl undisguised who can combine homely imagery and high sentence in her utterance. Richardson's challenge proved so successful that in large measure the equivalences between the two Pamelas became obliterated by the fame of Richardson's figure. Pamela the serving maid became the 'original', as in *Pamela II* she declares that she wishes to become.

So I, Madam, think I had better endeavour to make the best of those natural Defects I cannot master, than by assuming Airs and Dignities in Appearance, to which I was not born, act neither Part tolerably. By this means, instead of being thought neither Gentlewoman nor Rustick, as Sir *Jacob* hinted, (*Linsey-wolsey*, I think, was his Term too) I may be look'd upon as an Original in my Way; and all Originals pass Muster well enough, you know, Madam, even with Judges. (IV, 39)

Hovering within the word 'original' is the suggestion of eccentricity as well as the recognition of her low birth, her 'original', but here she is also claiming an originary status. She needs also to declare her independence from her 'author', but never can quite do so. There is here another point of likeness and of difficulty for Sidney and Richardson: that is the relationship of male writer and presumed female reader.

Like Richardson, Sidney was writing into a circle of female intimates, and a circle preoccupied with moral complexities and fine grained distinctions. Sidney writes to his sister of his book as a child 'done only for you': 'Your dear self can best witness the manner, being done in loose sheets of paper, most of it in your presence; the rest by sheets sent unto you, as fast as they were done' (I, ii–iii). Richardson told Aaron Hill that his writing of *Pamela* was spurred on by the interest and encouragement of his wife and a young lady then living in his family.[8] The expected intimate female audience is, in each case, part of the composing of the book. Both are 'written to the moment' of those first loved women readers. The erotic movement of each work is controlled by a desire for the responsiveness of women. In this these books are rare in post-medieval English literature – and rarer still in their open acknowledgement of the ordering presence of a known female readership.

In both works the writers make strong identification with women characters even while male characters blame the women for their beauty and the desire it arouses. In both works that beauty becomes a physical prison, within which the heroines are pinned by the violence and malice of others. They are then, insultingly, told that they produce the prison that contains them. So, Amphialus 'by a hunger-starved affection, was compelled to offer this injury' to Philoclea (ii, 419); he claims:

What then shall I say? but that I, who am ready to lie under your feet, to venture, nay to lose my life at your last commandment: I am not the stay of your freedom, but love, love, which ties you in your own knots. It is you your self, that imprison yourself: it is your beauty which makes these castle walls embrace you: it is your own eyes, which reflect upon themselves this injury.   (ii, 420)

Mr B., having tricked Pamela and being about to imprison her on his Lincolnshire estate, writes to her thus:

'The Passion I have for you, and your Obstinacy, have constrained me to act by you in a manner that I know will occasion you great Trouble and Fatigue, both of Mind and Body. Yet, forgive, me, my dear Girl; for tho' I have taken this Step, I will, by all that's good and holy, use you honourably. Suffer not your Fears to transport you to a Behaviour that will be disreputable to us both. For the Place where you'll receive this, is a Farm that belongs to me; and the People civil, honest and obliging.'   (p. 99)

Though nothing like as dextrous in argument as Amphialus, Mr B. succeeds in transferring the imprisonment from her to himself: he is 'constrained' by passion and her obstinacy; he attaches the word 'disreputable' to *her* presumed future rather than *his* own actual behaviour. Both Philoclea and Richardson's Pamela retort ironically upon this emotional strategy, and its pre-empting of the languages of property and independence. Philoclea indignantly comments: 'You entitle your self my slave, but I am sure I am yours. If then violence, injury, terror, and depriving of that which is more dear than life it self, liberty, be fit orators for affection, you may expect that I will be easily perswaded' (ii, 418). Pamela demands 'And pray . . . how came I to be his Property? What Right has he in me, but such as a Thief may plead to stolen Goods?' (p. 116). Mrs Jewkes ripostes: 'Why, was ever the like heard, says she! – This is downright Rebellion, I protest!'

The prison, and the falsehood of older women, men's agents, will later in the eighteenth century become a psychic necessity of the Gothic, as it was in medieval romance. The prison becomes a place of self-confirmation for the heroine. In *Pamela ii*, there is, further, a recognition that the constriction of women requires a symbolic image which will call attention to the prolonged childhood demanded of them. Women's language is itself, Pamela argues, the counter product of containment:

But how I ramble – Yet, surely, Sir, you don't expect Method or Connexion from your Girl. The Education of our Sex will not permit that, where it is best. We are forced to struggle for Knowlege, like the poor feeble Infant in the Month, who ... is pinn'd and fetter'd down upon the Nurse's Lap; and who, if its little Arms happen, by Chance, to escape its Nurse's Observation, and offer but to expand themselves, are immediately taken into Custody, and pinn'd down to their passive Behaviour. So, when a poor Girl, in spite of her narrow Education, breaks out into Notice, her Genius is immediately tamed by trifling Imployments, lest, perhaps, she should become the Envy of one Sex, and the Equal of the other. (IV, 320)

Pamela's terms glitter with double meanings and destabilize the taken-for-granted values of Mr B.'s world in which she is always an outsider. The word 'plot' itself, as we shall see, becomes a mark of Pamela's sedition in the autocracy of Mr B.'s household, as well as the well-ordered unrolling of story within a fiction. In the scene where Mr B., acting as accusor and judge, charges Pamela with 'treasonable papers', the lines between writing, amorous correspondence, the law, and the state are deliberately smudged (pp. 199–204). Pamela keeps her head, and her feet, in the midst of his devious appropriations and claims. He twice tells her that she must trust to his honour to come well out of her trial. His will is the only ordering principle of this social and verbal dictatorship. He has, earlier in the book, mocked the concept of honour as sound public reputation when Mrs Jervis speaks of his 'Reputation or Honour – '. 'No more, no more, said he, of these antiquated Topicks' (p. 69). Mrs Jervis, as good housekeeper, includes in her meaning of his 'Honour' the right governance of his estate and household. He rejects such concerns as old-fashioned, and in the trial scene 'Honour' seems to signify only a cavalier magnanimity outside the bounds of the law, whereas Pamela asserts 'I thought myself right to endeavour to make my Escape from this forced and illegal Restraint' (p. 200). Pamela has a little earlier been cutting about the aristocratic appropriation of words such as 'Honour', contenting herself instead with 'Honesty': 'My Honesty (I am poor and lowly, and am not intitled to call it *Honour*) was in Danger' (p. 187).

The social and emotional combat between them takes the form of conceits and repartee. Words such as 'plot', 'title', 'equal', 'liberties', and 'innocent exercises' in the dialogue passage below shift wittily across questions concerning social rank, social construction, civil order, literary construction, and the insurrectionary capacity of women. The repartee is expansive, allowing the reader time to savour the tussle of Mr B. (who speaks first) to take command of language. Pamela's intervening speech-tags – 'said I', 'said he' – exercise a retrospective shaping control over the conversation. The letter form puts Pamela in command of the narrative past. Moreover, she puts sardonic pressure on Mr B.'s language by calling attention to its terms: 'those *innocent* Exercises, as you are pleased to call them'. She exposes and so withers the sexual predation such phrases conceal.

I long to see the Particulars of your Plot, and your Disappointment, where your Papers leave off. For you have so beautiful a manner, that it is partly that, and partly my Love for you, that has made me desirous of reading all you write; tho' a great deal of it is against myself; for which you must expect to suffer a little. And as I have furnished you with the Subject, I have a Title to see the Fruits of your Pen. – Besides, said he, there is such a pretty Air of Romance, as you relate them, in your Plots, and my Plots, that I shall be better directed in what manner to wind up the Catastrophe of the pretty Novel.

If I was your Equal, Sir, said I, I should say this is a very provoking way of jeering at the Misfortunes you have brought upon me.

O, said he, the Liberties you have taken with my Character, in your Letters, set us upon a Par, at least, in that respect. Sir, reply'd I, I could not have taken these Liberties, if you had not given me the Cause: And the *Cause*, Sir, you know, is before the *Effect*.

True, *Pamela*, said he; you chop Logick very prettily. What the Duce do we Men go to School for? If our Wits were equal to Womens, we might spare much Time and Pains in our Education. For Nature learns your Sex, what, in a long Course of Labour and Study, ours can hardly attain to. – But indeed, every Lady is not a *Pamela*.

You delight to banter your poor Servant, said I.

Nay, continued he, I believe I must assume to myself half the Merit of your Wit, too; for the innocent Exercises you have had for it from me, have certainly sharpen'd your Invention.

Sir, said I, could I have been without those *innocent* Exercises, as you are pleased to call them, I should have been glad to have been as dull as a Beetle.   (pp. 201–2)

Pamela's dextrous chopping of logic ('the *Cause*, Sir, you know, is before the *Effect*') is laid beside her strong moral position. It gives the reader both a clandestine and an open pleasure. Pamela is 'naturally' intelligent. Mr B. indeed suggests this as an argument against the education of women. Men's power needs women's ignorance: Pamela is the equal of Mr B. in wit, in work, in the play of discourse, in everything except wealth and power. But the lack of wealth and power makes her own range of linguistic command dangerous to her. Her proverbial phrase 'dull as a Beetle' sets Mr B. thinking along the lines of her possible marriage to 'some clouterly Plough-boy'. She ripostes 'Sir, I should have been content and innocent; and that's better than being a Princess, and not so' (p. 202). Her ideal statement is both convincing and straight out of courtly pastoral. The idea of Pamela as 'the Ploughman's Wife' has a strong sexual charge for Mr B. It allows him fantasy identifications even as it exaggerates the social distance between them and demeans one who is demonstrating herself to be his verbal and moral superior. She is, moreover, threatening to take control of writing and to wrest 'the Catastrophe of the pretty Novel' from his control (p. 201). His plots and her plots conflict; it is she who devises the dramatic record of their conversation. 'Well', Pamela unguardedly remarks a little later, 'my Story surely would furnish out a surprizing kind of Novel, if it was to be well told' (pp. 212–13). She is presented as the teller of this tale; there is no open evidence of an organizing male author.

The tactical weakness in Pamela's position is that her writing, plotting, utterance, and body are all too closely contained: in a kind of physical conceit, she has sewn her letters into her garments and must undress to reach them. Her dress crackles with language: 'So I took off my Under-coat, and, with great Trouble of Mind, unsew'd them from it. And there is a vast Quantity of it' (p. 204).

Vestiges of the Renaissance fascination with cross-dressing, and with questions of how to describe the disguised self survive in *Pamela*, but there is none of the indulgence or the open pleasure in cross-gender description that is to be found in Sidney. This creates new difficulties for the male author disguised as a woman writer. Mr B. makes a fool of himself, and terrifies *Pamela*, by disguising himself as Nan, her fellow maid. Sidney's Zelmane (Prince Pyrocles dressed as a woman) is the more high-minded equivalent of Mr B. dressed as Nan. Both watch their beloved undress: '*Zelmane* would have put to her helping hand, but she was taken with such a quivering, that she thought it more wisdom to lean herself to a tree, and look on.' Invited to join the other ladies in their river-bathe, she excuses her/himself 'with having taken a late cold'; seeing Philoclea naked, '*Zelmane* could not chuse but run to touch, embrace and kiss her. But conscience made her come to her self' (I, 246–7). The delicate humour, directness, and eroticism of Sidney's description contrast sharply with Pamela's horrified realization that she has been duped in believing Mr B. to be Nan. Mr B.'s reactions are held entirely within her reading of them. Here the letter-form attempts to divest voyeurism of its glamour. 'But, I tremble to relate it, the pretended She came into Bed; but quiver'd like an Aspin-leaf; and I, poor Fool that I was! pitied her much. – But well might the barbarous Deceiver tremble at his vile Dissimulation, and base Designs' (p. 176). The titillation of the reader here is covert rather than wittily open as in Sidney. It lies in the close conjunction of affective words ('quivered', 'trembled') and words expressing moral disgust: 'vile Dissimulation, and base Designs'. The combination of declared revulsion and uninterpreted sensation is deeply secretive, as was Richardson's own position in the text.

Whereas *Arcadia* has an intimately confident and all-seeing writer, Pamela and Mr B. struggle to wrest control of plot and language from each other. But again the points of congruity, as much as the differences, between the two works articulate Richardson's challenges to his readers' assumptions. Pamela's questioning of terms unsettles the social contracts implicit in Mr B.'s language. More, she can reach assuredly across a linguistic register and series of discourses almost as inventive as those of *Arcadia*. *Arcadia* and *Pamela* are both marked by their extraordinary linguistic variety, and linguistic variety is essential to Richardson's reassessment of relations within society. The unaristocratic Pamela can command an ingenious intensity of language which asserts the value of the ordinary individual.

When in *Shamela* Fielding mocked the alternations in Pamela's language between italicized high apothegm and low-minded commentary, he achieved his affect by excising the intervening range of discourses to which she has access. Fielding's social suggestion is that no maid-servant could match aristocratic style. In the second half of *Pamela 1* there is some loss of the tremor across senses in Pamela's language. She loses her alertness to shifty signification, which was necessitated by her mistrust of Mr B.: for example, the word 'gentleman' ceases to be bandied provocatively about and settles into plain description. When her fear of the sham-marriage is withdrawn she can enjoy the word 'nuptials' unctuously and without reserve. But in *Pamela 11*, the dubiety re-awakens, with the strengthened shadow of an obliterated author in the argument. The clash of wits and courtesy here, the teasing of the reader, is held in the endoubled first-person of Pamela, who does the telling and purportedly controls the writing, and who yet is written, both by the contrivances of Mr B. and by connivance of Richardson's hand, plotting her.

The princesses in *Arcadia* are caught up in civil war, a war whose devastations undermine the pastoral state in which the book begins. Pamela, the rustic, is caught into a class and sexual power struggle which unsteadies Mr B.'s estate, though scarcely the country at large. In *Pamela 1* man is the master, woman the servant. In *Pamela 11*, within the less confrontational politics of the married state, the overweening claims of Mr B. are still pithily articulated by Pamela as going beyond constitutional powers: 'Could you ever have thought, Miss, that Husbands have a Dispensing Power over their Wives, which Kings are not allowed over the Laws? I have this Day had a smart Debate with Mr B.' (III, 390).

In *Pamela 11*, as in the second part of *Don Quixote*, readers' responses to the first part of the work become the action of the second. The question of Pamela's name is brought into the open and tied to the question of her equivocal class status as well as to the question of the book's own genre. One of the characters, bluff and snobbish Sir Simon Darnford, announces the literary connection: 'Methinks I like her *Arcadian* Name' (III, 140). This identification is soon followed by the very Cervantean episode of Sir Jacob Swynford's visit. Sir Jacob resolutely refuses 'to sit down at Table' with Mr B.'s girl: 'if she does, I won't' (III, 308). Sir Jacob is astonished by the hold that the unseen Pamela has established over her social superiors and over her husband: 'You talk in the Language of Romance', complains the forthright choleric Sir Jacob, 'and from the House-keeper to the Head of the House, you're all stark-staring mad ... I'm in an inchanted Castle, that's certain. What a Plague has this little Witch done to you all? – And how did she bring it about?' (III, 310).

Sir Jacob is gulled by the Countess of C. who presents Pamela as her youngest daughter, Jenny; the pregnant Pamela plays the role of the maiden Jenny. In this episode fun is more important than questions of propriety, but the fun brings out Pamela's disquieting power of flouting social categories. First, there is the matter of her name. Sir Jacob sneers: 'But, *Pamela* – did you say? – A *queer* sort of Name! I have heard of it somewhere! – Is it a Christian or a Pagan name? – Linsey-wolsey – half one, half t'other – like thy Girl – Ha, ha, ha' (III, 315).

When Pamela is presented as Lady Jenny, daughter of the Countess, the old man immediately traces the lineaments of high descent in her face, and, in her manners, generations of high breeding. Her intelligence, likewise, he sees as exclusive to great families. Only the next day is it revealed to him that Lady Jenny is Pamela, 'the Mistress of the House, and the Lady with the Pagan Name!' (III, 319). At the masked ball later, Pamela, dressed as a Quaker lady, knows that she has been recognized when 'a Presbyterian Parson ... bad me look after my *Musidorus* – So that I doubted not by this, it must be somebody who knew my Name to be *Pamela*' (IV, 95). The masquerade's jostling fictions of Christian sects and romance characters exemplify the mixed and unstable reference produced by disguise.

Pamela christianizes romance. She forgives Sir Jacob, the biter bit, and welcomes him to her household: 'And the Tears, as he spoke, ran down his rough Cheeks; which moved me a good deal; for, to see a Man with so hard a Countenance weep, was a touching Sight' (III, 320). As Mr B. remarks: 'Now she has made this Conquest, she has completed all her Triumphs.' Pamela is simultaneously 'an Angel' and 'a Witch'. She re-writes the eclogues of romance into hymns. She wishes to resolve contradictions and to be at one with herself. She can do this, however, only at the price of becoming extra-ordinary. She therefore cannot generate social change. She becomes a special case, an 'original', not evidence that cross-class marriages succeed and that serving girls may be the true equals of their masters.

This problem – shared by writer and character – of how to resolve what is disturbingly various within herself may lie behind Pamela's harping on Sir Jacob's phrase 'Linsey-wolsey'. The example raises questions of class, of sexual feeling, and of writing. Linsey-wolsey was a cloth woven from a mixture of wool and flax: such a home-spun fabric might seem a virtuous product of cottage industry quite to Pamela's taste. But it is a mixed fabric, ekeing out wool with flax, a shilly-shally mixture neither rich nor poor, and so

representing Pamela's awkward class-position running across the exalted and
the lowly rustic. Moreover, linsey-wolsey served in the sixteenth and seventeenth centuries as a metaphor for adulteration, and an emblem of the
mingled nature of sexual love, always edging over into base lust. The *Oxford
English Dictionary* cites Nashe: 'a man must not have his affection linsey-
wolsey intermingled with lust'. Linsey-wolsey is also 'a signe of inconstancie',
and displeasing to God.[9] Sylvester's du Bartas uses the adulterate fabric as
an image of his failings as a writer:

> I humme so harsh; and in my Works inchase
> Lame, crawling Lines ...
> And also mingle (Linsie-woolsie-wise)
> This gold-ground Tissue with too-mean supplies.[10]

So Pamela, in her desire for integrity and excellence, is made uneasy in
several ways by Sir Jacob's incidental insight.

The anger of the woman against the man, the servant against the master,
the poor against the rich, the lowly against the aristocratic, are all condensed
in Pamela. But so are the other aspects of that anger: the longing for alliance,
for acceptance and equality, which declare themselves as sycophancy more
often than as love. *Pamela II* is, in large measure, an attempt to control the
romance qualities of *Pamela I*, as well as to limit the social implications of
Pamela's rise. The immovability of privilege, the capacity of power groupings constantly to realign themselves and yet to produce the same privileges as
before, are examined in Mr B.'s behaviour as lover, husband, father, and
possibly polygamous man. Pamela may not suckle her own child; servant girls
continue to be tempted: Pamela has not saved them all, as the story of the
seduceable Polly shows. Polly is even denied the temptation and privilege of a
romance name and given a humdrum reduction of Pamela's own.

Yet Pamela, even in the midst of some curdled exchanges of courtesy,
insists on keeping her own name and not taking a title. She never turns out to
be a princess in disguise, or a lost scion of a noble house. She is sharp-eyed
about the claims of landed families and their assumptions that they will
possess the land eternally. Her claim to gentility is a Christian one; she is the
inheritor of that other romance tradition of 'gentillesse' described in
Chaucer's Wife of Bath's tale:

> Thy gentillesse cometh fro God allone.
> Thanne comth oure verray gentillesse of grace;
> It was no thyng biquethe us with oure place.[11]

Hardy, much later, would twist further the ironies in the tale of servant-girl
and master, by making that servant-girl, Tess of the D'Urbervilles, scion of a

lost great family whose title Alec has bought out, and who herself would now be happier as Durbeyfield. Richardson's Pamela resists any attempt – or Richardson resists it for her – to make her part of an aristocratic family by descent. Her aristocracy is derived from her literary associations only. Her consonance with Sidney's princess proves her title to high dignity at a literary level. Her bearing will be her entitlement to marriage into the landed gentry and to our respect. Her discursive range and her ordering predominance in the letter-form make hers the most authoritative voice, collapsing the claims of the aristocracy to govern language.

3

Truth and storytelling in *Clarissa*

JOHN A. DUSSINGER

A character who prefers death to a life not on her own terms may speak without guile. Partly owing to her reputation as Christian martyr, Clarissa, who could summon even Fielding's tears, has usually appeared free of the mendacity associated with Pamela's account of herself.[1] Yet despite this character's own frenetic assurances of intentional purity, Dr Johnson observed shrewdly that 'there is always something which she [Clarissa] prefers to truth'[2] and thus addressed the central epistemological dilemma while leaving open the question of whether her penchant for untruth is wilful or not.

To a large extent the question is unanswerable. Just as in the heat of the moment self-consciousness is inherently unstable and contingent, so Richardson's fictional narrative, which imitates this temporality, exploits the irresolvable tension between categorical, atemporal assertions about the world, on the one hand, and the character's limited, momentary account of an immediate situation, on the other. The aesthetic strategy of juxtaposing these two competing forms of discourse is made quite explicit in the author's preface to *A Collection of Moral and Instructive Sentiments*, which touts the 'improvements' of modern storytelling to represent specific moral qualities in action as opposed to the abstract maxims recorded by Plutarch from among his contemporaries.[3] But notwithstanding the new writing-to-the-moment realism, the universal statement – pithy sayings, oaths, sacred texts, absolute assertions – remains functional to Richardson's narrative style. McKillop's remark that the *Sentiments* 'was intended as a kind of rebuke to those who read for the story'[4] is misleading because Richardson believed that the aphorism, though detachable from the moment, articulates the design of the story. Moreover, since many of the sententious observations topically indexed in *A Collection of Moral and Instructive Sentiments* are not directly quoted from the novels but revised freely into general interpretations of behaviour, they co-exist with the narrative as 'spare parts' for widening the story's significance, and even changing its direction altogether. Rather than codifying the complex action of the novel dualistically in a quasi-Manichaean system of good and evil, of light and darkness, the moral sentiments often read like Blakean 'contraries', implying some higher synthesis as the only alternative to discord. The issue of Clarissa's sincerity as storyteller is really parallel to the issue of merging the universal aphorism with the particular scene represented: the truth is always out of reach, beyond language and the mind's reductive categories of experience.

Granted the epistolary contract, Richardson's characters have almost no moment when they are not somehow presenting themselves to a reader *within* the story; and thus, even in a novel whose plot carries individualism to a tragic extreme, there is nothing like the representation of consciousness found in Jane Austen's novels, where the third-person narrative often describes the heroine's solitary daydreaming. Rather, the illusion of subjectivity derives from the two kinds of discourse already noted – the non-temporal meditations, apothegms, proverbs, mottoes, and other autonomous sentences regarding the self; and the temporally reported speech, including both direct discourse and a variety of indirect discourse, which individualizes expression by word choice, emphasis, rhythm, and even spelling. As *Sentiments* makes clear, not only Clarissa but Lovelace, Anna Howe, James Harlowe, and other characters have a share in the general commentary; however, it is mainly the protagonists who have the burden of reported speech and who consequently lose themselves in the language of other characters.

Richardson's epistolary technique creates not one but at least three Clarissas: the proud examplar of her sex, vigorously self-assertive, with Anna's feminist spunk and even some of Lovelace's wit; the religious ascetic withdrawing from all worldly ambition, self-abnegating and sincere to the death; and the sentimental heroine, delicate, yielding, and erotically speechless, as seen through Lovelace's narrative. Each of these characters manifests a particular genre of literary language, but the first two are most at odds with each other.

Hardly an accidental effect, this problem of the heroine's character is even thematized in the presentation. From the beginning, Richardson draws attention to the difficulty of telling the 'whole story' and emphasizes that the character is usually absent at the moment. Yet the reporter who is present is also unreliable, always subjective in describing events according to a prescribed text, the character already generically determined. When Anna Howe enters *in medias res*, then, with the excitement over the duel between Lovelace and James fresh in everybody's mind, the implied reader belongs already to the gossips anxious to find out whether it is true 'that the younger Sister has stolen a Lover from the elder' (I,3; *1,2*). 'Public talk' forces Clarissa into the centre of the family conflict, but always she remains an enigma for the reader to fathom, or more accurately, to 'fill in' to answer his or her desires. Letters I–IV of the first volume comprise a narrative unit concerning the rumour about Clarissa's part in the feud, and nearly every paragraph of Anna Howe's letter educes witnesses to the recent events and mystifies the heroine with the community's inquisitiveness: 'I know how it must hurt you to become the subject of the public talk' (I,1; *1, 1*). What is remarkable about this technique of introducing information (a reflexive strategy used throughout the novel) is its way of complicating the story by querying its sources and media. From the beginning a relatively sincere I–thou relationship between writer and reader throws into relief the various public speakers at the periphery, but neither the 'inner' nor the 'outer' circles know exactly what has happened.

What we see represented in Richardson's complex epistolary technique, then, is the means itself of generating the text. If 'public talk' expresses the romantic wish–fulfilment of the conventional reader, the absent character resists fulfilment, closure, and thereby keeps the story in motion through seemingly endless unfolding of narrative layers. Fundamentally, while asking for information, Anna's first letter emphasizes the inherent difficulties of telling not only this particular story but *any* story, drawing us into a complex situation that spawns a variety of interpreters. Ostensibly for the sake of setting the record straight, Anna 'longs to have the particulars' from Clarissa herself; meanwhile, she reports what all the witnesses to the conflict are saying, capped by the bold insinuation that Clarissa has 'stolen a Lover' from Arabella. Whether Clarissa likes it or not, gossips have already inscribed her in their story of star-crossed love; and not even Anna, her most trusted friend, really wants to save her from this fate.

At the outset of *Clarissa* the correspondents seem nervously aware of the inherent difficulties in reporting, but still pretend that the objective truth is ever accessible. Anna's desire for 'the whole of your Story' (I,3; *1,2*) is no more realistic than Clarissa's promise in her first letter to 'recite facts only' (I,6; *1,4*); and in the end, when viewing the heroine's corpse, Anna remarks significantly: 'And is this All! – Is it All, of my CLARISSA'S Story!' (VIII,79; *IV,402*). Because character is always a marginal presence, a truth brought home by the utter vacuity of death, the 'whole' of the story can never be told.

Again, we see the tension between the atemporal, static identity signifying Virtue and the temporal, narrative subject who is continually becoming immersed in reported speech. According to *Sentiments*, from a global perspective the heroine is presumably as flawless as humanly possible: 'A pure intention, void of all undutiful resentments, is what must be my consolation, *says Clarissa*, whatever others may think of the measures I have taken, when they come to be known, vi.195 [vii.114]' (p. 102). But as if aware that the temporal presentation of herself inevitably undermines the fixed character of moral propositions, Clarissa remarks to Anna: 'I fear, I very much fear, that my unhappy situation will draw me in to be guilty of Evasion, of little Affectations, and of Curvings from the plain simple Truth which I was wont to delight in, and prefer to every other consideration' (III,206; *II,130*). Despite the preliminary encomiums on her innocence in Anna's opening letter, for instance, as a writer Clarissa immediately demonstrates a wily sense of the 'facts' and seems at least as interested in the craft as in the content of the storytelling. In response to her reader's curiosity, she is in the embarrassing role of gossip; and if not exactly relishing it, she at least does not regret the disparagement of a hateful elder sister and brother by a handsome aristocrat. Instead of reciting merely the 'facts', Clarissa editorializes freely, breaking into the other's discourse with parenthetical asides to Anna as confidante:

'So handsome a man! – O her beloved Clary!' (for then she was ready to love me dearly, from the overflowings of her good humour on his account!). 'He was but *too* handsome a man for *her*! – Were she but as amiable as *Somebody*, there would be a probability of *holding* his affections! – For he was wild, she heard; *very* wild, very gay; loved intrigue – But he was young; *a man of sense*: would see his error, could she but have patience with his faults, if his faults were not cured by Marriage.'
Thus she ran on; and then wanted me 'to see the charming man', as she called him.
(I,7; *I,5*)

Richardson wants us to sympathize with Clarissa's point of view here; but no matter how despicable Arabella may be, the reciter of the 'facts' compromises herself by compromising her own family to outsiders.

Safely away at the time of its occurrence and thus aloof from the ill-fated courtship, Clarissa also assumes a reporter's neutrality and relies on mimicry to condemn the speaker by her own words. An unattractive elder sister's jealousy suffices as a motive for all the insinuations of triumph ('He was but *too* handsome a man for *her*! – Were she but as amiable as *Somebody* ... ') over the heroine, but the mere replication of the other's language involves the writer as well as the speaker in a vicious sibling rivalry. Furthermore, Arabella's rationalization of Lovelace's character is itself based on report ('For he was wild, she heard; *very* wild ...') and on truisms about reforming a rake by marriage. Since Clarissa subsequently remarks that Lovelace is not physically displeasing, her quoting Arabella's desire for her '"to see the charming man", as she called him' may possibly betray more of an interest in him than she would care to admit. At any rate, the act of reporting her sister's speech and manner is less than innocent.

After mentioning Lovelace's repeated visits, Arabella attributes his delay in proposing marriage to his bashfulness; and apparently unable to restrain herself, Clarissa quips to her friend, 'Bashfulness in Mr. Lovelace, my dear!' (I,8; *1,6*). Circumstances soon dislodge the heroine from her privileged observation, but a moment like this one shows that she is not incapable of Lovelace's delight in the ridiculous. Such irony goes against the notion of the childlike person that the grandfather had rewarded in his will. Clarissa herself of course warns us that she is a Harlowe and thus hardly the sweet, timorous creature that Anna Howe and even Lovelace conjure up in their descriptions of a sentimental heroine; neither is she, in these moments, the ascetic Christian heroine impatient to die.

Since the bare presence of another is a threatening circumstance, Clarissa seldom writes without a cautious eye on her audience in the process. Initially, she enjoys portraying herself as an ingenuous, sociable person: 'You know, my dear, that I have an open and free heart; and, naturally, have as open and free a countenance; at least my complimenters have told me so. At once, where I like, I mingle minds without reserve, encouraging reciprocal freedoms, and am forward to dissipate diffidences' (III,300; *II,202*). Yet mingling minds without reserve is not an action represented in *Clarissa* or indeed anywhere else in Richardson's fiction. With a proper balance of frankness and tact, however, conversation between the sexes and between the various social classes may be mutually satisfying rather than a power struggle: 'A manly sincerity, and openness of heart, are very consistent with true Politeness, ii.331 [iii.67]' (*Sentiments*, p. 179).

Sincerity is not only a moral ideal in Richardson but a class ideology, an attack on the legitimacy of the ruling caste by proving its discourse to be cynical, without moral substance. Libertinism may be an evil on conservative religious grounds, but above all it reflects a hegemony that must be discredited for political reasons: 'The free things that among us Rakes, *says Belford*, pass for wit and spirit, must be shocking stuff to the ears of persons of Delicacy, v.377 [vi.295, 296]' (p. 112). In the spirit of the *Spectator* revolution in manners, the new standard of gentility is allegedly feminine: 'That cannot be Wit, that puts a modest woman out of countenance, iv. 146 [345]' (p. 214). Lovelace redeems himself in Clarissa's eyes by exhibiting the requisite delicacy: 'Even Lovelace declares, that he never did, nor ever will, talk to a Lady in a way that modesty will not permit her to answer him in, vii.222 [viii.145]' (p. 114). This evidence of his sensibility mitigates her willingness to correspond with him at the outset of the story. Presumably delicate feelings portend a moral disposition. Besides, despite her repeated complaints about Lovelace's role-playing, Clarissa is hardly above dissembling herself, having impersonated an elderly lady in a letter full of precocious wisdom (II,78–9; *1,295–6*). She is remarkably suspicious of servants and other working-class people, especially the clever ones whose coy sense of language threatens her sovereignty. Some of her most trying moments are her attempts to cope with the colloquialisms, slang, half-witticisms, garbled syntax, or 'provoking sauciness' (I,184; *I,135*) that designate the uneducated: in dealing with such people the task is not to uphold sincerity in communication but rather a hierarchy of manners to protect traditional class-consciousness. If Lovelace is the enemy from above, attempting to prove that all women are alike, namely whores, the servants are the enemy from below, attempting to prove the same thing to gain power over their mistresses.[5]

Although a dilemma may arise between sympathizing with Betty Barnes's egalitarian ideas of education, and preserving the necessary distance toward subordinates (II,111; *I,319*), the invasion of privacy is finally Clarissa's uppermost concern. When Betty rushes excitedly into her room, for instance, to announce that the family is waiting with Solmes below, Clarissa takes offence at the familiarity of her entrance and gesticulates with her fan. As on other occasions, however, no matter how irritating to her auditor, Betty does have a point: 'Bless me! said she, how soon these fine young Ladies will be put into *flusterations*! – I meant not either to offend or frighten you, I am sure' (II,187; *I,376*). Despite her protestation of innocence, Betty, of course, flaunts her momentary power over the heroine and and summons her choicest words for the occasion. Like her *stomachfulness*, Betty's *flusterations* may illustrate a view in *Sentiments*: 'Female words, tho' of uncertain derivation, have generally very significant meanings, vii.67 [408, 409]' (p. 215). Perhaps combining the idea of frustration as cause and being flustered as effect, *flusterations* is a useful neologism for an impertinent maid who delights in paralysing her mistress with fear ('I trembled so, I could hardly stand' (II,187–8; *I,376*)). Clarissa knows perfectly well Betty's intention, but is helpless to do anything about it: one of the heroine's worst tribulations while still in the family is to be affronted by tricky servants who mischievously carry out orders from above and then coldly observe the painful consequences on their young mistress.

Curiously, although the main action of *Clarissa* is a sexual assault, the subject of rape arouses only a few banal comments in *Sentiments* concerning just prosecution and punishment. One of the most ample categories, however, entitled 'Masters. Mistresses. Servants', focuses instead on an on-going class conflict that sometimes draws hero and heroine closer together in a political alliance. There is a nervousness about whether the lower orders are naturally good or whether they are prone to betray their employers. 'People in low stations have often minds not sordid, ii.59 [150]' (p. 159): 'Take number for number, there are more honest low people, than high, *ibid.*' (p. 159). Other assertions go so far as to allow only the disenfranchised the right to live: 'Were it not for the Poor, and the Middling, *Lovelace says*, the world would deserve to be destroyed, iii.189 [321]' (p. 181). But against this occasional sentimentalization of the poor, Richardson's text reiterates the theme that good masters make good servants and warns against a loss of authority: 'He that rewards well, and punishes seasonably and properly, will be well served, vi.260 [vii.182]' (p. 160): 'The art of governing the under-bred lies more in looks than in words, *ibid.*' (p. 160). Perhaps most urgent is the injunction to protect one's independence: 'The Master who pays not his Servants duly, or intrusts them with secrets, lays himself at their mercy, vi.260 [vii.183]' (p. 160). Reticence may go against the grain of a naturally open temper, but familiarity is the real danger: 'A Master's communicativeness to his Servants, is a means for an enemy to come at his secrets, ii.226 [309]' (pp. 159–60). Conversely, the subordinate is required to maintain deference toward the master at all times: 'Wit in a Servant, except to his companions, is sauciness, *Lovel.* vi.261 [vii.184]' (p. 161). Although frequently corrupting servants with bribes to carry out his plots, Lovelace agrees in principle with Clarissa about the need to keep them at a safe distance.

At Harlowe Place the heroine already suffers humiliations at the hands of servants, from the sly Betty Barnes to the unfaithful Joseph Leman, whose illiterate messages suffice to incriminate them. By way of contemning both upper and lower classes at one stroke, Clarissa praises Betty Barnes underhandedly for a natural wit comparable to that not only of ladies of fashion but even of the university-educated young gentlemen: 'I have heard smarter things from you, than I have heard at table from some of my Brother's Fellow-collegians' (II,111; *I,319*). For instance, to repress her servant's egotism Clarissa unluckily ascribes her 'liveliness or quickness' to the nature of women in general: 'The wench gave me a proof of the truth of my observation, in a manner still more alert than I had expected: If, said she, our Sex have so much advantage in *smartness*, it is the less to be wondered at, that *you*, Miss, who have had such an education, should outdo all the men, and *women* too, that come near you' (II,111–12; *I,319*). Clarissa then makes the chilling remark: 'I was willing to reward myself for the patience she had made me exercise, by getting at what intelligence I could from her' (II,113; *I,320*) – and this from one who has just explained to the girl the difference between *ingenious* and *ingenuous*!

If Clarissa only feigns intimacy in her conversation with Betty here, moments before, however, mistress and servant did come dangerously close while exchanging proverbs about poverty, suffering, and health; and the heroine does not blush to record the effect on the girl: 'She was mightily taken with what I said: See, returned she, what a fine thing scholarship is!' But as the conversation drifts to Betty's inadequate childhood education and her subsequent 'great improvements', the underling's comical affectation of snuff-taking does not completely detract from her criticism of pedants:

Your servant, dear Miss; dropping me one of her best courtesies: So fine a judge as you are! – It is enough to make one very proud. Then, with another pinch – I cannot indeed but say, bridling upon it, that I have heard famous scholars often and often say very silly things: Things I should be ashamed myself to say – But I thought they did it out of humility, and in condescension to those who had not their learning.

(II,III; *I,319*)

By now there is something amiss in the tone: Betty is making too much sense, and Clarissa can no longer depend on the girl's undiluted admiration of her 'scholarship' in mouthing proverbs. Before things get out of hand, Clarissa makes a condescending remark on the liveliness of women's imagination in general and on Betty's 'smartness' in particular. Several entries under 'Vivacity' in *Sentiments* warn against Betty's natural bent: 'Lively talents are oftener snares than advantages, i.186 [194]' (p. 210).

While intelligence among the working class is potentially sinister, trustworthiness may reflect simply an ineffectual naiveté. Just as the quick-witted servant is subversive, so a 'clown' like the tenant farmer Anna Howe sends to inquire after Clarissa proves to be an honest, humble, and loyal retainer; but he is also duped by Widow Bevis into surrendering a valuable letter to the enemy. Perhaps most remarkable in this scene is the way servants are foregrounded – Clarissa being absent at church and Lovelace eavesdropping within earshot from a closet – to represent the conflicting attitudes of clever mimicry and dumb ingenuousness.

Although pretending to defend his rights as Clarissa's husband, Lovelace feels obliged, nevertheless, to bribe the Hampstead maidservant into complicity:

Lovel. Well, child, if ever you wish to be happy in wedlock yourself, and would have people disappointed, who want to make mischief between you and your Husband, get out of him his Message, or Letter, if he has one, and bring it to me, and say nothing to Mrs. Lovelace, when she comes in; and here is a guinea for you.

Peggy. I will do all I can to serve your Honour's Worship for nothing [Nevertheless, with a ready hand, taking the guinea]: For Mr. William tells me what a good gentleman you be. (v,240; *III,158*)

The messenger announces his solemn mission exactly as ordered, but his rustic idiom gives him away: 'I must speak to her her own self'; 'He will speak to Mrs. Harry Lucas her own self'; 'Nay, and that be all, my business is soon known. It is but to give this Letter into your own *partiklar* hands – Here it is' (v,240–2; *III,159–60*). Against the widow's vanity of appearing too 'fresh and ruddy' to be mistaken for Clarissa 'bloated, and in a dropsy', Lovelace rejoins wryly: 'True – but the Clown may not know That.' Despite his shrewd manipulations, however, in trying to reward him with a half-guinea, Lovelace underestimates the cottager's simple allegiance to his mistress: '*Widow*. How shall I satisfy you for this kind trouble? *Fellow*. Na how at all. What I do is for Love of Miss Howe. She will satisfy me more than enough.' But as if to obviate sentimentality, this servant also has a Falstaffian humour for drinking and amorous play, allowing Peggy to retreat only after an unexpected *double entendre*, '*For if he could not make sport, he would spoil none*', and a hearty 'smack, that, she told Mrs Bevis afterwards, she might have heard into the parlour' (v,242–4; *III,160–1*).

For the sake of conveying information, a character's undesirable social behaviour within the story may be very useful to the narrative itself. If Betty's liveliness is a handicap in a servant, it nevertheless enables her to give distant happenings an immediacy through reported speech, a talent Clarissa had displayed while rendering Arabella's mistaken trust in Lovelace. Dissatisfied with her own subordinate role, Betty gleefully compensates with the power of impersonating Clarissa's worst enemies: 'The insolent Betty Barnes has just now fired me anew, by reporting to me the following expressions of the hideous creature, Solmes – "That he is *sure* of the coy girl; and that *with little labour to himself*"' (I,279; *I,206*). For the moment, in compensation for her own servitude, Betty indulges vicariously in the suitor's misogynistic fantasy of power.

From what we have seen in this mistress–servant dialogue, then, rather than any personal quirkiness it is the heroine's enforced situation that largely explains her always preferring something to truth. Unless at the simple level of communication once enjoyed, say, with her grandfather, circumstances almost always prevent the frank discourse that Clarissa believes is her wont. For instance, the difficulty, if not impossibility, of ever telling her story to the world becomes painfully apparent at the time of her arrest for a bogus £150 debt, with numerous onlookers to add to the public disgrace. This episode represents the only time in the novel when Clarissa is actually out in the open air and speaking to disinterested people rather than to the usual conniving subordinates. If her case is ever to be taken from the dark interiors of house and home, this might be the opportunity to make good her threat in the famous 'penknife scene' ('The LAW only shall be my refuge!' (VI,63; *III,289*)) of seeking litigation to redress her grievances against Lovelace.

But when she is brought up close to even the most disinterested public, her exposure reveals only the futility of telling the 'whole story' to the most sympathetic audience. A sensitive plant with a broken stalk, the heroine is remote from the everyday world and fails to comprehend the legal nomenclature of the officers in charge:

Action! said she. What is that? – I have committed *no bad action*! – Lord bless me! Men, what mean you?

That you are our prisoner, Madam.

Prisoner, Sirs! – What – How – Why – What have I done? . . . *Suit!* said the charming innocent; I don't know what you mean.

Perhaps as might be expected in a predatory world, the reactions from the crowd are mixed and class-oriented, with only one or two educated men speaking up on her behalf: 'The people were most of them struck with compassion. A fine young creature! – A thousand pities! cried some. While some few threw out vile and shocking reflections! But a gentleman interposed, and demanded to see the fellows' authority.' Once assured of the officers' legitimacy, however, this fatherly spokesman simply advises the heroine to co-operate with the authorities: 'He pitied her, and retired.' Another gentleman pleads that she not be abused. The thought of Clarissa's being carried off 'through a vast croud of people' causes Belford, the narrator, to gasp: '*All this was to a Clarissa*!!!' (VI,249–51; *III,427–8*). But no amount of pity can save the heroine from the punitive laws against her alleged indebtedness.

Notwithstanding the unquestioned political and economic power of the male over the female, throughout this story women are seen to be locally worse enemies than men; and while detained at the Rowlands's, Clarissa has to submit to insults from Sally Martin, who is 'fond of gratifying her jealous revenge, by calling her *Miss*' to emphasize cruelly that the heroine is unmarried as well as not a virgin. Clarissa's only defence is bewilderment at her interlocutor's street slang: 'You amaze me, Miss Martin! – What language do you talk in? – *Bilk my lodgings*! – What is that?' (VI,252; *III,429*). On another occasion, the prostitute returns to taunt Clarissa for being without her wardrobe: 'you are a little *soily*, to what we have seen you'. The sympathetic Belford interjects: '*Insolent devils! – How much more cruel and insulting are bad women, even than bad men!*' (VI,265; *III,438–9*). In contrast to Richardson's perspective, however, Belford's view conveniently overlooks the male-dominated economic system that prompts such competitive behaviour between women in the first place.

Notwithstanding a character's penchant for being honest, the task of reporting events, as Richardson knew, is always contingent on the particular moment and on the inherent vagaries of language. Clarissa's sincerity as storyteller, we have seen, is in doubt not only because she may have something to hide but, more significantly, because language inevitably leaves something out, an insight Jane Austen brought to fiction: 'Seldom, very seldom, does complete truth belong to any human disclosure; seldom can it happen that something is not a little disguised, or a little mistaken.'[6]

Aphorisms, as non-temporal universal statements, are relatively free of such exigencies; and by their very distance from the domestic world, they usually exert an ironic effect whenever directed toward the apparently random circumstances of a story, as in the famous opening sentence of *Pride and Prejudice*. Proximity to the warm moment, on the contrary, obviates this oral freedom. Characters as storytellers have no choice but to present themselves to their reader while in the act of describing what happens, and this sense of audience qualifies whatever is said. Thus no matter how sincere her ideal of personal integrity, Clarissa can never tell the 'whole story' because, as Richardson's elaborate typographical apparatus reminds us, any narrative is circumscribed by the conventions of language. This contingency of reporting is most transparent in discourse involving power relations, particularly in the dialogue between master or mistress and servants, where even the exemplary character finds herself in the rake's position of toying with others. Although usually regarded as the antithesis of sincerity, role-playing, as Clarissa discovers, is the requisite condition of being in the world, inescapable not only in talking to others but also in setting pen to paper.

4

Remapping London: *Clarissa* and the woman in the window

EDWARD COPELAND

Near the end of Clarissa's life, a mischievous account of her behaviour in London gets abroad to the Harlowes. Mr Brand, their clergyman spy, reports that a lady living 'up one pair of stairs', 'over against the house where she lodgeth', has seen Clarissa from her window engaged in suspicious conversations with Lovelace's intimate friend, Robert Belford. He 'hath often been seen with Miss (*tête à tête*)', writes Brand, 'at the *window* – In no *bad way*, indeed', Brand hastens to add. 'But my friend's wife', he assures the Harlowes, 'is of opinion, that all is not *as it should be.*' As to Clarissa's daily forays out of her Covent Garden lodgings 'to *prayers* (as it is said)', writes Brand, 'my friend's wife told me, that nothing is more common in London, than that the frequenting of the Church at morning prayers is made the *pretence* and *cover* for *private Assignations*' (VII, 285–7; IV, 238–41).

The voice of the woman represents a voice heard repeatedly in Richardson's novel: the accent of the canny, streetwise Londoner ready to mark any sparrow that falls in its peculiarly urban frame of reference. Her language in *Clarissa* is what Mikhail Bakhtin calls the language of 'impersonal going opinion', 'always superficial and frequently hypocritical', but a language with which the novelist has no easy relationship: 'sometimes abruptly exposing its inadequacy to its object and sometimes, on the contrary, becoming one with it, maintaining an almost imperceptible distance, sometimes even directly forcing it to reverberate with his own "truth", which occurs when the author completely merges his own voice with the common view'.[1] The language of the Bakhtinian marketplace, the intrusive street language of *Clarissa*'s London, provides a running check on all the struggling languages of Richardson's correspondents.

Richardson insists that we grant the Londoner at least grudging respect. The woman in the window, for example, misreads her London signs grossly, but instead of laughing at her, we laugh at Brand, the credulous yokel. In fact, as soon as the gossips who report this tale learn Clarissa's true situation they are anxious to make amends: '[They] were very much concerned to think any-thing they said should be made use of against her: And as they heard from Mrs. Smith, that she was not likely to live long, they should be sorry she should go out of the world a sufferer by their means' (VII, 295; *IV, 244*). Brand has no such commendable remorse. In Fielding's and Smollett's novels, however, a Londoner's accent inevitably carries in its rhythms the yoked dangers of misrule and corruption. The streets speak to Tom Jones with a cudgel to the back of his head. In *Humphry Clinker* (1771), a Covent Garden bawd polishes cherries for the gentry by passing them through her 'ulcerated chops'. In *The Beggar's Opera* (1728), Gay's Polly sings of the 'fair flower in its lustre' sent to Covent Garden, where '(as yet sweet)' it 'rots, stinks, and dies, and is trod under feet'. Graphic artists also follow the well-worn path. Hogarth's *Morning* (1738) depicts the piazza as a receptacle for all the moral refuse of the city – irresponsible gentry, a riotous mob, and the starving poor (see figure 1).

Samuel Scott, however, a contemporary of Hogarth, Fielding, Smollett, and Richardson, presents us with a view of Covent Garden much closer to that enjoyed by Clarissa's idle gossip (see figure 2). In Scott's large oil, *Covent Garden Piazza and Market* (*c.* 1749), in the Museum of London, we look west, from the vantage of a first-floor elevation, across the market towards St Paul's church on the east side of the piazza. Beneath our eyes we find a depiction of London's hectic, busy flower and vegetable market in full operation: lively figures engage in the anonymous lifting and hauling of market produce; others pause to strike bargains; vegetables lie stacked for convenience, not elegance; and the nobility and gentry, who occupy centre stage in Hogarth's more focused picture, are now relegated to the edges of the action, identifiable only by their slightly brighter clothing.[2] The anonymous efficiency of Scott's commercial London remains relentlessly impersonal. In Scott's painting, for example, a brawling man and woman in the lower right hand corner collect a small but casual audience – nobody takes much notice; idle, anonymous people stand about watching other idle, anonymous people. Clarissa confirms the point in a letter to Anna Howe: 'I remember, my dear, in one of your former letters, you mentioned London, as the most private place to be in' (III, 155; *II, 92*).[3] A loaded cart rolls out of the right side of our view up James Street; a hackney coach rumbles down King Street (the same street in which Clarissa takes refuge with the Smiths); wagons wait in line to be loaded and unloaded – all this busy, orderly commercial activity taking place under a clear golden light that extends its optimistic glow to an infinite horizon.[4]

On the right side of Scott's painting (the north side of the piazza) in one of

1   William Hogarth, *The Four Times of Day: Morning* (1738)

2　Samuel Scott, *Covent Garden Piazza and Market* (*c.* 1749)

the windows of the first floor of that block of buildings, we spy two women, themselves idle onlookers, observing the action in the piazza from a viewing position analogous to our own. Their position informs ours: they possess precisely the same frame of reference as we do – after all, they can presumably see us in our window as well as we can see them in theirs. Placed above the scene, seemingly out of the fray, they are, like ourselves, market shoppers out to select and 'buy' meaning from the richly stocked market below. On the other hand, we and the two women in the window are compromised by the consumerism implicit in our positions in Scott's semiotic paradigm. We are caught in the same buoyant consumerism we observe below us: like the two women, we are at the mercy of 'going opinion' for our selections of meaning.

So far as Richardson's Londoners are concerned, Lovelace and Clarissa are just two more tourists in town for a wedding visit; at worst, as one laconic street witness remarks, Clarissa is simply another recruit for 'Mother *Damnable's* Park' (v, 24; *ii, 522*). Such cool London appraisals force the reader to reevaluate less disinterested languages – outraged father, anxious friend, scheming lover, even the accents of the suffering heroine herself. In a novel where every correspondent wields an ideologically freighted pen, observant Londoners seem often, and refreshingly, more right than wrong. A sedan chairman in the street, for example, witnesses Clarissa's escape from Mrs Sinclair's and comments, perceptively enough, 'That he'd warrant, she had either a bad husband, or very cross parents' (v, 23; *ii, 522*). The three foolish ladies of Hampstead, Mrs Moore, Miss Rawlinson, and the Widow Bevis, have a surprisingly accurate picture of Clarissa's ignorance of her own heart. The Smiths, who run a hosier's shop in Covent Garden, befriend Clarissa, and, when Lovelace forces his way into their house, reprove his intrusion with great good sense: 'Sir', says Mr Smith, ' 'tis not like a gentleman, to affront a man in his own house' (vii, 132–3; *iv, 126*). When Clarissa orders her coffin delivered to her room to serve as a desk, the morbidity of the act shocks every Londoner who sees it, and reasonably so.

The language of commerce is the language of truth: in Clarissa's London, the coaches run on time.[5] Hackneys ply the streets; sedan chairs come on call; coaches can be hired by the day as can a boat and a waterman; taverns provide refeshment and a place to write; churches keep regular hours for daily prayer. Most important, letters come and go: 'I think there can be no objection to your going to London,' Anna Howe writes to the heroine: 'There, as in the centre, you will be in the way of hearing from every-body, and sending to any-body' (iii, 173; *ii, 105*). Regular post, penny post, private messenger, all systems of communication are centred in London (see figure 3).[6] With her second and final escape, the heroine and Miss Howe abandon 'Wilson's', the

3   Postal routes in 1756

private letter exchange in Pall Mall that Lovelace has suborned, for alternative ways to correspond. The great London inns provide safe places for receiving and directing their mail. 'I will send my Letters by the usual hand', Miss Howe writes to Clarissa, 'to be left at the Saracen's Head on Snow-hill: Whither you may send yours (as we both used to do, to Wilson's)' (VI, 182; *III, 377*). 'Direct ... to Mrs. Dorothy Salcomb, to be left, till call'd for, at the Four Swans Inn, Bishopgate-street', Clarissa instructs Mrs Hodges (VI, 123–4; *III, 334*) (see figure 4). She asks Lady Betty Lawrance, Lovelace's kinswoman, to send any correspondence 'to the Belle-Savage on Ludgate-hill, till called for', knowing that even if Lovelace should see the address, her hiding place will remain secure (VI, 120; *III, 332*) (see figure 5). Lady Betty takes no chances and scratches out the address, but taunts Lovelace by telling him that 'it was probable, [it] was only a temporary one, in order to avoid me: Otherwise she would hardly have directed an Answer to be left at an Inn' (VI, 226; *III, 410*).

The order of London's efficient systems regularly opposes the disorder of Lovelace's anarchic imagination. Clarissa sends for a sedan chair: 'This startled me', Lovelace confesses: 'A chair to carry her to the next Church from Mrs. Sinclair's, her name not Sinclair, and to bring her back hither, in the face of people who might not think well of the house! – There was no permitting That' (III, 324; *II, 220*). He avoids discovery by taking her to St Paul's in his own coach. Growing anxious, Clarissa tries for a sedan chair again: 'I will only go to St. James's Church', she writes to Miss Howe, 'and in a *chair*; that I may be sure I can go out and come in when I please, without being intruded upon by him, as I was twice before' (IV, 189; *II, 373*). Lovelace sends Will, his servant, this time to give directions privately to the chairmen. Clarissa tests her situation one more time: 'I will go out, and that without him, or any attendant', she writes to Miss Howe (IV, 198; *II, 379*). She orders Dorcas to call a chair: 'You must not go, Madam!' cries Lovelace, who seizes her hand and blocks the way (IV, 201; *II, 381*). When a horrified Anna Howe discovers the secret of Mrs Sinclair's house, she writes to Clarissa, 'Did you never go out by yourself, and discharge the coach or chair, and return by another coach or chair? If you did [Yet I don't remember that you ever wrote to me, that you did] you would never have found your way to the vile house, either by the Woman's name, *Sinclair*, or by the Street's name, mentioned by that Doleman in his Letter about the lodgings' (V, 32; *III, 2–3*). London and its systems operate in utter truthfulness. The rules are as dependable as those of fairy tales: if Clarissa names the street, 'Dover-street', to a chairman, she will discover Lovelace's plot. If she sends her letters to a proper posting inn, she will get her mail.[7]

4   T. H. Shepherd, *The Four Swans, Bishopgate* (*c.* 1855)

5   The 'Belle-Savage'

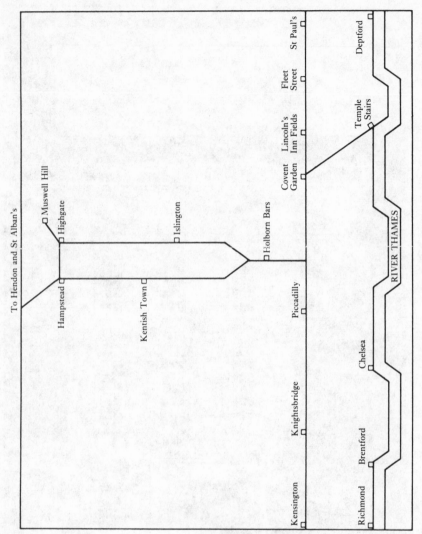

6 Transportation patterns in *Clarissa*

In short, Richardson's novel gives us a guidebook London, a city of services provided. It is, in fact, a London very much like that of Defoe's contemporary guide, *A Tour Thro' the Whole Island of Great Britain* (1724–7), in which we find a city given shape by its systems of transportation and services.[8] Such is still the order of London, notes Nicholas Shakespeare in his recent *Londoners* (1986): 'To stake out a border is to become tangled in several different maps: one marking the square mile of the City, another the taxi driver's six-mile circle from Charing Cross; and, in a widening ripple, those outlining the London postal and telephone areas, the London Underground and bus routes, the Metropolitan Police district.'[9] Guidebooks, like maps, foster in their users the joint illusion of control and power. For us, the familiar map of the London Underground offers a convenient example: its clean geometry makes sense out of a formidable tangle of rail lines laid down over what is in reality a distinctly ungeometric topography. Defoe's *Tour* brings an analogous order to the 'monstrous growth' of eighteenth-century London by supplying the city with recognizable corners. In the east, says Defoe, the edge of the city is at Deptford; in the west, at Knightsbridge and Kensington; and in the north, at Kentish Town and Islington, with the northern villages of Highgate and Hampstead set at its outermost suburban reaches; in the south, the boundary lies at Southwark and its nearby villages.

In *Clarissa*, Richardson's characters move securely and efficiently about Defoe's imagined square of order (see figure 6). On the eastern border, for example, we find Mrs Townsend, the smuggler who agrees to hide Clarissa in Deptford: 'a populous village; and one of the last, I should think', writes Anna Howe, 'in which you should be sought for' (IV, 153; *II, 346*).[10] (Margaret Anne Doody calls my attention to the delightful topographic pun in Mrs Townsend's name.) The Thames supplies a convenient means for Clarissa to avoid a threatened visit from Lovelace: in a boat hired at Temple Stairs in the morning, she travels to Chelsea, dines at 'Brentford-Aight', a river island near Brentford, on to Richmond, then to Mortlake where she drinks tea at a place recommended by her waterman, and at last, home to Covent Garden in the evening by Temple Stairs (VII, 199; *IV, 175*). As for the northern boundaries, early on Clarissa and Lovelace take an 'Airing' on Hampstead Heath (an exercise recommended by Defoe as one of the suburban pleasures of London), going there by the circle tour of Hampstead, Highgate, and Muswell Hill, returning home to Mrs Sinclair's through Kentish Town (IV, 268; *II, 430*).[11] Later, when Clarissa takes refuge with the Smiths in Covent Garden, she twice makes the round of the northern suburbs on her own, returning home both times through Islington. At Defoe's western limits, Lovelace sets up camp at the Rose Tavern in Knightsbridge where during Clarissa's last illness he paces from Kensington Palace 'to the Gore' (current

7 T. H. Shepherd, *Lincoln's Inn Chapel* (*c.* 1829)

8 'St Dunstan's Fleet-street'

9   P. Sandby, *The West Front of St Paul's, Covent Garden*

site of the Albert Hall) as he awaits Belford's hourly messages from Clarissa's bedside (VII, 363–4; *IV, 296*).

The city is demystified, made accessible in *Clarissa*. Contemporary readers, in fact, journeyed to Hampstead to commemorate Lovelace and Clarissa's stop for refreshment at a popular tavern, the Upper Flask, on the way to their Hampstead Heath 'Airing'.[12] The guidebook temptations of the novel persist: we can follow Clarissa's footsteps through Hampstead's streets to Jack Straw's Castle at the top of the village where, with tears in her eyes, the heroine relinquished her final attempt to escape London. We can stand on the west portico of St Paul's, Covent Garden for the claustrophobic experience of reliving Clarissa's arrest for debt in that very spot: 'Looking about her, and seeing the three passages, to wit, that leading to Henrietta-street, that to King-street, and the fore-right one, to Bedford-street' (VI, 250; *III, 428*). Eighteenth-century readers could visit her churches, inspect her inns, walk down King Street where she lived, take a boat to Brentford-Aight.

In short, *Clarissa*'s readers become active participants in the systems of London. When, for example, the heroine lists her daily schedule of church attendance in town, Richardson expects us to confirm the locations and the

○ LOVELACE'S LONDON

Pall Mall

1. The Cocoa Tree
2. The King's Arms
3. 'Wilson's'
4. *St James Park*
5. *St James*, White's
6. *Soho Square*, Belford's address
7. *Dover Street*, Mrs Sinclair (false address)
8. *Albemarle Street*, Lovelace's cousins
9. *Monmouth Street*, used clothing for disguises
10. *Piccadilly*, taverns during Clarissa's last days
11. *Suffolk Street*, The Eagle
12. *St Martin's Lane*, Tomlinson's address

Lovelace's Churches

13. Chapel Royal
14. St James's, Piccadilly
15. St Anne's, Soho
16. St George's, Bloomsbury
17. St Martin's-in-the-Fields
18. St Giles's-in-the-Fields
19. Kensington Gore
20. Rose Tavern, Knightsbridge

◇ CLARISSA'S LONDON

Covent Garden

1. *King Street*, the Smiths' address
2. St Paul's
3. The Bedford Head
4. *Fleet Street*, undertaker's shop
5. *Temple Stairs*, waterman
6. *Snow Hill*, Saracen's Head
7. *Bishopsgate*, The Four Swans
8. *Ludgate Hill*, The Belle Savage
9. *Holborn Bars*, Hampstead coach
10. *High Holborn*, sponging house

Clarissa's Churches

(2) St Paul's, Covent Garden
11. Lincoln's Inn Chapel
12. *St Dunstan's*, Fleet Street
13. *Norfolk Street*, attractive lodgings
14. *Fleet Street*, The White Horse Inn

10 Lovelace's London/Clarissa's London (using John Rocque's *A Plan of London* (1769))

times: 'once at Lincoln's-Inn chapel, at Eleven; once at St. Dunstan's Fleet-street, at Seven in the morning, in a chair both times; and twice at Six in the morning, at the neighbouring Church in Covent-garden' (see figures 7, 8, 9). The author-as-editor prudently footnotes the time of the service at St Dunstan's Fleet-street to prevent our hasty intervention with better knowledge: 'The Seven o'clock Prayers at St. Dunstan's have been since discontinued', he writes (VI, 193; *III, 396*). Lovelace's imaginary parade through the streets of London from prison in Newgate to trial at the Sessions House receives a similar corrective footnote: 'Within these few years past, a passage has been made from the Sessions-house, whereby malefactors are carried into the court without going thro' the street.' As a public-spirited citizen, Richardson adds that 'Lovelace's triumph on their supposed march shews the wisdom of this alteration' (IV, 258; *II, 423*). We are expected to recognize King Street, where Clarissa takes refuge in Covent Garden with the Smiths, as a street of respectable tradesmen – a grocer, a stationer, three haberdashers, a linen draper, three tailors, a perukemaker, buttonseller, cabinetmaker, fruiterer, distiller, and two gentlemen, according to contemporary account.[13] Even coach schedules become our responsibility: when Anna Howe urges Clarissa to throw herself into the protection of Lovelace's kinswomen, she writes, 'You should put yourself, if in town, or near it, into the Reading Stage-coach, which inns somewhere in Fleet-street' – she can't remember where (VI, 235; *III, 416–17*). Any reader possessing a copy of the *Complete Guide to ... London, and Parts adjacent* (1749) could conveniently determine that the Reading stage leaves from 'The White Horse in Fleet-street, everyday'. In the back of this volume, the reader could also find advertised two novels (from the same publisher) to take on the journey: *Pamela: or, Virtue Rewarded* and *Clarissa: or, The History of a Young Lady*. Moreover, the White Horse lay directly across Fleet Street from passages leading into Salisbury Court, Richardson's London address during the writing of *Clarissa*, providing, no doubt, a pleasant shock of recognition for Richardson's London friends and family.[14]

Running at ideological cross-purposes to this vision of a modern, efficient, commercial London, however, we find that the two protagonists, Lovelace and Clarissa, use an imagined map of the city based on a competing traditional ideology, that of 'Town' and 'City'.[15] In *Clarissa*, the two protagonists divide the city between themselves, drawing the dare-you-to-cross-it line at the east–west division of St Martin's Lane (see figure 10). When Doleman, Lovelace's tool, suggests that the heroine would probably prefer lodgings on the west side of town to lodgings in Norfolk Street, a street leading off the Strand halfway between the churches of St Mary le Strand and St Clement Danes, Clarissa corrects him: 'I seemed to prefer those in

Norfolk-street, for the very reason the writer gives why he thought I would
not; that is to say, for its neighbourhood to a City so well-governed as London
is said to be. Nor should I have disliked a Lodging in the heart of it, having
heard but indifferent accounts of the liberties sometimes taken at the other
end of town' (III, 178–81; *II, 111*).

Under Lovelace's spell the West End, that topographic sink of corruption,
bubbles again: 'I cannot but say', he tells Belford, 'that the Westminster Air is
a little grosser than that at Hamstead . . . and I think in my heart, that I can say
and write those things at one place, which I cannot at the other; nor indeed
any-where else' (v, 267; *III, 178*). His haunts are all west of St Martin's Lane
– two clubs in Pall Mall, the King's Arms and the Cocoa Tree, and another,
White's in St James Street.[16] He fixes Clarissa's and Anna Howe's postal
exchange 'at Mr. Wilson's in Pall Mall', an arrangement which enables him to
monitor their correspondence. He takes his walks – and plots another
abduction – in St James's Park. When Clarissa asks for directions to a church,
'the Royal Chapel at St. James', he tells her, is where 'he oftenest went to,
when in town'. Mrs Sinclair's nymphs recommend St James's, Piccadilly, and
St Anne's, Soho, as being convenient to Mrs Sinclair's, 'and another in
Bloomsbury', the new and fashionable St George's, though they prefer St
James's, they admit, for 'the good company, as well for the excellent
preaching' (III, 301; *II, 203*). On this topographic hint, we are left to deduce
the location of the false 'Dover-street' as somewhere in the area between St
James's and St George's. During Clarissa's last days, when Lovelace is
waiting for hourly dispatches from her deathbed, he sticks to his side of the
line, as Belford confirms in a letter to their mutual friend Mowbray: 'You will
find him between Piccadilly and Kensington, most probably on horseback,
riding backwards and forwards in a crazy way; or put up, perhaps, at some Inn
or Tavern in the way' (VII, 424; *IV, 341*).

Clarissa takes just as firm possession of the east side of St Martin's Lane by
her round of churches: St Paul's in Covent Garden, the Chapel at Lincoln's
Inn Fields, and St Dunstan's in Fleet Street.[17] She shops in Fleet Street,
buying her coffin, 'her house', at a draper's after morning prayers at St
Dunstan's (VII, 248–9; *IV, 210*). Her posting inns, the Saracen's Head, the
Belle Savage, and the Four Swans, are all chosen east of the significant
dividing line. In fact the division is so well established, that when Clarissa's
cousin, Colonel Morden, invites Belford to dine with him on the same day
that Lovelace has arranged to dine with Belford, Belford continues to meet
Colonel Morden on Clarissa's side of the line at the Bedford Head in Covent
Garden, and Lovelace on his side, at the Eagle, near the Haymarket in
Suffolk Street (VIII, 187; *IV, 484*).

However, the division of the city is finally an empty one, much as its traditional simplicity tempts both Richardson and his protagonists to put their faith in it. Such ideological divisions inevitably give way to 'going opinion' or street wisdom. The working systems of London refuse co-operation as they regularly cross the all-important line of St Martin's Lane with no regard whatsoever for the struggles of the two protagonists. A constable in the 'wicked' West End, for example, tries to rescue Clarissa from Mrs Sinclair's house; another on the steps of her own parish church in Covent Garden arrests her for a debt sworn against her by Mrs Sinclair. Clarissa can scarcely understand his language, the language of the London systems: '*Action!* said she. What is that? – I have committed *no bad action!* – Lord bless me! Men, what mean you?' 'You *must* go with us', the constable tells her: 'We have a Writ against you.' A gentleman interposes, inspects the writ, and tells her: 'You *must* go with these men, Madam ... They have authority for what they do' (VI, 250; *III, 427–8*). Sally Martin, Mrs Sinclair's accomplice, satisfies a group of protesting onlookers that the lady will be 'exceedingly well used', that 'the people she had lodged with, loved her: But she had left her lodgings privately', upon which they disperse, untroubled by the inevitable turning over of the wheels of justice. 'O!' say 'one or two' in the crowd, 'had she those tricks already?' (VI, 251; *III, 428*). Nor does Richardson question a law designed to get people to pay their debts; it is the *haut bourgeois* Belford who is shocked by Clarissa's arrest.[18] Reading as canny Londoners ourselves, we recognize the power of the London systems and the terrifying danger that lies in wait for anyone unable to negotiate them.

At the conclusion of the novel, the Londoner's voice of 'going opinion' is the only untouched survivor. Both major protagonists, Clarissa and Lovelace, are driven out of London, literally as well as figuratively. Belford announces Clarissa's death and Lovelace's exile from London in the same sentence: 'I have only to say at present', he writes to Lovelace, 'Thou wilt do well to take a Tour to Paris; or where-ever else thy destiny shall lead thee!!! – ' (VII, 425; *IV, 342*). Until it is lost from sight, his eyes follow the hearse bearing Clarissa's body down King Street. We as readers, survivors ourselves, remain in London to peruse Clarissa's will with Belford, witness its probate, affirm the I-could-have-told-you's of what happens to Mrs Sinclair, what happens to Arabella and James, what happens to the Harlowe parents, Anna Howe, and so on. Even Lovelace's dramatic final words, 'LET THIS EXPIATE', drop on Belford's doorstep with bathetic finality as they arrive from Italy, stamped, sealed, and delivered by the efficient Foreign Post.

But as Margaret Anne Doody perceptively recognizes in a recent essay, Richardson does not level his guns on London: 'Clarissa finds everything she wants at the end in London ... [She] has no yearning to spend her last days among green fields and purling brooks and shady groves.'[19] Moreover, as Eaves and Kimpel, Richardson's biographers, observe, *Clarissa* was conceived in London, in Salisbury Court, nearest neighbour to 'victuallers, tallow chandlers, apothecaries, engravers, bakers, glaziers, pawnbrokers, cabinet-makers, silversmiths, periwig-makers, tailors, watchcase-makers, physicians, poulterers, surgeons, and even a clergyman and two people described as gentlemen'.[20] Extracted from Lovelace's plots and machinations, the London of *Clarissa* presents a picture of up-to-date convenience and homely comforts. In fact, whenever Richardson as editor of Defoe's *Tour* sees the chance to aggrandize the city or correct a negative impression left by Defoe, he does so. In the 1748 edition of the *Tour*, Defoe's qualified claim of 1725, that London possesses 'perhaps the most regular and well-ordered Government, that any City, of above Half its Magnitude, can boast of', becomes in Richardson's grander emendation, 'the best regulated that any City can pretend to'. Moreover, claims Richardson, 'of late Years it boasts of several new Regulations, as to Beggars, Lights, Pavements, &c. which turn out greatly to its Advantage' (II, 100). The Penny Post in Defoe's first edition of the *Tour* is simply an institution which will take a letter for a penny from Limehouse in the east 'to the farthest Westminster' several times in a day, but for Richardson, in 1748, letters go triumphantly 'to the neighbouring Villages, as *Kensington, Hammersmith, Chiswick*, &c. Westward; *Newington, Islington, Kentish-town, Hampstead, Holloway, Highgate*, &c. Northward; to *Newington-butts, Camberwell*, &c. Southward; and *Stepney, Poplar, Bow, Stratford, Deptford, Greenwich*, &c. Eastward, once a Day' (II, 109).

The map of London, its public landmarks, its churches, inns, and parks, the business of its streets *seem* to give the option of freedom to Clarissa. It is there for the taking, as Richardson suggests in the novel and in his emendations of Defoe's *Tour*, which he turns from an informal ramble into a practical 'guide', tidying Defoe's enthusiasms – the Post Office, the water supply, hospitals, charities, prisons, libraries, schools, shipping – into sixteen chapters neatly headed and indexed as to contents. By accommodating the city to an imaginary world of stable signs and symbols, Richardson gives London shape, triumphing over the amorphous absence of direction so detested by critics like Smollett and the Fielding brothers.

But London, as part of its modern definition, supplies no knight in shining armour to help the heroine. The great impersonal systems of Defoe's London, and Richardson's, and the painter Samuel Scott's as well, are, in fact, the horror of this 'monster city' as well as its glory. The maligned last volume of *Clarissa* has always, to me, seemed its most 'modern' contribution to fiction, as close to Beckett as to eighteenth-century fiction. It offers a literary experience so powerful, and so frustrating too, that surely no one has ever left it with neutral feelings. In it, with Richardson's Londoners, we are witnesses to a shattering departure from moral order. Perhaps we take comfort in the system of punishment and reward that Richardson offers us, or perhaps we find a competing satisfaction in the Marxian readings of Terry Eagleton or Christopher Hill, also offered by Richardson, though in a less declarative strategy.[21] Either way, we find ourselves involved in London. It is the paradox of Bakhtin's 'common language': a language that is at one time inadequate 'to its object' and at another, one with the author's 'own voice'. As Belford says of Sally Martin and Polly Horton, Mrs Sinclair's whores: 'The wretched women, it must be owned, act but in their profession' (VI, 269; *III*, 442). In the last volume of the novel, the city and its systems are the only thing we have left, the letters pressing this truth on us with all the busy energy of Samuel Scott's painting. But with the hum and bustle, the practicality and efficiency of London's systems, the language of London in *Clarissa* suggests, finally, to me at least, a chilling vision of anomie – a world filled with people, and at the same time, a world despairingly empty.

5

Lovelace and the paradoxes of libertinism

JAMES GRANTHAM TURNER

On goûte une douceur extrême à réduire par cent hommages le coeur d'une jeune beauté, à voir de jour en jour les petits progrès qu'on y fait ... à forcer pied à pied toutes les petites résistances qu'elle nous oppose ... Mais lorsqu'on en est maître une fois, il n'y a plus rien à dire. (Molière, *Dom Juan* I, ii)

Having *her*, I shall never want a subject. Having lost her, my whole Soul is a blank ...
O Return, Return! (Lovelace to Belford, *Clarissa* VI, 196; *III, 388*)

If we had to choose a single word to characterize Richardson's Lovelace, it might be 'vapour'. Most of his outrageous libertinism, he claims, is 'vapour' – posturing without substance, improvisation in the realm of pure wit, 'to shew my invention' (III, 162; *II, 98*). The pleasure that he seeks in seduction, as he explains to his accomplice Joseph Leman, is cerebral and aesthetic:

I love dearly to exercise my invention. I do assure you, Joseph, that I have ever had more pleasure in my contrivances than in the End of them. I am no sensual man; but a man of spirit – One woman is like another – (III, 228; *II, 147*)

The woman in question was rejected as a marriage-partner because she was a tradesman's daughter, and died hideously in childbirth; but for Lovelace this was 'a youthful frolick', an exercise in volatility and 'spirits' as opposed to mere body. He swears, in the same self-justificatory letter to Leman, that his pursuit of Clarissa is utterly different from such displays of 'invention'. I will suggest, however, that Lovelace cannot maintain this distinction, and cannot escape the destructive contradictions that typify libertine attitudes to sex and marriage. He must force Clarissa into sexuality (to prove that 'every Woman is the same'), and yet sex is empty and disgusting for him – 'a vapour, a bubble!'[1] He seeks a profound intimacy with her, and yet cannot imagine sexual love within marriage, since he fears in a partner precisely the 'vapours' and volatility that he enjoys in himself; seeing Clarissa weep, he confesses to

70

being 'terribly afraid I shall have a vapourish wife, if I *do* marry' (III, 281; *II, 187*). 'Not', he adds, 'that I shall be *much at home with her, perhaps, after the first fortnight, or so.*'

Such paradoxes, I would argue, are central to erotic libertinism – that is, to the *mélange* of Ovidian seduction-theory and Epicurean philosophy that Richardson found in the court wits of Charles II and in the seducer-heroes of Restoration drama and early eighteenth-century fiction. Put simply, these antecedents of Lovelace are torn between two roles; they proclaim their allegiance to Wit and Sense, but they are unable to reconcile the two components of this libertine character, intellectual brilliance and passionate sensuality. They show their wit, and their freedom from conventional beliefs, by adopting a sensualist, materialist and determinist philosophy that denies intellect and freedom altogether. Simultaneously, they submit all appearances and all behaviour to a cynical, penetrating, Machiavellian rationalism that subordinates pleasure to calculation, and that reveals the hollowness of the 'life of sense' they ostensibly espouse. Abstract Reason, in Rochester's great *Satyr* against mankind, is condemned as an *ignis fatuus* that leads into a wilderness, whereas 'right reason', the intellect adapted to the service of the animal senses, must be the sole arbiter of the individual; one must dine when one is hungry, not when the clock dictates – a dead mechanism that enforces dead social conventions. And yet Rochester's poem deconstructs its own sensualism, since the physical is nothing but 'dirt' and the animal a metaphor for human aggression and corruption. Elsewhere, Rochester shows how his restless intellect destroys the life of stable sensuous comfort. In the Song 'Absent from thee I languish still', perhaps addressed to his wife, he conjures up a vision of steadfast and secure love precisely in order to justify abandoning her and pursuing casual affairs: his 'Fantastick mind' must experience 'The Torments it deserves to try, / That tears my fixt Heart from my Love'. (Rochester's syntax is as deliberately ambiguous as his tone.) In the absence of other models, Lovelace evidently bases his conception of marriage, and of the future 'life of honour' he imagines with Clarissa, on poems such as these.

Libertine sexuality cannot be understood simply as a surrender to spontaneous physicality; it is inseparable from the cerebral triumph over the opposite sex, from mastery exercised through tactical reason. Thus Horner in Wycherley's *The Country Wife* (to limit ourselves to familiar examples from Restoration comedy) seduces the City wives to prove the proposition made in the first scene – that the greatest prudes are the greatest lechers in private – and then constructs an elaborate network of secrecy and blackmail that demonstrates his skill as 'a *Machiavel* in Love' (IV, iii). Dorimant, in Etherege's *The Man of Mode*, plans every detail of an ostensibly spontaneous argument-scene and then executes it precisely as planned, explicitly using metaphors of clockwork to reinforce that sense of control which has obviously become his principal source of pleasure (I, i; II, ii). Lovelace, in the same spirit, frequently calibrates his experience with Clarissa against the set of procedures and maxims he 'always' obeys. Even his most spontaneous behaviour is presented as if it were a controlled experiment to test a general law: 'Nor are women ever angry at bottom for being disobeyed thro' excess of Love. They like an uncontroulable passion . . . Don't I know the Sex?' (III, 309; II, 209). As Clarissa herself realizes, Lovelace pursues her in order to prove that, despite anything they may say, women really want to be seduced and even raped by 'boisterous and unruly' men of violent spirit (III, 130; II, 73).

This experimental and tendentious approach to seduction has one important corollary; it undermines the libertine's claim to originality. The intense assertion of individual rebellion and individual libido turns out to be quite conformist, since it aims to prove an existing theory, an established (if scandalous) ideology of female submission and female arousal. It confirms a script already written. So Lovelace's assertion that all women can be won by sexual violence is repeated almost verbatim from Ovid's *Ars Amatoria*, and had been endlessly reiterated in Renaissance dialogues, Restoration lampoons, and Augustan satires; it underlies Pope's notorious generalization that 'Ev'ry woman is at heart a Rake'.[2] We must conclude that Lovelace is motivated by a kind of neoclassical respect for authority. In his experiments on female virtue, and in his attempts to imagine an amorous future with Clarissa, he seeks to validate not only a libertine sexual ideology but a libertine literary tradition.

As several critics have remarked, Lovelace is obsessed with the methodical intellectual control of phenomena, and yet the methodical and the cerebral are what he most dreads: 'I must banish Reflection, or I am a lost man.'[3] Here again Richardson has constructed his protagonist out of contradictions central to libertinism. The 'Man of Sense' was fascinated by the application of method to sexuality, and by the 'Mechanick' philosophy that explained all reality in terms of primary drives and repulsions, independent of traditional morality.[4] But he was equally a man of the world, concerned with social success, seductive grace and fashionable *souplesse*: 'dull methods' and mechanical behaviour inspired the greatest horror and scorn.[5] Satire against the artificial spark or false wit runs throughout Restoration comedy: thus the puppet-like Sir Fopling Flutter is contrasted with the lithe and powerful Dorimant, and the philosophical rakes ('Gentlemen of Wit and Sense') in Thomas Shadwell's *The Virtuoso* attack would-be wits as 'the only Animals that live without thinking', having only 'a Form, a Fashion of Wit, a Rotine of speaking, which they get by Imitation' (I, i). The rake-hero must think intensely, while living as if he had 'banished reflection'; the fop makes himself subhuman (an automaton, less than an animal) by too much conscious invention, too visible an effort at wit. As Lady Fidget remarks in *The Country Wife*, 'the depraved appetites of witty men' lead them to the opposite of what they ostensibly desire, since, although they 'use to be out of the common road, and hate imitation', they actually end up repeating the commonest and grossest experiences (v, iv). The goal of the court wit or *libertin honnête homme* (as we learn from the *Mémoires de Grammont*) was to be 'inimitable' without being eccentric, to seduce by recombining the polite conventions into a wholly original effect, 'brilliant' and 'incomprehensible'. Failures were despised for their mechanical imitation, their '*Routines d'Expression*', their *méthode* without talent.[6] Rochester's phrase is even more trenchant and vitalistic: in *A Ramble in St James's Parke*, he declares war on 'abortive Imitation' (l. 57).

This concern with the quality of imitation, with the *reproduction* of behaviour in a way that must be wholly methodical and yet wholly devoid of mechanism, has implications both psychological and aesthetic. It creates the fear that he who runs his affairs like clockwork may himself be a machine: Dorimant, for example, is particularly anguished by those moments when he is himself confounded by the machinations of others, reduced to impotent silence. Jane Barker responds to Rochester's misanthropic *Satyr* by presenting contemporary life as an overwrought '*Clock-Work*', a system of tension, noise and contradiction that 'seldom *strike[s] true*'.[7] And Rochester himself, writing to his wife, confesses that his libertine life is really an exercise in method, and that (as in the lyric 'Absent from thee') such 'methods ... seeme so utterly to contradict' his own deeper need for love and security.[8] Lovelace, as we shall see, experiences these anxieties to the full.

By generating such ambivalence around the issues of method, mechanism and imitation, libertinism effectively brings into question the very assumption it is supposed to uphold – the absolute autonomy of the individual. Both in France and in England, the libertine clearly expresses the desire to be independent, inimitable and 'singular' – a concept often used by contemporaries to explain Rochester's flamboyant career.[9] Reflecting on the seventeenth-century representation of Don Juan, Coleridge finds him a sublime figure because he lives and dies by the principle that 'Self-contradiction is the only wrong'; his extravagant sexuality expresses his need to be loved in and of himself, and not for any accidental or exterior quality (*Biographia Literaria*, ch. 23). And yet, according to the materialist philosophy of the libertine, the individual is a product of blind drives and random circumstances. Indeed, Claude Reichler suggests (in a recent study of 'l'age libertin' in France) that the central problem of libertinism, once it had rejected traditional religious beliefs, was to maintain an authentic self in a world increasingly constituted by 'representations'. Reichler traces the oscillation of the libertine character between two extreme positions – a fierce individualism that underestimates the power of social forces, and a compliance to social conventions which, though intended to be ironic and self-liberating, eventually traps the self within the mask.[10] Thus the libertine could justify his excesses by explaining the self as a reflection of social expectations – the excuse of cynical seducers like Crébillon's Versac and Laclos's Valmont (himself, of course, a follower of Lovelace). This half-ironic theory of identity is more than just a screen for personal indulgence, however; it corresponds to a deep-seated belief that the self is indeed determined by external forces, that the self is indeed contingent and therefore *reproducible*. Hence the anxiety over 'imitation'. Lovelace articulates this contradiction at the heart of libertine identity-theory, some-times with exuberance (*'Lovelace's in every corner, Jack!'*) and sometimes with barely-concealed anxiety: 'Is there but *one* Lovelace in the world? May not *more* Lovelaces be attracted by so fine a figure?' (v, 70, III, 83; *III, 31, II, 38*).

The paradoxes of libertinism thus converge on questions of 'represen-tation', and above all on the question of language, the mediating force – or the obstacle – between physical desire and rational self-consciousness. The libertine remains profoundly uncertain whether language (writing, imagin-ation, 'wit') is an accessory to seduction or a substitute for it. Gallant pretence maintained the former ('A *Song* to *Phillis* I perhaps might make, / But never Rhym'd but for my *Pintle's* sake'), but candour recognized the latter: 'But now, alas! for want of further force, / From action we are fallen into discourse.'[11] In coarser libertine texts, like those Restoration brothel-lampoons where the clients 'fancy at least they swive with Quality', imagin-ative projection is a crude compensation for social and sexual failure. High erotica such as Nicolas Chorier's *Satyra Sotadica* (1660) or Julien de la Mettrie's *L'Ecole de la volupté* (1747), on the other hand, develop a philosophy of sex in which the image takes priority over physical reality. Indeed, compared with the mental idea the physical may be dismissed as a paltry thing, subject to age and exhaustion, leading to what the arch-pornographer Chorier called 'Veneris nausea'.[12] By recognizing that *foeda est in coitu*, high libertinism can break away from simplistic naturalism and join the more sophisticated side of the old debate For and Against Fruition, promoting a refined and cerebral eroticism. Lovelace's frequent denunciations of 'the crowning act', the 'vapour' of physical fruition (IV, 139; *II, 337*), make him not an exception to the libertine tradition but a central example.

Given this highly-charged and problematic connection between personal identity, sexuality and representation, we would expect the libertine to be unusually concerned with the aesthetics of self-presentation. 'Abortive Imitation' and compensatory discourse must be replaced by something more vital and authentic. Thus the narrator of the *Mémoires de Grammont* announces that his style will be as singular and 'inimitable' as the hero he tries to reconstruct: writing only for pleasure, he will barely trouble with 'chronological order and the proper arrangement of facts', and instead will offer 'fragments, just as they occur to my imagination, regardless of their order or status (*sans égard à leur rang*)' (p. 2). (However confidently done, such a project is doomed to failure, since an 'inimitable' subject is by definition impossible to capture in words.) It is in this context that we must study Lovelace's self-referential preoccupation with the act of writing. Through 'invention' and 'contrivance' he tries to create an authentic libertine self, but he remains, as we shall see, crucially dependent on conformity to previous definitions of the libertine character. Even when he asserts his absolute originality and independence of method, he does so in terms borrowed from his literary predecessors: 'Regardless, nevertheless, I shall be in all I write, of connexion, accuracy, or of any-thing but of my own imperial will and pleasure' (III, 34; *1, 516*).

It is important to recognize, at this point, that the term 'libertine' referred to an aesthetic as well as a sexual or philosophical stance, a style of writing as well as a mode of behaviour. Lovelace's antecedents tried to align the aesthetic and the erotic, but they do not necessarily coincide. Dryden and Oldham, for example, use 'libertine' to denote the free mode of translation that Pope would later use in his *Imitations of Horace* – a form of imitation that is fruitful and energetic rather than 'abortive'.[13] For Pierre Corneille, to abandon the unities in drama is 'libertine'.[14] And Mme de Sévigné – one of the few French authors whom Richardson acknowledges and discusses, precisely because she raised issues of propriety and style – uses the word to denote a delightful improvisatory freedom of style. She refers continually to 'le libertinage de ma plume', and particularly praises those letters written by her daughter 'when you have no subjects', when she is free to write 'lettres toutes libertines'.[15]

In this sense, Clarissa herself is 'libertine'. Richardson has left behind the servant-girl's pertness and homiletic gravity of Pamela, and has created for Clarissa a style of penetration and freedom, the aristocratic lady's epistolary manner that had been brought to perfection by Mme de Sévigné. She is a worthy successor of Congreve's heroines, a potential leader of the *salon*. Even in distress her letters breathe intimacy, wit and alertness; her sentences are elegantly varied, judiciously combining deliberate structure and casual upper-class colloquialism, sharpened by crisp aphorisms and vivid sketches of character.

Indeed, Clarissa has affinities of mentality as well as of style with the spirited heroines of Restoration comedy and worldly fiction, sexually virtuous but free enough in wit, 'libertine' enough in style, to match the rakish hero. She admits writing 'freely' about her family (I, 7; *I, 5*), and her early letters in particular enjoy a delicious freedom of expression, a stinging sarcasm created out of the restricted vocabulary of politeness; the delight is a painful one, of course, since her verbal freedom can never be translated into action, and cannot halt the encroachment of James or Lovelace. Discussing Lovelace with her confidante, she slips into a Millamant-like tone that suggests not just intelligence but amusement and even conspiratorial pleasure in his addresses: 'Bashfulness in Mr. Lovelace, my dear!' ... 'The man, you know, has very ready knees' ... 'What will not these men say to obtain belief, and a power over one?' ... 'What shall I do with this Lovelace?' (I, 8, 239, 259, 309; *I, 6, 176, 184, 228*). He is not only 'the man' but the 'contradictory creature', the 'impatient creature', the 'artful wretch' – all terms that with a tap of the fan could turn from insult to endearment. Her flustered response to a supposed offer of marriage – 'Would he have had me catch at his first, at his *very* first word?' (III, 70; *II, 28*) – sounds like Millamant during the proviso-scene, a parallel all the more poignant since Lovelace is deliberately preventing their confrontation from evolving into a Congrevean courtship ritual. Even her tragic perplexity is lightened by stylistic dash and poise, with a tinge of drawing-room slang: 'I am strangely at a loss what to think of this man. He is a perfect Proteus ... Don't think *me* the changeable person, I beseech you' (III, 141; *II, 82*). (Imagine what Anne Bracegirdle – or Edith Evans – would have made of the Proteus sentence.) Her expressive talent, exercised hitherto on the family, is obviously stimulated by her first encounters with Lovelace (whose faults and virtues she sums up as Mirabell did Millamant's), and it flares up intermittently throughout his attempts to stupefy her.

The horror of Clarissa's predicament increases when we see her as a worldly heroine in a Restoration-comedy situation that has been grotesquely hardened, translated into a realm where the comedic resolution is impossible, and where her 'libertine' style and grace must fight to the death with the 'libertinism' of male depredation. The roaring father is a Sir Sampson who cannot be tricked off stage, the mother is a Lady Woodville fearing a Dorimant in every bush, and Clarissa herself is a 'country wife' (even without marriage) whose predicament reproduces that of Margery Pinchwife – locked up and threatened both by her gothic guardian and by her pseudo-liberating lover, for whom she practises the skills of secret correspondence. At one point, indeed, Clarissa exploits the limitations of Lovelace's astuteness in a way that redefines him, not as Horner, but as the blundering Mr Pinchwife: 'he had cunning enough to give me, undesignedly, a piece of instruction' – to avoid showing anger, since her anger would serve his purpose as well as her desire (I, 19; *I, 14*). This turning of the tables, which starts with an urbane exchange of aphorisms, combines the quick apprehension of Margery with the high breeding of another character from *The Country Wife*, the heroine Alithea. Richardson maintains the parallel with Wycherley's comedy when Lovelace later comes to realize that he has been excluded from the role of rake-hero; after Clarissa's escape he imagines stratagems that would explicitly make him like Horner (VII, 20; *IV, 42*). It is Clarissa's wit, more than her virtue, that gives her the chance to exert some control over the drama: her snubbing of Solmes, for example, is a grim version of the triumph of Millamant over the rustic Sir Wilful – except that, of course, she will be deprived of the rewards that this comedy-routine leads us to expect.

Again, the comedy-heroine is expected not only to trounce the clownish alternative suitor, but to grill her future mate with merciless wit and penetration. (It is Clarissa's 'penetration' that Lovelace later uses to justify his proceeding 'by the Sap', that is, by secret military tunnels [III, 33; *I, 515–16*], and his rape of her unconscious body may be read as a crude physical counterpart to this quality that he fears in her.) Thus Alithea criticizes her suitor Harcourt, and Harriet in *The Man of Mode* accuses Dorimant of arrogance and 'Affectation', paralysing him (at least for a few scenes) by an adroit mimicry of his characteristic poses that turns them into mechanical 'Routines' – precisely the fate he tries to impose on other women (III, i; III, iii; IV, i). In the same spirit, Clarissa 'penetrates' Lovelace, seeing in him the disabling contradiction of the upstart where others see only aristocratic confidence: 'for persons to endeavour to gain respect by a haughty behaviour, is to give a proof that they mistrust their own merit: To make confession that they *know* that their actions will not attract it. – Distinction or Quality may be prided in by those to whom distinction or quality is a *new* thing' (I, 193; *I, 142*). She delivers her observations with the appropriate elegance, confirming that in the psychological realm it is *she* who is the aristocrat and *he* the parvenu – a precise reversal of the social position of their families. We cannot enjoy this potentially comic 'penetration' and role-reversal, however, because at the same time Clarissa senses an ominous inner vacuity in Lovelace, an insecurity that could erupt or implode into violence: 'Some people may indeed be afraid, that if they did not assume, they would be trampled upon. A very narrow fear, however, since they trample upon themselves who can fear *this*' (I, 193–4; *I, 142*).

Even before we encounter Lovelace's own letters, then, Richardson has allowed his heroine to fix him with her own 'libertine' freedom and penetration.[16] As the novel develops she continues to exercise her intelligence on the character he presents to her, reinterpreting it as an inauthentic simulacrum. She exposes his vain desire to show his 'address', the 'half-menacing strain' of his compliments, the 'lines of his own face' that condemn him by contradicting his words, the histrionicism that makes his anger '*manageable*' rather than real, and his general habit of 'visibly triumphing . . . in the success of his arts' (I, 193, 239, 275; III, 5, 13; *I, 142, 176, 202, 495, 501*). After her capture they still play the game of scrutiny, like the alert and predatory couples of comedy, 'great watchers of each other's eyes; and indeed . . . more than half-afraid of each other' (III, 156; *II, 93*). Clarissa continues to play the tragic Millamant, verbally outmanoeuvring her partner/opponent by sheer force of wit: 'he might be surprised at my warmth, perhaps; but really the man looked so like a simpleton, hesitating, and having nothing to say for himself' (III, 67; *II, 26*). Lovelace himself recognizes her power to reduce his speech to silence and to disrupt the trained seducer's well-oiled sequence of moves: 'When I see my Angel . . . what will become of all this vapouring?'; 'My divine Clarissa has puzzled me, and beat me out of my play' (III, 33; IV, 354; *I, 515, II, 492*). Her tone becomes inevitably darker after her violation, but the dynamics are the same: 'abandoned man! – *Man* did I say? . . . well may'st thou quake; well may'st thou tremble and falter, and hesitate, as thou dost!' (V, 321–2; *III, 219*). Only her resolution to die gives her a more effective role.

Thanks to the narrative design of *Clarissa*, the reader approaches Lovelace's writings in a spirit not only of excitement – anticipating the depravity already hinted by the Preface – but of critical scrutiny. Clarissa's sharp diagnosis of his insecurity prepares us to read Lovelace's writings as theatrical overstatements that conceal a fundamental lack. Anna Howe, too, raises questions about this young man who 'has always a pen in his fingers when he retires'. 'What can be his subjects?' she asks. Certainly something wicked that would contaminate both him and us, if we were unlucky enough to read it. And why should he devote his time to such a domestic and sedentary, such a *female* activity (I, 67–8; *I, 49–50*)?

Lovelace himself will often admit to exaggeration and posturing, sometimes with an agreeable touch of humour – after one particularly heroic rant, his dog comes in to see if he is feeling well – and sometimes with disarming frankness. He claims at one point, in words that closely parallel Richardson's diagnosis of his own 'nervous disorders', that if he did not scribble away so furiously he would go mad.[17] His tone and rhythm will often suggest hollowness or vacillation, even in declarations of imperious mastery. His verbal swagger, as Clarissa suggests in one of her aphorisms, 'proclaim[s] the profligate's want of power' as well as his 'wickedness' (III, 21; *I, 507*), and even his fiercest manifestations of libertine ruthlessness suggest a lack of control, a slippage of the authorial self. It is not the least of the paradoxes that constitute Lovelace, that a man so proud of his contrivance and foresight, such a '*Machiavel* in Love' (to echo his acknowledged model Horner), should be almost hysterically spontaneous and improvisatory in his self-expression. He subordinates the world to his 'invention', and aims to rewrite Clarissa according to his master-scenario, and yet he is curiously unwilling to reread what he has written, let alone to revise it (I, 206; *I, 152*). He elevates the Will into the supreme determinant of text, behaviour and morality; indeed, Margaret Anne Doody suggests that his will is so overdeveloped that it cuts him off from the physical-sensuous world and damages his capacity to love. And yet he admits that 'I must write on, and cannot help it.'[18]

Writing to fill a void, we should recall, was already an acknowledged effect of the libertine character, displayed most famously in Rochester's 'Upon Nothing'. Mme de Sévigné, as we have seen, had praised those 'libertine' letters written without a subject, and more recently Pope had used the concept of 'writing on nothing' to justify the rakish posing of his own early correspondence; in a fabricated letter supposedly written in his youth, he claims a kind of virtuoso freedom from the constraints of subject and method, a spontaneous and elegant trifling.[19] Lovelace redeploys this topos, but with a curious variation. Anna's question ('What can be his subjects?') proves more complicated than she realized. His first letter to Belford promises that, though he cannot join him, he can at least write – 'and as well without a subject, as with one. And what follows shall be a proof of it' (I, 196; *I, 144*). A letter that declares his love, but that reports no progress in the seduction, must in libertine terms have no subject, and Lovelace does indeed sign off with a Rochesterian flourish to this effect: 'thus, Jack, as thou desirest, have I written. – Written upon Something, upon Nothing.' (I, 206; *I, 151*).

But Lovelace is actually rather uncertain whether or not he has a 'subject' in Clarissa. In a revealing autobiographical moment, he tells Belford how his earlier idealization (and disillusion) came from inflaming his imagination with poetry, wanting to have an experience to match his authorial fervours; the problem was that 'many a time have I been at a loss for a *subject*, when my new-created goddess has been kinder than it was proper for my plaintive Sonnet that she should be' (I, 198; *I, 146*). It is resistance rather than surrender that gives him a 'subject', an opportunity to project onto the inaccessible beloved the qualities of sublimity. It might seem that the young Lovelace was arrested at an archaic pre-libertine stage: who would write Petrarchan sonnets in 1720? But in fact the need for resistance was recognized in the most sophisticated forms of libertinism. Reichler suggests that the seducer-hero is trapped in precisely this 'double impasse' – a circle of idealization, mastery, disillusion and blame that can be broken only by entering another endless path, the quest for an unattainable object.[20] Molière's Dom Juan, in a famous speech that I have chosen as an epigraph, explains how he loves to overcome resistance 'day by day' and 'foot by foot';

but once he has conquered 'there is nothing more to be said'. Dom Juan reveals the self-cancelling quality of the libertine pursuit, which must fail if it succeeds and succeed if it fails; unless it is thwarted, it must inevitably – indeed, methodically – lead to a linguistic and emotional vacuum. Lovelace transforms Dom Juan's complaint into his fantasy of a future extra-marital life with Clarissa, in which *he* becomes the inaccessible one, perpetually abandoning her and perpetually returning to renewed passion (III, 281; *II, 188*). Only then would they be 'always new to each other, and having always something to say'.

The question of 'subject' brings us to the conceptual tangle at the centre of libertinism – the relation between language, sexuality and individual identity. Does the seducer pursue his victim only to show his 'invention'? Is writing a tool of seduction or a substitute, and is this substitute valued more highly than the act itself? Is the self created by its own free will, or is it determined by external forces, an 'abortive Imitation' produced by social expectations and 'Rotines' – determined, in fact, by a pre-existent discourse or script? After Dom Juan's monologue, Sganarelle shrewdly remarks that it sounds like something repeated by heart, spoken 'like a book'.

Lovelace repeatedly gloats over the 'illustrious subject' that Clarissa provides 'to exercise [his] pen upon' (III, 26; *I, 510*), as if the chief motivation of his pursuit were to stimulate the act of writing – precisely what he denies in his self-justificatory letter to Joseph Leman. Since he conspicuously fails to convert the real Clarissa to participating in his scenario (she refuses to turn into one of Dorimant's victims, a compliant Belinda or a ludicrously tragic Mrs Loveit), we must conclude that writing does become all-important for him, a compensatory realm or an imaginary act of dominance. But Lovelace also presents himself as the passive agent or mouthpiece of a 'subject' outside himself: 'See what grave reflections an innocent subject *will produce*' (I, 234; *I, 173*, my emphasis). In an extreme version of this conceit, he imagines that Conscience has stolen his pen and written moral reflections into his text; he then proceeds to beat and choke this female conscience-figure to death (V, 223–4; *III, 146–7*). At times, too, he seems to blur the boundaries of life and art, confusing two distinct meanings of the word 'subject' (a topic for writing and a person or autonomous self): 'I never had a subject I so much adored; and with which I shall probably *be compelled* to have so much patience, before I strike the blow; if the blow I do strike' (III, 65; *II, 24*, my emphasis again). These vacillations between different conceptions of the active subject, accompanied by bursts of paranoia and sadism, reveal a strange vacuity in Lovelace's own sense of himself. They culminate in his lament after Clarissa's escape – the passage that I have chosen as my second epigraph (VI, 196; *III, 388*). He promises Belford to write down – or to invent – everything about her, 'to tell thee her thoughts, either what they are, or what I would have them be'. 'Having *her*,' sealing her into his private world so that no gap appears between sexual possession and imaginative elaboration, 'I shall never want a subject'. But 'having lost her' his own status as a 'subject' collapses or evaporates: 'my whole Soul is a blank'.

Writing for Lovelace is not (as Anna Howe thought) a sedentary and reflective process, but a form of action – precisely because he ignores the boundaries that separate imaginary scripts from real events, and invests his whole identity in their fusion. His nervous disorder inspires furious inventiveness because the alternative is a 'blank'. He wants Clarissa to be a fiction, a Pygmalionic statue, an author's character who would simply *be* what he dictates: 'I might have had her before now, if I would. If I would treat her as flesh and blood, I should find her such' (III, 308; *II, 208*). (The word 'treat' expresses exactly his confusion of script and behaviour.) The irony is that, when he *does* attempt to force her into his image, he is not at all clear what he wants her to be, what kind of 'subject' he desires in her.

Lovelace's dilemma is particularly acute because he is using her to discover, not the secret of Clarissa Harlowe, nor even the secret of 'woman', but the answer to what he is himself. He fails to treat her as the conventional 'flesh and blood', not only because the autonomous and self-possessed heroine refuses to conform to his script, but because he himself recoils from the body and denounces sex in Dom-Juan-like terms, as a routine leading to nothing. Clarissa must satisfy his childlike demand for a source of identity outside himself, but since he has already invested in the libertine character she must also be proved a sexual object, the conventional 'woman' to his conventional 'man'.[21] This consummation must be both the focus of his activity and the source of his dread, since she will then mirror the essential void or vapour within himself. Belford's advice to Lovelace articulates this impasse within libertinism: 'I should dread to make further trial, knowing what *we* know of the Sex, for *fear* of succeeding' (III, 243; *II, 158*). Lovelace evidently takes these words to heart. He repeats them in full, begins to justify himself in terms of traditional male roles, and then veers nervously off in another direction. He tries to pass Belford's insight off as a digression, pretending to 'return to my principal subject' – when in fact he has never left it (III, 277–9; *II, 184–5*).

Lovelace is intensely conscious of the disintegrating effect of Clarissa as 'subject', who undermines both his cult of the Will and his authorial mastery. In the letter that crows over Clarissa's abduction, for example, he repeats his inviolable vow of revenge; he cannot forswear himself, and so he cannot 'hesitate a moment' in his resolve to seduce her. But the point is undermined in the making, since in the same breath he recognizes that 'I *must* be

forsworn, whether I answer her expectations, or follow my own inclinations,'
and in the next breath he is justifying precisely the hesitation he has just
declared unthinkable (III, 31–2; *1, 514*). He remains trapped in these
oscillations throughout the letter, subjectless and centreless, shuttling
between fantastic exultation in her ruin and abject reverence for her nobility.
He breaks off to apologize for 'rambl[ing] ... too far from the track I set out
in' – even though, again, he has not actually drifted from his declared topic –
and recognizes that his stylistic incoherence comes from being 'in such a
situation, that I know not what to resolve upon'. But he tries to establish a
'libertine' freedom in the text which will compensate for those paralyses of
will that destroy the libertine character. The letter ends with a flourish
designed to persuade us that all his vacillation is deliberate caprice – the
declaration, already noted, that his writing will disregard everything but 'my
own imperial will and pleasure' (III, 33–4; *1, 516*).

The effect of this exit-line is quite different from the airy virtuosity he
intends, however. Lovelace's pen moves freely under contradictory impulses
and associations, but it is a freedom without control, a style of convolutions,
fragmentations and dislocations. Word-order and sentence-structure crack
apart. He boasts of the natural simplicity of his contrivances in strained,
inverted phrases: 'No Machinery make I necessary. No unnatural flights aim I
at' (IV, 352–3; *II, 491*). In the abduction letter, likewise, his style reflects the
struggle to say, on paper, that he intends to seduce Clarissa: 'that I *do* intend it
I cannot (my heart, my reverence for her, will not let me) say' (III, 31; *1, 514*).
Lovelace is caught here between two modes of courtship, illicit and honourable, but he is also torn between two conflicting principles of libertine
philosophy: that 'Self-contradiction is the only wrong', and that true freedom
can be found only in surrender to passion and spontaneity. This strain
produces the shifts and fissures of the Lovelacean text, which in turn give him
the sense that his pen is stolen from him at times, that he does not write, but is
written.

For the reader equipped with Clarissa's sharpness of vision, but given
access to those letters that she could never see in full, Lovelace is most fully
revealed in his inability to control his own text. In one letter of triumph over
the Harlowes, for example, he seizes upon a metaphor to express the
difference between contemptible '*tame Spirits*' and wild, free, antinomian
libertines; the Harlowes are cowardly and sadistic spiders, 'self-circum-
scribed tyrant[s]' (III, 63; *II, 22–3*). But associations of voluptuous cruelty
immediately take over his mind, forcing him to reverse his metaphor with
himself as the exultant spider – thus unwittingly levelling himself with the
Harlowes. In triumphing over Belford he reveals, again unwittingly, the
circularity and self-cancellation of the libertine pursuit: Belford (like Marlow

in *She Stoops to Conquer*) can desire only common wenches, and had asserted 'like a paltry fellow' that 'all women are alike'; Lovelace despises such plebeian pleasures, and glories in the challenge of capturing a high-born lady. But his self-differentiation immediately collapses, since the whole point of his quest is to 'abase' the lady and so to demonstrate precisely the doctrine that makes one a 'paltry fellow' – the identity of all women in their sex (III, 72; *II, 30*). The cynical letter to Joseph Leman repeats this article of libertine belief.

In another exultation, rewriting a scene in which he simultaneously bullied and fawned on Clarissa – 'take me to yourself: Mould me as you please: I am wax in your hands' (III, 139; *II, 80*) – Lovelace casts himself as a sublime erotic adventurer, a magnificent Jove about to incinerate the terrified Semele. But again these images slip out of his control. He invokes the standard Ovidian/libertine justification of male violence, the conventional thesis that women like to be overpowered by 'boisterous spirits' ('all the Ladies I have met with till now, loved to raise a tempest, and to enjoy it'). But at the crucial moment of masculine display the causative power is transferred to 'the Ladies', who *raise* tempests where we would expect them to *be* stormed. Lovelace's libertine activism dissolves into a dependence on local circumstance ('Lord send us once happily to London!'), and even the Semele-metaphor turns limp in the execution. He *would* have fulfilled his sublime role, 'had not my heart misgiven me'. The thought that brings on this collapse of masculine resolve, and this perpetual deferral of the heroic gesture, is the fear that *she* might be the real libertine: 'she might abandon me at her pleasure' (III, 163; *II, 98*).

In constructing the character of Lovelace, Richardson refuses to simplify the relation between 'action' and 'discourse'. Writing is never just a transparent vehicle of truth, nor an efficient tool to change the world, nor a masterful compensation for failure; it shares in each of these functions and mingles them together, so that falterings in action will produce tremors and dislocations throughout the text, and incoherences of tone forewarn us of psychological contradictions that will later be acted out with full destructive force. Writing calls for scrutiny, the active participation of the reader, the 'penetration' that Clarissa brings to conversation and behaviour. The tragedy is that she cannot extend this freedom to Lovelace's letters, and so penetration cannot be mutual.

Lovelace has been marked by suspicion ever since Anna Howe raised her questions, which pointed to a contradiction between the nature of writing (passive, feminine) and the character that he projects. When we are allowed into his text, after long and almost prurient expectation, we find that her suspicions were both right and wrong: in the short term she is wrong, since his letters actively contribute to his plotting, but in the long term we do come to see a passivity in the very act of constructing a character of absolute power. And libertine writing also comes to seem 'female'. More than one critic has noticed the paradox that 'Clarissa's writing is "masculine" whereas Lovelace's is "feminine" '.[22] Even when he explicitly differentiates himself from the opposite sex, the texture of the writing belies him. He claims, for example, that if he were a woman he would cry when Clarissa wounds him – though he seems uncertain whether this display would have shown women's greater capacity to feel or to deceive; instead of producing tears he produces a handkerchief ('*That* I could command, but not my *tears*'), but at the crucial moment he cannot 'command' his style to leave out feminine details, cannot resist telling us that it is a 'white cambrick' handkerchief.[23] In the abduction letter, again, he strives to create a portrait of a woman entirely in his masculine power; language and flesh are both subservient to his 'imperial will'. Clarissa is *described*, for the first time in the novel. But the scene of description – the equivalent of Medley's luscious account of Harriet in *The Man of Mode*, or Fielding's gloating introduction of Sophia in *Tom Jones* – rapidly turns into something quite different. First, Clarissa's 'flesh' becomes a morgue-like 'wax'; then the details of her dress crowd onto the page and take over the authorial persona, transforming him into a breathless fashion editor (III, 27–8; *I, 511–12*). The great seducer disappears in a cloud of Brussels lace and primrose-coloured paduasoy.

To posit an essential passivity at the heart of Lovelace's libertine self-presentation helps to explain, not only his moments of stumbling inarticulacy, but also (paradoxically) his violent assertions of imperious selfhood. He complains of being '*obliged*' to assume 'airs of Reformation' that alarm not only his libertine companions but his libertine self, since he feels so subdued and unrakish after approaching her (more precisely, after coming near her father's walls); he is likewise '*obliged*, by thy penetration, Fair-one, to proceed by the Sap' (III, 31, 33; *I, 514, 515–16*; my emphasis). She is in his power, he declares repeatedly and with mounting stress, and yet 'every time I attend her, I find that she is less in *my* power; I more in *hers*' (III, 32; *I, 515*). For all this, *she* must pay.

Just as Dorimant, in Etherege's comedy, is forced to acknowledge to Medley his moment of lost control, redeemed only by promises of a greater revenge (III, iii), so Lovelace admits to Belford that he is tongue-tied and 'out-talented' by the advantages she won over him (III, 76; *II, 33*); this refers to the occasion, already noted, when Clarissa had described him as a 'simpleton'. His account of the exchange, and the inevitable fantasy of revenge that follows, both reveal an ontological insecurity that belies the active, combative role he assigns himself: 'what an abject slave she made me look like!' he exclaims, as if his identity depends on an audience even when they are alone together. He goes on to threaten that 'I could have told her something that would have humbled her pretty pride at the instant, had she been in a *proper* place, and *proper* company about her' (III, 75; *II, 32*). He could articulate this 'something' (presumably some devastating sexual fact of life) if he were only in the 'proper' social setting – a paradoxical word when applied to a London brothel – but meanwhile he cannot even articulate it to himself. He seems a creature of the geography of libertinism, rather than an autonomous 'subject'.

This impression of passivity lingers even after he has moved to the [im]proper location at Mrs Sinclair's; his accessories seem to carry on the action to its violent conclusion, even when he vacillates himself.[24] At times the automotive quality of his inventions fills him with joy as well as anxiety. Before leaving for London, his heart may 'rise to my throat, in half-choking flutters', but still ' 'Tis a plotting villain of a heart', full of 'joy when any roguery is going forward! – I so little its master! – A head likewise so well turned to answer the triangular varlet's impulses' (III, 280; *II, 186*). Lovelace disowns both his head and his heart here, leaving the reader in some doubt where he himself can be located; but the surrender of identity is treated with comic verve. (This is also the point where he indulges in the Rochesterian fantasy of leaving the 'vapourish' Clarissa after a few weeks.) In the passages written by 'Conscience', however, the full horror breaks out. In a text set off in 'sentence' marks and stuck on with wax to the main letter, Lovelace admits that he is 'afraid of the gang of my cursed contrivances', and '*compelled* to be the wretch my choice has made me!' The paradox of libertine freedom could hardly be taken further. Richardson has created a subject/victim who can perceive and express his own futility and yet seems powerless to change it: 'Upon my soul, Jack, it is a very foolish thing for a man of spirit to have brought himself to such a height of iniquity, that he must proceed, and cannot help himself; and yet to be next to certain, that his very victory will undo him.' Lovelace falls into the chasm that yawns for all Machiavels in love and all philosophical Don Juans, the narrow seam that separates the 'method' of the brilliant seducer from the mechanization that destroys all spontaneity. Now, he realizes, 'I am a machine at last, and no free agent' (V, 223–4; *III, 146*).

Lovelace's solution, of course, is to invest ever more heavily in the libertine character, stiffening his resolve by referring, only half-ironically, to the heroic wickedness that conventional society expects of him: 'Am I not a *Rake*, as it is called? And who ever knew a Rake stick at any-thing?' 'Were I now to lose her, how unworthy should I be to be the Prince and Leader of such a Confraternity as ours! – How unable to look up among men!' (III, 162, 57; *II, 97, 18*). But this assumption of a pre-scripted or prefabricated libertine identity, with its attendant cluster of misogynistic attitudes, hardly solves the essential problem – the surrender of responsibility for the formation of one's own being.

Lovelace is concerned with the 'figure' he will make in 'Rakish Annals' (v, 220; *III, 144*), not only in the semi-burlesque displays put on for Belford, but in his imaginary confrontations with Clarissa herself. His tone is sometimes defensive ('what can a Lover say to his Mistress, if she will neither let him lye nor swear?'), and sometimes petulantly vengeful: 'If I forgive thee, Charmer, for ... these contempts, I am not the Lovelace I have been reputed to be; and that thy treatment of me shews that thou thinkest I am' (III, 53, 51; *II, 15, 14*). The ironies here are dizzying. In one case she is blamed for *not* giving him the standard faithless-lover role, in the other case (from the same letter) she is blamed because she *does* assume him to be the conventional libertine. When Laclos's Valmont shifts the blame to his victims or to the way of the world, we always read it as a cynical manoeuvre, but Lovelace seems genuinely indignant and genuinely unaware of the contradiction that sustains his pursuit of Clarissa and reduces it to stalemate: on the one hand, he tries to force her into his own script, to impose a prefabricated character on her (much as her father wants to tame her by ordering 'patterns' from London, not realizing that she designs her own clothes and embroiders her own material); on the other hand, he continually casts her in the active role of initiator, of definer, of 'subject'. Even when 'Conscience' holds his pen, he presents himself as the victim of a larger circumstance: 'Why was such a woman as This thrown in my way?' 'What a happy man ... had I been, had it been given me to *be* only what I wished to *appear* to be!' (v, 224; *III, 146*). The fate he wishes on Clarissa – to be a fiction wholly controlled by the Will, with no gap between projected appearance and inner essence – he really desires for himself.

Lovelace's 'imperial will' appears to be founded on the anxiety of dependence. He fears, and craves, the function that he has himself imposed on Clarissa – that of mirroring him and solving the question of his own identity. This mirroring cannot be simply the flattering reflection of a well-established male ego, since according to libertine ideology she must be forced to represent the 'vapour', the sexuality that he despises. Conventionally he has to conduct women – 'from step to step', as in *Dom Juan* – to the point where 'all tests are got over, and we have completely ruined them' (IV, 268; *II, 430*), even though this is the point where he himself is annihilated. But Lovelace also seeks a different kind of intimacy, difficult to articulate and impossible to reconcile with libertine possession and destruction; he wants his 'steps' to lead to a 'familiarized' state (IV, 145; *II, 341*) – a confusing term, because it is unclear whether he means the contempt that follows seduction, the mutuality of an established couple, or the incestuous bonds of family. His contradictory demands can be gathered from his incongruous shifts of tone. He insists that

Clarissa must fail his seduction-test and prove 'flesh and blood' like the rest, but he also longs intensely for her to pass it; as he elaborates his ultra-conservative theory of female virtue as superiority to sexual temptation, he breaks off to exclaim 'my Clarissa out of the question' (III, 84; *II, 39*). He sounds here, not like the humble suitor or the arrogant seducer, but like the proud father.

Proud *mother* might be a more accurate analogy, since Lovelace persistently identifies his own sensibility with the female. To escape the dilemma of depending on a 'sex' that he is compelled to reduce to nothing, the hyper-masculine rake attaches himself to other 'feminine' qualities – no less conventionally assigned, but not directly equated with sexuality. We have seen how his heart rises in 'half-choking flutters', how his masterful description of the newly-captured heroine dissolves into satin and ruffles. 'Libertines', he himself claims, are different from other men because they are 'nicer'; having more of the supposedly-female quality of fastidious discretion, they are (paradoxically) entitled to be harsher in their judgements of the women they ruin.[25] Lovelace speculates about dressing up as a woman (having imagined separate churches for men and 'girls', he then imagines himself crossing these self-made boundaries as a transvestite); he describes his first venture into libertinism as 'a pretty *lady-like* tyranny', and calls his early resolution to destroy women his 'maiden vow' (I, 198; III, 52, 65; *I, 146; II, 15, 24*). He thus justifies a grotesque and vengeful misogyny by invoking a sort of insider's privilege: his absurd claims to 'know the sex' (which always accompany his libertine declarations that all women can be reduced to one thing) derive their authority from the fact that, like Tiresias, he 'has a good deal of the soul of a woman'. His original bashfulness now converted into impudence, his original tenderness now turned to simulation and contrivance, demonstrate a 'likeness' between himself and woman that is proved, or authorized, by quoting Pope's celebrated maxim that 'Ev'ry Woman is at heart a Rake' (III, 106; *II, 55*). What he means is evidently that every rake is at heart a woman. Lovelace's transference of blame to the female, his projection of anxiety, even make him forget the double standard and claim for himself the absolutist morality normally imposed on woman alone: 'Who, that has once trespassed with them, ever recovered his virtue?' (I, 234; *I, 172*).

The libertine simultaneously identifies with the female and reinforces his masculinity by projecting his most vulnerable characteristics onto her. Passivity and contradiction were the chief qualities ascribed to women in male ideology; it is precisely these qualities that constitute the inner world of Lovelace himself. For a a man floundering in contradiction, it is acutely important to be able to force women into a contradictory posture, and to intensify the triumph by pretending to find this delightful: '*The Sex! The Sex, all over*! – Charming contradiction! – Hah, hah, hah, hah!' This is the outburst that brings in the worried dog, who *hears* Lovelace perform as he writes.[26]

Kierkegaard defined Mozart's Don Giovanni as the perfect seducer because 'his life is a perpetual vanishing, like music', a flow of pure amoral energy, independent of any system of judgement or representation; it can only be captured in the abstract medium of music.[27] Lovelace would have been attracted to this romantic revision of libertinism. He aspires to the condition of pure performance, spontaneity, 'uncontroulable passion', unstoppable energy of sound. His greatest fear, in the imagined future, is of having nothing more to *say*. But he remains trapped within precisely those forces that are transcended in the Kierkegaardian version of the libertine myth: the cerebral, the imitative, the ideological, the social. Richardson has created, in Lovelace's vapouring and sounding off, a tonal-dramatic effect as distinctive as that of Mozart's protagonist. But the acoustic presence of Lovelace is quite different from the grandeur and precipitancy of Don Giovanni; it is a fluttering, stalling music, with nervous changes of tempo and dynamics, moments of unexpected delicacy interrupted by the grand march played too loud. Lovelace's tone betrays his tensions, and his tensions derive, I have been arguing, from paradoxes inherent in the libertine tradition. His dog can hear what Clarissa has already heard, the trouble and insecurity that vibrate within the representation of seductive confidence. Lovelace's self-image corresponds, in fact, to the vision of the 'decentred subject' proposed by recent literary theory; he is an empty space on which various contradictory discourses leave their trace.

6

Richardson's *Meditations*: Clarissa's *Clarissa*

TOM KEYMER

Job in petticoats

In December 1746, Aaron Hill urged Richardson to rename *Clarissa* 'The *Lady's Legacy*', and amplified his suggestion in an elaborately drafted title-page.[1] The title's reference to Clarissa's inheritance of her grandfather's estate (which she at one stage describes as 'the original cause' of her misfortunes: V, 51; *III, 17*), and thus to the socio-economic implications of the novel, has been thoroughly plotted.[2] As its later phrase 'Published in Compliance with the Lady's Order on her Death-Bed' makes clear, however, it denotes not only what Clarissa inherits, but also what she bequeaths: her own history, left to posterity for its edification. The ambiguity seems happy enough, but Richardson, though finding the title 'very promising', nevertheless rejected it, precisely because of its emphasis on this fiction of the text's self-generation: '*The Lady's Legacy*, it cannot now be properly called, as it might at first', he explained to Hill, 'because in the last Revisal, I have made the Sollicitude for the Publication, to be rather Miss Howe's than hers.'[3] Perhaps with memories of Pamela's undoing in the anti-Pamelist satires (which had detected in her narrative a similarly incriminating hint of apologetics, and used it to parody her story as one of 'feign'd innocence'),[4] Richardson preferred to play down Clarissa's role in raising a monument to her own virtue, and defensively modified the novel. In the published texts of 1747–8 and 1751, the idea of 'a compilement to be made of all that relates to my Story' (VIII, 109; *IV, 425*) remains her own, and is outlined in her will; but it becomes a memorial to Clarissa both instigated and assembled by her friends, rather than her own legacy to the world. Technically, at least, she is innocent of self-proclamation.

Instead, Clarissa turns her back, hermetically, on the world, and prepares to leave it, telling Anna that she has 'more important things to do' than to justify herself in narrative (VII, 45; *IV, 61*); and it was this exemplary endeavour that Richardson chose to emphasize in what, after the cautious revisions of 1746–7, became her only literary legacy. The will records a volume that is impeccably unworldly: Clarissa bequeaths to one pious widow, Mrs Norton, 'my book of *Meditations*, as I used to call it; being extracts from the best of books', and entitles another, Mrs Lovick, to take a copy of the book, 'which she seemed to approve of, although suited particularly to my own case' (VIII, 107; *IV, 423*). In the event, Mrs Harlowe takes possession of the original, 'as it was all of her dear daughter's handwriting; and as it might, when she could bear to look into it, administer consolation to herself' (VIII, 121–2; *IV, 434*); and the legacy is heard of no more. Its text remains largely unknown to the reader of *Clarissa*, with the exception of a few samples included in the correspondences that form the novel. Having read several meditations on visiting Clarissa's lodgings during the period of their composition, Belford transcribes three in letters to Lovelace, avowedly as a spur to his conscience. Each is a collage of about a dozen scriptural verses drawn up and applied by Clarissa to her own case on specific occasions: the first adapts verses from various chapters of Job to lament her imprisonment at the debtor's gaol (VI, 392; *IV, 6–7*); the second, entitled 'Poor mortals the cause of their own misery', turns to Ecclesiasticus and Psalms in response to a recriminating letter from her sister (VII, 93–4; *IV, 96*); and the third returns to Job to complain, according to Belford, at 'some new instances of implacableness from her friends' (VII, 126–7; *IV, 120–1*). Another collection of verses from Job is appended to a letter from John Harlowe, where Clarissa has stitched it '*with black silk*', thereby identifying it as a direct response to his accusations (VII, 100–1; *IV, 101*). Finally, Lovelace quotes a fifth, obtained on his unsuccessful attempt to surprise Clarissa at her lodgings: headed 'On being hunted after by the enemy of my soul', it draws on appropriate psalms to protest at his continued pursuit (VII, 152; *IV, 140*). Despite this evident relevance to the business of the novel, however, no more of the book than these five extracts appears. But it was not lost. Like another fictive item from Mrs Harlowe's reliquary for which Richardson contrived a disconcerting parallel existence, the Vandyke taste portrait '*drawn as big as the life by Mr. Highmore*' and puffed in a note to the original edition (1st edn, III, 260), it found its way eventually into the reader's world. Late in 1749, six months after publishing the second edition of Clarissa's epistolary history, Richardson printed the legacy, in separate form, as *Meditations Collected from the Sacred Books; And Adapted to the Different Stages of a Deep Distress; Gloriously surmounted by Patience, Piety, and Resignation. Being those mentioned in the History of Clarissa as drawn up by her for her own Use.*

Meditations is one of the most obscure items in Richardson bibliography.

Sale, in 1936, could locate only two copies, one of which is now in the Rothschild Collection in Trinity College, Cambridge.[5] The volume is a small octavo, dated 1750, and consists of a five-page advertisement by 'the Editor' of *Clarissa*, a three-page preface signed 'Cl. Harlowe', and, on the following seventy-six pages, the meditations themselves, to a total of thirty-six. The advertisement briefly outlines Richardson's reasons for issuing the volume and explains its relation to the novel, quoting several paragraphs of Belford's plot-summary (VII, 124–5; *IV, 119–20*) to enable readers unfamiliar with *Clarissa* 'to judge of the aptness and force of the Meditations as here applied' (*Meditations*, p. iii). Interestingly, the mask of authorial disavowal is lowered as Richardson becomes unusually explicit about the feigned authenticity of the text: the advertisement ends by noting the preservation, within the volume, of 'all those marks of genuineness which are necessary to give greater efficacy to the Example proposed to be set by the Heroine', and cites as a case in point 'the following Preface ascribed to Clarissa' (p. v). From here on, however, the volume scrupulously maintains the appearance of a found work. Clarissa's preface provides a short retrospective introduction, accounting for her composition of the book during a period of spiritual turmoil, and is immediately followed by the text of the meditations. Each is similar in character to the examples from the novel, being a collage of verses adapted from one or more of Job, Psalms, Ecclesiasticus and the Wisdom of Solomon, with marginal references supplied. (Job is immediately apparent as the main source, although a number of the central meditations are based principally on Psalms, and the Apocryphal books are more heavily used towards the end.) The volume's organization reinforces the link with *Clarissa*: the first twenty-six meditations are dated and arranged in order of supposed composition, and each is preceded by an editorial introduction or 'historical connexion' designed to place it in its fictional context, usually including precise references to pages or letters in the first edition. Only in the ten more abstract and didactic meditations of the last phase are dates and situations left unspecified. The five meditations from *Clarissa* reappear, in their original order, as nos. VIII, XII, XIII, XVII, and XVIII.

The meditations are dated between 18 June and 29 August, and thus coincide with the point in the novel at which Clarissa more or less ceases to narrate. During the period of their composition, Anna repeatedly urges her to write a memoir of just the narrative type that she has so obviously abandoned: a closed, continuous and authoritative account, clearly organized in terms of a consistent self, a coherent sequence of cause and effect, and a categorical moral gloss. 'The villainy of the worst of men, and the virtue of the most excellent of women, I expect will be exemplified in it, were it to be written in the same connected and particular manner, in which you used to write to me', she predicts in a letter requesting, even after Clarissa's reluctant final foray into circumstantial narrative, 'the full particulars of your Story' (VI, 185; III, 379–80). Her expectations of this narrative's usefulness are clear enough: its retrospective organization and didactic rhetoric will guarantee its efficacy as both an alarm to the unwary and a definitive vindication of its author. Her view of the relation between writing and experience, likewise, is wholly unproblematic: the one, in the ideal form of the 'connected and particular' memoir, will simply distil, and permanently guarantee, the essential truths of the other.

Clarissa, however, is by this time less sure, either of the inherent connectedness of experience or of the reliability of self as an organizing principle. The mad papers written in the immediate aftermath of the rape present a series of vivid emblems for what Terry Castle has called a 'traumatic loss of faith in articulation, and the power of the letter to render meaning'.[6] In a later passage, Clarissa looks back on several days spent 'under a strange delirium; now moping, now dozing, now weeping, now raving, now scribbling, tearing what I scribbled, as fast as I wrote it' (VI, 174; III, 372). In the crisis of returning consciousness, coherent discourse appears at once unattainable and invalid. 'What she writes she tears', reports Lovelace, 'and throws the paper in fragments under the table, either as not knowing what she does, or disliking it' (V, 302; III, 204): in every sense, language is ruptured. Writings are scratched through, torn, or otherwise aborted; in one, punctuated largely by dashes, the familiar letter visibly collapses beneath the weight of an experience too devastating to admit of explanation in the conventional, ordered syntax in which Clarissa has previously made sense of the world, and leaves her, having 'sat down to say a great deal', able to write 'nothing at all' (V, 303; III, 205). The fragmentation, both syntactical and material, attests a crisis in which language can no longer encompass life:[7] Clarissa's complaint at wrongs 'beyond the power of *words to express*' (V, 322; III, 220) is entirely without hyperbole. But the crisis is also one of self. Her failure to reduce her experience to the linear arrangements of narrative occurs simultaneously with a radical questioning of subjectivity as an organizing principle, and a new acknowledgement of its tendency to reduce the most scrupulously undertaken explanations to the level of special pleading: having recognized the inherent resistance of the world to 'connected and particular' rendition, she makes the logical next step of questioning the subjective basis on which her constructions of it have previously been founded. 'But still upon *Self*, this vile, this hated *Self*!' she exclaims, in interruption of an early attempt to resume her letter-narrative: 'I will shake it off, if possible' (VI, 107; III, 321). The only valid discourse will be self-less and uncompromised by extenuation: like Daniel Deronda, with his impossible ambition 'to shift his centre till his own personality would be no less outside him than the landscape',[8] she hopes to displace the origin of her writing, to make it impersonal and objective. 'It is difficult to go out of ourselves to give a judgment against ourselves', she tells Anna; 'and yet, oftentimes, to pass a *just* judgment, we ought' (VII, 103; *IV, 103*).

The problem continually exercises Richardson's narrators: 'Self', as Harriet Byron notes, 'is a very wicked thing; a sanctifier, if one would give way to its partialities, of actions, which, in others, we should have no doubt to condemn' (*Grandison*, II, 1). But whereas characters in *Grandison* notoriously address the discrepancy between event and its mediation in narrative by offering their readers, on critical occasions, not their own accounts but minutes taken by a concealed stenographer, Clarissa devises a more subtle remedy. By the time of Anna's request for the memoir, she has recovered the ability to write coherently; but her refusal to grant it betrays a residual scepticism at the efficacy of the 'connected and particular' manner as a register of experience, and at the impartiality attainable in first-person narrative. By advocating, instead, the composition of an epistolary history, she provides the next best thing to the objectivity to which she now scrupulously aspires: a diverse collection of subjective versions, in which no single viewpoint will have pre-eminence. In excusing herself from writing any retrospective apology, she turns to Job for endorsement of her challenge to the legitimacy of narrative self-justification: '*If I justify myself, mine own heart shall condemn me: If I say, I am perfect, it shall also prove me perverse*' (VII, 45; *IV, 60*). The epistolary 'compilement' will enable her to avoid any such compromising gesture, and to confirm her own integrity precisely by refusing to assert it: 'it will be an Honour to my Memory', she tells Belford, '. . . that I was so well satisfied of my Innocence, that, having not time to write my own Story, I could entrust it to the relation which the destroyer of my fame and fortunes has given of it' (VII, 70; *IV, 79*).

Revealingly, however, Clarissa has altered the cited text, substituting 'heart' where Job reads 'mouth'. The implication of the original is that self-justification is simply impossible: words will inevitably subvert the very claim they are enlisted to make. But for Clarissa it is not the mouth, or the utterance itself, that will condemn her, so much as simply the heart, the monitor within. Linguistic self-presentation is dangerous, but not impossible: she now distrusts, and has relinquished, conventional narrative media, open as they always are to the accusation of rhetorical distortion, but she has not given up her quest for purer and less vulnerable forms of discourse. Even as they demonstrate the fragmentation of the 'connected and particular' manner and of the epistemology on which it is based, the mad papers in fact open the way to new modes of composition: in one, Clarissa articulates her story by means of a hauntingly ambiguous allegory;[9] in another, by amassing a series of mock-biblical images of corruption and decay (v, 304–6; *III*, 206–8). In this respect, their significance is not just negative: like the rape itself, the fragmentation of discourse which accompanies it prepares Clarissa for the redefinition of self and experience in a new literary form, marking the point of a shift from realism to abstraction, and from epistolary narrative to meditation.

In the final third of the novel, meditation takes over as the dominant form of Clarissa's spiritual and literary activity. The process by which her devotion to the exercise of holy dying[10] brings with it new patterns of understanding and opportunities for expression is meticulously documented. In pursuit of spiritual readiness, she turns incessantly to scripture: in the hands of the whore Sally, her Bible falls naturally open at Job and Ecclesiasticus, where Clarissa has 'doubled down the *useful places*' (vi, 265; *III*, 439). Job and Ecclesiasticus are revealing choices, given the consolatory power conventionally ascribed to the wisdom books: within Richardson's circle, Patrick Delany urged that these texts should be 'perpetually perused, and perfectly remembred: and, by being so, will be a sure and lasting fund of direction, consolation and support … throughout all emergencies in life'; another contemporary theologian found Job 'singularly well adapted to administer Comfort in the Day of Adversity … to private Persons in Distress'.[11] As a genre characterized by its attempt to wrest meaning from a hostile or disorderly world, wisdom literature offers the afflicted a comforting conceptual structure in terms of which to understand their suffering. With their complaints at captivity, persecution, calumny and (in the crucial cases of Job and Psalms 38–41) physical defilement, furthermore, the books provide a language of lament peculiarly suited, in meaning and intensity, to Clarissa's case, enabling her not only to endure, but also to articulate, her experience. Having virtually abandoned the effort to document her life in epistolary narrative, she discovers in biblical wisdom a form that replaces the 'minute particulars' of circumstantial realism with a luminous and cogent symbolism, and thus makes available a newly emphatic medium in which to define her wrongs and vent her grief. More importantly still, Job and Psalms, her main sources, offer salutary examples of patience, types of afflicted integrity who themselves confront the challenge of arbitrary suffering, and ultimately find meaning in it as a necessary process of mortification. By modelling herself on them, Clarissa can make sense of her own afflictions and at the same time approach, imitatively, the eventual state of pious resignation expressed in her quotation from Psalms, '*It is good for me that I was afflicted*' (viii, 5; *IV*, 346). In sum, her chosen texts provide patterns of understanding, conduct and language by which she is able to reconstruct a sense of her life as coherent, and thus bring it to its exemplary conclusion.

Her pursuit of these benefits becomes obsessive: not content even with perpetual perusal, she rewrites her sources in application to her own case, rearranging verses to bring the texts into new juxtapositions, and occasionally even inserting pastiche phrases of her own. By changing pronouns throughout from masculine to feminine, she seals the act of linguistic appropriation, and thereby refocuses the original texts' laments at physical and spiritual affliction on her own specifically female history of sexual oppression and rape. Belford describes the practice as 'the method she takes to fortify her mind' on one occasion when, troubled by a censorious letter from her uncle, she searches the wisdom books for passages of particular consolation and relevance, and recasts them in two meditations of complaint, 'with intention to take off the edge of her repinings at hardships so disproportioned to her fault' (VII, 93; *IV, 96*). The effect is to signify her own conformity to sacred example: where she gathers verses to lament her imprisonment at Rowland's, he is struck not only by 'the noble simplicity, and natural Ease and Dignity of Style' thus made available to her, but also by the force of the analogy with Job, which he pursues having borrowed a Bible 'to compare the passages contained in it by the book, hardly believing they could be so exceedingly apposite as I find they are' (VI, 391, 393; *IV, 6, 7*). Her concern in a third meditation, he suggests, is not just to adapt biblical sentiment, but to re-enact the pious endurance of biblical type. 'On every extraordinary provocation', he notes, 'she has recourse to the Scriptures, and endeavours to regulate her vehemence by sacred precedents. "Better people, she says, have been more afflicted than she, grievous as she sometimes thinks her afflictions: And shall she not bear what less faulty persons have borne?"' (VII, 126; *IV, 120*). By abandoning her own language and appropriating theirs, Clarissa takes imitation of example to extraordinary lengths; but her thoroughness has its desired effect. When she locks away her papers, she first removes the completed volume of meditations, 'saying, She should, perhaps, have use for that' (VII, 355; *IV, 290*): in her last days, she need only review its text to complete her devout preparations for the grave.

The importance of *Meditations* for *Clarissa* lies in its development of this story of spiritual progress, and in its display of the new literary practices by which the progress is sustained. Clarissa's preface explains the redemptive value of the meditations: collecting them, she reports, was 'an employment that *divinely* comforted me. And when collected, the frequent recourse I had to them in the different stages of a progressive, and very heavy distress, gave me still greater comfort' (*Meditations*, p. vi). As she presents them, they in the first place secure, and subsequently record, her spiritual transcendence. Once completed, the volume reminds her 'that the gradations from *impatience* and *despair*, to *resignation* and *hope*, and from thence to *praise* and *thanksgiving*, are not only more natural, but, to a truly contrite heart, more easy, than I, in my darker state, had apprehended it to be' (p. viii): it does so by documenting her triumphant passage through these 'gradations', and by demonstrating them (as the shifting grammar suggests) to combine in a single spiritual path. The process begins soon after the rape when, having, as the preface recalls, 'great grief, and, at times ... great impatience in my grief', she turns to scripture, adapting the famous curse of Job 3 in her first meditation, and following it with similar compilations from elsewhere in Job and from various psalms of lament, in which she redefines her situation in violent and densely-patterned images of darkness and captivity. 'This kind of spirit', she continues, 'I indulged, as I fear, too much ... having, as I thought, so good an example in the impatience which the Holy Man I have mentioned gave way to in the early stages of *his* Affliction' (pp. vi–vii). Job perfectly meets her expressive needs, his own direct encounter with the impossibility of matching experience in expression enabling her to write with new force: 'O that my grief were thoroughly weighed, and my calamity laid in the balance together!' Meditation VIII opens, 'For now it would be heavier than the sand of the sea: Therefore my words are swallowed up' (pp. 16–17). The resonances are best illustrated by Meditation V, which draws on the anguished imagery of Job 9 not only to allude elliptically to the rape, but also to protest at the vilifications to which it has exposed her: 'If I wash myself with snow-water, and make my hands never so clean; yet shalt thou plunge me in the ditch, and mine own cloaths shall abhor me' (p. 11). But the same evocative language of suffering and defilement pervades all the early meditations. 'My breath is corrupt, my days are extinct, the grave is ready for me', the second complains: ' ... I have said to corruption, Thou art my father: To the worm, Thou art my mother and my sister ... / I stretch forth my hands unto thee – Hear me speedily, O Lord; my spirit faileth. Hide not thy face from me – / And why dost thou not pardon my transgressions, and take away mine iniquity?' (pp. 4–5). Likewise, Meditation III, written on a failed attempt to escape from the house at 'Dover Street', is preoccupied by corruption and isolation, as though to recover some transcendent meaning from the particular situation. 'Thou hast laid me in the lowest pit, in darkness, in the deeps', it laments. 'Thy wrath lieth hard upon me, and thou hast afflicted me with all thy waves. / Thou hast put away mine acquaintance far from me: Thou hast made me an abomination unto them. I am shut up, and I cannot come forth.' Again, it appeals for the comfort of revelation: 'How long, Lord, wilt thou hide thyself?' (p. 7).

   In the figures of scripture, experience thus takes on a certain intelligibility: by lifting it to a level of intense poetic abstraction, Clarissa sheds the specific and local, and begins to explain it in the larger moral terms of darkness and evil. But the sources of *Meditations* offer still more significant patterns of coherence. From the earliest meditations, a narrative begins to emerge, in which her suffering ceases to be arbitrary, and takes on the character of a divinely sanctioned trial: 'God hath delivered me to the ungodly, and turned me over into the hands of the wicked!' she writes in Meditation IV: 'I was at ease; but he hath broken me asunder' (p. 9). The complaints accumulate: 'God hath cast me into the mire, and I am become like dust and ashes' (p. 13); 'the arrows of the Almighty are within me; the poison whereof drinketh up my spirit' (p. 17). But as they do so, they lend a special eminence to Clarissa's case, as she writes in apostrophe to the Harlowes: 'If indeed ye will magnify yourselves against me . . . Know now, that God hath overthrown me, and hath compassed me with his net. / He hath fenced up my ways that I cannot pass. He hath set darkness in my paths' (p. 31). In such passages, the random and inexplicable cruelty of her antagonists can appear in a new light, as part of the pattern of a Christian ordeal. In consequence, the cry of despair becomes increasingly a defence: that she has been selected for the distinction of trial.

With these redefinitions of her life as one of divine affliction, Clarissa begins to use not only the language but, increasingly, the story of Job to impose coherent shape on the experiential chaos epitomized in the mad papers. She ends her preface with an apology for having 'taken the liberty of substituting the word *her* for *him*, and to make other such-like little changes of words', a liberty she hopes 'will be thought pardonable' (p. viii). Her little changes, however, carry the deepest implications: by adopting and redeploying Job's words, she also adopts the precedent of his life, which hers now appears to reiterate. Analogies become inescapable, and in this respect Belford's consultation of the Bible to compare her case with those of her 'sacred precedents' is exemplary. By her use of Job, she is able, as one introductory passage approvingly notes, to 'sanctify the afflictions' she has experienced (p. 30), implicitly awarding herself the same status of suffering integrity, and rewriting her life after its model, often with ostentatious precision. In Meditation VI, for example, she adapts the lamentation of Job 29 to recall days 'when the Almighty was yet with me! When *I was in my father's house*', equating her own charitable acts with Job's ('I delivered the poor that cried, the fatherless, and him that had none to help him'), and drawing a contrast with her present undeserved suffering: 'But now my soul is poured out upon me. The days of affliction have taken hold of me' (p. 13). On occasion, Richardson's passages of 'historical connexion' intervene to point applications of this sort: an early example identifies Lovelace as the 'plague' of Meditation II, and Mother Sinclair and her cronies as the 'dragons, and birds of the night' with whom Clarissa is 'an inmate' (p. 4).

Cumulatively, the effect is to keep continually in play the parallel between Clarissa's own history and the text in terms of which she now rewrites it. As a type of suffering humanity, Job has an evident applicability to Clarissa's case.

Meditations, however, probes beyond this simple reading, to find in its source a set of more specific analogies, and to draw on them in its redefinition of the history. As one contemporary commentary makes explicit, Job is not simply 'a pious good man resigned and patient under all the severest strokes of fortune ... but a pious good man, persecuted by the devil in so many shapes, and afterwards reproached for all his piety from a quarter, he had so little reason to expect it from'.[12] His life is a trial of his integrity by an adversary intent on proving the hollowness of virtue, who brings the trial to its climax by touching him 'in his flesh': the same commentator identified this final assault as 'the highest test of his sincerity, an experiment if he stood it, that were decisive of his virtue',[13] terms which aptly suggest its relation to Lovelace's pose of libertine empiricism. In fact, the analogy originates in Lovelace's reminder to Belford that 'Satan, whom thou mayest ... call my instigator, put the good man of old upon the severest trials' (III, 86; *II, 40*); but it becomes central to *Meditations*, in which every allusion to 'the wicked', 'the destroyer', 'the enemy' (pp. 9, 29, 41) makes way for a simple redefinition of Clarissa's life as a trial of virtue by vice. Job's plight, however, involves more than Satanic persecution: as commentators throughout the 1740s regularly noted, the narrative of his sufferings is quickly consumed, in the body of the text, by an acrimonious debate on the question of his integrity. Garnett even identi-fied the comforters as Job's family, 'his own kindred deriding and insulting him',[14] to point out how his physical affliction is aggravated by unjust accusations of its deservedness; another commentator read the whole text as a rhetorical struggle, a 'grand Dispute' conducted in the alternating speeches of Job and the comforters on the question '*Whether* JOB *was really the upright and religious Man he appeared to be, or at the Bottom, but an Hypocrite and Dissembler with God and Man.*'[15] Job's victimization, in short, is rhetorical: he is not only 'oppressed with Sufferings' but also 'traduced by Calumny',[16] a condition that provides Clarissa with her most telling resource, allowing her to redefine censure and misrepresentation simply as the last phase of her own trial. Like Job, she is accused of responsibility for her suffering; and she uses Job's words to deny it. Medi-tations V, XIII, XIV and XVII develop the analogy most fully, by referring Job's complaints at calumny to the Harlowes, who 'write bitter words against me', or 'break me in pieces with words' (p. 38); but it is implicit throughout. By appropriating Job's language she stresses these two conformities between her own life and his, defining herself in the role not simply of the righteous sufferer, but of the righteous sufferer maligned and misrepresented. The meaning of her life becomes fixed by analogy: reinterpreted and rewritten according to the model of Job's trial, it takes on a new and arresting significance. She is a latterday Job, tested by adversity; Lovelace is the Satan sent to try her; the Harlowes become the comforters, compounding her sufferings by reading them, maliciously, as retribution.

These analogies established, the rest of the story writes itself: like Job, Clarissa need only wait. 'I was the sooner convinced', the preface records,

that I ought patiently to bear the chastisement which I had incurred. And so, by degrees, more chearful prospects opening upon my benighted mind, I looked forward to the promises of divine pardon and reconciliation, which are everywhere to be met with in the Sacred Books. And then the Meditations carry a more comfortable appearance; as I was then less impatient, and of consequence more resigned to the dispensations of that Providence, which I found must be my ONLY refuge.   (p. vii)

Consequently, the meditations in their next phase abandon their complaints at violation and calumny, instead identifying suffering, and the admission of guilt, as the way to redemption. 'In thy sight shall no *one* living be justified' (p. 24), she writes in Meditation XI, and returns to the language of pollution in Meditation XX: 'What is man, that he should be clean? And he which is born of woman, that he should be righteous? / Behold *God* putteth no trust in his saints: Nor are the heavens clean in his sight. / How much more abominable and filthy is man, which drinketh iniquity like water?' (p. 44). In the recognition of sin and chastisement as stages of a progress towards God, she confirms the Job-like pattern of her life as a path through adversity and suffering to redemption: as she writes in a rare departure from scripture, 'There is a shame which bringeth sin; and there is a shame which bringeth glory and grace' (p. 38). Given the new interpretation offered by sacred precedent, her affliction has become a mark not of reprobacy, but of election: 'For gold is tried in the fire; and acceptable men in the furnace of adversity' (p. 33).

Armed with this redefinition of her life, Clarissa brings it to its logical conclusion in a language which precisely answers that of the opening complaints: darkness, captivity and defilement are met by light, deliverance and healing. The introduction to Meditation IX cites the text as evidence of her endeavours 'to possess her soul in patience and peace, in order to fit her mind for the Change, which, from her low and weak state, she had reason to believe would soon happen' (p. 19). In it, she already finds the offer of redemption: 'For *thou hast* looked down from the height of *thy* sanctuary ... To hear the groaning of the prisoner; to loose *her* that is appointed to death. / Blessed *are they* whom thou chastenest, O Lord, and teachest out of thy Law; / That thou mayest give rest from the days of adversity' (p. 20). In Meditation XXI, she quotes Psalm 51 for a precise answer to the snow-water image of Meditation V: 'Thou shalt purge me with hyssop, and I shall be clean: Thou shalt wash me, and I shall be whiter than snow' (p. 47). From this point on, the progress is complete. The introduction to Meditation XXIII finds 'all her

pious doubts and fears ... now dispelled by the sun-shine of Divine Grace'
(p. 50), and the same idea is invoked in the preface. The explanation of her
life offered by sacred precedent affords a new clarity of view: 'I was graciously
enabled to look back upon those distresses which had been so grievous to me,
as so many mercies manifested by the Divine Goodness to draw me to
Himself' (pp. vii–viii). The last meditations triumphantly reiterate this newly
established history, reading at times like an elaborate gloss on Clarissa's
coffin (which is inscribed with some of the same texts). In Meditation XXII,
'The snares of death compassed me round about; and the pains of hell got
hold upon me. I *found* trouble and heaviness, and I called upon the Name of
the Lord: / *Saying*, O Lord, I beseech thee, deliver my soul! / *And Thou, Lord*,
deliveredst my soul from death; mine eyes from tears; and my feet from
falling' (pp. 48–9). Meditation XXV confirms this retrospect with a sequence
from Psalm 30, and the conceit dominates even the more abstract meditations
of the last phase. In Meditation XXXV, Clarissa adapts Elihu's consoling
explanation to Job of God's ways, that '*Tho' he hath sometimes* visited in his
anger, yet he knoweth it not in great extremity' (p. 75); and she concludes the
final meditation assured of victory in her trial: 'Turn again unto thy rest, O my
Soul! for the Lord hath rewarded thee!' (p. 76). She has been purified,
healed, and saved.

    It would misrepresent the character of *Meditations* to suggest that Clarissa
sets out deliberately to rewrite her life in a new narrative medium. Rather,
Richardson presents her as reaching desperately, like Job, for meaning,
writing 'to the moment', and only incidentally, in her endeavours to conform
to the piety of scripture's righteous sufferers, arriving at her redefinition of
the history. At first, Job simply supplies a peculiarly apposite and intense
language of complaint. Gradually, however, the heightened language takes on
the character of a privileged discourse which, within the novel, Belford likens
to 'a rich vein of golden ore, which runs thro' baser metals' (VI, 391; *IV, 6*): it
allows her to detach herself from the constraints of 'connected and particular'
narrative, and, instead of documenting her experience in all its detail and
diffusiveness, to replace the complex history with a simple fable of trial and
redemption, and thus to suffuse it with a new moral clarity. In this respect,
Meditations is a kind of spiritual autobiography, rendering experience coherent by reading it in terms of a divinely engineered masterplot; but it goes
much further. As the fragmentation and rearrangement of sacred texts takes
over as her chosen means of signification, Clarissa effectively reconstitutes
herself in the image of her exemplar, so that her own experience appears
simply as a recapitulation of his, radiant with the same meanings. The
narrative of *Meditations* is in this respect not just spiritualized and sanctified,
but typological: pared of the contingencies of time and place with which the

novel is so preoccupied, it discovers a core of meaning in her life's conformity to that of the great archetype of suffering virtue, Job. By immersing her own language, self and experience in his precedent, Clarissa enables herself to understand her life in new terms, and to record that understanding in the oracular form of her own 'Book of Clarissa': the gesture redefines her, irresistibly, as the female Job.

Reading *Meditations*

The violence of Lady Bradshaigh's reaction to Clarissa's death is well known: 'it will hurt my heart, and *durably*', she announced.[17] Richardson consoled her on her mock bereavement with lectures on the vanity of life, turning for illustration not to the newly published novel, but to material deleted from it: 'I had formed a meditation for my divine Girl on this very Subject, which would have been an apt Answer to all you have said, when you have generously lamented her early Death', he told her, 'but I omitted it in the History, as I did several other Meditations … because of my undesirable length.'[18] The letter is fragmentary, but Richardson is clearly preparing to cite Meditation XXXVI, 'An Early Death not to be lamented'. 'Omitted' is an equivocal term, but seems to indicate that at least some of the passages first printed in *Meditations* were originally designed for *Clarissa*, and subsequently withdrawn. Numbers can only be guessed at, but *Meditations* almost certainly preserves a large amount of material deleted from the pre-publication manuscripts that circulated among Richardson's quorum of sample readers between 1744 and 1747: the references made in the novel's first edition must have been to a book already substantially, if not wholly, written.

Having reassembled this omitted material, however, Richardson hesitated even to publish it separately. The text is clearly prepared for public sale: its title-page bears the usual booksellers' names, and the advertisement reports that, although he had transcribed the meditations only 'for the use of some select friends', they, on reading them, 'were urgent with him to give them to the public,' and had persuaded him to do so (p. i). Printing, however, did not necessarily entail publication, and he remained undecided even as he committed this passage to press, despite the continued intercessions of his friends. Lady Bradshaigh was one mover: 'The meditations you design to print, I should be glad to see published,' she urged late in 1749, 'and as you say they are connected with the history, it is pity the public should not be obliged with them.'[19] But by 1 January, when Richardson sent copies to Edward Young and his housekeeper, Mary Hallows, he was still not ready to publish. The collection had been printed only at the desire of friends, he wrote, and in only a small number: 'Your approbation, or the contrary, will give me courage to diffuse it, or to confine it to the few hands for which it was designed; notwithstanding the booksellers' names in the title page.'[20] Young promptly pressed him not only to publish it, but also to restore it to the next edition of *Clarissa*, in which it would 'much add to the verisimilitude, and pathos, and sublimity of the work'.[21]

Richardson, however, followed neither advice, and appears for some months to have proceeded no further in distributing the text. It is clear from both his description and his treatment of *Meditations*, moreover, that he was disinclined to recognize the volume for what Young and Lady Bradshaigh took it for, and what it inescapably was: a supplement to *Clarissa*. Instead, he presented it simply as a devotional work, while underplaying its fictional dimension. His explanation to Young of his motives for circulating the work is typical:

> But reading it to a little assembly of female friends one Sunday night, one of whom was labouring under some distresses of mind, they were all so earnest with me to print it, that person in particular who is my wife's sister, that I could not resist their entreaties; and as they were all great admirers of Clarissa, I thought I could not do better than, by historical connexion to the piece, point the use of them in a distress so great as my heroine's is represented to be.[22]

By this account, the volume is designed not as a new contribution to the epistolary 'compilement', but as a manual of consolation for the afflicted. Its status as a document from the world of the novel becomes merely incidental: Clarissa's authorship and the passages of historical connection are not invitations to put *Meditations* back into *Clarissa* so much as exemplary demonstrations of ways and contexts in which it might, instead, be put to immediate 'use' in the reader's own spiritual life. Interestingly, Richardson practised what he preached in this respect, and reserved the work, initially, for the bereaved. Theirs were the 'few hands' for whose use it had been prepared: having set the manuscript to work on his wife's sister, and been urged by her and others to publish it 'to all such as labour under great afflictions and disappointments' (p. i), he selected as recipients readers most likely to use it as intended, at the same time resisting calls for publication or restoration to the novel. When Lady Bradshaigh made such a call, Richardson simply sent a copy to Young, who (according to Mary Delany) was 'in great trouble' at his stepdaughter Caroline Lee's sudden death in November 1749;[23] and when Young responded by urging publication 'for the sake of all the afflicted, to whom it will be the richest cordial',[24] he seems to have done nothing until sending a copy to Aaron Hill's daughters, probably on Hill's death in February 1750. In July, Astraea Hill apologized for her dilatoriness in acknowledging 'ye excellent Manuel of Divine Meditations', and thanked him for providing 'such strong and beautiful Aids, to strengthen and suport our Too too weak Minds by'.[25]

During the summer, however, he at last began to distribute it more widely. On 14 July, Ann Donnellan thanked him for a copy: 'I have received infinite pleasure, and something better, from the collection of sublime sentences which you have so ably made the divine Clarissa apply to in her deepest distresses.'[26] The Rothschild copy, originally Jane Collier's, is dated 'Aug: 1750'; and in September Mary Delany's sister Anne Dewes acknowledged receipt of another, and joined Young and Lady Bradshaigh in pressing for dissemination to a wider audience which, she reassured him, with deft aim at both his social and his evangelical ambitions, could only applaud: 'They must be of great use and pleasure to all who read them; and the few friends to whom I have shewed those you favoured me with, are greatly pleased with them, especially Lady Anne Coventry, aunt to the Duke of Beaufort, a lady of singular piety and religion, who has been a widow, and, like Anna the prophetess, walked in the house of God these forty years.'[27] Richardson held firm, but in October had still not finally decided against publication. When Sarah Chapone thanked him for 'the fair Sufferer's Meditations, which, together with her History, render the whole a complete System of Knowlege and Duty', and added her voice to the clamour for publication, he responded that he had 'not yet published the Meditations', but that she might 'command two or three more of them, for any Friend'. She was quick to accept, requesting one for each daughter and a third for a Miss Laurence, 'a true Admirer of Clarissa, to which, in a very great Measure, it may be imputed, that she preserves her Principles in a very disolute Family'.[28] Miss Laurence had sent to her bookseller for a copy and 'was greatly chagrined when she found, they were not to be purchas'd'; but neither was Richardson to be swayed. No meditations were added to the new edition of *Clarissa* published in April 1751, and Richardson's 'not' had become a 'never' when, the following year, he sent his Dutch translator 'a little Piece . . . mentioned in the work as Clarissa's Meditations; which I have never yet published'. Stinstra was flattered at inclusion in so select an audience: they pleased him the more, he wrote, 'because you said that they have never been published, and you distribute them only among your friends'.[29]

Richardson nowhere records a final resolution to suppress the piece, but his procrastination was decisive enough. A late note on the covering letter to Young identifies the gift as 'Clarissa's Meditations; a little piece, hitherto (July 30, 1758,) unpublished';[30] and unpublished it remained. Other members of Richardson's circle no doubt received copies, but Clarissa's meditations can never have reached the wider readership of her epistolary history, and probably no more than the small number originally mentioned in the letter to

Young were ever printed. Despite sustained pressure from his closest friends and literary advisers, Richardson neither put the work on sale, nor included it in any subsequent edition of *Clarissa*, confining it instead only to readers known to him or otherwise possessed, like the vigilant Miss Laurence and the angelic Lady Anne, of impeccable credentials as Clarissa's 'true Admirers'. In the light of the responses of these readers, his suppression of *Meditations* is all the more remarkable. In arguing for separate publication or incorporation within *Clarissa*, they merely followed the internal logic of the work, treating it as an appendix to, or even a completion of, the 1747–8 text, much as Richardson himself encouraged them to treat the 1751 volume of *Letters and Passages Restored from the Original Manuscripts of the History of Clarissa* (which provided, for readers of the first edition, much of the material added to the third). Richardson, on the other hand, consistently resisted that logic, playing down the volume's fictional associations at every turn. By excluding it from every edition of *Clarissa*, and, when at last persuaded to print it separately, withholding it from the public and designating it simply as a didactic manual, he effectively denied the implications of *Meditations* for the novel in which it had originated, and with which it retained such obvious links. Had it not been for its potential as a devotional instrument, he might well have suppressed it completely.

We can only guess at the reasons for this behaviour. *Clarissa*'s length may indeed, as he told Lady Bradshaigh, have required the initial omission of all but five meditations. But any need to cut a handful of pages from a total of over two and a half thousand explains neither their continued exclusion from the 1751 edition, which added an entire volume expressly (and to some extent genuinely) 'to restore many Passages ... omitted in the former merely for shortening-sake' (I, ix), nor the suppression of the separately printed collection. More revealing is his explanation that he omitted them for fear that their religious emphases might threaten 'one of his principal Ends; which was, to engage the attention of the *Light*, the *Careless*, and the *Gay*' (*Meditations*, p. ii). The inclusion of many more meditations would certainly have made *Clarissa* more obtrusively religious (though as it stands it hardly panders to the frothy); perhaps more damagingly, domination of the concluding volumes by what amounts to a theological explication of the entire novel might have dulled the attentiveness of readers to other implications of the text. *Clarissa* throws up various analogies, the conflict between Satan and Job being just one: Tarquin and Lucretia, Satan and Eve, Lothario and Calista are other pairs occasionally invoked as precedents relevant to the case of Lovelace and Clarissa. But these analogies are never more than hints: they provide points of reference against which to measure an endlessly complicated encounter, but are inadequate to explain it fully. The meditations, however, take the

Job-theme further: from their viewpoint, *Clarissa* begins to look, retro-
spectively, like little more than allegory. Intriguingly, William Warburton,
who wrote the second preface to *Clarissa* and instigated, in his *Divine Legation
of Moses demonstrated* (1738–41), a protracted debate on Job now remembered
only in footnotes to *Tristram Shandy*,[31] wanted to reduce the novel to precisely
these terms. Having received a copy of the second instalment, he offered a
preface for the third, which would complement the existing piece's 'general
criticism on the *species of the Fable*' with 'a more particular examination' of
Clarissa,

> in which we find that too great a sensibility & impatience under the force put on her
> selfe satisfaction necessarily & fatally drew after it that long & terrible attack & combat
> on her Virtue which here so entangled her in the miseries of life that nothing could free
> her from or make her tryumphant over them but divine grace which now comes, like
> the God in the catastrophe of the Ancient fable, to clear up all difficulties.[32]

Whether Richardson accepted this offer may be worth investigating: there are
certain parallels between Warburton's letter and *Clarissa*'s Postscript, as well
as a very Warburtonian ring to the passage on the 'dispensation . . . with which
God, by Revelation, teaches us, He has thought fit to exercise mankind' (VIII,
280; *IV, 554*). But whatever Warburton's role, Richardson was evidently
disinclined to accompany the final three volumes with so schematic a reading
of their contents, and no Job-like synopsis appears. By ignoring Warburton's
recommendation and omitting the bulk of Clarissa's meditations, he could
inhibit his readers from understanding the text too reductively, and keep the
typological interpretation at arm's length.

Many critics, of course, would not credit Richardson with such tact; and
one might point, conversely, to indications that he originally arranged
Meditations very much as a key to *Clarissa*. According to the advertisement,
the work serves to point out the novel's 'principal design and view' (p. i), a
function to which many of the introductory passages explicitly contribute:
one, for example, reports that 'Clarissa was to be an example of suffering
virtue, according to the Christian System. She was to be tried as gold in the
fire of affliction' (p. 30). As an integral part of *Clarissa*, the meditations might
have upset its balance, but in the marginal role of a separately published work
they could have done little damage, and might even, as such passages suggest,
have been intended as a salutary commentary. Thematic reductiveness,
therefore, cannot wholly account for Richardson's anxiety to allow them no
public circulation, even in this marginal role. That he was unhappy at other
implications, however, is evident from Young's letter, which urges him to
incorporate the entire sequence in *Clarissa*'s third edition on the grounds that
'now her character is established, your reason for not inserting it at first

ceases'.[33] What Young meant remains unclear from Richardson's prefaces and letters; but *Clarissa* itself offers ample evidence that, far from supporting the character of its heroine, *Meditations* might equally be thought to compromise it. The five included meditations, in fact, become a major focus of controversy within the novel, which offers not one unified model but two antithetical models for reading them. In Belford's reading, they offer compelling evidence of Clarissa's transcendent virtue; but when Lovelace reads them, he finds nothing but a devastating new rhetoric, the brilliant last word in Clarissa's efforts to affirm that transcendence. Lovelace is an eloquently sceptical reader, building on his complaint at being '*manifestoed* against' in the planned epistolary history (VIII, 144; *IV, 451*) a cogent challenge to the legitimacy of Clarissa's use of sacred precedent. Having read Meditation VIII, he complains at the delusive power of the language plundered by her, insisting that 'death is no such eligible thing, as Job in his *calamities*, makes it', and that Clarissa 'has found the words ready to her hand in honest Job; else she would not have delivered herself with such strength and vehemence' (VII, 15, 14; *IV, 39, 38*). More important, he complains at the wilfulness of the interpretations advanced by each meditation, as though to alert Belford that their coherent meanings are not renditions of some truth inherent in Clarissa's life, but fanciful constructions projected, arbitrarily, onto it. Meditation VIII, he wryly insists, 'is finely suited to her case (that is to say, as she and you have drawn her case)' (VII, 14; *IV, 38*) – which is to say, partially in every sense: it has no special claim to definitiveness, but merely adds to the manifesto. Meditation XVIII, likewise, is at root not representational but rhetorical, as the successful effect, on Mrs Lovick and Mrs Smith, of 'this collection of Scripture-texts drawn up in array against me' (VII, 154; *IV, 141*) only serves to confirm. Lovelace enacts his dissent by subjecting the meditations to his own subversive interpretations, thereby further unsettling the illusion of typological affinity. Disruptively assuming that Clarissa's images of captivity, 'the *Gin*, the *Snare*, the *Net*, mean matrimony, I suppose' (VII, 153; *IV, 140*), and taking 'the arrows of the Almighty are within me' to mean, 'in plain English, that the dear creature is in the way to be a Mamma' (VII, 14; *IV, 38*), he attempts to reduce the meditations to the semantic instability of the 'connected and particular' form, and to prove that scripture, like anything else, can be made to mean anything. Finally, he parodies Clarissa's method by appropriating an entire meditation, and establishes its power to misrepresent by using it to convince his family of his penitence. 'It is', he tells Belford, 'as suitable to my case as to the Lady's, as thou'lt observe, if thou readest it again' (VII, 118; *IV, 114*).

It is not, perhaps; but Lovelace's critique usefully indicates the more troubling implications of Clarissa's compositional practices, and opens another way of reading *Meditations*: not as the trace of an exemplary spiritual progress, but rather as an elaborately contrived proclamation of the writer's own apotheosis. In refusing to write the memoir requested by Anna, Clarissa cites Job's paradox, '*If I say, I am perfect, it shall also prove me perverse*', to stress her pious repudiation of rhetoric. But her wholesale appropriation of Job in *Meditations* makes that repudiation look merely expedient: rather than giving up the effort to say 'I am perfect', it might be alleged, she has simply found a better way of setting about it, a new and more coherent rhetoric which leaves behind the troublesome 'particulars' of narrative and advances to the higher ground of symbolism and typology. As a spiritual exercise, addressed to herself or to God, the result is innocent enough; but when addressed to other readers the invocation of precedent that worked initially to provide Clarissa with a consoling interpretation of her own life begins to appear, instead, as a sustained effort at imposing that interpretation on the world. At times, Clarissa even seems to confirm the rhetorical status of the meditations. In the novel itself, where she recommends the institution of the epistolary 'compilement' (including Lovelace's narrative) as the best available means of transmitting her story to the world, she presents the collection of letters as a hostile medium in which she is nevertheless prepared to rest her case, 'with the same truth and fervour as he did, who says: – *O that one would hear me! and that mine adversary had written a book! – Surely, I would take it upon my shoulders, and bind it to me as a crown!*' (VII, 46; *IV*, 61–2). The quotation recalls Job the maligned sufferer, whose pious embrace of calumny is the ultimate sign of his innocence. But in Meditation VIII (also included in the novel), she quotes a very different verse of Job's, momentarily forgetting the spiritual purposes of her writing and placing the text, instead, in the rhetorical context emphasized by Lovelace. 'O that my words were now written! O that they were printed in a book!' she exclaims: 'That they were graven with an iron pen and lead in the rock for ever!' (*Meditations*, p. 17). If *Clarissa* is the adversary's book, then *Meditations*, the verse suggests, is her own definitive utterance, and will inscribe her perfection in absolute and timeless form.

In the very act of expressing her own Job-like condition of suffering integrity, in short, Clarissa can hardly avoid repeating what the Book of Job ultimately identifies as its protagonist's great fault: 'that he justified himself rather than God' (Job 32.2). Caught between private prayer and public protest, the devotional and the rhetorical, *Meditations* is fraught with tension: inherently, its piety is countered by a strong undertow of presumptuousness. The problem is all the more critical in view of Richardson's anxiety, in the final instalment of the novel, to make his heroine wholly innocent of proclaiming her own integrity, and his awareness of it was always acute. There is a perverse consistency to his methods of addressing the crux.

Initially, he simply stressed Clarissa's eventual reluctance to allow *Meditations* any public role. She closes her preface, prudently, with an appeal that her adaptation of her sources 'will be thought pardonable, as the Collection was made for my own particular use' (p. viii), thereby preparing the reader to understand the text as exclusively private and devotional; in her will, she makes the same emphasis, and carefully limits its dissemination. In the third edition of 1751, in which Richardson consistently and in many ways reductively revised the text in reinforcement of her exemplary status,[34] he made only one substantive change to the group of included meditations, but a highly significant one. In the first edition, Meditation VIII concludes, as in *Meditations*, with Job's appeal, 'O that my words were now written ...' (1st edn, VI, 253); but in the third Richardson removed this entire verse and replaced it with an irreproachably pious dictum of Elihu's, to make Clarissa stress, with new humility, not the uniqueness but the ordinariness of her case:

> *But behold God is mighty, and despiseth not any.*
> *He giveth Right to the Poor – And if they be bound in fetters, and holden in cords of*
> *affliction, then he sheweth them their work and their transgressions –*
>
> (VI, 392; *IV, 7*)

In so doing, he dealt with one particularly awkward passage. But the deleted verse is only the most obvious sign of an ambivalence at work throughout *Meditations*, which as a whole is so radically at odds with this straightforward new tone of humble self-effacement that suppression of the entire text, rather than of a single verse, may eventually have been Richardson's only option. In the event, he simply put into practice, with intriguing symmetry, Clarissa's own defensive treatment of the text, by restricting it to a mere handful of her 'true Admirers' and suggesting that even they read it simply as a manual of devotion and consolation. Clearly, he did not share Young's confidence that her character *was* safely enough established for the remaining meditations to become public, either in the novel's third edition or even in separate form. By allowing the collection only this most marginal and limited of existences within the devotional practices of his own circle, he confined it to a sphere in which its capacity to impinge on the novel could hardly have been weaker, effectively sacrificing it to the debilitating insistence on Clarissa's unimpeachability which, by 1751, had become his first priority. Instead of graving her words in the rock for ever, he more or less erased them.

We cannot, of course, restore *Meditations* to *Clarissa*, whatever its place in the original manuscripts. But the novel notoriously resists simple textual definition. Between 1744, when Richardson began to circulate the first handwritten copies, and 1761 (the year of his death), when he seems to have planned a new revision,[35] its text was in a state of recurrent flux, each version bringing together elements from the total set of *Clarissa* material in significantly different forms and combinations. *Meditations* may be considered as part of that flux: as a work written in the person of the protagonist, repeatedly referred to or quoted in the text, but fully incorporated in no published edition, it belongs with, though not in, the novel. In this context, it has an important bearing not only on *Clarissa*'s religious and spiritual themes, but also on the primary action in which its characters are engaged: the attempt to fix self and experience in language. The old saw, dating back to Sarah Fielding,[36] that any possible reading of the novel is anticipated within the text, is very appropriate to this last attempt of Clarissa's. We may read *Meditations* sympathetically, as Belford does, sceptically, as Lovelace does, or even therapeutically, as Mrs Harlowe does (and as did the daughters of Aaron Hill). But only by chance is reading it an option at all.

7

Identity and character in
Sir Charles Grandison

MARGARET ANNE DOODY

Disguise is important in Richardson's narrative, and the handling of disguise and revelation is an important aspect of his narrative art. Characters frequently wonder who another character is. In *Pamela* both hero and heroine adopt disguise of some sort at important junctures. Pamela becomes another woman, jokingly to be identified as perhaps her own sister, but momentarily unrecognizable in her country garb. Mr B. also becomes another woman, another servant, when he disguises himself as the drunken maidservant Nan in order to attempt Pamela in her chamber. Both of these characters identify themselves emblematically by the disguises they adopt (Pamela is rural innocence, Mr B. is drunken weakness, degraded conscience). The hero and heroine also absorb these new identities which at one level were only show; they find out something about themselves in adopting their strange garb.

Richardson draws on his own precedent set in *Pamela* in his use of disguise and his concern with personality and personal identity in his two later novels. In *Pamela* we are shown stable characters capable of development, capable of learning through the disguises they momentarily assume. In *Clarissa* disguise is a reflection of a radically unstable world. In *Sir Charles Grandison*, that novel which was to be a pendant to *Clarissa* and a contrast to it, Richardson is unwilling to approach the construction of novelistic character in the same manner; disguise in its obvious manifestations is much less important, and the philosophical background has altered, so questions of identity are different. Yet in writing *Grandison*, Richardson was necessarily aware of the precedent that he himself had set in *Clarissa*. In *Clarissa*, Richardson investigates both the dangers and the benefits of disguise, examining not only in his villain–hero but in his divine Clarissa the benefits of protean alteration, of shape-changing imagination. In some respects the most 'philosophic', most speculative of Richardson's novels, *Clarissa* makes one of the central mysteries of its story a mystery which taxed English philosophers of the Enlightenment – the mystery of personal identity.

David Hume, treating 'Of Personal Identity' in his *Treatise of Human Nature* (1738), had set out the sceptical position:

I never can catch myself at any time without a perception, and never can observe anything but the perception.

...I may venture to affirm of the rest of mankind, that they are nothing but a bundle or collection of different perceptions, which succeed each other with an inconceivable rapidity, and are in a perpetual flux and movement.[1]

There is no stable self, just a collection of perceptions; the only constant is these perceptions' great mobility and variety:

The mind is a kind of theatre, where several perceptions successively make their appearance; pass, re-pass, glide away and mingle in an infinite variety of postures and situations.[2]

Hume's mobile and image-conscious language in some respects accords very well with Richardson's. But Richardson's position is closer to that of John Locke and Locke's exponents. Locke had set forth his position in his *Essay concerning Human Understanding* (1690). In 1769, one of Richardson's contemporaries, Bishop Edmund Law, contributed a pamphlet, *Defence of Mr. Locke's Opinion, concerning Personal Identity*, an essay that was to become almost canonically attached to Locke's *Works* in the later eighteenth century. Law elaborates Locke's position that persona and personality are in a sense only necessary legal fictions. They represent that which is to be accountable to the law. As Locke had indicated, person is mere invention, and personality is merely 'a Forensick term'.[3]

The word person standing for a certain guise, character, quality, *i.e.* being in fact a mixed mode, or relation ... it stands for that particular quality of character, under which a man is considered, when he is treated as an intelligent Being subject to government and laws ... All difficulties that relate to a man's *forgetting* some actions, &c. now vanish, when a person is considered as a character and not as a substance ... and it amounts to no more than saying, a man puts on a mask – continues to wear it for some time – puts off one mask and takes another.[4]

Locke's position on personality rests on a sombre base of guilt and judgement, but it reaches towards light and freedom in that particular Augustan insistence upon variety, and upon our varying even (perhaps especially) from ourselves. Hume's theatre is a desolate void, a metaphor which must not be entertained; Locke's social and private consciousness involves an inevitable masquerade which gives pleasure. A man puts on a mask – puts it off and takes another. Richardson enjoyed this kind of variableness, and in *Clarissa* he set out to explore it. Richardson's novel investigates various relations of person to law, person to guilt, persons to other persons at different existential moments. The heroine is the first impersonator of the story, for we early hear that she has, some while before the story opens, written a letter impersonating an older lady, in order to give advice to a wrongheaded mother. That is, Clarissa has impersonated authority in order to stimulate guilt and lay down the law which will free the daughter in the case (II, 78–9; *I, 295*). She picks up a mask and puts it off again.

Person, beginning in guilt, results in the mobile splendour of an examinable but not completely knowable variability. Hume saw that we are all like novelistic characters: 'The identity, which we ascribe to the mind of man, is only a fictitious one'[5] – we are all fictions. To Hume, fiction means delusion, and all images of such fictions, including the image of the theatre of consciousness itself, are reminders that life is inconsistent, nugatory, unreal. Richardson, who believed in a creative God and the Creator Spiritus, is able to accept the fictional nature of our perpetual construction of reality. *Clarissa* is perpetually hospitable to the fluid and mobile; its very narrative structure questions the authority that sustains consistent certainty.

Nobody of any great importance in *Clarissa* has a stable character, or is drawn in the terms the eighteenth century recognized as clear character drawing. Anna Howe in the initial volumes makes the most valiant attempts at drawing boundaries around other persons, delineating them as stable entities. She thus does some of Richardson's narrative work, apparently, while really providing the sort of temporary pseudo-stability that he can undermine. Anna gives us, for instance, the most lengthy single account of Roger Solmes, as she claims that one of her own talents 'is to give an ugly likeness'. She writes several pages on the subject, and is proud enough of her work, and as she says 'silly enough' when her mother makes inquiries 'to read Solmes's character to her' (I, 170–3; *I, 125–7*). Anna writes a complete 'character', a solid neo-Theophrastean piece of observation of a real individual, setting his qualities out complete. But Anna's character-drawing cannot capture the Solmes we come to know; it merely gives us a starting point. This 'character' does not and cannot capture the Solmes who through the pressure of events begins to discover in himself erotic capacities expressed in sadism. Solmes too is changeable; how could a drawer of 'character', no matter how talented, have found in him what he could not yet know, a mask he had not yet tried on? In *Clarissa*, Richardson shows the individual's identity being produced by memory, by action, by the imagination of the future – all of these acting 'to the moment'. The fictions of each person about personal identity are invariably inadequate, but God-formed identity is found in the active process of being and becoming, not in an absolute given. A birth of full form would be a still birth. Simple legal identity is always, in Richardson's *Clarissa*, a still, dead thing. Or at least it is so without the personality behind it – or rather, that perpetually mobile complex of personalities that cannot be covered or named by any legal identity, or public fiction. People sit lightly to their names in that novel. 'My name *was* Clarissa Harlowe: – but it is now *Wretchedness!*' (VI, 250; *III, 427*). The fiction-making mind just consents to touch upon the name and personate what it might be. We impersonate ourselves, changing the mask, recreating the impersonated entity from moment to moment. Personality is always in the making.

In *Sir Charles Grandison*, on the other hand, Richardson recognizes that too much of the protean unfixes order and leads to breakdown and madness – as indeed in *Clarissa* personal metamorphosis does for the two central characters. In *Grandison* the protean and the mad are drained off, as it were, into Clementina, the one major character who is not a structuring epistolary narrator. Madness may be peculiarly helpful to the individual who has suffered from repression and suppression, but it is a dangerous remedy, and protean fluctuating action is here seen as symptomatic of something gone amiss. Disguise, in a few instances where it is employed in this novel, is seen as dishonest and sexually dangerous, without the redeeming features it had in *Clarissa*. Jeronymo della Porretta going on his amours in disguise is shown to be asking for trouble and to deserve the sexual crippling that results.

Civil life at its highest, seen in its most expansive terms of social and individual development, requires a large measure of stability in its members. In particular, it requires that its male members remain stiffly erect, firmly constant, without dangerous shape-changing playfulness; one cannot imagine any male character in this novel, no matter how degraded, doing what Mr B. did when he assumed the garb and persona of the drunken maid Nan. Culture requires a higher respect for male privilege. The central personage of this novel, the hero whose name is given to the title, is a man at the centre of his culture, a member of the progressive liberal gentry, one of the new founding fathers in the making – and not, like Lovelace, a disillusioned aristocrat conscious of the death of his order. Sir Charles stands for social order and the attractions as well as the possibilities of stability.

In the name of such valuable stability, a demand for frankness is made of all members of the community. 'Frankness' reaches a very high level of value in this novel, although the novel fully recognizes that frankness puts limits on identity and the possibilities of identity, as well as forming it. 'Frankness' means acknowledging to the group (as best one can) one's feelings, hopes, wishes, real desires – and that cannot be done without acknowledging the group's right to speak on the matter, to arrange, to judge, to reshape the individual's emotions and wishes into some socially acceptable form. Frankness means giving up something, as well as giving up the self. When Clementina della Porretta, secretly suffering from unacknowledged and suppressed love for Sir Charles, tries to escape from her parents' house to see Sir Charles, she momentarily conceals herself. She dresses in the garb of her servant, just as Clarissa escaped from the brothel in the garb of the servant Mabel. But Clarissa escaped through acting ambiguously, remaining in the borrowed persona, saying nothing when addressed (IV, 94; *III, 311*). When Clementina, mistaken for a servant, is addressed by the servant Camilla, she replies: 'Don't be angry with me, Camilla', and is of course recognized at once (II, 202). She innocently thwarts herself by speaking as herself from within the borrowed garb when addressed, the very point at which the less frank Clarissa wisely remained silent. Clementina is naive, but she also proves her worth here by showing dramatically that she values frankness above her own wishes. She forsakes disguise and is at once swallowed up again by the community that claims her.

Characters major and minor in *Grandison* may at moments prefer being found out, being discovered, to acting frankly, for acting frankly can seem masochistic. To act or speak frankly is usually to invite sessions of constructive self-criticism. Harriet Byron's cousin and confidante Lucy Selby was once in love, in a past era before the story begins. Lucy, we hear, kept silent about her love as Clementina, Harriet's rival for Sir Charles's love, will do. Lucy, however, was soon found out, and submitted in an exemplary manner to the group:

You sighed in silence, indeed: But it was but for a little while. I got your secret from you; not, however, till it betray'd itself in your pined countenance; and then the man's discovered unworthiness, and your own discretion, enabled you to conquer a passion to which you had given way, supposing it unconquerable, because it would cost you pains to contend with it.   (I, 67)

This is a somewhat chilling statement, and none the less so for its exhibition of Harriet the heroine as policeman of her cousin's emotions. (Harriet will be paid back for that when she has to confess her own passion to Charlotte and Lady L., who likewise get her secret from her.) The group letting in daylight upon the soul of the individual encourages her to conquer libido; the group supplies through shame and exhortation the means of making the sufferer consent to endure pain for a social good. The sufferer is always instructed that the social good is chiefly her own good. The novel both jokes about the pain such group pressure causes and makes the pain quite evident, raising doubts about the almost totalitarian vision of social judgement at the same time that it evokes the need for communal values and responsibilities. The questions and issues are not played out with the kind of close attention to individual

personality that we find in *Clarissa*. This novel is not similarly concerned with
the mobile nature of personality and identity. Instead, *Grandison* focuses on
the problems of knowing, the nature of the object to be known.

Are people knowable? The eighteenth century in general had a strong wish
to believe that yes, they are. Fielding states the case for clarity in his 'An Essay
on the Knowledge of the Characters of Men' (1743), a treatise which is
consistent with the delineation of character found in Fielding's novels. Some
men are deceitful and wear disguise, it is true: 'while the crafty and designing
Part of Mankind ... endeavour to maintain one constant Imposition on
others, the whole World becomes a vast Masquerade'. But each masquerader
'if closely attended to ... very rarely escapes the Discovery of an accurate
Observer; for Nature, which unwillingly submits to the Imposture, is ever
endeavouring to peep forth and shew herself'.[6] Nature unerringly displays
the symptoms of the diseases of the mind, as she does those of the body.
Juvenal had said '*no Trust is to be given to the Countenance*', but 'the Satyrist
surely never intended by these Words ... utterly to depreciate an Art on
which so wise a man as *Aristotle* hath thought proper to compose a Treatise'.[7]
The defect lies in our reading of the signs:

> The Truth is, we almost universally mistake the Symptoms which Nature kindly holds
> forth to us; and err as grossly as a Physician would, who should conclude, that a very
> high Pulse is a certain Indication of Health...
>
> In the same manner, I conceive, the Passions of Men do commonly imprint
> sufficient Marks on the Countenance; and it is owing chiefly to want of Skill in the
> Observer, that Physiognomy is of so little Use and Credit in the World.[8]

Human beings are knowable; the face is readable. All that is needed is a skill
in studying the symptoms and their precise indications; we err in our
judgement of a plain and legible world only through ignorance which science
and application can correct. Such a view is borne out in the authorial
narration and the story of *Tom Jones*, which might be subtitled 'Adventures in
the Knowable World'.

Most of the personages in *Grandison* act for part or all of the time as if they
believed everything Fielding says in his 'Essay' – and they are usually right so
to do. Great emphasis is given to countenance and manner. Harriet makes
discoveries through clear-headed observation of details of person and
behaviour. Not blinded by the flattery of Fenwick, Greville, or Sir Hargrave
Pollexfen, she sees their symptoms of lust, self-love and bad temper. True,
Harriet is misled in engaging her servant William Wilson, 'a well-looking
young man ... well-behaved, has a very sensible look, and seems to merit a
better service' (I, 97–8). Wilson has been planted in the home of Harriet's
cousins by Sir Hargrave Pollexfen, who uses Wilson to abduct Harriet from
the masquerade. If Harriet was misled, however, it was partly because she did

not read the signs aright. She and Mrs Reeves were both too taken with
Wilson's good looks (thus proving themselves feminine and fallible). Yet their
judgement was not altogether wrong, it proves; the repentant Wilson presents
himself as very much what Harriet had thought he was. He is a man of good
parentage and 'of a goodnatured disposition', amiable and willing to please.
These very consistent qualities made him weakly compliant to a bad master.
The full character, however, was always there to be read.

'Character' means sign, mark, a symbol consistently indicating a stable
meaning – as in the characters of written or engraved or printed letters. A
human 'character' is or ought to be a consistent collection of legible traits that
consistently indicate the same human entity. Richardson, naturally enough,
used the word 'Character' in all its contemporary senses in each of his novels.
The word, however, seems to be slighted or denied in *Clarissa*, and to occur
much more insistently and persistently in *Grandison*, with special force and
perhaps special enforcement.

Sir Charles Grandison is not without its own subtlety even as it expresses the
deepest yearning for stability – for steadfast rest of all things firmly stayed
upon the pillars of rational piety and benevolence. The novel longs for and
tries to create a world of knowable characters. Yet there are moments in the
novel which temporarily accommodate a desire to de-stabilize the well-
balanced open world, and moments when the counter-yearning for the
unknowable, for impenetrability, is recognized.

One scene in *Grandison* in particular embodies and exorcizes the desire to
be unknowable, and to find the unknowable. At the Masquerade (which we
hear about only later through Harriet Byron's embarrassed description to the
Grandisons), people flout the standards of frankness and stability. Instead,
they adopt disguise that is acknowledged as disguise. They are *known* to be
disguised. The absence of the pretence of the real seems more perturbing
than anything else. Harriet proclaims her sense of guilt and alienation:

What would my good grandfather have thought, could he have seen his Harriet, the
girl whose mind he took pains to form and enlarge, mingling in a habit so
preposterously rich and gaudy, with a crowd of Satyrs, Harlequins, Scaramouches,
Fauns, and Dryads; nay of Witches and Devils; the graver habits striving which should
most disgrace the characters they assumed, and every one endeavouring to be thought
the direct contrary of what they appeared to be.   (II, 427)

Charlotte Grandison flippantly responds 'Well then, the Devils, at least, must
have been charming creatures!' (*ibid.*). Charlotte's remark comically illus-
trates and endorses the prevailing view of character-reading as a relatively
simple science. If the codes are simply reversed, then one should read in
reverse. If everyone is 'the direct contrary' of the appearance, then the
appearance is again a useful guide, and the 'Devils' will reliably be taken as

'charming'. Charlotte here comes closest of any character in *Sir Charles Grandison* to parody of the straightforward reading and valuation of character so much indulged in throughout the novel.

No one else seconds Charlotte's onslaught on simplicity, although her sister Lady L. wonders whether it would be possible to save the masquerades as an amusement by insisting that 'decorum' should be observed, 'and every one would support with wit and spirit the assumed character'. Consistency in acting, conscientious living up to the character, might make the masquerade adaptation of another persona into a safe pastime, she thinks, because such a pastime would be morally consistent, parallel to the adoption of one's constant character in daily life. But Harriet's remark has already prepared us for Sir Charles's disapproval; Harriet felt guilty, not in relation to the potential approval of a still-living grandmother, but in relation to the imagined but powerful disapproval of the dead grandfather. Patriarchs cannot countenance such a business. Sir Charles assures Caroline L. it would be impossible 'to collect eight or nine hundred people, all wits, and all observant of decorum'. We cannot rely upon other people's desire to regularize the game. Unruly hordes ('eight or nine hundred people') will take liberty for licence. It were better to ban such displays, which make evident the instability of human character and offer a shrine for worshipping unknowability. As the patriarch in the making, Sir Charles must make every effort to support simple characters and simple character-reading. Deviousness and disguise threaten his imperial control, and the values for which he stands. We must have a constant solid notion of our own character, and of each other's character.

'Character' is a word on everyone's lips in *Sir Charles Grandison*. Even the bad value it, and male characters of all kinds are especially apt to bring it forward. Captain Salmonet and Major O'Hara, those two sleazy and suspect officers and would-be gentlemen (respectively brother-in-law and husband of young Emily's fallen mother, Mrs Jervois) insist upon the word as vehemently as any Grandison. Captain Salmonet vouches for O'Hara: 'De man of honour and good nature be my broder's general cha-*ract*-er, I do assure your Lordship.' We are informed that 'He spoke English as a Frenchman ... but pronounced the word character as an Irishman' (III, 20). (To pronounce the word 'character' as an Irishman is already to be a suspect character.) Everyone has a character to others – even Sir Charles. Everyone is visible according to the sign put out to ensure an answerable public reputation. Emily Jervois's mother says 'Sir Charles Grandison is a very fine gentleman', and Captain Salmonet responds 'De vinest cha-*ract*-er in de vorld. By my salvation, everybody say so' (*ibid.*). Public repute responds rightly to the symptoms of solid worth; even the language of these bullies and spongers cannot injure the unalterable fact of Sir Charles's fine character.

To have an established character is to have something to live up to – or down to – but in any case to live with permanently. A character has solidity, complete form; it is known by its marks and signals. Small clear signs constantly present are valuable because immensely reassuring; hence the tolerance the novel accords, and the emphasis it gives, to little traits or foibles that are characteristic, such as Lord G.'s collecting china or shells, or Aunt Nell's dressing in pink and yellow ribbons. The novel's language constantly turns the inside outwards. That which is internal, perhaps related to ineffable changeable personality, is rendered in metaphors of the external, and stabilized by being related to character. Sir Charles speaks of his desire not to declare a passion early in a courtship, which would 'drive a lady into reserves'; he would prefer to take advantage of the 'innocent freedoms' of friendship in order 'to develop the plaits and folds of the female heart' (II, 429). In this metaphor the female heart (inner) becomes the female dress (outer); emotional personality becomes characterological. Sir Charles has just told his bachelor cousin that 'Bachelors ... and maids, when long single, are looked upon as houses long empty, which no-body cares to take' (II, 428), an image that neatly allows literal three-dimensionality (for houses are three-dimensional)[9] but firmly relates the uncommunicative bachelor or old maid to something visible, public and stable, easily readable in terms of real estate. The image renders the persons characterologically readable through external signs, rather than considering the mysterious inwardness of private self.

The house image is of course important in the novel as a whole. Grandison Hall proves the ideal correlative of Sir Charles; the house is handsome, noble, elegant, spacious, and the entire estate mirrors its owner: 'The gardens and lawn seem from the windows of this spacious house to be as boundless as the mind of the owner, and as free and open as his countenance' (III, 272). The estate belongs to Sir Charles and reflects him, as he in turn embodies that estate. It would not seem amiss to suggest that the estate has formed Sir Charles, giving him the idea of the dignity he must express. He has always had an established character to hand, despite the deviations from dignity and grace of his slightly rascally father, for whose errors Sir Charles is busily compensating.

Character has to be made, or rather revealed clearly to the eyes of another, before it is character. Sir Charles says 'I have sometimes ... allowed persons, at first acquaintance, a short lease only in my good opinion ... And by this means I leave it to every one to make his own character with me' (II, 428). Sir Charles keeps thinking in terms of real estate; a new acquaintance is like one of his tenants, an uncertain one to be given 'a short lease'. Not knowing he is being tested by this invisible landlord, and that his lease may soon expire, the new acquaintance will give himself away in conversation which Sir Charles initiates: 'I enter directly with frankness, into conversation with him.' The 'frankness' entices the other into masochistic frankness, while concealing the fact that conversation is a test, presumably scientifically designed to permit maximum characterological reading. The innocent acquaintance will freely reveal the symptoms which, as Fielding believes, nature holds forth. A character's being made *with* another is merely character revealing itself.

Character can, however, be 'made' in another sense; that is, the ideal character may be presented first in the mind of a person who then looks about to find a human being who fills the bill and really does represent the character. In looking for a servant, every employer does this. Sir Charles goes through this process when he is looking for that 'upper servant' a wife – not for himself but for his uncle, Lord W. He thinks of the ideal type of woman to serve his uncle's purposes: she should be a woman over thirty, of a serious turn, one who would feel under an obligation to the man who gave her consequence by marrying her, a suitable nurse, and so on. Once he has created this list of specifications, the fulfilment of such a character comes to mind, and Sir Charles does Miss Mansfield and her family a good turn by marrying her off. 'But I had her not in my thoughts when I proposed to my Lord the character of the woman he should wish for' (III, 60). Character is something like an empty shell, a carapace that can be truly inhabited by the right person, no masquerader but someone acting perfectly in character.

Yet the concept of 'character' as public and social does not and must not preclude a sense of depth and of some sort of mystery in the personages we meet within or without the pages of Richardson's novel. If everybody is knowable and utterly frank, then all these characters run the danger of being boring. A society of frank solid characters might be a society of intense inanity. The representative of that danger seems to be the stupid young Mr Singleton encountered early in Harriet's career in London. His name signifies singularity, even eccentricity, and we are told he is 'the object of ... ridicule, even down to his very name' (I, 42). But his true singularity lies in his extreme submissiveness to the group; 'humble, modest, ready to confess an inferiority to every one', Singleton is perfectly happy to be dissolved in the group personality. He laughs readily at everyone's jests 'since he takes his cue from their smiles'. There is no happier character in the entire novel than laughing Mr Singleton, inoffensive and constantly pleased. Suppose the family of love, the family of harmony were so tediously knowable as to allow no suspense or expectation? Some sense of mystery must counteract the comic mediocrity of plain characters serving the group interests.

One of the novel's earliest suggestions of mystery in the human heart and complexity in human behaviour is offered in the presentation of Mrs Oldham, who appears only in the long flashback narrative provided by the Grandison sisters. Mrs Oldham was the mistress and housekeeper of the girls' and Sir Charles's rakish and arbitrary father, Sir Thomas Grandison. On Sir Thomas's death, Mrs Oldham must immediately leave her apartments and offices in the manor in Essex. The Grandison daughters, who have long resented her, now have the opportunity to wreak their spite upon an erring woman who had supplanted their own mother and taken the affection that was not given to them. Mrs Oldham stands before the Grandison girls in tears; they do not even ask her to sit down. Caroline asks pointedly 'And so you have put yourself into mourning, madam? . . . Your weeds, I suppose, are at your lodgings?' Caroline is so offended at Mrs Oldham's appearance in black garments that she taunts her with having assumed the garb of a mourning widow, which she will don in full as soon as she is out of their sight. The Grandison girls, in effect, accuse Mrs Oldham of having assumed a disguise, going in masquerade as the widow of their father. Mrs Oldham replies with dignity: 'Indeed, ladies, I am a *real* mourner: But I never myself assumed a character, to which it was never in my thought to solicit a right' (II, 363). Mrs Oldham, with her strong sense of decorum, proves her right to some sort of public reputable 'character', however diminished, since as she points out she did not assume the wrong 'character'. She is not masquerading, and she is 'a *real* mourner'.

Sir Charles repairs the harshness of his sisters by polite attentions to Mrs Oldham. He chooses for the sake of propriety 'to consider her only as one who has executed a principal office in this house', even though he is fully aware that this housekeeper has had a long-standing affair with his father, to whom she has borne two male children. As he ceremoniously conducts the weeping Mrs Oldham through the house, and silences his petulant sisters with grand displays of magnanimous charity, Sir Charles invents his own kind of virtuous masquerade. Since piety demands that he should draw 'A kind, a dutiful veil' over his father's faults, he throws the veil over Mrs Oldham also, and decks her in another character. Yet everyone present understands the charade for which the erring lady must be grateful.

Shortly after his advent upon the scene at the Essex manor, when he first encounters Mrs Oldham and rescues her from his sisters' indignation, Sir Charles utters the important moral statement which he makes to Mrs Oldham: 'No one can judge of another, that cannot be that very other in imagination, when he takes the judgment-seat' (II, 365). The sisters are stricken with awed admiration 'at a goodness so eclipsing'. Sir Charles's elaboration of the Golden Rule seems to anticipate the ethical philosophy of Adam Smith, who in his *Theory of Moral Sentiments* (1759) bases moral response upon the individual's capacity to sympathize, to feel 'what, by bringing the case home to himself, he imagines should be the sentiments of the sufferer'.[10] It is our moral duty to encourage sympathetic imagination: 'to feel much for others, and little for ourselves ... to restrain our selfish, and to indulge our benevolent affections, constitutes the perfection of human nature'.[11] The first edition of Smith's *Moral Sentiments* appeared five years after the last volume of *Grandison*, and might almost have been based upon it. Smith's theory, like Richardson's novel, allows for or even demands some sharp checks upon both emotion and sympathy. The sufferer from a violent passion can only hope to obtain sympathy 'by lowering his passion to that pitch, in which the spectators are capable of going along with him. He must flatten ... the sharpness of its natural tone, in order to reduce it to harmony and concord with the emotions of those who are about him.' We admire 'that recollection and self-command which constitute the dignity of every passion' and are 'disgusted with ... clamorous grief' while we must 'reverence that reserved, that silent and majestic sorrow, which discovers itself only in the swelling of the eyes, in the quivering of the lips and cheeks, and in the distant, but affecting, coldness of the whole behaviour'.[12] It is the duty of the sufferer to act with propriety, and sympathy will (naturally, Smith thinks) be withheld from an improperly emphatic passion. (Smith's assumptions seem extremely British, and people from other cultures might not feel the disgust or the admiration he depicts.) The doctrine of sympathy proves a doctrine of spectatorship; it is the sense of imagined spectators which makes a man's conscience respond with remorse or a sense of blameworthiness to bad actions and with self-respect and self-applause to his benevolent deeds. Sir Charles does not have to imagine invisible spectators, for the spectators always surround him, and he must always act correctly for their benefit, in displaying and restraining personal emotion and in his exemplary responses to the emotion of another.

Sir Charles announces that he has a moral duty to imagine another's case to be his own – but he can only *say* that he does so. We cannot see him undergoing the metamorphosis implied in the novel use of the verb 'to be' – to 'be that very other in imagination'. This moment would seem to be Grandison's equivalent to a moment in Clarissa's life described by Anna Howe in her memorial 'character' of her friend at the end of *Clarissa*. When 'a large circle of Ladies' was censuring 'a generally reported indiscretion in a young Lady' Clarissa suddenly impersonated the absent victim of censure: 'Come ... let me be Miss Fanny Darlington' (VIII, 199; *IV, 493*). Clarissa actually undergoes that metamorphosis, and enacts someone else's part; it is one of our last glimpses of her, splitting herself into two in the personality flux that is so vital an aspect of *Clarissa*. Sir Charles cannot say, 'Come ... let me *be* Mrs Oldham for a moment.' Clarissa performs the action, the impersonation of another, but Sir Charles must not lose his character in that of another – else how could he remain in 'the judgement-seat'? It is his duty to remain within his own character, guarding it as 'de vinest cha-*ract*-er in de vorld'. Sympathy cannot move outwards too far towards identification, for boundaries would thus dissolve, and all signs and propriety – including property – would be lost.

Indeed, as Mrs Oldham and Sir Charles go through the rooms of the Essex manor, one is increasingly impressed with the extent to which Sir Charles is not Mrs Oldham. Mrs Oldham is the beneficiary of and the principal figure in the virtuous show he produces. Sir Charles and Mrs Oldham walk through the house with the girls, compelled to follow in her train, walking 'as stately, and as upright, as duchesses may be supposed to do in a coronation-process-ion' (II, 367). Yet the object swept up in this rehabilitating parade and offered another social 'character' still remains capable of individual unshared and internal emotion. She recaptures opacity. When they arrive at 'the chamber in which Sir Thomas died, and which was his usual apartment, Mrs Oldham turned pale, and begged to be excused attending them in it. She wept' (*ibid.*). In her pallor and weeping she provides symptoms of inner response, but that inner response is not susceptible to total definition. The rooms of the house are thrown open to inspection in this miniature judgement-day and Mrs Oldham has lost her 'short lease' indeed, but she is not entirely knowable. The whole unsharable history of her sexual relation to Sir Thomas is forcibly brought to her mind at the scene of his death, the room and the bed which were also the scene of their love. The history of that illicit love lingers privately recorded in her mind, and is unsharable, not to be articulated, free from the laws that demand 'frankness'. Mrs Oldham provides a helpful example (at one remove from the central characters) of the power of what cannot be said. She will not and cannot make the inner into the entirely outer.

The Grandison girls are eager to peer into every corner and container in the house, hoping to find evidence of venal misconduct on Mrs Oldham's part. They wish to spy into Mrs Oldham's closets and drawers, chiefly in order to find out what clothes and jewels she got from their father, and to embarrass her; they have also an unspoken curiosity to find out what their father's mistress looked like when she was acting the role of a mistress. Sir Charles puts a stop to their peering and prying with the memorable rhetorical question 'Ought not the private drawers of women to be sacred?' He makes them blush, and they command Mrs Oldham 'to lock up the chest' (II, 373). Private drawers, chests, closets – these indicate the right of the private soul not to be fully characterized, not to be fully read and scrutinized. No one can claim total authority over another person's character to the extent of demanding the right to scrutinize and supervise everything.

Richardson might be accused in this instance of ignoring some of the social dimensions of the social problem displayed. The Grandison girls are too hard on Mrs Oldham, and too censorious, because women have been taught to place a high value on chastity and to police other women who break the sexual rules. It is the males who demand that their women shun these licentious women, for otherwise all women might become promiscuous, or at least careless, if they were not cognizant of the punishments which they must administer to each other. His gender gives Sir Charles a very different relation to his father's mistress than that endured by his sisters. Yet his moral maxim about moral imagination, limited as it is in his own case, sends a ripple through the settled codes; character-knowing is complicated, even while the maxim supposes that knowledge is possible. The presence, both opaque and ephemeral, of Mrs Oldham on the scene questions rules of all kinds, gives a shake to moral and characterological certainties. Richardson evidently hoped to achieve a similar shake with the introduction of the passionate Olivia, who was not to fit into the customary patterns of virtuous lady or fallen woman. But working with this passionate Italian proved more difficult than bringing Mrs Oldham on the stage for a few trembling moments.

Sir Charles himself always has to assume that everyone is knowable. He certainly wants other people to make themselves knowable – through consistent behaviour and frank self-delineation. Yet the eighteenth century's strong preference (even mania) for rational personality, legible Characters of Men, and reasonable social behaviour could become oppressive. Richardson recognizes the oppressiveness, though it is a sleight of nationalism for him to locate the centre of such oppressiveness in Italy. Italy, which we know through the della Porretta family, is a realm of group tyranny. It is no wonder that in Harriet's nightmare Italy proves to be 'a dreary wild, covered with snow, and pinched with frost' (VI, 149). Clementina has been frozen by the authoritarian group order of her family. She has been petted, kept perpetually a child, and she is also treated as if absolutely everything about her were not only knowable but absolutely known. She is supposed to be naive, unthinking, transparent. In such a family of concerned patriarchs, she has little room to manoeuvre.

When Clementina first falls into love-melancholy, she rather pointedly begins to talk to an invisible and *undefined* presence: 'she bent forwards, and, in a low voice, seemed to be communing with a person in the closet' (III, 127). Her maid Camilla asks to whom she is talking, but is not answered. Determining to let rational light in on this nonsense, Camilla then 'stept to the closet, and opened the door, and left it open, to take off her attention to the place, and to turn the course of her ideas; but still she bent forwards towards it, and talked calmly as if to somebody in it' (*ibid.*). When her mother enters, Clementina 'shut the closet-door, as if she had somebody hid there'. Clementina desires to keep things hidden; not only Sir Charles but she

herself constitutes the 'somebody' hidden behind her closet-door. She has a
private closet, a closed space, within herself. Like Mrs Oldham, Clementina
has a secret space of hidden matters, though the 'closet' has now risen to a
higher metaphorical level. 'Ought not the private drawers of women to be
sacred?' The della Porrettas have their own concept of love, but very little idea
of privacy or autonomy, especially for women. Clementina finds in madness
the only really effective way of guarding herself. She becomes opaque and
puzzling to her family (though much less so to us, for we can better read her
symptoms). She rebels against being over-determined and over-known. She
resents everyone, including Sir Charles, who takes it upon himself to
diagnose her condition and to prescribe for it.

Clementina in her madness disguises herself from herself and others, and
adopts a different role from the customary and desired one. She loses her
'character'. Her madness points out the dangers of familial and communal
pressure. When such pressures operate over-insistently to induce an artificial
conformity, the unnatural constraint can lead to eccentricity, imbalance,
explosion. There are limits to the desirability or even the possibility of socially
restructuring an individual. These limits may be tested, but should be
honoured, no matter how desirable it may seem, for instance, that someone
like the feeble rake Everard Grandison should be reformed through communal pressures such as disapproval, teasing, scolding, and familial propaganda.
The revolt of madness is one extreme reaction to social shaping; the other
extreme reaction is a perfectly happy and utterly flabby acquiescence in the
life of the group, in the manner of Singleton. If insanity does not result,
perhaps inanity may.

Grandison thus poses for the author the problem of showing a way to avoid
the extreme reactions of mad revolt or insipid compliance. Richardson
presents in this novel a strong moral and narrative value which acts as a
counter-agent to too much enforced harmony, frankness, and emotional
levelling. This value, at once moral and aesthetic, is 'reserve'. Reserve is a sort
of moral disguise, without the suggestion of iniquity or fragmentation denoted
in this novel by the adoption of physical disguise. Physical disguise means
tampering with one's own character and with the social order, whereas
reserve carries no such threats. The concept of 'reserve' is both consistent
with the idea of character and a corrective of it, as it permits variety and depth
and counteracts monotony and shallowness.

All the central characters here are reserved, and are accused of being
reserved. Harriet Byron, taking her stand on 'the frankness of my own heart',
criticizes Sir Charles very early in their acquaintance: 'I do not love that a man
so *nearly* perfect . . . should have reserves to such a sister. Don't you think . . .
that this seems to be a *kind* of fault in Sir Charles Grandison?' (I, 185). Harriet

has her own reasons, not clear to herself, for wishing Sir Charles to be clear and frank, especially about his love engagements. The train of her thought is clear in the suggestion she starts to herself: 'Very likely, he would be as reserved to a wife' (I, 184). Her speculation hints at her real attraction to Sir Charles and her real uneasiness about him. Reserve creates anxiety, poses the possibility of risk. Harriet herself seems guilty of reserve at times; Sir Charles's sisters accuse her of 'affectation and reserve' in their 'attack' upon her in her dressing room, though the sisters can make Harriet acknowledge and drop her reserve and admit the truth about her feelings. In their ability to triumph over reserve, the Grandison ladies prove themselves true sisters to Sir Charles, who is always able to get behind someone else's reserve when he wishes to do so. Sir Charles says to Lady Beauchamp 'a man of common penetration can see to the bottom of a woman's heart ... You are not, madam, such Mysteries, as some of us think you' (IV, 280).

The penetration of reserve, the probing to the heart, are masculine acts, and the language reminds us that 'reserve' is sexually attractive. Sir Charles's boast unites him oddly with old Sir Rowland Meredith, another male who is sure of his success in understanding women. He has one sure criterion: 'By the softness or harshness of the voice ... I form a judgment of the heart, and soul, and manners of a Lady ... I am hardly ever mistaken' (I, 36). Pompous and naive as Sir Rowland may be, his certainty points to the simplicity of knowing, to the clarity of characterological symptoms which partly support Sir Charles's certainty also. Sir Charles's boast raises the by now familiar paradox of this novel, for if a man can always 'see to the bottom of a woman's heart' then everything becomes again plain, flat and undifferentiated. There needs to be some reserve, some mystery, somewhere. Not to have reserve or to perceive any is to be a social imbecile. The pleasure lies in penetrating reserve, getting through the social veil, finding the hidden closets, the private drawers, and this pleasure cannot be extended by someone who does not know how to assume reserve. Yet the conscious assumption of reserve comes perilously close to cunning and disguise. Harriet Byron must balance reserve and frankness in order to be interesting and good. Richardson was dissatisfied with the comments of readers who thought that Harriet was simply indiscreet. Lady Bradshaigh objected that it would be more prudent in Harriet not to be so communicative: 'I think her *frank heartedness* hurts her *delicasey* [*sic*] ... I shou'd still have admir'd her more, had she suffer'd in *Silence*.'[13] Richardson defends Harriet; the whole issue, he insists, can be summed up in the question 'was she to be honest, or not?'[14] Yet Richardson is well aware that the honesty which dismisses reserve entails aesthetic as well as social danger. It is the duty of every good character, inside a novel and out of it, to cultivate some reserve. Without reserve, intimacy is not possible, for intimacy is known when reserve is laid aside. At some points every individual should be temporarily unknowable. Reserve is the quality which balances society's intrusive rights; it is also the aesthetic quality which keeps uniformity and boredom at bay. Through conscious reserve we may vary from ourselves without radical instability, and can thus reassure others as well as ourselves, through healthy variation, that the mind and heart will not be wearied by the flatness of the known.

In *Grandison* Richardson also chooses to tackle the same aesthetic (and moral) problem by constant strong use of a principle of narrative multiplicity. Richardson sets himself the task of creating a great variety of imaginary persons who will resemble each other but be different; he thus extends to us the pleasing possibility of difference contained within the similarity that rational society enforces. In particular, Richardson in this novel is noticeably fond of creating 'twin' characters who are not identical. Harriet has two rake suitors – Mr Greville and Sir Hargrave (and the one is mistaken for the other at the masquerade). The Grandisons have two old aunts: Aunt Nell and Aunt Gertrude. Charlotte has two serious suitors, Lord G. and Sir Watkyn Williams. Emily's mother has two defenders, Captain Salmonet and Major O'Hara. Clementina has two stern powerful brothers, both of whom are referred to only by title: the Bishop and the General. (Her humane and emasculated brother Jeronymo is referred to differently, by name, and has a different role in the narrative.) Characters arise to our sight out of multiplicity; they belong to a crowd, even though they are distinct. In *Clarissa*, the character who is one of three children, Clarissa, is (in some sense) in love with the now orphaned only child, Lovelace. In *Grandison*, the same situation occurs, but here in reversal it is the male who is one of three, and, unlike Clarissa who differentiates herself sharply from her brother and sister, Sir Charles is extremely closely attached to and identified with his siblings. He lords it over them, but he shares their lives, their interests, and their name – all three children have the same name retold with slight variants in each case: Caroline, Charles, Charlotte. Harriet, an only child and an orphan, is, unlike Lovelace, solidly wedged in a family situation that pleases her, and her surrogate siblings reduplicate – there is not only Lucy but Nancy.

The presence of such crowded multiplicity of persons, types and relationships holds out the hope that the world is various enough to please. Despite resemblances, monotony can be avoided. The principle of varying multiples, like the principle of reserve, encourages the belief that the goodness valued by society can be maintained without sacrifice to oppressive conformity. All can fit in, yet all are different, so that the knowable world need not be dull. The reassurance of similarity can be combined with the stimulation of difference. Yet, once admitted, difference, like closeted reserve, is seen to produce confusion or unhappiness – or to be the result of confusion and unhappiness. The Christian religion comes in 'twin' forms – Catholicism and Protestantism – a fact resulting from confusion and misery on the national scale and creating unhappiness for individuals. The heroines come twinned. Harriet has competition in Clementina, not only for Sir Charles's heart, but also for the reader's affection and loyalty. Richardson takes the risk that some readers will be dissatisfied, unhappy at the way the story turns out, as one heroine must lose. The reader's loyalty will be tested only if she or he thinks there are strong differences between the two women, but suspense as to Sir Charles's choice can follow only if the reader thinks that both women are 'worthy', i.e. in some sense the same.

In Richardson's correspondence during the writing of *Grandison*, we can see that the spirit of his novel was upon him. He plays games of reserve and multiplicity with his closest correspondents. His 'reserve' as author consists both in his pretending that he does not know how the story will turn out, and in his holding back, or holding out on his correspondents, regarding the true ending. His love of and belief in the variety of multiplicity (a belief partly indoctrinated by his own novel) emerge in his proposals for a number of different endings. Sir Charles might be killed in a duel, or drown. Or Clementina might die. There are further interesting possibilities; Richardson suggests he might 'make a glorious Exit for Harriet (I never yet killed a Woman in her *Regal* month) and bequeath her Husband, and her surviving Child, to Clementina'. Killing Harriet off after she has given birth to Sir Charles's child would make the novel interesting:

I can draw, I fancy, a charming Child-bed Death. A glorious 'Trial' for Sir Charles! ... What Scenes, what busy Scenes would here be! ... Domestic Happiness is a tame thing to the World around us.[15]

This imagined ending, which involved Harriet's death-bed request to Sir Charles that he marry Clementina as his second wife, did not please Lady Bradshaigh at all. She protested vigorously:

And now I resume to tell you, you are *very cruel*. ... Before I receiv'd your last, I threaten'd *death* to that *Savage*, that [was] for killing either Har[t]: or Clem: but I did not think I had been threatening the *Father* of the Innocents. but if you *had* set your Heart upon '*killing a Woman in her Regal Month*' (the expression of a Canibal [*sic*]) surely you wou'd have done right, to have chosen the *less* happy of the two ... It is most Strange to me, that you cannot shew us a Woman Tryumphant in *Life*. I thought you reckon'd it Tryumph sufficient that she cou'd bring her self to offer her Husband to Clem: 'that wou'd fetch her up with a Witness', were your words. Which tho' I very much disapprov'd, seems now *nothing*, comparitively [*sic*]. I cou'd compound for *any thing* now. But death, death, death, is your *darling*! Misery, deep *distress*, is what your Soul pants after.

After this strong expression of protest against Richardson's fondness for dying ladies and his reluctance to show us 'a Woman Tryumphant in *Life*', Lady Bradshaigh proceeds to parodic ridicule:

O fie, what tenderness do you shew! You are *too Humane*. Wou'd it not be more suiteable [*sic*] to your Taste to kill Clem[a]: *before* her *Regal Month*. Charlott [*sic*] may also die in Travail of her first child. *That will be quite new*. I donot [*sic*] think you can resist that Temptation. In short, I think you had better kill them *all*, and (like Tom Thumb the great), make it the most 'Tragical Tragedy, that ever was Tragedized'.[16]

One might expect Richardson to be seriously annoyed by the reference to Fielding's play, but in fact he himself adopts Bradshaigh's gibe in his *Letter to a Lady* explaining why there would be no further instalments of the novel:

in scenes of life carried down nearly to the present time, and in which a *variety of interesting characters* is introduced, all events cannot be decided, unless, as in the History of *Tom Thumb the Great*, all the actors are killed in the last scene.[17]

The massacre of the innocents initiated by Richardson and developed by Lady Bradshaigh is a mode of eliminating the tensions supplied by variety. In their joint production, imagining the stage of *Sir Charles Grandison* littered with corpses (particularly of female child-bearing corpses) Bradshaigh and Richardson attack and parody the social demands for uniformity and knowability. When is a person a more satisfactorily knowable object than when a corpse? The extreme return to transparency, tranquillity and stability is a return to the calm uniformity of the undifferentiating grave.

Richardson suggested another solution to the ending of the story, a solution to which Bradshaigh alludes when she refers to Harriet bringing herself 'to offer her Husband to Clem'. Richardson teased some of his female correspondents that the appropriate solution to Sir Charles's predicament ought to be bigamy, or, as he calls it, 'Polygamy'. He imagines the polygamy solution as suggested by Harriet herself, in what would certainly have made an unusual ending to the story, a '*Strange Catastrophe*'. In making this 'grateful Compliment' to her sister excellence, Harriet might 'shew a Magnanimity uncommon to Northern, to Western, and to all but *Eastern* women'.[18] Lady Bradshaigh rose to the bait, scorning this solution, and pointing out that it would be humbling to Clementina and 'look like Tantalizing arrogance in the proposer, being an English woman and bound by law not to make *good* what she proposes'. There is 'No great magnanimity in such an offer', and Eastern women have polygamy '*imposed* upon them by *Tyrany* [*sic*]'.[19] The 'Polygamy' solution is unrealistic and illegal, and reflects the sex-biased tyranny from which Richardson is not free. Lady Bradshaigh is always quick to react against the idea that the two heroines can be made identical and interchangeable; she insists that Sir Charles sees and values the difference in clearly preferring Harriet: 'I say, "It is impossible, for a man to be *Equally* in love with two *Angels* at the *same* time," I laid my whole weight upon the word *Equally*.'[20] Richardson has set the problem of the equal and thus similar heroines, and wittily defends the polygamy scheme. After all, Sir Charles evidently loves both women at the same time, and the Bible not only exemplifies polygamy in the Old Testament but endorses female inferiority in the New:

The Apostle says, Woman was made for Man, not Man for Woman. It would be the greatest of Indelicacies for a Woman to be thought to love two Men at the same time equally – But – Let me, as a Problem only – Yet I will not – Tho' – [21]

As soon as he thinks of the 'unthinkable' reverse case, Richardson jokingly recognizes that it would constitute a thinkable case for the court of love, and that there is another novel to be written upon that interesting 'Problem' too. In *Grandison* he invokes Otway's *The Orphan* (v, 539), a play in which the only happy ending would be to allow Monimia (mono-anima, the one) to have two husbands.

The 'Polygamy' solution plays up the possibilities of multiplicity and variety, but only to collapse them into unity. Reserve is also at an end, that final 'reserve' whereby a person reserves the love of another to herself. Harriet's tendency to communicativeness could go no further than for her to communicate not only her love but her beloved. The 'strange Catastrophe' of such magnanimity turns all that is private, emotional, sacred and enclosed into what is public, frank, profane (or pagan) and open. The 'Polygamy' scheme acts like a parody of the values the novel inculcates, of submission to the group, of valuing others beyond the self, of privileging order and frankness without disguise, without keeping anything back. The strange stimulus of the sexually inventive turn, like the imagined bloody catastrophe, rapidly turns into a tranquillizing retreat to the undifferentiated. That which was plural and puzzling becomes undifferentiated and uniform, putting an end to the entire game of character and reserve. If everyone becomes frank and unreserved to that extent, then there is neither story nor character, only a pictured idyll of human perfection rendered unproblematic, like Houyhnhnm life.

Richardson was grateful, and with reason, to Sarah Chapone, who did not join in the disapproval that other women had expressed for Sir Charles's 'two-fold attachment' to both heroines, but instead congratulated the novelist upon its significance:

I believe you design'd to convey a fine conceal'd moral or Doctrine, which ever you please to call it, by shewing that in real life, the heart of man is subject to such various impressions – entangled by such inexplicable intricacies – either from his own passions – or the inroads of others – that some fluctuations there may be even in the best heart before it has solemnly engaged itself to one object, and also, that nothing less than the sacred tye of Marriage could in the nature of things secure one Man to one Woman.[22]

Marriage puts a limit to the wandering off into the undifferentiated: Richardson's plot teaches 'that *that* appropriated kindness – that incommunicable affection which cannot proceed beyond it's [*sic*] chosen object, is only to be expected from the restraining Grace and blessing of God'.[23] Marriage supports difference, and thus upholds the value of the individual character by insisting on an 'incommunicable affection' (in some senses an ungenerous affection) which cannot be given freely to all but must be held in reserve. As Chapone's commentary shows, Richardson had chosen the right story for his themes. The answer to Sir Charles's problem (the love of many) must be marriage (the choice of one, the privileging of one individual in especial intimacy). The very foundation of society which is marriage shows the limit of the extent to which society can take charge of individual life and demand utter frankness and submission to the group. If the group control is a tyranny, it offers paradoxically the possibility of the freedom of wandering from one to another, of 'fluctuations', and we may at times feel nostalgic for the old days, before individuality, 'ere one to one was cursedly confin'd'. The Grandisons may be a 'family of love' but they are not permitted to be like the seventeenth-century sect, the 'Family of Love', whose members shared property and spouses. The presentation of Olivia is a partly nostalgic tribute not to the power of passion (for that, if tamed, is supposed to exist in marriage) but to the power of everything that is offered outside limitation and outside the 'sacred tye' that binds one to one alone. The reader is supposed to admire Olivia; Lady Bradshaigh, always the champion of Harriet, marriage and individual value, insisted she could not possibly do so: 'nothing yet appears to me, but a very ill-minded Woman, Introduc'd to add glory to your Hero ... nothing but a preparation of Miss Blandy's cou'd create a love for such a Woman as Olivia'.[24] So unreserved that she offers herself unasked, Olivia must of course be defeated, and defeated by Harriet. Character and difference win victory over the allurements of undiscriminating and undifferentiating sexuality.

The 'love story' of Charles and Harriet and Charles and Clementina supports the values of variousness and differentiation in showing (as Chapone points out) the heart and mind being formed through entanglements and 'various impressions'. In speaking for the value of 'intricacies', and 'fluctuations' in creating character, Sarah Chapone sets Richardson's novel happily above the rigidity he himself feared for it. She also assures him that as an artist he had achieved the variety in unity, the harmonized diversity, that the novel is trying to present as the highest value:

such is the Skill of *This* intellectual Painter – that by certain imperceptable [*sic*] Strokes, He identifies his various characters, while the Standing Lineaments are the same in each character of the same kind, yet it is impossible to mistake one for another.[25]

Without relying on the fluctuating unstable personality traced in the major personages in *Clarissa*, Richardson had created solid but differentiated characters. Each character has a character, and has an identity. Richardson thought a great deal about his characters in *Grandison*, and discussed in detail his formation of them. He not only identifies them by their various signs, but also identifies himself with them from moment to moment:

Here I sit down to form characters. One I intend to be all Goodness; All Goodness he is. Another I intend to be all Gravity; All Gravity he is. Another *Lady G*-ish; All *Lady G*-ish is she. I am all the while absorbed in the character. It is not fair to say – *I*, identically I, am any-where, while I keep within the character.[26]

Richardson enjoys the meta-characterological pleasure of characterization. He forms these characters, all the while being none. What is 'character' if one can be absorbed in it, and then detached from it and absorbed in another 'character'? Character in the novel is preserved in consistency, but the author – and to some considerable extent the reader – may fly above 'character' while the author's and reader's own personalities, hearts and minds are being formed by the experience of diversity. Richardson wanted debate, argument, various readings:

It is not an unartful Management to interest the Readers so much in the Story, as to make them differ in Opinion as to the Capital Articles, and by Leading one, to espouse one, another, another Opinion, make them all, if not Authors, Carvers.[27]

The reader must be bewildered by the multiplicity, making choices which may vary from reader to reader, and in the same reader from time to time. The novel, like the world, is thus never really knowable at any one moment. If the vision of character apparently held up in *Sir Charles Grandison* is sometimes like a clear but solid carapace, the readers and Richardson are to exhibit a fluid and animating set of reactions and responses that free them from passive obedience. They are liberated (as author, as reader) from their very prescribed duties as exhorters or receptacles of exhortation. In order to form the reader's character, the novel must present itself as various and fluctuating, catching readers and making them weave and wander through change, reacting changeably.

   The capacity for such meta-impersonation in Richardson ('all the while absorbed in the character') and (by implication) in the reader casts a strange light on the idea of hard-formed character that Grandison as hero represents.

The stability of Grandison Hall under its chief may be held out as a vision of a social ideal, but the act of writing (or of reading) the novel holds out the promise of growth and validation through delightful instabilities. As Keats says, 'What shocks the virtuous philosopher, delights the camelion Poet'[28] – or reader. Character is something the chameleon novelist can assume, form, inhabit for a moment, and then discard. 'I, identically I' is a hard matter to discover. In the acts of reading, as of writing, the 'I' may go into abeyance. The protean Richardson and his reader may laud stable character, but they themselves are not bound to it. Even while they praise 'character' and stable identity, they are released into permitted play with character. Author and reader fly above character, touching down and informing one and then another and flying off again. 'Character' becomes what we create and read, an imagined being which satisfactorily allows the unstable 'identical I' to find its paradoxical freedom.

8

The pains of compliance in
Sir Charles Grandison

CAROL HOULIHAN FLYNN

On the eve of Harriet Byron's wedding to Sir Charles Grandison, Charlotte Grandison presents a pretty domestic scene. When Harriet's grandmother, Mrs Shirley, retires from the party, Harriet, 'beauty in full bloom', attends 'beauty in ruins', providing physical support for her 'tottering parent'. After admiring the 'striking' picture, Charlotte offers the history of Mrs Shirley's infirmity:

The old Lady's lameness is owing, it seems, to a strained sinew got in leading up a dance, not many years ago, proposed by herself, in order to crown the reconciliation which she had brought about, between a couple that had, till then, been unhappy; and which her good-nature and joy made her not sensible of till she sat down. Pity, pity, that any-thing should have hurt so benign, so chearful, so benevolent, a woman! Why did not Harriet tell us this circumstance? It would have heightened our value for her: And the more, if she had told us, as is the truth, that she never considers it as a hurt (so honourably come by) but when she thinks she is troublesome to those about her.

(III, 215)

   Richardson's peculiar version of *discordia concors* reveals the '*contradictory vagaries*' (III, 148) of his domestic ideology. In promoting social harmony, Mrs Shirley, the model of female excellence, leads up a dance too strenuous for her own good. When she strains a sinew, literally undone by her 'good-nature and joy', she goes against her own true nature, the physical frailty that reasserts itself when the dancing ends. (The faults of women, Richardson warns elsewhere, 'lie in the bone'.[1]) Mrs Shirley is such an excellent woman that even in pain she sublimates her suffering by 'never consider[ing] it as a hurt (so honourably come by) but when she thinks she is troublesome to those about her'. This heightened sensibility enables her to sacrifice her own feelings for the common good. Such sublimation strains the sinew even more, exacting the cost of domestic reconciliation.

   Richardson would no doubt bristle at such a strained analysis of a pleasant

133

anecdote. Mrs Shirley is one of his most unequivocally praised characters, exemplary to the core, designed for our admiration and wonder. Yet his description invites a more critical wonder, for our exemplary model is also a ruin, tottering victim to her talent for sacrifice. When Charlotte celebrates (without irony) the 'old Lady's' heroic grace, she is demonstrating her own hardly-won domestication, but again it is a domestication that reminds the reader of the inequities of Richardson's system. Like so many of Richardson's feminine characters, Charlotte, the pert Lady G., must struggle against her own nature, suppressing sharp wits to accommodate Lord G.'s sweet and reasonable dullness, achieving in the 'matronizing' process domestic peace. This essay will consider the costs of the domestic reconciliation that Richardson exacts from his female characters and readers, concentrating particularly upon *Sir Charles Grandison* and Richardson's own correspondence. To situate Richardson's dilemma contextually, I will discuss briefly an earlier experiment in domestic form, Defoe's family 'instructions' that reveal eighteenth-century society's contradictory desires for mutual subordination and voluntary compliance. Both Defoe and Richardson, creating the newly reconciled 'self' for their domestic fictions, endorse compliant behaviour that strains against the belief in the individual that their culture was inventing. The early English novel becomes a site of their struggle, exposing in its irreconcilable differences the strains of domesticity.

While he emphasizes the pains of compliance in order to 'heighten our value' for feminine accommodation, Richardson also leaves us with a detailed account of the contradictions implicit in the 'civilizing process'[2] he officially endorses. His novels and letters record – endlessly – a struggle that he cannot resolve. Almost coyly, in his letters and novels, threatening never to stop teasing his reader into frustrated acts of compliance, Richardson calls attention to the inequities of a system that demands individualism and hierarchy, equality and subordination. His ideology prescribes harmony, but inevitably produces dislocation. Game veterans like Mrs Shirley end up with strained sinews for their pains, but less adroit practitioners like the divine Clementina della Porretta run mad in attempts to escape such contradictory demands. 'Pity, pity, that any-thing should have hurt so benign, so chearful, so benevolent, a woman!' Much of Richardson's discourse manufactures just this pity that his culture both depends upon and denies.

The inevitable frustrations Richardson creates for his compliant heroines can be seen in a most revealing vision. Reporting the details of her courtship, Harriet Byron lays down her pen to a well-deserved rest that is 'broken and disturbed by dreadful, shocking, wandering dreams'. She sees herself married to the best of men, then not married, rejected, then rewarded, 'dragged out of a subterraneous cavern' expecting to be punished for her 'audaciousness, and for repining at my lot', only to be turned at last into an angel of light. A 'dear little baby' is put into her arms, sometimes hers, sometimes Lucy's, sometimes Emily's, and at another time Clementina's. Sir Charles, 'the man', rejects her and her baby, saying '*so* sternly ... that he thought me a much better creature than I proved to be: Yet methought, in my own heart, I was not altered'. In another part of her 'resverie' Sir Charles loves her dearly, 'but when he nearly approache[s] me, or I him', he changes into a ghost, flitting away from her embrace. Finally Sir Charles, most shockingly, is assassinated by Greville. 'But such *contradictory* vagaries never did I know in my slumbers. Incoherencies of incoherence!' (III, 148–9).

Much is going on in this spectacular series of dreams. On a psychological level, Harriet is certainly 'project[ing] her unconscious antipathy' for Sir Charles's notoriously doubled love,[3] but she is also dreaming through the confusions and incoherencies of her culture's ideological imperatives. Equally expecting to be punished for her audacity and to be elevated as angel of light, Harriet reveals the pains of the civilizing process. Uncertain of her worth as long as she is ruled by such an arbitrary code, she subjects herself to the criticism of a hero shadowy at best, ghostly, mercurial, 'flitting' away from her need for more substantial connection.

Harriet is experiencing the pains of compliance. While she can claim 'in my own heart, I was not altered', she falls down at her accuser's feet in the next sentence. Her worth depends upon his judgement rather than her substance. The notion of alteration is crucial to Richardson's entire treatment of that sex he purports to exalt, for their exaltation depends upon their voluntary transformation of their very nature.

It is generally agreed that women became domesticated in the eighteenth century. No longer seen as naturally and irredeemably gross, they were allowed to be tractable creatures capable of improvement. As Randolph Trumbach suggests, 'it was ceasing to be thought that all women were potentially whores (and that married women, especially, required watching)'.[4] The newly domesticated woman would rather learn to watch herself, to gaze upon her own actions and judge herself accordingly. While voluntary compliance would seem to offer more freedom, it makes more subtle demands upon its subjects, imposing a sternly subjective self-discipline. Such a self-imposed surveillance accommodates a cultural code that almost by definition can never be satisfied, since the refined product goes against a nature that always threatens to reassert itself. When conduct writers such as Defoe and Richardson set out to manufacture codes for self-measurement, they offer the reconstructed subject patterns to follow 'voluntarily', for as both writers agree, there will be no 'upper servants' in their improved domestic structure, but instead conveniently compliant women born to serve with dignity and grace.

Issuing contradictory demands for freedom and limitation, equality and subordination, Defoe and Richardson deliver a dual message: proper behaviour must be learned, restraint against fallen nature must be developed, but that behaviour must also appear voluntary and natural. Liberty is measured by 'Christian Limitation', an elastic talent for suppression that 'Affective Individualism' depends upon, an ability to elicit 'Moderation where we have no positive Restraints imposed'.[5] While they outlaw physical coercion (although Richardson will titillate Lady Bradshaigh with hints about the need for 'fear' in marriage),[6] arbiters of female conduct require an 'affectionate' compliance that strains against the natural rebellion that they suspect of (and inspire within) their subjects.

Conduct discourse, in fact and fiction, narrates a struggle for power, for an individuation that depends upon a suppression of the will. Ironically, once the woman is regarded as an individual, with a will that must be sacrificed for the good of others, once her compliance is deemed both necessary and voluntary, the individual who must be curbed is also called forth. To agree to her reconstruction, the lady need claim, however precariously, a sense of self, even if it is a self to be denied. Consciousness so hardly won expresses itself obliquely. In waking life, sinews strain while in dream-life, angels and caverns, babies and corpses, illustrate the cost of voluntary compliance. Mrs Shirley might 'never consider' her lameness 'as a hurt (so honourably come by)', but this suppressed hurt subjects her none the less to the 'neat crutch-stick' under her arm.

In his *Family Instructor* (1718) Defoe demands just this 'voluntary' and 'conscious' compliance in his histories of dramatically unsettled households. The ideal domestic situation, voluntary surrender to God's and the godly husband's will, is best expressed by simple spokesmen: the poor peasant giving thanks for his meagre bounty, the tender child of six asking to be instructed in God's and Papa's ways. The real circumstances of Defoe's examples tend to cancel unwitting gestures of faith, revealing instead the code's discrepancy. Individuation would seem to depend upon a calculated suppression of free will and sexuality. Although he carefully speaks out against physical measures to produce his domestic subjects, Defoe none the less finds it necessary to rely upon the metaphysical powers of God the Father to instill within his subjects voluntary obedience. Lacking the simple faith of the old and feeble, or the young and idiotic, his less willing subjects are brought to the patriarchal good through 'accidents' providentially plotted, that result in maiming, illness, fever, and madness. Once chastened, necessarily abject, his exemplary models assume their domestic duties with all the ardour appropriate to affective domestic structures.

The struggle for voluntarily offered compliance can be seen in Defoe's depiction of the trials of two religious husbands saddled with independent and rebellious wives. The men, a 'citizen' and a 'friend' from the country, compare notes on their attempts to 'instruct' their households. The country friend struggles to bring his wealthy, aristocratic bride to acknowledge God's (and his) authority. Several hundred pages of insubordination and mockery culminate in her flight from the household. The young wife proves so determined to escape her husband's authority that she finds herself rashly imagining that she would rather poison her spouse than relinquish her power. In a dream she carries her desires too far, and sees herself not only poisoning her husband but setting her house on fire, destroying her husband, her household, and her children. The vision sends her into a guilty fever. She emerges from her temporary madness into a state of grateful, chastened repentance, ready at last to comply.

The citizen's tale is more complicated, for his wife is not the typical young and fashionable chit in need of correction, but a religious helpmate, not rebellious, not irreligious, but bored and irritated by her husband's 'performance' of his function as family instructor. She calls his instruction 'a piece of cold insignificant stuff ... an abomination', so maddening her husband that he stops family prayers altogether. What is at issue here is not conduct so much as subservience to the husband's authority. The wife objects to her husband's 'lordly' posture towards her, his demand for authority that he disavows whenever he preaches the democratic doctrine of 'mutual subordination'. And while Defoe himself, preaching mutual subordination, attacks the 'positive restraints' necessary to evoke compliance, he manages to reform this dangerously critical wife quite severely. His method exposes the very problem that consciousness insists upon. To bring his rebellious wife to her senses, he drives her out of them, containing most efficiently her sensible rebellion.

When Defoe's fractured family divides, 'all appearance of order and duty is lost'. Three children might join their mother upstairs for prayers, but their support is invalidated by the power the father can wield. In retaliation, he holds services downstairs, officially locking the mother out of the family circle. The struggle between husband and wife escalates until the wife goes mad, spends a year in an asylum, and returns home humbled, with a loss of memory, but 'in a very good disposition as to the religious part'. Dulled compliance, however, does not satisfy the citizen. Since she cannot remember offending her husband, she is not capable of true repentance. He looks upon her 'as one dead'.[7]

'Dead' the wife is a disappointment, but 'alive' she threatens to destabilize a domestic order that depends upon a voluntary compliance completely divorced from merit. As Richardson emphasizes in the marriage of the saucy, superior Lady G., the wife must support and encourage her husband, however inferior. The artificial elevation is necessary if his superiority is to be deemed tolerable. While Richardson in his letters and novels preaches against unequal marriages, he does not allow post-nuptial re-evaluations of marital fitness. Lord G. might appear fit only to oversee the fortunes of his butterflies and china, but by definition, he is able to lord it over his more intelligent, caustic wife. His right resides in the order of things, an order depending upon a subjugation of energies that must be consecrated to the good of the domestic whole.

The problem of consciousness, of vitality itself, is more rigorously explored by Richardson in *Clarissa*. When Clarissa dies, she satisfies in death a society that depends upon the 'dead' compliance that she withholds in life. 'To live like Sir Charles, and to die like Clarissa, what a full complement of felicity that would be!' Mr Thomas Edwards is thanking Mr Richardson 'for those most excellent instructions which you have given the world!' (*Correspondence*, III, 72). His compliment unconsciously approaches the problems that Richardson presents to the reader he works hardest at affecting, his girl, better dead than disorderly. For while Clarissa's death is supposed to be tragic, it is also advantageous to the society that (alive) she so severely unsettles.

Richardson laboured hard to bring his female readers to a consciousness of duty that he appears to have delighted in frustrating. In an epistolary exchange circling the problem of filial obligation, he incited Hester Mulso to compose several hundred pages designed to 'force Richardson to make clear distinctions which he avoids doing'.[8] His evasion is typical. In his letters, as in his fiction, Richardson seems compelled to stir up a desire for certainty that he refuses to satisfy. To make clearly apparent the ideology he is working with (and against) would not only resolve the dilemma he explores, but would lose him his most interested readers. His girls and ladies would appear to enjoy *not* hearing the law laid down absolutely, preferring instead to play within the circumscribed boundaries Papa allows.

While Richardson's tone varies with each female correspondent, his insistent assertion of authority remains constant. He battles against Miss Mulso, tantalizes Lady Bradshaigh, a woman particularly susceptible to his threats of naughty schemes of polygamy and wife-beating, and cajoles Susanna Highmore. Sarah Westcomb, the meekest, comes in for the greatest amount of abuse. In fact, it is her very conformity and compliance that would seem to invite his most critical attention.[9]

One exchange of letters testifies to the strain her compliance creates. While caring for an invalid mother and visiting friends, Miss Westcomb has been an inattentive correspondent. To explain her epistolary lapse, she enumerates her holiday pleasures – the delights of rowing and fishing and reading and prattling – and then submits 'readily' to Richardson's judgement: whether these were censurable amusements or not (III, 281–5). Tongue in cheek, Richardson mocks her ingenuous recital of her days' activity while chiding her negligence. In a 'scolding letter', the neglected papa 'won't call you so much as a punctilious daughter'. It is, after all, 'the duty of a father, as you own, to tell his children of their faults' (III, 292–3). Westcomb responds to his letter with a vexed complaint begging more forgiveness. Making much ado about her small lapses, she insists that she was not 'intentionally faulty', and making a distinction that Clementina also uses, begs that he censure the head rather than the heart of the 'affectionate, yet hardly-treated, S. Westcomb'. 'How you have teased me, you dear naughty Sir, you!' she scolds. 'My poor mamma, and all here, suffer for it. She asks me, what makes me so fretful and peevish? I answer, Papa' (III, 297–8).

The ingenious tormenting[10] continues. Papa taunts his dear girl, asking for her 'voluntarily promised letter ... But I was but a papa!' Richardson complains that Westcomb treats him as if he were 'guilty of a naughty ingenuity; as if I took a pleasure in torturing, mangling, perverting your meanings to my own disadvantage!' Defending his fears for her safety, he reminds her that 'I know you to be near a forest where there was a great wild bear who had cubs to purvey for her devouring maw' (III, 300–3).

When Richardson calls up visions of devouring bears, he playfully exaggerates the monitory style that informs his more serious fictions while approaching the contradictions that his fictions create. For all her punctilio, Clarissa 'took a great fancy to a young Lion, or a Bear', which she fed with her own hand. Like a lap dog, it followed her everywhere. 'But mind what followed: At last some how, neglecting to satisfy its hungry maw ... it resumed its nature; and on a sudden fell upon her, and tore her in pieces.' Who is to blame? The lady, most surely. 'For what *she* did was *out* of nature ... what *it* did was *in* its own nature' (V, 304–5; III, 206); yet what '*she*' did was expected of her by her society becoming, against its nature, civilized. In taming young lions and bears, Clarissa, exemplary model for her sex, does only what she has been educated to do, a vocation that Lovelace exploits without mercy. But then, what makes Lovelace such a powerful adversary is an essential conformity that depends upon young ladies bred to tame his conventional lapses. Not he as much as his society exercises its 'hungry maw'.

When writing to Miss Westcomb, Richardson demonstrates his own insatiable hunger for compliance. Playfully suggesting that his friend should stay out of the woods, lest she be eaten by a bear, or worse, a rake, he teasingly frightens her into submission, becoming in the process, rakish, sadistic, coy. Inciting rebellion, he then blames her smallest lapse. As Miss Westcomb notices, Richardson blames her 'for being vexed instead of sorry'. But his denunciation produces just that state. After mock-pathetic reiterations of obligations unmet, Miss Westcomb closes by begging Richardson that he 'be assured that you can never be, intentionally, neglected or slighted by' his 'humble servant' (III, 309–10). It is difficult to imagine how the ever compliant daughter could not slight her obligations. Papa's maw is never filled.

The correspondence literally depends upon the fiction of Miss West-comb's dreadful lapse. Once discovered to be faulty, and then vexed by the unfair discovery, she will work even harder to please impossible-to-please papa. Her apologies simply inspire more complaints to be apologized for:

But now comes the formidable article of not writing after promise. Oh! what a terrible word! What shall I say? What can I say? Why nothing; but yet I think I could excuse it a little. Yet once more, self-justifier, be quiet – not another syllable: a promise broke is a promise broke, and nothing I can urge will make it less so. Well, if ever I go to Ankerwyke again, I will (Oh! bless me, here is another promise coming) sit up all night rather than not save my word; but even then I do not know how I shall keep it, for we never go to bed till late, and rise pretty early. Here let me ask, if you are not a naughty and undutiful papa, to tell me with a Madam, I cannot bear to be slighted ... What a style is this to me! for pray, Sir, am I not your daughter? do I not owe infinite favours to you?   (III, 308–9)

Miss Westcomb vowing filial piety to the naughty Papa becomes the ideal daughter owing infinite infantile favours regardless of their reception. As Richardson cautioned his Miss Highmore, 'the want of duty on one part justifies not the non-performance of it on the other, where there is a reciprocal duty' (II, 217). Turning 'mutual subordination' and reciprocity on its head, Papa seems determined to test his daughters' inclinations to rebel against demands designed to subvert their sense of duty.

Miss Westcomb's habit of confessing her faults is crucial to her papa's civilizing process. In their letters, and in their interviews, his girls 'tell' their faults, putting themselves under surveillance while seeking an absolution that will transform self-acknowledged 'lowness' into headily imagined heights. Harriet's dream of subterranean caves and stellar glory schematizes the polarities of such a domestic vision. But even Richardson's best women eventually balk at telling all. Mrs Frances Sheridan cautions Richardson against demanding too much compliance from his 'young folks', too much 'open and ingenuous' behaviour. While 'nobody, like you, has the art to penetrate into the secrets, and unwind the mazes of a female heart; and if I am not mistaken you can deal corrosives and lenitives with an even hand', Richardson must expect none the less, his confidants to 'lock up mouths' to protect themselves (IV, 161–3). To open shut mouths, Richardson vexes his correspondent into the confessional mode. 'But patience will hold out no longer', Miss Westcomb cries, 'my vexation rises to my pen; and, for relief, must throw itself off this way' (III, 295). 'Who knows what a lady is till she is provoked' (III, 299), Richardson crows, delighted that he has engaged his daughter in punctilious combat.

Faults upon faults, vexations upon vexations arise within the filial exchanges. When Miss Westcomb complains that Papa's teasing makes my poor mamma suffer, Richardson rejoins with a call to 'redoubled duty':

> To think that your dear, your indulgent mamma should suffer for what you call (for what you own to be) your fretfulness, your peevishness, on this occasion; and when I told you too, that if you would excuse my scolding letter, I would excuse you, affects me.
>
> Pray let me hear that by your redoubled duty you set all right with so tender a parent ... or else you will add a concern to my heart, greater than even any you could give or have given to it by your neglects of ... Your truly paternal friend.   (III, 305)

Here Miss Westcomb faces a favourite Richardsonian dilemma. In her efforts to comply, she inevitably makes somebody unhappy. Like the more spectacularly dramatic characters, Pamela, Clarissa and Clementina, she suffers from a desire to please the contradictory demands of authority figures that want nothing more or less than 'the heart' of their subjects. Centre of the domestic universe (no matter how small), the girl responds to contradictory demands that eventually satisfy nobody. To retain her centrality and to satisfy an impossible-to-please papa, Miss Westcomb turns peevish, teasing in turn a 'tender' mama who must also be appeased. To make amends, she must now redouble her duty to please both figures and lose more of herself in the process. No wonder Richardson warned Miss Highmore 'that in such a world as this, and with a feeling heart, content is heroism!' (II, 252).

To bring stiff-necked subjects to their duty, Richardson, much like Defoe the conduct writer, is not averse to employing the heavy hand of God. As Defoe illustrated in his *Family Instructor*, to rebel against the father, God or man, is to court chastisement. Pert wives fall sick with guilty fevers, rebellious sons cry out for their fathers on their deathbeds, stubborn matrons lose their inflexible minds in the service of a higher good. Richardson more subtly strains the sinews of his victims. Since Clarissa so deliberately designs and enacts her final mortal statement, it can be interpreted as a triumph of will, a lasting sign of her integrity and her power. Her significance is framed, however, by her author's intentions. Dead she is a monument, but she is also out of the way. Although she continues to stir up trouble in her posthumous demands, Clarissa once mortally silenced, even as she wears her 'book' as her 'crown', loses control of her published self. It takes only a few footnotes inserted by the

Richardsonian author to turn a vengeful angel into a *memento mori* designed to keep less divine rebels in their place.

Clementina, less conscious of her resistance, demonstrates more pathetically that in her dependent position, any independent action that she takes against her family can be denied or reinterpreted. As Margaret Anne Doody suggests, Clementina, like Clarissa, is in opposition to her family, but she does not know it.[11] She knows only that something is terribly wrong. The house has become a world turned upside down, disordered by her unconscious desires. Superficially the conflict in the Porretta household centres on the issue of religion. Sir Charles's Protestantism unsettles the staunch Catholic temper of the Italian (and therefore passionately exotic) family. But at the true centre of the Porretta family is the more familiar domestic product, not the exotic Italian, but the commonplace girl herself, as Clementina seems to recognize:

> This house is not the house it was: Who, but I, is the same person in it? My father is not the same: My brothers neither: My mamma never has a dry eye, I think: But *I* don't weep. I am to be the comforter of you all! And I *will.* – Don't weep! Why now you weep the more for my comfortings! . . . I would make you *all* happy, if I could.
>
> (II, 209–10)

Just this impossible obligation of making *all* happy 'disorders' her mind. In an attempt to reconcile all opposing wills, she necessarily loses her own. As Sir Charles insists, women were designed to be '*dependent,* as well as *gentle,* creatures; and of consequence when left to their own wills, they know not what to resolve upon' (II, 280–1). When Clementina is left to her own will, her desire for Sir Charles conflicts with her divided loyalties to her parents, brothers, confessor, and God. She not only loses resolution, but finally loses her mind. She interprets her own madness as 'punishment for [her] pride . . . the hand of God' (II, 631).

God's conveniently heavy hand blots out the contradictions of Clementina's situation. To escape the strain of her family demands, she suffers a considerable loss of memory, which her suitor the Count of Belvedere calls 'her absence'. Significantly, her absence of mind presents no obstacle to the lover-like Belvedere, who would apparently rather have a blankly submissive wife than a consciously rebellious one. Her family, however, more like Defoe's citizen, who looks upon his docile wife home from the asylum as 'one dead', are more demanding in their love, and need more conscious compliance. They are determined to restore her senses the better to enjoy them, and show a willingness to give up their earlier resistance to Sir Charles's proposals if that will make their child whole. Clementina, however, in her desire to please all, realizes that the original family demands for religious conformity cannot be so easily relinquished. She remains faithful to their initial objections:

Shall I not, if it please God to restore my memory, be continually recollecting the arguments which you ... formerly urged against an alliance with this noblest of men, because he was of a religion so contrary to my own, and so pertinacious in it? And will those *recollections* make me happy?   (II, 566)

For Belvedere, Clementina's 'absence of mind was no obstacle' (II, 558); for Clementina, recollection restores consciousness of the contradictions that erased her memory in the first place. Like Clarissa refusing to marry Lovelace to please society's regard for appearances, she has incorporated her family's initial demands more thoroughly than they would wish, reflecting in her 'self-denial' a *self* that stubbornly confronts the conflicting demands for compliance that 'shatter' her 'reason'.

If I thought I could make [Sir Charles] happy; if I thought I should not rather punish than reward him; if I thought I could be happy in myself, and my soul would not be endangered; if I thought I could make you and my papa happy, by giving my hand to him; God knows that my heart would not make the least scruple. But madam, the Almighty has laid his hand upon me. My head is not *yet* as it should be.   (II, 573)

In polarizing her dilemma, Clementina clarifies the opposition between head, or consciousness, and heart. Since her desire to comply cannot withstand her consciousness, her only solution is loss of consciousness, madness in a head 'not *yet* as it should be'.

Clementina's struggle never completely ends. The hand of the Almighty is replaced eventually by the hand of Sir Charles, god-like author of 'proposals' that ensure her submission to her family's objections to her taking the veil (and losing her estate). Meanwhile the god-like author, Richardson, announces that *he* prefers to leave his heroine in an indeterminate state. Has he not been complaisant to his readers, he boasts in his Appendix, 'to leave to them the decision of this important article?' He confides that from what he has already heard from his audience, 'a considerable time will pass before this point will be agreed upon among *them*'. But as always, in his letters and in his fiction, Richardson proves incapable of allowing such latitude. Unable to trust his gentle readers to their own devices, he intrudes a page later to 'add' that Clementina is 'mistress of her own will. By the power Sir Charles, in the articles he drew, stipulated for her, we know she will make herself happy in acts of beneficence; and, as he has foretold, will see every-thing in a chearful light, that before appeared to her in a cloudy one. What will be the result?' (III, 468–9). Since Richardson's muse demands marriage, the result is not difficult to envision. 'Will' here, as elsewhere, bends to the authorial, patriarchal imperative to resolve the irreconcilable differences – at least in an imagined appendix.

Harriet Byron, less highly strung than the divine enthusiast Clementina, displays the subtler difficulties of accommodation that compliance creates. Her ophaned status helps here. Freed from contradictory family demands, she need please only her Grandisonian 'sisters' and those mammas and papas like Lady D. and Sir Rowland willing to bow to her ultimate wishes. Her quite visible desire for Sir Charles is privileged, replicating an adulation that preoccupies almost every character in the novel. Once Clementina refuses Sir Charles, leaving him to the noble English Harriet, it would seem that Harriet's will is not only allowed, but nurtured, for to love Sir Charles is to love perfection itself. But even Harriet, 'Defective ... in the way of Vivacity', must be 'reined in' by her Lord.[12] She learns what it is to be 'Nobody' (I, 280), a creature of 'raised' humanity but severely lowered 'self-consequence' (I, 285). In an interesting, somewhat strained scene, we can see better what Richardson means when he assures the reader that Clementina 'is mistress of her own will', for in the new domestic order, the will must – voluntarily – wither away.

   Christmas is almost upon us, and Harriet is making preparations 'to benefit and regale our poorer neighbours, and Sir Charles's tenants'. Forming herself 'on the example of the late excellent Lady Grandison', she is blessed by her servants with their tears. Observing that Grandisonian servants 'live in paradise', Harriet wonders at the efficient harmony of the operations. Laws have been drawn up at the low servants' own request to enable each body to know its own duties. Noting visible manifestations of Sir Charles's goodness – a servant's library in three classes: divinity and morality, housewifery, history (true adventures, voyages and innocent amusement), a special library of gardening kept by Sir Charles; and an apothecary on call to physic the tenants – Harriet then reports the natural adoration that her husband enjoys. According to Mrs Curzon, the housekeeper, to honour Sir Charles, servants and tenants 'pull off their hats to the ground, and bow their whole bodies ... the good women courtesy also to the ground', while his servants 'love him as they attend him at table' and 'watch his eye in silent reverence'. Harriet confesses here, tears of joy trickling down her cheeks, that she is 'Proud of my inferiority'.

   The letter shifts, as Harriet describes an unexpected meeting with Dr Bartlett. He has returned without the other gentlemen, and afraid that he is not well, Harriet follows him upstairs to tell him her apprehensions. After he gracefully confesses his indisposition, adding that her attention has made him well, she joyfully tells him 'what had passed between Mrs Curzon and me', and repeats with delight the public praise of her good man. Dr Bartlett adds to the adulation, lauding Grandison's attention to the bricklaying, carpentry and sawing on the estate. While Harriet delightedly listens to reports of Sir Charles's 'management and intentions', she forgets her company below. Sir Charles's arrival reveals just how mindful his (and any proper) wife must be to the demands of her 'company'.

That moment (without any-body's letting me know the gentlemen were returned) into the Doctor's apartment came Sir Charles. My back was to the door, and he was in the room before I saw him. I started! Sir, Sir! said I, as if I thought excuses necessary.

He saw my confusion. That, and his sudden entrance, abashed the Doctor. Sir Charles reconciled us both to ourselves – He put one arm round my waist, with the other he lifted up my hand to his lips, and in the voice of Love, I congratulate you both, said he: Such company, my dearest Life! such company, my dearest friend! you cannot have every hour! May I, as often as there is opportunity, see you together! I knew not that you were! The Doctor and I, madam, stand not upon ceremony. Pardon me, Doctor. I insist upon leaving you as I found you –

I caught his hand, as he was going – Dear, dear Sir, I attend you. You shall take me with you; and, if you please, make my excuses to my aunt, for leaving her so long alone, before you came in.

Doctor, excuse us both; my Harriet has found, for the first time, a will. It is her own, we know, by its obligingness.

He received my offered hand, and led me into company: Where my aunt called me to account for leaving her, and begged Sir Charles would chide me.

She was with Dr. Bartlett, madam, said he: Had she been with any other person, man or woman, and Mrs. Selby alone, I think, we would have *tried* to chide her.

What obliging, what sweet politeness, my dear grandmamma!   (III, 285–9)

It is appropriate that Harriet, having found her 'will to oblige', should write this way to the dear grandmamma, sufferer of the strained sinew. Sir Charles's sweet attention here is no less crippling to the 'inferior' Harriet who is, in this scene, obliged to account for her every domestic minute. Sir Charles's easy acceptance of the conference between Dr Bartlett and his wife suggests the gross impropriety of conferences less sacred; 'Such company, my dearest Life! such company, my dearest friend! you cannot have every hour!' For the rest of the hours, Harriet must monitor herself, attending to the needs of all others, complying to their desire, lest she be seen as selfish, uncaring, inattentive. Under surveillance – under the watchful eyes of Mrs Selby, Sir Charles, and greatest critic of all, herself, Harriet is learning to oblige, forming in the process a will that refines individual desire into a rage to comply. Short of madness – or death – there could be few alternatives.

9

Richardson's 'speaking pictures'

JANET E. AIKINS

Shortly after her fatal flight from home to the waiting carriage of Robert Lovelace, Clarissa Harlowe writes of a shock that has broken her heart. The affront is not her rape, as we might expect, but her father's terrible curse, and she explains its horror by saying that 'the Curse extends to the life beyond this'. She learns of her father's action in a letter from her sister who also tells her that her 'whole-length picture, in the Vandyke taste' has been removed from the parlour at Harlowe Place (III, 257–60; *II, 169–71*). As Bella's letter makes clear, the banishment of the portrait is as dreadful as the paternal curse itself. This is not all we hear of the picture, for it is mentioned again in Clarissa's last will and thus becomes a part of the document with which the estranged daughter assumes a final, patriarchal authority over her 'estate' both in this life and the next. The property Clarissa distributes includes not only this painting but also the collection of Harlowe family portraits, along with other pictures, drawings, and works of figured embroidery that display either the 'person' or the mind and artistic skill of Clarissa, their creator. These telling references point to the special status of pictorial art within Richardson's novel. Here, as in all of his fictions, we view the pictures in the text and the texts within the pictures that the narrative figures forth. Whatever their form, such images hint at a powerful visual aesthetic governing Richardson's method as a 'painter' of character in words.

Discussions of the parallel between verbal and visual art were familiar in Richardson's day, and he raises the subject in *Clarissa* through an elliptical reference to Alexander Pope's second moral essay. Robert Lovelace adopts one of its lines, 'every woman is a Rake in her heart' (III, 106; *II, 55*), to explain the contradictory nature of his 'Charmer'. In the poem, Pope uses portraiture as a metaphor for the elusive nature of women whom he, as a poet, is attempting to 'paint'. He suggests that any one woman can be accurately depicted in a variety of contradictory costumes and attitudes, as was true in fashionable pictures of the time. The Fannia who is 'leering on her own good man' in one canvas can elsewhere appear as a naked and vulnerable Leda. In the first instance she is the stimulated viewer, in the second she becomes the helpless object of a lecherous gaze, but she remains the same 'person'.[1]

As his paraphrase reveals, Lovelace misconstrues the poem whose claim is that woman's nature is mysteriously various, not simply that all women are alike and easily understood. In the same letter, he compares himself to the blind seer Tiresias who 'can tell what they think, and what they drive at, as well as themselves' (III, 106; II, 55). Lovelace's sense of alliance with the Greek visionary inadvertently forecasts his own downfall, since Tiresias was blinded for viewing a goddess in the nude, an action which Clarissa's rape will tragically mimic. Here, and at many other points within the text, Richardson invites us to consider what it means to 'see' this woman whose visual aspect is so powerful. The narrative thereby becomes a form of verbal portraiture which creates a series of visual illusions in the mind of the reader. While the parallel between verbal and visual art remains on the level of metaphor in Pope's poem, Richardson uses it as a method for storytelling.

Throughout his career as a writer, Richardson fancied himself as a painter in words. His decision to illustrate *Aesop's Fables* in 1739 and *Pamela* shortly thereafter[2] grew from his belief in the visual effect of language, a notion which appears frequently in his correspondence. For example, in a letter of 1748, he directed Edward Moore to 'behold' Lovelace's death as it is painted within *Clarissa*: 'See him in his following Delirium Spectres before his eyes! His lips moving, tho' speechless – *wanting* therefore to speak – "See him in convulsions, and fainting away."' Richardson also claimed that letters from friends caused him to experience such visualization; he told Sarah Westcomb that when reading hers, 'I have you before me in person: I converse with you, and your dear Anna, as arm-in-arm you traverse the happy terrace' – as if the terrace itself took pleasure in the touch of the women's feet and Richardson could feel it. In a comment to Lady Echlin about *Sir Charles Grandison* he claimed that he intended 'to provoke friendly Debate' about the characters.[3]

Richardson's idea of writing a fiction in order to prompt a 'debate' about its characters directly recalls what the painter and prominent art theorist Jonathan Richardson had written in 1715 about the active, biographical effect of a portrait on a viewer: 'Upon the sight of a Portrait, the Character, and the Master-strokes of the History of the Person it represents, are apt to flow in upon the Mind, and to be the Subject of Conversation.' Seeing a portrait is less an exercise in identifying a feigned image with an original than a direct and sometimes disturbing experience of the complex 'person' whom the portrait depicts. As in 'writing to the moment', a successful portrait must therefore capture movement and action, for 'The Air of the Head, and the

Mien in general, gives strong Indications of the Mind.'[4] This comment by
Jonathan Richardson clearly anticipates Clarissa's belief that in writing about
people, the 'air and manner often express more than the accompanying words'
(I, 7; *I, 5*), and it is likely that her creator drew some of these ideas directly
from art theory, for he enjoyed friendships with painters and art theorists
including Joseph Highmore and Joseph Spence.

These men shared a belief that the highest aim of portraiture is an
embodiment of abstract qualities rather than a depiction of the subject's
features. One of Joseph Highmore's essays raises this issue directly. 'Of two
portraits of the same person', he wrote, 'the less like may possibly be the
better picture' because it captures 'nature in general' in addition to particular
physical likeness.[5] The banishment of Clarissa's portrait suggests that it
succeeded in doing both, for it was all too potent a representation of Clarissa's
body and soul for her guilty family to have to see. Also, as the Harlowes were
vividly aware, the power of a picture depends not merely on the painted forms
but on the state of mind of the spectator. Moreover, a portrait can only
persuade a viewer to accept its illusion as 'reality' if its scale and position in a
room conspire in the deception. In Joseph Highmore's words, 'the best
portrait that ever *Titian* drew, if hung up in a frame, on the side of a room,
would not deceive; that is it would not be taken for the person represented,
which, however, it infallibly would, if placed where that person must be
expected'. Highmore's purpose in making this speculation is 'to shew how
necessary the concomitant circumstances either of a picture, or of nature are,
in order to produce the proper effects of the one, or the other, on the
spectator'.[6]

Richardson's fiction is centrally concerned with the complexity of being a
'spectator' of both art and life. In the verbal pictures he creates within his
texts, and in the actual illustrations he commissioned for *Pamela*, he makes us
first visualize his characters and then realize the extent to which our mental
sight is subjective – the product of 'concomitant circumstances' that range
from the ocular to the social, moral, and political. His novels offer a form of
portraiture in that they attempt to represent imaginatively characters' physical
features while also capturing the elusive qualities that transcend physical
substance. As Richardson well knew, any portrait, whether visual or verbal,
must acknowledge what Jonathan Richardson had asserted in his essay on
connoisseurship:

as time never stands still, neither do our bodies continue the same, but are ever
changing ... we are always stepping on: so it is with our minds, ideas are continually
arising ... these pass away to give place to others, so that the scene within is eternally
shifting from what it was.[7]

Both bodies and minds are 'ever changing' so that in a painting, as in an epistolary narrative, the artist must somehow record the psychological and optical reality that, as Jonathan Richardson wrote, 'things have a different view every moment'. This fact is central to the knowledge that Pamela gains in the process of narrating her adventures to her parents, and a survey of Richardson's 'speaking pictures' must therefore begin with his first fictional heroine.

The most important event in Pamela's life is marked by a visual experience. On her wedding day, she revises her former 'view' of the world around her, and we share her sight. She exclaims, 'What a different Aspect every thing in and about this House bears now, to my thinking, to what it once had! The Garden, the Pond, the Alcove, the Elm-walk. But, Oh! my Prison is become my Palace; and no wonder every thing wears another Face!' (p. 293). Pamela comes to this realization as she and Mrs Jewkes sit upon a 'broad Style' which serves as a convenient emblem of her transition from maidservant to wife and as a trigger to our visual memory of an earlier scene which this one echoes. As Pamela remarks, 'Mrs Jewkes was quite another Person to me, to what she was the last time I sat there!' Here she is referring to the thirty-sixth day of her 'Imprisonment' when she had found the doors open and had inadvertently escaped from her entrapment simply by walking out of the house: 'before I was aware, [I] had got to the Bottom of the long Row of Elms; and there I sat myself down upon the Steps of a sort of broad Stile' (p. 158). On this earlier day, Pamela had revealed her ambivalence about leaving Mr B.'s home by stopping to reflect on her actions, and in the midst of her debate she was interrupted by the sight of 'a whole Body of Folks, running towards [her] from the House, Men and Women, as in a Fright'. The obvious explanation for the disturbance did not at first occur to her; only slowly did she realize that the household thought she had consciously attempted to escape, and as she tells us, 'I sat still, to let them see I had no View to get away' (p. 159).

In these two parallel incidents, Richardson makes us see with a kind of multiple vision. In the earlier scene, we picture Pamela on the stile, and the group of runners, and share both her dawning realization of what the view before her means and the runners' awareness of what the sight of Pamela at a distance means to them, however mistakenly. Later, on her wedding day, her sitting on the same stile triggers a memory of the earlier moment of complex seeing. Along with Pamela, we contemplate several discrete 'views' of her in a single instant, so that as time collapses within Pamela's mind, we realize her intense mental conflict. Our point of view is thus fragmented, much as it is in a painting that depicts several figures in complex relation to each other. Although such effects in Richardson's novels have often been compared to the drama, the affinity here is to the stasis of visual art. The force of the incident arises not from its depicted action but from the reader's simultaneous awareness of separate points of view recorded in a single, suspended moment.

In such scenes, our attention is insistently directed to the sight of Pamela's body, and recent commentators have explored the social implications of this choice. They have argued that dress is a sign of 'distances' between economic classes and between particular individuals, and that the heroines's change in clothing signals her triumph in overcoming both through marriage.[8] However true this may be, such explanations overlook the purely visual phenomena that Richardson wants us to observe. For example, although Pamela's distress at Mr B.'s forward behaviour may result from their difference in class, what she herself complains about is the term 'speaking Picture' and other 'bad Names' that Mr B. calls her including 'artful Creature, painted Bauble', and 'Gewgaw' (pp. 144–5). 'Speaking picture' is of course Philip Sidney's definition of poetry as a form of painting, and its use here suggests both Pamela's powerful visual eloquence and her discomfort at being viewed.[9] In another example, Sir Simon Darnford and his friends pay Mr B. a visit, and Pamela is forced to make her appearance by walking down a long path that gives the company the most extended view they can have of her progress through the garden. As she explains, she was required to enter from 'the longest Gravel Walk in the Garden, so that they saw me all the Way I came, for a good Way; and my Master told me afterwards, with Pleasure, all they said of me' (p. 242). Here, both literally and figuratively, Pamela grows larger in the eyes of her social superiors as she approaches them from a distance.

Richardson exposes the subjective nature of seeing. He thereby highlights Pamela's own difficulty in viewing the world accurately and describing its appearance in 'speaking pictures' of her own. In his final revision of the novel, he stressed this aspect of the story by adding, early in the story, young Pamela's comment to her parents, 'Now, if I shall not tire you, I will give you some little account of the characters and persons of these four ladies; for when I was hardly twelve years old, you used not to dislike my descriptions.' What follows is a satiric and at times even savage visual depiction of the four 'fine ladies' who visit Mrs Jervis.[10] By including these passages, Richardson turns our attention from the objects Pamela sees to the highly subjective nature of her gaze and its effect upon the story that she tells.

Her first encounter with Monsieur Colbrand is an excellent example of her constrained vision, for she describes the man as 'the most hideous Monster I ever saw in my Life'. She not only mentions his 'foreign Grimaces', and awkward bodily gestures, but girlishly imitates his accented voice. This account follows shortly after her encounter with the apparent bulls who turn out to be mere cows, so that we know she tends to see terrifying creatures where there are none. Indeed, she depicts Colbrand as a 'Giant of a Man, for Stature ... large-bon'd, and scraggy'. She focuses particularly on his 'great staring Eyes, like the Bull's that frighten'd me so'. She claims that he has 'Vast Jaw-bones sticking out; Eyebrows hanging over his Eyes', a total of three scars, 'two huge Whiskers, and a monstrous wide Mouth; blubber Lips; long yellow Teeth, and a hideous Grin'. However unpleasant he may be, Pamela's words may more truly be said to depict her own horrified state of mind as she looks upon him. She ends her description of the encounter with a final imitation of his voice: 'He said, He fright de Lady, and offer'd to withdraw' (pp. 147–8).

The portrayal of Colbrand is a particularly interesting example of Richardson's *ekphrasis* or his attempt to prompt a visual image in the reader's mind,[11] for in his revisions of the text in the 1750s, he transformed this already potent description from a single to a double mental image by a slight change in wording. He moved the 'He said' from the start of the paragraph so that with no intrusion from Pamela, we read, 'I fright de young lady, said he.' With this minor alteration, two radical changes occur. The switch from the third to the first person suddenly transforms the retrospective narration into an event presently occurring, as if Pamela has momentarily forgotten where she is as she pictures the odious man in her mind. Moreover, when we hear his actual words, 'I fright de young lady', following the cruel account of his 'foreign grimaces', an image of Pamela's own rudely grimacing face leaps to our minds, for what else could prompt his remark about her fear? Although we may picture different details, all readers here turn a mental gaze from Colbrand's ugly face to Pamela's terrified one so that what we see is both Colbrand's grimace and Pamela staring back.[12]

At her best, Pamela is less a teller than an illustrator, and in its sixth edition Richardson gave the novel actual illustrations to complement hers. He eventually commissioned Hubert François Gravelot and his pupil, Francis Hayman, to complete the series of engravings, but he began the project in 1740 with a more modest effort to add to the second edition a pair of frontispieces by William Hogarth. Aaron Hill wrote to him at the time, 'The designs you have taken ... seem to have been very judiciously chosen; upon pre-supposition that Mr. Hogarth is able (and if any-body is, it is he), to teach pictures to speak and to think.' Ultimately the Hogarth designs were not used, and the Introduction to the second edition suggests that they were rejected for 'having fallen very short of the Spirit of the Passages they were intended to represent'.[13]

On the basis of such evidence, commentators have speculated that Richardson did not approve of Hogarth's interpretation of the novel and that he would have preferred the elegant, baroque style of Gravelot and Hayman for his genteel servant girl. T. C. Duncan Eaves argues that their graceful engravings show us 'Pamela as Richardson saw her', and not as the 'graphic "Shamela"' that Hogarth might have created. Marcia Allentuck calls the Gravelot and Hayman illustrations 'oversimplifications' resulting from Richardson's trying to impose on the reader genteel images which the text itself subverts.[14] These comments underestimate the integral relation of the engravings to Richardson's already highly visual text; the significance of Hogarth's disappearance from the project is not that Richardson objected to his style, if he did, but that Richardson in 1742 had abandoned a plan for two frontispieces in favour of a series of twenty-nine illustrations, an unusually large number for an English work of the period, as Eaves points out.[15]

Richardson hints at what led to this extraordinary change of direction when he quotes a comment from Aaron Hill who preferred his own fancied images of Pamela to 'any *figur'd Pretence to Resemblance*' that an artist might supply. In seeing the Hogarth engravings for the first time, he and Hill had shared the startling experience of viewing images that contradicted the 'Pamela' they each had visualized, however differently. In reaction, Richardson might well have abandoned the idea of illustrating his text; instead, he chose to invest in a much larger and more costly series of illustrations which do not diminish but dramatically expand the startling discrepancy between the reader's mental pictures and those on the page. His action was not a rejection of Hogarth but of the frontispiece as a genre too limited in power. Aaron Hill had remarked that frontispieces are 'commonly' disappointing because they depict 'negligent *shadows of form*', and Richardson had come to agree with him.[16]

Whatever they may have looked like, Hogarth's proposed designs could hardly have been any more shocking than the narrative itself in which the heroine creates highly exaggerated and often grotesque 'descriptions' of people and events for the pleasure of her parents. Moreover, the Gravelot and Hayman engravings draw attention to Pamela's difficulties both in seeing and being seen. Often they slyly enhance the comic variations between what she describes and what we would actually view if present. For example, when we finally see the 'hideous' Colbrand (figure 11), what we view is not the sexually imposing monster Pamela described but a handsome and valiant protector. In Volume I, the engraving diverts attention from Pamela's eager chatter to Mr B.'s penetrating gaze as she describes her bundles of clothes to Mrs Jervis (figure 12). He peeps out from behind a curtain, on the other side of which the decorative end of the bell pull seems to peer at her, as if to hint that many eyes are upon the heroine, including ours.

Richardson sharpened such effects in the presentation of the sixth edition by carefully placing each illustration opposite the particular words it glosses.

11   'Pamela fleeing from Lady Davers', designed by Francis Hayman and engraved
      by Hubert François Gravelot, in *Pamela*, 6th edn (London, 1742), II, 267

12   'Pamela revealing to Mrs Jervis her wishes to return home', designed by
Francis Hayman and engraved by Hubert François Gravelot, in *Pamela*, 6th edn
(London 1742), I, 123

Rather than numbering the engravings as pages in the volume, Gravelot included on each one a notation of the volume and page number across from which it appears. We are thus to read each engraving as the visual equivalent of the discourse it faces, not an illustration of characters and action. The image of Pamela angling is an especially powerful example of this pictorial narrative strategy.[17] At the top of the page facing the engraving we read the end of a sentence: 'by a simple Wile'. The 'Wile' to which it refers is Pamela's trick of hiding her letters from Mrs Jewkes in the garden. The two go fishing, and Pamela likens herself to the carp played on the string and says she will instead grow horsebeans in the garden rather than depriving the fish of its liberty. What we see in the image, however, is not merely the graceful Pamela flinging the carp into the water but also a surprisingly normal looking Mrs Jewkes, quite mild in comparison to the 'broad, squat, pursy, fat Thing' (p. 107) Pamela had earlier described, holding the end of the fishing line as if to hint that she is being 'played' by Pamela with her 'simple Wile'. The picture does not display 'Pamela throwing the carp into the stream', as Eaves describes it, but Mrs Jewkes literally and figuratively on the hook. To see the full 'image' in the text we must thus match the carefully chosen segment of printed narrative with the engraving it faces, an effect over which Richardson as the printer had full control.

By reading each engraving as an integral part of the page of text, a thematic coherence among all the pictures emerges. In some way each one deals with an aspect of the visual experience that constitutes human relations. Eaves is right in determining that Joseph Highmore's later series of *Pamela* paintings is far more successful as a sequential and causally connected narrative, recording the major incidents in Pamela's story like a Hogarth progress;[18] however, the Hayman and Gravelot series possesses its own coherence as an essay on the interdependence of literal and figurative seeing. As such, it suggests Richardson's awareness of this issue as central to his novel's interest.

The scope of this paper does not allow for comment on all the engravings, but even a brief survey suggests the range of their concern. In the first illustration we view Mr B. looking to 'see' how Pamela is 'come on in [her] Writing' (I, 4). Neither he nor she can face the other; instead, they 'view' each other through objects they each hold. She examines her pen while he admires a page of her writing which he holds and which displays, as he says, her 'pretty Hand', her 'tolerable' spelling, and 'my good Mother's Care in your Learning'. Another image shows us Mr B. reading 'sweet Confusion' in Pamela's eyes, blushes, and bosom (I, 358). Behind her we see a sundial which suggests that like a device for visually measuring time, Pamela's changing physical appearance is a measure of her unseen thoughts. Elsewhere we see Pamela resolve to 'watch all [the] Motions' of the fortune teller who rubs a tuft

13 Joseph Highmore, *The Harlowe Family* (c. 1745–7)

of grass on her hand to make the unseen lifeline visible, while Mrs Jervis, too, is 'watchful' over them both (I, 373). In still another image we see Sir Jacob survey Pamela 'from Head to Foot' (III, 377) and exclaim, 'Had my rash Nephew seen this lovely Creature ... he'd never have stoop'd to the Cottage, as he has done.' Sir Jacob mistakes Pamela for an elegant lady, not realizing that he is actually looking upon Mr B.'s 'cottage' wife. Several engravings depict moments of recognition or 'witnessing' such as Pamela's startling sight of her father (II, 89), her marriage before 'the few Witnesses present' including the reader (II, 175), her appearance at the Masquerade (IV, 108), and her giving up Mr B. to her rival (IV, 210) with 'God' as her 'Witness' and a symbolic ray of sun hitting the mirror shown within the engraving (IV, 210). Again and again, the images demonstrate the multiple ways in which the substance of daily life consists in our varied responses to the sensory impressions that come through the eyes.

The pictures in the text and the texts in the pictures thus reveal Richardson's view of both fiction and life as 'visual art'. In *Pamela* he probes the discrepancies between what we see in the world and the verbal and mental pictures of it that we create. In *Clarissa*, however, he explores the nature of portraiture in particular by urging us to construct a mental image of its complicated heroine. Indeed, in a painting of 'The Harlowe Family', Joseph Highmore recorded his friend's narrative solution to the paradox that any portrait – whether visual or verbal, actual or imagined – offers a static depiction of the constantly changing 'person'.

Scholars have speculated that Highmore intended 'The Harlowe Family' (figure 13) to be the first of several, sequential illustrations of *Clarissa* because he had earlier painted such a series of *Pamela*;[19] however, the painting is self-contained in that it records in a single image the primary issue, both visual and moral, that informs Richardson's text – the resonant meaning of 'family'. As Richardson noted, we view in the picture 'the accusing Brother, and the accused Sister, on her return from Miss Howe's, as represented in the beginning of vol. I'.[20] Clarissa hovers in the background, her empty chair an ominous hint of her future. The angry James stands with his back to us, above his seated family, prematurely assuming the authority he will inherit as the only male child. His rigid body divides the mother from the father (as happens emotionally in the novel), while his father's gouty foot appears between James's legs, thereby forecasting James's own intemperance. We cannot see his full face, but in his father's scowling visage, placed in close juxtaposition with Bella's plump one, we see a representation of James's features both in their angry expression and in the jowly shape his face is likely to assume at his parent's age. Highmore's picture thus collapses time and explores the flux within the human 'countenance', a term used often by

Richardson for the complex and sometimes shifting facial features which embody human 'character'. The painting implies that the father mirrors something both present and potential in the son's face before him, and like the novel which it represents, it depicts the 'family' as a biological, political, and social entity with tragic power over the individual 'person' – body and mind.

In this work, Highmore alludes visually to the first image in William Hogarth's 'Marriage-à-la-Mode' series painted in 1743, and in doing so he makes clear his understanding of Richardson's subject. Highmore gives to Mr Harlowe the very features, wig, hand positions, and elevated gouty foot of Hogarth's Baron who is arranging a marriage between his son and the daughter of the wealthy merchant for the sake of her dowry. The facial resemblance is unmistakable. Moreover, Clarissa stands in the same position on the canvas as the merchant's daughter whose body is being traded in the marriage agreement. As Highmore's allusion to Hogarth confirms, control over Clarissa's body is a primary concern in her story, and to make this theme more compelling, Richardson creates for the reader a powerful *ekphrasis* of the heroine. That is, he achieves an illusion of her palpable substance through careful visual description

From the beginning, Richardson urges us to think of what it means to 'see' Clarissa. In the first letter of the novel we learn that a terrible event has 'pushed [her] into blaze' so that 'Every eye ... is upon' her (I, 3–4; *I, 2–3*). Later on, when Arabella taunts Clarissa with her family's anger, she says, 'it is wished you may be seen a beggar along London-streets' (III, 259; *II, 171*), a sentence that anticipates the many scenes in which Clarissa cringes under the eyes of crowds in the streets, at doorways and windows, or at the entrance to a carriage.[21] Throughout her life, Clarissa has been celebrated not merely for her virtue but for her physical beauty, a reputation that draws every eye to her in church or on the street and that brought Lovelace to the Harlowe door. Reading the text thus invites a tangible encounter with Clarissa's 'person', and in each 'view' of her, we are asked to see both the 'WOMAN in her charming person' and the 'ANGEL that shines out in such full glory in her mind' (VII, 299; *IV, 248*).

Our visual image of Clarissa depends in part upon what Highmore called the 'concomitant circumstances' in which she is placed, and the Harlowe house is one of the most important both literally and figuratively. In leaving it, she departs in a single gesture from the building, the Harlowe family, and the reach of Mr Harlowe's gaze. When Clarissa herself describes the house, she details both its architectural layout and her own imagined cringing under the eye of a viewer seeing her flee from it: 'For, as to the front-way, you know, one must pass thro' the house to That, and in sight of the parlours, and the servants hall; and then have the open court-yard to go through, and, by means of the iron-gate, be full in view, as one passes over the Lawn, for a quarter of a mile together' (II, 283; I, *447*). Here Clarissa asks us to picture an advancing line of sight with her own body steadily at the point of the perspective, like a camera following a travelling object.

The account of her actual 'flight' also details the eyes that are upon her, and in this case, too, they are products of Clarissa's imagination. She writes, 'Now behind me, now before me, now on this side, now on that, turn'd I my affrighted face, in the same moment; expecting a furious Brother here, armed servants there, an enraged Sister screaming, and a Father armed with terror in his countenance' (II, 333; *I, 484*). According to her hallucination, she 'sees' in multiple directions simultaneously and seems stopped on all sides while she runs at top speed. The description approximates what Joseph Spence admired in Pope's account of Ulysses's shipwreck: a 'Great View is compleatly contracted into a few Lines ... We are, in a manner, surrounded with it on all sides; and which ever way we turn our Eyes, we cannot look out of it.'[22] When Francis Hayman painted Clarissa's escape from home (figure 14), he positioned her body to suggest this sublime action and in doing so depicted the heroine's insoluble moral dilemma. This picture, Hayman's only known illustration of Richardson's second novel, appears to have been completed between 1753 and 1754. In the composition the heroine seems at first glance to lean reluctantly away from the garden door towards Lovelace, who pulls her towards a distant carriage. However, a second look reveals that her prominent left foot is positioned so that if she were to take a forward step, she would actually move *away* from both the garden and Lovelace himself. Her stance and longing gaze at the garden door imply that she wants to move in several competing directions at once.

In deciding to paint this particular scene, Hayman selected a moment of exceptionally powerful visual effect within the narrative. In this fleeting instant, Clarissa's fate turns on her not being seen by anyone in the Harlowe household. Moreover, for Lovelace the view of Clarissa in this tense moment is so potent that he is later compelled to reconstruct it in what he calls a 'faint sketch' of 'her admirable person with her dress' which he sends to Belford. He remembers particularly the 'cuffs and robings curiously embroidered by the fingers of this ever-charming Arachne' (Clarissa herself) and a 'white handkerchief wrought by the same inimitable fingers' that 'concealed – O Belford! what still more inimitable beauties did it not conceal!' (III, 28; *I, 511–12*). In Lovelace's eyes, the clothes meant to 'conceal' her body ironically reveal the 'person' beneath. The 'running pattern of violets and their leaves' which the Arachne Clarissa has herself crafted not only seem startlingly real to him but enable him to view her internal organs as if, like a

14 Francis Hayman, *Robert Lovelace Preparing to Abduct Clarissa Harlowe* (c. 1753–4)

powerful Tiresias, he had a superhuman vision. He exclaims, 'I saw, all the way we rode, the bounding heart (by its throbbing motions I saw it!) dancing beneath the charming umbrage.' The images of flowers on her dress seem alive to him and make the substance of her body palpable to both Lovelace and the reader. In a like moment, he speaks of the 'gaudy propriety' of two of Clarissa's pieces of framed embroidery. Although these pictures literally depict 'Abraham offering up Isaac' and 'Samson and the Philistines', his oxymoron ('gaudy propriety') suggests that he perceives the image of Isaac as a portrait of Clarissa, and the sensual Samson, as a portrait of himself (VI, 101–2; *III, 317*). His visual memory of the framed embroidery, like his memory of Clarissa's decorated clothing, is equivalent to a mental encounter with the woman herself.

In such moments, Richardson also urges the reader to picture the heroine's body, for he tells her story as a series of struggles either to escape the view of others, or, by contrast, to see or be seen. In the first two volumes, her family cruelly banishes her from their 'presence', not even allowing her to do needlework before her mother. We perceive her physical weight when she bursts through a door and her family seems just to have vanished, leaving her sprawling 'flat on my face' (II, 206; *I, 390*). At another point, we picture Clarissa retreating behind a 'sash-door', then behind its glass, and then behind a 'silk curtain' so that Bella 'should not see me' through it (II, 47; *I, 271*). After the fire incident, she is desperate to avoid being 'seen' by Lovelace, while he stands helplessly before her glass, threatening to break it 'for not giving me the personal image it was wont to reflect, of *her*, whose idea is for ever present with me' (V, 25; *II, 524*). The fire episode is especially powerful because it enables Lovelace to see her not merely as a two-dimensional image but as a three-dimensional form, her 'scanty coat giving the whole of her admirable shape, and fine-turn'd limbs' (IV, 368; *II, 502*).[23] It is not surprising, then, that Richardson chose the word 'interview' for their fatal meeting at the garden door or that Clarissa calls Lovelace her 'betrayer', for both are words of 'showing' or 'seeing' (II, 334; *I, 485* and V, 326; *III, 223*). To know the heroine, we must picture her body and consider what it represents in sexual, familial, economic, and even spiritual terms. It is for this reason that portraits of Clarissa, of her family and friends, and embroidered pictures made by Clarissa's fingers assume such a prominent role in her will.

In a novel whose central, tragic event concerns a young woman's envied inheritance of her grandfather's house and land, it is striking that her will includes only minimal description of the estate and features instead so many details about her collection of paintings and embroidery. As she bestows each item on the friend of her choice, it becomes, in effect, a 'representation' of Clarissa herself. Through this activity she perpetuates her own existence

beyond death, which is the symbolic goal of any portrait. Her bequest
includes the family pictures which Bella had angrily coveted, a 'gown and
petticoat of flowered silver of my own work', her embroidery of flowers, her
own 'little miniature picture set in gold' done by a 'famous Italian master', her
'picture at full length' which is in her 'late Grandfather's closet', several other
'finished and framed pieces of needle-work', and a 'locket, with the miniature
picture' of Anna Howe that she has worn on her 'person' the entire time we
have known her, as if it were part of her body. Richardson takes great care to
enable us to visualize details of size, style, colour, location, and artist of
objects in the lengthy list, and whether the object depicts Clarissa's features
or is simply associated in some way with her body, each offers differing
'representations' of the woman herself through every act of bestowing them
on others (VIII, 100–4; IV, 418–21). We are in this sense surrounded by
multiple 'portraits' of Clarissa as we move through the text. Few of these
representations provide an actual likeness of her features; instead, they fulfil
Jonathan Richardson's idea that a portrait should be an embodiment of 'the
Character, and the Master-strokes of the History of the Person it represents'
which 'flow in upon the Mind' of the person who views it.

Richardson prepares us to interpret the will in such terms with Bella's
curious account of the abrupt banishment of Clarissa's portrait and framed
needlework. The letter in which she describes the terrible event is intended to
mortify the 'rebel' sister by bringing her the news of her father's fatal curse.
Bella succeeds in her purpose, for Clarissa says that 'this dreadful Letter *has
unhinged my whole frame*' (III, 266; II, 176), with italics added in the third
edition to suggest a pun on the idea of Clarissa herself as a framed image. In
the letter, Bella assumes the role of a connoisseur and says that Clarissa's
portrait was formerly valued for the 'imputed dignity … of your [Clarissa's]
boasted figure' – a dignity which Bella implies is not inherent in either the
picture or the woman but which is 'imputed' by the viewer. According to
Bella, Clarissa's family also looks upon her drawings and framed embroidery
as depictions of their maker's active hands, for as Bella says in a very peculiar
phrase, they were formerly valued 'for the magnifying of your dainty
finger-works'. Bella tells her sister that the portrait, and Clarissa's own
creations have been 'taken down' from her 'late parlour' and 'nailed up' in her
closet, declared to be as dead to the family as the cursed daughter herself. By
implication, then, the woman, the visual images depicting her, and those
made by her are all to be treated as bad art, thrown into a closet to perish in
obscurity (III, 259; II, 170–1). The pictorial representations are as powerful as
the presence of Clarissa herself.

Here as in all of his novels, Richardson instils special significance in
objects crafted in various media including embroidery, painting, drawing, and

even landscape gardening.[24] Both the skill to create art and the talent of tastefully collecting it serve as indicators of a character's position in the moral, social, and political hierarchies. We notice, for example, that Mr B.'s study not only gives access to his garden but contains a collection of valuable pictures, a hint of his innate virtue. In *Sir Charles Grandison*, Richardson portrays the graciously designed Grandison estate as a representation of the heart and face of Sir Charles. The new Lady Grandison writes of her dwelling and her husband, 'The gardens and lawn seem *from the windows of this spacious house* [my emphasis] to be as boundless as the mind of the owner, and as free and open as his countenance' (III, 272). Harriet's words indicate that to appreciate either the estate or the face of the man who possesses it, the viewer must be properly positioned inside the house and gaze through its well placed windows, and by the time she writes these words, she has achieved this 'place' both literally and figuratively. In these examples, skilful connoisseurship is a sign of moral superiority. Considered in such terms, the two full-length pictures of Clarissa that are mentioned in her story offer a telling contrast with each other.

The first is her banished portrait. When the novel was originally published, Richardson included a footnote to inform the reader that this portrait was actually 'drawn as big as the life by Mr. Highmore and is in his possession'.[25] That the portrait is life-sized and in 'the Vandyke taste' sets it apart from the very different taste in English painting practised more typically by Highmore and other native artists, including Charles Jervas, Francis Hayman, Arthur Devis, and the early Thomas Gainsborough. While Van Dyck as a court artist produced life-sized, formal pictures, with fully expressed figures and much psychological detail in the face, these later English painters favoured small-scale pictures, suitable for modest rooms, with figures whose clearly artificial features and delicate bodies are best described as doll-like. Richardson invites us to visualize Clarissa's second 'picture at full length', the one in her 'late Grandfather's closet' (VIII, 103; *IV, 420–1*), as a work in this native English manner.

Clarissa's portrait in 'the Vandyke taste' is exactly the sort of work to be commissioned by the socially aggressive Harlowes, who hoped to secure their position in the aristocracy by constructing a Dutch garden and by giving their daughter's 'person' in marriage to the odious Solmes whose estate was contiguous with hers. They prefer the styles of art imported from abroad in the previous century and favoured by the court. By contrast, her grandfather's aesthetic choice reflects his more modest good taste and his affection for Clarissa. He prefers the diminutive native art which is suitable for the privacy of a closet, suggesting his desire to sense his granddaughter's presence in his most personal moments. Not only were the canvases of such English paintings relatively small, but the scale of the figures in them shares an affinity with the proportions of book engravings, clearly intended for private contemplation. They differ both visually and ideologically from the portraits by such court artists as Sir Godfrey Kneller whom Sir Charles Grandison's vain and profligate father had commissioned to paint one of the six diverse pictures of himself that adorn his son's estate (III, 279). Richardson's third novel is the one that most fully records his view of the ideological potency of art both as a form of creative activity and as an object for the collector's appreciation.

Richardson published *Sir Charles Grandison* in 1753, the year in which Francis Hayman and others formed a Committee of Artists in an early effort to found a British academy comparable to those on the continent. Also in 1753, Hogarth published his controversial *Analysis of Beauty*, a rival attempt to support English painting and to discourage teaching painting by the European method of copying the Old Masters.[26] In a number of its details, Richardson's last novel can be read as a contribution to this movement in favour of native art, for it portrays the superiority of the English Sir Charles Grandison over all that continental civilization has to offer.

The novel rewards Sir Charles for his goodness with his marriage to 'the *Flower of the British world*', Harriet Byron (III, 252). By contrast, Sir Charles's first love, Clementina, is beautiful and noble, but her devout Catholicism has made her an unsuitable partner for Sir Charles since she fails to be British in any sense of the word. Richardson uses Clementina's aesthetic skill as an index of this larger, political problem. Like Clarissa, Clementina draws, but when she does so at the height of her madness, her doodlings are of artificial images. Dr Bartlett writes, 'Sometimes she draws: But her subjects are generally, Angels and Saints. She often meditates in a map of the British dominions, and now-and-then wishes she were in England' (II, 254). She is out of touch with reality in her visions of saints and angels, and the closest she can come to attaining the Englishness of Sir Charles is by 'meditating in' a map of Britain as an empire. The curious wording, which attributes a religious dimension to cartography, calls attention to the hopelessness of her efforts to unite with the heroic Englishman. Later she shows him an unfinished piece of her needlework and tells him that 'the drawing was my own too, after – after – I forget the painter'. When she asks his opinion of it, he reluctantly points out 'a disproportion that was pretty obvious' (II, 489). Here Richardson depicts Clementina as an amateur artist of the school attacked by Hogarth, for she draws after the Old Masters rather than from life and what she produces is not only incomplete but exhibits a failure in perspective.

In the disproportion of Clementina's drawing, Richardson hints at both her distorted mind and her misplaced faith. Her failure as an artist thus signals her more significant inability to learn the English language and adopt its culture and religion as her own. Clarissa, by contrast, had created a piece of flowers in needlework which she bequeaths to her Cousin Morden because his father had been 'very earnest to obtain' it and 'carry it abroad with him' (VIII, 103; *IV, 420*). In this detail, Richardson reverses the more common balance of aesthetic trade in his day and thereby pays a high compliment to his fictional heroine. In a similar spirit, he implies that the Grandison estate, which is 'considerable, and improving', is an indication of Britain's growing national strength. The young 'Grandison' is a gentleman of a new generation. His life is a corrective to that of his dissolute, aristocratic father, and the description of his home reveals the principles that guide him and that Richardson hopes will guide the British nation. He says to Clementina, 'My capital mansion (I value it for not being a house of yesterday) tho' not so magnificent as your palace in Bologna, is genteel, spacious, convenient' (II, 589–90). He allies himself not with the court but with the country gentry in his domestic life, for he calls his home a 'mansion', not a 'palace'. He values it because it is not new, not 'a house of yesterday', and yet throughout the novel he is occupied in its redecoration. It is 'spacious' without being 'magnificent', 'convenient' or liveable, and above all 'genteel'. Its gentility thus resides in its smaller proportions that bear a stylistic affinity to the small-scale English portrait of Clarissa that hangs in a place of honour in her grandfather's closet.

Richardson expected his readers to recognize the implications of these aesthetic choices, for all three of his narratives urge us to understand the complex subjectivities of sight, whether figurative or literal. In *Pamela* we witness the imperfect efforts of the heroine to create 'speaking pictures' of the shifting sights around her. By providing actual illustrations of the novel, Richardson encouraged his readers to trust their own visualizations rather than wholly accepting the images Pamela so handily supplies. What draws our attention is the heroine's fallible perspective, however sympathetically Richardson portrays it. In *Clarissa* he attempts an even more daring project, for he asks us to imagine what it means to 'see' both the body and the soul of the heroine. Through his multiple efforts to make us picture her, he explores the social, economic, sexual, and spiritual significance of the physical body or 'person' as Clarissa calls it when she debates with her mother its place within a happy marriage. In *Sir Charles Grandison*, however, Richardson implies a gentle critique of his idealized portrait of Clarissa. Unlike Lovelace whose offending gaze destroys the woman he so often calls a 'goddess', Sir Charles 'addresses himself to women, *as* women, not as goddesses; yet does honour to the persons, and to the sex' (III, 139). He is a hero who recognizes the potential tragedy of valuing excessive styles of art over the more genteel forms that capture nature. The young Grandison's gift is that of infallible perspective. All three of Richardson's narratives thus teach us to visualize 'person' and event from the views so carefully crafted by the characters and, ultimately, by their creator.

10

Unravelling the 'cord which ties good men to good men': male friendship in Richardson's novels

DAVID ROBINSON

Among the numerous relationships which Samuel Richardson depicts in his novels, different types of friendships abound: those between married couples, lovers, siblings, between a young person and an older advisor, and of course between people we would normally think of as 'friends'. In this last group, Richardson's women obviously outshine his men. As Janet Todd remarks in *Women's Friendship in Literature*, 'At the very beginning of the classical English novel, Samuel Richardson created two women [Clarissa Harlowe and Anna Howe] whose friendship became the pattern in life and literature.'[1] Todd's reading of *Clarissa* as the story of the heroine's 'conflict between patriarchal obedience and female autonomy' perceptively illuminates this model friendship between women, revealing its crucial importance in the novel.[2] A deep, intimate friendship between two women, because it encourages women's independence of and separation from men, clearly poses a threat to the established sexual order. It is my contention that male friendship, as it develops over the course of Richardson's three novels, proves to have a similarly subversive potential, calling into question prescribed definitions of masculinity and male identity. Negligible in *Pamela*, it becomes significant in *Clarissa*, and finally unsettling and experimental in *Sir Charles Grandison*. Yet Richardson studies are almost devoid of discussions of male friendship.

Partly, this omission results from Richardson, his characters, and his critics taking male friendship for granted. This tendency is evident in two discourses on women's friendship found in *Clarissa*, one of which, because it is written by the admirable although hot-tempered Colonel Morden, seems to be at least partially endorsed by the author. The Colonel writes:

Friendship, generally speaking, Mr. Belford, is too fervent a flame for female minds to manage: a light that but in few of their hands burns steady, and too often hurries the sex into flight and absurdity. Like other extremes, it is hardly ever durable. Marriage, which is the highest state of friendship, generally absorbs the most vehement friendships of female to female; and that whether the wedlock be happy, or not.

What female mind is capable of two fervent friendships at the same time? – This I mention as a *general observation*, but the friendship that subsisted between these two ladies [Miss Harlowe and Miss Howe] affords a remarkable exception to it: which I account for from those qualities and attainments in *both*, which, were they more common, would furnish more exceptions still in favour of the sex.

(VIII, 167; *IV, 468–9*)

This passage echoes an earlier letter, also addressed to Belford, in which Lovelace expresses his thoughts on female friendship:

Verily, Jack, these vehement friendships are nothing but . . . mere apes of us! . . . when a *man* comes in between the pretended *inseparables*, friendship is given up, like their music and other maidenly amusements . . .

Thou hast a mind, perhaps, to make an exception for these two ladies. – With all my heart. My Clarissa has, if *woman* has, a soul capable of friendship. Her flame is bright and steady. But Miss Howe's, were it not kept up by her mother's opposition, is too vehement to endure. How often have I known opposition not only cement friendship, but create love? . . .

But this I pronounce, as a truth, which all experience confirms, that friendship between women never holds to the sacrifice of capital gratifications, or to the endangering of life, limb, or estate, as it often does in our nobler sex.

(V, 254–5; *III, 169*)

These two pieces both treat male friendship as the norm and female friendship as an anomaly. Yet they clearly say as much about the former as about the latter, although what they say is not very convincing. Morden and Lovelace assume that men are better suited for the 'fervent . . . flame' of friendship than women; yet good female friendships are commonplace in literature, while comparable male ones are much rarer. Both writers also imply that while marriage and romance 'absorb' and invalidate 'the most vehement friendships of female to female', they do not interfere with the friendships of male to male; yet one could cite numerous examples of two male friends fighting over the same woman. Finally, Lovelace makes the common male assumption that taking physical risks is a proof of true friendship; whereas a much stronger proof, in fact the requisite of friendship, is the courage to take emotional risks, a quality which women display far more consistently than men. Obviously there is a great disparity between the popular myth of male friendship, as expressed by Morden and Lovelace, and its realities. If we are truly to understand the interactions among Richardson's characters, we can no longer afford to take this relationship for granted.

When one examines male bonds more closely, one immediately finds that many 'friendships' exist in name only: the word often has no substance behind it; the relationship to which it refers is scarcely more than indicated. This is the case in *Pamela*, a novel almost completely devoid of male friendship. Mr B.'s 'friends', his mostly rakish companions from his pre-Pamela days, appear briefly only once or twice and then vanish from the story. What little effect they have on Mr B. is a negative one, as when they disrupt his wedding day and prevent him from having dinner with his new bride. Mr B. must dine instead with these unwanted guests and even accompany them on the road in order to get rid of them, leaving Pamela to write in her journal and walk in the garden with Mrs Jewkes. (Interestingly, the leader of these intruding rakes is Sir Charles Hargrave, whose name – and perhaps character as well – Richardson splits in two and reuses in his last novel, calling his hero Sir Charles Grandison and his villain, such as he is, Sir Hargrave Pollexfen.) As for the male characters who appear more often in *Pamela*, Mr Peters and Sir Simon, they are neighbouring gentry, not friends. Their intercourse with Mr B. is confined to polite socializing and nothing more. The only possible friend of whom we hear is the dying Mr Carlton, to whom Mr B. pays a comforting visit. It is only in relation to this character that love between two men is mentioned in the book. Mr B. writes of Mr Carlton, 'I know he loves me', and Pamela writes that Mr B., 'by his kind expressions, I find, loves him [Mr Carlton]' (pp. 314–15). Yet we never see this supposed friend. His illness is a device to demonstrate Mr B.'s generosity and to keep him away from home so that Lady Davers can terrorize Pamela. Once this purpose is served, Mr Carlton conveniently dies. Neither his nor any other male character's relationship with Mr B. or with another provides an example of anything approaching a true friendship between men. It is a relationship wholly missing from Richardson's first novel.

A similar lack is evident in *Pamela II*. Mr B.'s supposed friends are men such as the lawyers Mr Turner and Mr Fanshaw, whom Pamela describes as 'very free, very frothy, in their Conversation; and by their laughing at what they say themselves, taking that for Wit, which will not stand the Test' (IV, 6). When pressed by her husband to give her opinion of these men, she expresses her disapproval of them, concluding half apologetically, half ironically with, 'But you'll pardon me, good Sir, for speaking my Mind so freely, and so early, of these *your Friends*' (IV, 7). Of course, what Pamela is saying to her husband is that these men are *not* his friends. Yet neither she nor anyone else seems to notice that no men in *Pamela II* play this role. There are no male friendships in the book.

This situation changes in *Clarissa*, however. The leading male character, Robert Lovelace, develops a prominent and believable friendship with his correspondent Jack Belford. In this relationship we see Richardson struggling with a received form – the rake's friendship – attempting to expand, deepen, and transform it. Yet most critics, however perceptive their observations on other aspects of *Clarissa*, miss the subtle development of this relationship over the course of the novel. Janet Todd dismisses Belford as 'a man [Lovelace] frequently despises and always ignores', while Morris Golden classes Belford among 'the sober, respectable men of sense' who contribute 'little of significance' in Richardson's works.[3] Neither critic takes any notice of the strength of the connection which exists between Lovelace and Belford, a connection which approaches a mutual dependency and compulsion. However angry Lovelace may grow with Belford, he cannot stop corresponding with him. 'I threatened above to refrain writing to thee', he states. 'But take it not to heart, Jack – I must write on, and cannot help it' (IV, 362; *II, 498*). A little later he remarks, 'But for this scribbling vein . . . I should still run mad' (V, 28; *II, 525*). Clearly, these letters provide a much-needed outlet for Lovelace, but, significantly, they are not journal entries. They are Lovelace's primary form of communication with another man, Belford, who is as anxious to read the letters as Lovelace is to write them (e.g. IV, 126–7; *II, 327–8*). The question is not, as most critics suggest, whether or not the two men have a relationship, but rather, what exactly are its characteristics? How do the men behave and interact?

To answer these questions, one must first understand Lovelace's most fundamental character trait – his desire for power and control – which he demonstrates most obviously, and obsessively, in his relationship with Clarissa. Rejecting the suitor's subservient role, Lovelace demands complete control over both Clarissa's outer and inner life (even going so far as to read her private letters in order to discover her unvoiced thoughts and feelings). More than anything, he wants to make Clarissa submissive – he has erotically charged fantasies of her humbled and broken (IV, 21–2; *II, 251–2*). Yet this desire for power is not limited to his relationship with the heroine. As Golden writes, '[Lovelace] is so dominated by his fantasies of superiority that almost any incident or train of ideas in which he engages develops into one of them.'[4] He attempts to assert his superiority over almost every character he encounters.

As with many men, this desire for power is intimately tied to issues of masculinity and femininity. In speaking of Clarissa, Lovelace asks Belford, 'Yet is she not a *woman*? Cannot I find one yielding or but half-yielding moment, if she do not absolutely hate me?' (IV, 223; *II, 398*). In his mind, to be a woman is to yield. Not surprisingly, therefore, he rarely yields to anyone. Similarly, because Lovelace conceives of conscience as a female, a 'varletess', he feels himself a real man only when she has been banished from his breast (IV, 226–7; *II, 400*). When conscience softens him, dissuades him from his cruel purposes, his masculinity is threatened. 'How does this damn'd love unman me!' he complains to Belford (V, 28; *II, 526*). Lovelace unquestioningly accepts, and is trapped by, traditional notions of masculinity, femininity and acceptable gender roles. Consequently, he desperately fears and avoids even the appearance of weakness.

One manifestation of this fear which considerably limits the degree of intimacy Lovelace can achieve with another man is his inability to empathize. In some cases he will not even acknowledge the suffering of another person, as when he complains of Belford's 'tedious whining over thy departing [uncle]' and later asks, 'Is not thy Uncle dead yet?' (IV, 128, 304; *II, 329, 456*). Even in the case of Belton's horrifying illness and death, where Lovelace does express concern for his former companion, he still keeps the situation at a distance from himself (both literally and figuratively) and only sympathizes; Belford, on the other hand, puts himself in the sufferer's place and learns from the experience – he empathizes. Lovelace cannot allow himself to go that far, because empathizing means sharing another person's pain and weakness, and weakness is antithetical to Lovelace's concept of manhood and to his very identity.

These elements – Lovelace's desire for power, his notions of masculinity, even his inability to empathize – help explain why Clarissa's undoer needs to feel superior even to his male friends. In his own words, 'this is certain, that in every friendship, whether male or female, there must be a man and a woman spirit (that is to say, one of them, a *forbearing* one) to make it permanent' (V, 255; *III, 169*). Lovelace, of course, must be the man spirit, the superior one, and thus feels entitled to call himself Belford's 'master', and to 'command' him (III, 278; I, 206; *II, 185*; *I, 152*). He even unabashedly admits to Belford the motive behind this behaviour, his desire for superiority: 'with such others as Belton, Mowbray, Tourville, and Thyself, I ... valued myself on being the Emperor of the company; for, having fathomed the depth of them all, and afraid of no rival but thee, whom also I had got a little under (by my gaiety and promptitude at least) I proudly ... delighted to give Laws to my little Senate' (VII, 13; *IV, 37*). As a self-styled emperor, he seeks out subjects, not friends.

However, what makes his relationship with Belford different is that both men know Belford is not really Lovelace's inferior. As the 'master' admits in the previous quotation, he fears a rival in Belford. Importantly (at least for men who subscribe to traditional definitions of masculinity), each man knows that the other is undaunted by physical danger. As Lovelace puts it, 'I know thou as little fearest me, as I do thee, in any point of manhood' (V, 329; *III, 225*). However much he may pretend otherwise, he knows he has a formidable match, or near-match, in Jack Belford.

For a while, Lovelace is able to keep the upper hand through his 'gaiety and promptitude': his superior looks, his wit, his social charm. But as Clarissa begins to thwart his desires, robbing her persecutor of his superiority, his relationship with Belford changes and deepens. What had been an unbalanced, hierarchical arrangement becomes a much more interesting and volatile interaction between equals. Again, what makes this development possible is Lovelace's unprecedented and growing vulnerability, caused by Clarissa's unconquerable resistance. This successful challenge by a member of the 'weaker sex' completely undermines the would-be emperor's superiority. One of the first signs of the resultant change in his relationship with Belford is that his friend's good opinion begins to matter to Lovelace. For example, he writes to Belford:

> I am sensible, that my pleas and my reasonings may be easily answered, and perhaps justly censured; but by whom censured? Not by any of the Confraternity, whose constant course of life, even long before I became your General, to this hour, has justified what ye now, in a fit of squeamishness, and thro' envy, condemn. Having therefore vindicated myself and my intentions to YOU, that is all I am at present concerned for.
>
> Be convinced, then, that *I* (according to our principles) am right, *thou* wrong; or, at least, be silent. But I *command thee to be convinced*. And in thy next, be sure to tell me that thou art.   (IV, 24–5; *II, 253*)

Despite his posturings and commands, Lovelace is asking for his friend's approval. He needs to 'vindicate' himself to Belford.

The balance of power in the relationship continues to shift even further in Belford's favour as Lovelace's relationship with Clarissa further deteriorates. The rake's ever-ready wit begins to fail him, and he grows less and less able to endure his friend's criticisms and rebukes, repeatedly charging Belford not 'to rally' and triumph over him, because he 'cannot bear it' (e.g. VI, 67; *III, 292*). When Clarissa escapes him for good, Lovelace also finds he needs Belford's services as his advocate. He writes at one point, 'I would have thee attend her ... and vow for me, swear for me, bind thy soul to her for my Honour, and use what arguments thy friendly heart can suggest, in order to procure me an answer from her' (VI, 75; *III, 298*). Instead of giving orders, he now begs favours.

Not surprisingly, Lovelace has difficulty accepting this new power arrangement. He does not relinquish his superior position gracefully. One of his defences is to mock Belford's homely appearance, which he contrasts to his own physical beauty. Much of this mockery seems playful, as Lovelace likens his friend to various animals, including a dog, a bear, and even a rhinoceros (III, 73, 61; VII, 285; *II, 30, 21; IV, 237*). Yet there is a serious side to these remarks, a longstanding sexual rivalry which Lovelace makes explicit in passages such as the following:

> What indeed made me appear to be more wicked than thou, was, that I being an handsome fellow, and thou an ugly one, when we had started a game, and hunted it

down, the poor frighted Puss generally threw herself into *my* paws, rather than into *thine*. And then, disappointed, hast thou wiped thy blubber-lips, and marched off to start a new game, calling me a wicked fellow all the while.

In short, Belford, thou wert an excellent *starter* and *setter*. The old women were not afraid for their daughters, when they saw such a face as thine. But, when *I* came, whip, was the key turned upon their girls.   (VIII, 149; *IV, 455*)

In this cruel letter, Lovelace reacts to the loss of his precious superiority with a typically masculine sexual competitiveness, boasting of his greater success with women, his sexual prowess. But the assumption underlying such a strategy is that Belford still measures himself by his sexual 'triumphs' over women – in other words, that he is still a rake. Accordingly, Lovelace repeatedly makes him out to be, as he puts it, 'as bad a man as myself', and defends himself to Belford 'as arguing Rake to Rake' (VII, 3; V, 221; *IV, 30*; *III, 145*). In this way, Lovelace attempts to return the relationship to the old arena of sexual competition, where he feels confident of besting Belford, and to invalidate his friend's increasingly painful reproaches as coming from a fellow sinner, a partner in crime.

Understandably, Belford objects to this unfavourable characterization of himself, and to some extent he is justified. He truly is attempting to repent and reform. Nevertheless, at times he goes too far in blaming his correspondent and exonerating himself. For instance he once writes,'I always loved you. It has been my misfortune that I did: For this led me into infinite riots and follies, of which otherwise, I verily think, I should not have been guilty' (VIII, 140; *IV, 449*). When Lovelace disputes this contention, Belford more or less acknowledges the truth of his friend's argument and accepts responsibility for his own crimes, as well he should. All previous sins aside, his conduct towards Clarissa is far from blameless. Although he tries to persuade Lovelace to be good to the heroine, Belford none the less displays an unmistakeably voyeuristic curiosity, as when he writes: 'But, nevertheless, I should be desirous to know (*if thou wilt proceed*) by what gradations, arts, and contrivances, thou effectest thy ingrateful purpose' (IV, 25; *II, 254*). Clarissa herself calls him to account for this fault, wishing he had assisted her earlier:

I find, Sir, by this expression, that he had always designs against me; and that you all along *knew* that he had: Would to Heaven, you had had the goodness to have contrived some way, that might not have endangered your safety, to give me notice of his baseness, since you approved not of it! – But you gentlemen, I suppose, had rather see an innocent fellow-creature ruined, than be thought capable of an action, which, however generous, might be likely to loosen the bands of a wicked friendship!

(VI, 297–8; *III, 463*)

Belford's subsequent assistance to Clarissa is certainly admirable, but it does not clear him of having been an accessory to her undoing.

As for his relationship with Lovelace, Belford is by no means above taking advantage of his friend's vulnerability to exact a measure of revenge for past abuses. For example, in response to one of Lovelace's 'raving' letters, Belford writes to

... congratulate thee on thy *expected* rage and impatience, and on thy recovery of *mental* feeling.

How much does the idea thou givest me of thy deserved torments, by thy upright awls, bodkins, pins, and packing-needles, by thy rolling hogshead with iron spikes, and by thy macerated sides, delight me!

I will, upon every occasion that offers, drive more spikes into thy hogshead, and roll thee down hill, and up, as thou recoverest to sense, or rather returnest back to *senselessness*. Thou knowest therefore the terms on which thou art to enjoy my correspondence. Am not I, who have all along, and *in time*, protested against thy barbarous and ungrateful perfidies to a woman so noble, entitled to drive remorse, if possible, into thy hitherto callous heart?   (VI, 290; *III, 457–8*)

In this and other letters, Belford seems motivated as much by spite as by morality to try to compel Lovelace to repent for his crimes. Yet at the same time, while getting even with Lovelace verbally, Belford '[does] not forget the office of a friend': he convinces Clarissa that Lovelace did not have her thrown in jail, and tries to persuade her to agree to marry her former captor, or at least 'to give [him] her last forgiveness personally' (VII, 379; *IV, 307*). Belford has his friend's ultimate welfare at heart – he wants to see him a reformed man, cured of his moral ills. It is only that Belford wants to administer the unpleasant treatment himself in order to enjoy his patient's pain and discomfort.

Because Belford now has a means of resisting his friend's domination, he and Lovelace can interact on a more equal footing, and their relationship seems to work for a while. But the longer Lovelace is apart from Clarissa, the tenser the two men's friendship becomes. While Belford tries to be a friend to Lovelace but not 'to his actions to the *most excellent of women*', his commitment to protecting Clarissa moves him closer and closer to a violent clash with the man whose passion for the heroine has become an all-consuming obsession (VI, 283; *III, 452*). As Lovelace sees that his friend's first loyalties now lie with Clarissa, he warns, 'Take care – Take care, Belford – I do indeed love you better than I love any man in the world: But ... the matter is grown very serious to me. My heart is bent upon having her. And have her I will, tho' I marry her in the agonies of death' (VII, 84; *IV, 89*). His declaration of the strength of his feelings for Belford is striking; yet it is outweighed by his determination to 'have' Clarissa no matter what the consequences or cost. Given Lovelace's increasing desperation, a physical confrontation seems inevitable.

Clarissa's death, however, averts this outcome and allows the men's friendship to overcome the tensions between them. Although they quarrel over Lovelace's letters again before he departs for Europe (he wants them returned; Belford refuses), Lovelace demonstrates that he now values his friend more highly than he does having his own way. 'But, at last', Belford writes, 'all was made up, and he offered to forget and forgive every-thing, on condition that I would correspond with him while abroad ... and particularly give him, as I had offered, a copy of the Lady's Will' (VIII, 187–8; *IV, 484*). With Clarissa irretrievably gone, Lovelace has no incentive to quarrel with his best and only friend. As a result, their leave-taking (as described by Belford) is quite tender:

> He and I parted with great and even solemn tokens of affection; but yet not without gay intermixtures...
>
> Taking me aside, and clasping his arms about me, 'Adieu, dear Belford! said he: May you proceed in the course you have entered upon!... if I live to come to England, and you remain fixed in your present way, and can give me encouragement, I hope rather to follow your *example*, than to ridicule you for it ... And when thou thinkest thou hast made thyself an interest *out yonder* (looking up) then put in a word for thy Lovelace.'   (VIII, 191–2; *IV, 486–7*)

Touched by his friend's warmth, Belford declares to Lovelace's uncle, 'I do love him, my Lord' (VIII, 192; *IV, 487*). The feeling, we are shown, is mutual, although it seems more strongly felt on Belford's side. In one of Lovelace's last letters, the once thoughtless and selfish rake writes to his friend:

> On reperusing yours in a cooler moment, I cannot but thank you for your friendly love, and good intentions. My value for you, from the first hour of our acquaintance till now, I have never found misplaced; regarding at least your *intention*. Thou must, however, own a good deal of blunder of the over-do and under-do kind, with respect to the part thou actest between me and the Beloved of my heart. But thou art really an honest fellow, and a sincere and warm friend.   (VIII, 234; *IV, 519*)

Some of the old pride lingers, but the sentiment is clear. Against all expectations, and despite Lovelace's fundamental need for superiority, he and Belford overcome the masculine desire for power and fear of vulnerability, the most common – in fact almost universal – obstacle to male friendships in eighteenth-century literature.

But how strong a friendship do they actually achieve? At one point, as tensions mount between the two men, Lovelace expresses a very open-minded attitude towards their difficult relationship. 'Reformation', he observes, '... is coming fast upon thee. Thy Uncle's slow death, and thy attendance upon him, thro' every stage towards it, prepared thee for it. But go thou on in thy own way, as I will in mine. Happiness consists in being pleased with what we do' (VI, 343; *III, 496*). While Clarissa lives, this is hardly Lovelace's philosophy. His 'heart [is] bent upon having her', even if it necessitates violence against her or anyone who protects her, including Belford. It is only Clarissa's death that enables the friendship to survive. And even if one ignores this point by focusing solely on the period after she dies, Lovelace and Belford's relationship is still far from exemplary or even satisfactory. True, what had been a conventional rake's friendship, rife with competition and sexual rivalry, does evolve into a more co-operative relationship allowing for demonstrations of affection, but only slightly and for the briefest of times. Almost as soon as Lovelace and Belford achieve a kind of harmony, the former travels to Europe and is killed. (One could even argue that the two men's signs of mutual affection are not all that significant, but instead are rather conventional, occurring as they do during parting scenes: right before Lovelace's departure for the continent, and before his fatal duel with Colonel Morden.) The new, more interesting stage of their friendship – in which they relate affectionately with, and directly to, each other, without using women as either a bond or a battleground – does not progress beyond a beginning.

The reason for this sudden termination of the relationship is that it is impossible for a good man, which Belford has become, and a bad man, which Lovelace still is, to have a harmonious friendship. At the end of the novel, it seems as if Lovelace is on the verge of repentance when he says that on his return to England he might follow Belford's example. But he is not another Mr B.; Richardson does not attempt to reform him. Instead he kills off this memorable villain. In *Clarissa*, Richardson makes more out of a conventional rakish friendship than could ever have been expected, but he does not experiment with any new kind of intimate male bond.

In *Sir Charles Grandison*, however, Richardson attempts just such an experiment, basing a male friendship – that between Sir Charles and Jeronymo della Porretta – on a female model. Yet he encounters a great deal of difficulty in accomplishing this task, difficulty which arises from Sir Charles's close resemblance to Lovelace, particularly in their fundamental need for superiority. As Morris Golden demonstrates at length, although on the surface Sir Charles and Lovelace might appear to be polar opposites, the best and worst of men, respectively, closer examination of their characters reveals a striking similarity,[5] Miss Howe once remarks of Lovelace, 'To have Money, and Will, and Head, to be a villain, is too much for the rest of the world, when they meet in one man' (VI, 145; *III, 350*). Remove the words 'to be a villain', and one has a remark that applies equally well to Sir Charles Grandison. Lovelace, one could say, is Sir Charles's evil twin. Both men are wealthy, intelligent, aristocratic, charming, and exceptionally handsome. And both men share the same fault: an excess of pride, a desire for power, a need always to occupy the superior position in a relationship.

In Sir Charles's case, superiority takes the form of being a patron to all and a friend to almost none. Although he is able to enumerate the necessary elements of friendship – he writes that 'trust, confidence, love, sympathy, and a reciprocation of beneficent actions, twist a cord which ties good men to good men, and cannot be easily broken' – what Sir Charles understands in theory he does not apply in practice (II, 45). Specifically, he allows no one to reciprocate the 'beneficent actions', the good deeds, which he performs. He is like a man who, when out to dinner with friends, always insists on picking up the bill. A pleasant treat once in a while, the gesture becomes frustrating and humiliating if made a regular, irreversible practice. Yet this is exactly the role which Sir Charles continually assumes, using his power to help others as a means of also subordinating them. As Margaret Anne Doody writes, Richardson, in the protagonist of his last novel, 'embod[ies] and authori[zes] privilege and power. Sir Charles, already at twenty-six visibly a patriarch in the making, fulfills the English dream-image of the country gentleman on his estate. Inordinately handsome, learned without pedantry, and utterly self-assured, Sir Charles organizes the world around him with a ruthlessness that terrifies some of the objects of his unstoppable benevolence.'[6] Because he never steps down from his throne, never accepts a favour, never treats anyone as an equal, Sir Charles has no friends, only beneficiaries.

For example, the supposedly intimate relationship between the hero and his brother-in-law Lord L. is marked far more by politeness than by warmth. In Sir Charles's presence Lord L. is respectful and restrained; in fact, one barely notices his existence. Only when Sir Charles is gone and Lord L. is alone with his constant companions Lady L. and Charlotte (and sometimes Harriet) does he grow more animated, conversing freely, trading quips, and acting more like another sister than like a brother-in-law or husband. And like the sisters, he is frustrated by the unapproachability of their brother. 'Whence is it', he asks them,

that we are all three insensibly drawn in, by each other's example, to this distance between him and us? – It is not his fault...

MISS GR. He came over to us all at once so perfect, after an eight or nine years absence, with so much power, and such a will, to do us good, that we were awed into a kind of reverence for him.

LADY L. Too great obligations from one side, will indeed create distance on the other. Grateful hearts will always retain a sense of favours heaped upon them.

(I, 444)

Although Lord L. does not blame his brother-in-law for the situation, he none the less feels, as do so many other characters, unable to get close to the man who has become his patron.

Yet if Lord L.'s relationship with Sir Charles is a disappointment, for a large part of the novel the appearance of a close friend for the hero seems imminent in the person of Edward Beauchamp. Richardson raises the reader's expectations through a prolonged and extensive build-up in which Dr Bartlett and Sir Charles repeatedly praise Beauchamp long before he appears in the novel in person. The following declaration of the doctor's is typical of their laudatory remarks:

> I long, Ladies, to have you all acquainted with this other excellent young man. You, Miss Byron, I am sure, in particular, will admire Sir Charles Grandison's, and my Beauchamp: Of spirit so manly, yet of manners so delicate, I end as I began; He is a second Sir Charles Grandison.   (I, 464)

The last phrase, 'a second Sir Charles Grandison', is used on several occasions to refer to Beauchamp. It cannot help but make us anticipate another perfect Christian man like the hero. We are also told that 'from a sympathy of minds', there has grown between Sir Charles and Beauchamp 'an intimacy that will hardly ever end' (I, 460). Sir Charles even says to Harriet, 'I love my friend Beauchamp above all men' (II, 114). Short of beatification, nothing could raise the character higher in our estimation than he now soars. We eagerly await the arrival of this intimate friend and equal of Sir Charles Grandison.

His appearance, however, is thoroughly anti-climactic. After receiving a second-hand account of Beauchamp's arrival at his father's house – an account written by Harriet, but told to her by Sir Charles – we are introduced, or rather not introduced, to this character in the next letter. While Sir Charles presents him to the members of the Grandison household, the most we learn is that, in Harriet's words,

> Mr. Beauchamp is an agreeable, and, when Sir Charles Grandison is not in company, a handsome and genteel man. I think ... that I do but the same justice that every-body would do, in this exception. He is chearful, lively, yet modest, and not too full of words. One sees both love and respect in every look he casts upon his friend; and that he is delighted when he hears him speak, be the subject what it will. (II, 344)

Beauchamp is described minimally and almost entirely in comparison or relation to the hero, apart from whom he hardly seems to exist. He rarely speaks, and when he does, it is almost always in order to praise Sir Charles. He is seldom described as doing anything in particular. In fact, as soon as he arrives, Sir Charles leaves, taking the focus of the story with him and leaving

Beauchamp on the periphery. Throughout the remainder of the novel we scarcely see the two 'friends' interact. After a volumes-long drum-roll, Beauchamp makes his entrance and promptly merges into the hero's chorus of admirers.

Only one male character, Jeronymo della Porretta, achieves a kind of intimacy with Sir Charles, and like everyone else, he, too, is subordinated by the protagonist. But in Jeronymo's case, the unusual nature and degree of his subordination makes possible, at least for a time, an intimacy not found among any of the other men, one in which sexuality plays a much more noticeable role. Sir Charles describes the early history of the two men's relationship in a letter to Harriet as follows:

> I became intimate with Signor Jeronymo at Rome, near two years before I had the honour to be known to the rest of his family ... but [he] had contracted friendship with a set of dissolute young men of rank, with whom he was very earnest to make me acquainted. I allowed myself to be often in their company; but, as they were totally abandoned in their morals, it was in hopes, by degrees, to draw him from them: But a love of pleasure had got fast hold of him; and his other companions prevailed over his good-nature...
>
> Such a friendship could not hold, while each stood his ground; and neither would advance to meet the other.

The two men parted company until, after an unspecified period of time, an accidental meeting occasioned the renewal of their friendship. According to Sir Charles,

> [The relationship] however held not many months: a Lady, less celebrated for virtue than beauty, obtained an influence over him, against warning, against promise.
>
> On being expostulated with, and his promise claimed, he resented the friendly freedom. He was passionate; and, on this occasion, less polite than it was natural for him to be: He even defied his friend ... [The] result was, [we] parted, resolving never more to see each other.

Yet, as if in punishment for disobeying Sir Charles's warning about the unnamed lady, Jeronymo is waylaid and dangerously wounded by a rival lover, only to be saved by Sir Charles, who, by a lucky coincidence, passes the scene of the ambush and intervenes before Jeronymo's assailant can administer the *coup de grâce*. Concluding this history, Sir Charles tells Harriet that

> being told, by the surgeon, that he owed his preservation to me, O Grandison! said [Jeronymo], that I had followed your advice! that I had kept my promise with you! – How did I insult you! – Can my deliverer forgive me? You shall be the director of my future life, if it please God to restore me.   (II, 120–1)

Jeronymo could hardly be more explicit in granting Sir Charles power over him, a relationship he henceforth reaffirms by frequently addressing his friend as 'my deliverer' and 'my preserver'.

It is important to note that although Jeronymo acquiesces in his sub-ordination only after the hero saves his life, Sir Charles has attempted to occupy a superior position from the very beginning of their relationship. Although they meet at first as equals, Sir Charles immediately tries to control Jeronymo, specifically in his choice of friends. Each man, however, 'stood his ground'. To Sir Charles, this situation means that they cannot be friends. He implies that they need to compromise, by which he really means not that they should meet each other half-way, but that Jeronymo should abandon his position while he himself does not budge. Faced with a resolute opponent, Sir Charles cannot maintain the friendship, and the two men part. When they meet again, Sir Charles once more tries to control Jeronymo, ironically (as we shall see) by warning him against women, and Jeronymo rebels. Fate punishes this rebellion, and brings the young Italian to regard Sir Charles as his 'deliverer', who will be 'the director of [his] future life'.

Jeronymo is now relegated to an obviously, and even graphically inferior position in regard to Sir Charles. The images we have of the two men strongly reinforce their inequality. While Sir Charles traverses Europe in the peak of health, Jeronymo languishes bed-ridden in his chamber, suffering from the improperly cared-for wounds he received from the assassins, undergoing dangerous and painful operations, and generally being 'in a very bad way' (II, 257). Even out of bed, Jeronymo needs 'crutches, helps, [and] wheeled chair' to get about (II, 238). He is thus not only spiritually subordinated to the hero, but also physically inferior to and dependent on him as well.

The sexual aspect of this subordination begins to emerge when one realizes that as in *Clarissa*, issues of power and superiority are closely related to notions of masculinity, notions which are even more important in Richard-son's last novel because of the peculiar nature of its male protagonist. Terry Eagleton enquires:

How could meekness, chastity, sentiment and benevolence, qualities bound up with the passive, powerless woman, survive transplanting to the political arena? The answer to this question is Richardson's last novel, *Sir Charles Grandison* ... *Pamela* and *Clarissa* have foregrounded the woman, pressing deep into new dimensions of feeling; it is now time for that tide of feminization to be recuperated by patriarchy and centred on a man ... In the figure of Sir Charles Grandison, then, Richardson will give us a womanly man, for whom power and tenderness are fully compatible.[7]

In theory, at least, Richardson creates this strong yet gentle man; it is certainly what he attempts.

Nevertheless, some conventional ideas about sex roles have a profound impact upon the author, because anxiety lest Sir Charles appear feminine haunts the novel. It is not enough that Sir Charles always be superior to others, and thus avoid the vulnerability and weakness – considered feminine traits according to sexist ideology – which equality with, or subordination to, another person implies. He must also be clearly and visibly masculine, which Richardson takes great pains both to tell and to show the reader. Numerous characters use the adjective 'manly' to describe Sir Charles and his behaviour. Of course, the epitome of manly behaviour is the use of physical force. Thus Richardson shows us Sir Charles's manliness by having him, despite his strict adherence to Christian virtues, successfully engage in several duels, each time disarming his opponents. In these and other instances, the author attempts to distinguish his protagonist from the common round of Englishmen, among whom, according to Sir Charles, 'A wretched effeminacy seems to prevail', and about whom he asks, 'Can there be characters more odious than those of a masculine woman, and an effeminate man?' (II, 10; III, 247). The speaker's answer, which he proceeds to argue, is of course an emphatic 'No!' Richardson thus impresses upon the reader that however 'womanly' some of his hero's qualities might be (such as his tenderness or his charity), Sir Charles is none the less indisputably masculine.

No such claim can be made for Jeronymo, who is not only subordinated but also feminized by the indomitable protagonist. In his account of the attack on the young Italian, Sir Charles writes, 'His wounds proved not mortal; but he never will be the man he was.' Because of his affair with the 'lady, less celebrated for virtue than beauty', in which he defied Sir Charles, Jeronymo is unmanned by a wound in the hip-joint (II, 121). As with Uncle Toby's mysterious wound in Sterne's *Tristram Shandy*, Jeronymo's injury suggests emasculation, as well as sexual inferiority. In this respect, it functions similarly to Belford's ugliness in *Clarissa*. However, there is an important difference between the two men's conditions: only Belford is made to seem sexually unappealing. To a man like Lovelace, who is most strongly attracted to a combination of physical beauty and vulnerability, Belford's ugliness and 'manliness' would inhibit desire. Lovelace is unlikely to be 'seduced' by his friend – and, in fact, try as he might, Belford is unable to get Lovelace to return his friendship with equal affection. Jeronymo's condition, on the other hand, increases his attractiveness by making him not only vulnerable, but also 'womanly'. His emasculation thus encourages a sexual bond with Sir Charles which Belford's ugliness discourages in his relationship with Lovelace.

Jeronymo's feminization is emphasized in other ways besides his wound. One small example are his tears – in the two men's emotional parting scene, only Jeronymo cries, not Sir Charles (see also II, 625). More significant is the intensity and demonstrativeness of the young man's affection for his 'preserver'. For instance, his ardently and repeatedly voiced wish is for Sir Charles to be his brother. He once writes, 'Would to God you could have been my Brother! That was the first desire of my heart!' (III, 5). He seems to see a marriage between his sister, Clementina, and Sir Charles less as a union between the two of them than as a connection between Sir Charles and himself. At times, in his letters, Jeronymo sounds like a melancholy or beseeching lover, as in the following:

Dear Grandison, love still your Jeronymo! Your friendship makes life worthy of my wish. It has been a consolation to me, when every other failed, and all around me was darkness, and the shadow of death. You will often be troubled with Letters from me. My beloved, my dearest friend, my Grandison, adieu!   (III, 5)

Sir Charles, though he expresses his own love for Jeronymo, never begs, or even asks, for Jeronymo's love in return. Also, while Sir Charles may write 'my beloved friend', he never writes 'My beloved, my dearest friend', as does Jeronymo, in which expression the use of 'beloved' becomes ambiguous: is it an adjective or a noun? Is Jeronymo writing 'my beloved dearest friend' or 'my beloved'? The ambiguity, although subtle, is important; it characterizes most of Jeronymo's relationship with Sir Charles, as he is simultaneously subordinated and feminized by his patron.

Of course Sir Charles, disgusted as he professes himself to be by effeminate men, and anxious about his own masculinity, cannot but feel uneasy returning his friend's emotional declarations of love, suggesting as they do a sexual component to their friendship which could be more easily denied were Jeronymo more masculine. (It should be noted, however, that although Jeronymo is feminized, Sir Charles would not necessarily consider him effeminate, as he would consider, for example, a lisping fop.) His expressions of friendship, delivered with an attempt at ardour, usually resemble the following: 'Jeronymo! my dear Jeronymo! one of the most amiable of men! how precious to my soul will ever be the remembrance of his friendly love!' (II, 635). Compared with Jeronymo's avowals of love, Sir Charles's are almost always either stilted and melodramatic, as in the previous attempt (in which Sir Charles seems to express what a friend ought to feel, not what he actually does feel), or restrained and relatively unemotional. And even when Sir Charles does manage a convincing expression of affection, he still does not return Jeronymo's love with equal intensity.

One can find a precedent for this type of relationship in *The Nicomachean Ethics*, where Aristotle writes, 'in friendships that involve superiority ... the superior friend should get more honour, and the needy friend more gain;

because honour is the reward for virtue and beneficence, whereas the remedy for need is gain'.[8] 'This condition', he avers, 'offers the best prospect even for unequal parties to be friends, because their inequality can be compensated [by the inferior's showing greater affection].'[9] Richardson seems to have chosen this arrangement as a model for Sir Charles's friendships: Sir Charles's friends shower their benefactor with praise and admiration in return for his assistance. In fact, a metaphor of Aristotle's applies especially well to Sir Charles and Jeronymo's relationship. The philosopher writes:

One might introduce here the relation between lover and beloved, or between a handsome person and an ugly one. This is the reason why lovers sometimes make themselves look ridiculous by demanding to be loved as much as they love; if they were equally lovable, this would be a reasonable demand, but when they have no such qualification it is ridiculous.[10]

According to Aristotle, it would be only natural for Jeronymo to love more and Sir Charles to love less. After all, Sir Charles is the hero, the perfect man, superior to everyone else in the book; he deserves more love by virtue of his greater 'lovability' – his supreme merit and unparalleled beauty. Interestingly, in the marriage of Sir Charles's sister Charlotte and Lord G., Richardson tries to show that this type of unequal relationship does not work. Perhaps it is unacceptable there because the female is superior to the male, while in Sir Charles and Jeronymo's relationship, the feminized character is subordinated to the masculine character.

However, Sir Charles's failure or unwillingness to love Jeronymo as much as Jeronymo loves him should not prevent us from realizing how affectionate the two men really are with each other, and how nearly intimate they at one time become. Sir Charles is more demonstrative with Jeronymo than with anyone else in the novel, with the possible exception of Harriet and Clementina. Their correspondence and conversation are filled with expressions of endearment. Sir Charles, to Jeronymo, in addition to being 'my deliverer' and 'my preserver' is also 'my dearest Grandison', 'the friend of my soul', 'my beloved friend', 'my dearest, my best friend', and even 'the man [he] love[s]' (II, 224, 226, 229, 243, 156). Likewise, Jeronymo, to Sir Charles, is 'my kind Jeronymo', 'my dear Jeronymo', 'my friend Jeronymo', 'my dear friend Jeronymo', 'my ever-valued friend', and 'my beloved friend' (II, 199, 224, 201, 215, 233). If Jeronymo seems more fervent in his endearments, and Sir Charles more reserved, this difference is in keeping with the type of relationship described by Aristotle, as well as with their roles of benefactor and beneficiary. Even so, Sir Charles's affection does at times subdue his superiority, as when he calls himself, in speaking of Jeronymo, 'the friend who loves you, as he loves his own heart' (III, 12). This is a simple, tender, and sincere expression of love for his closest friend.

What Richardson is trying to create here is a new kind of friendship between men. Not only does he make Sir Charles a 'womanly' man in some respects, but he also makes his friendship with Jeronymo 'womanly', basing it on the model of Clarissa's relationship with Anna Howe. Janet Todd calls this type of relationship a 'sentimental friendship' – although 'passionate friendship' might be a more accurate description – and describes it as 'a close, effusive tie, revelling in rapture and rhetoric ... providing close emotional support ...'[11] Unlike the distance and 'manly' reserve which characterize most male relationships, Sir Charles and Jeronymo's friendship is notable for the strength and frequency with which the men express their love for each other. Clearly, Jeronymo's feminization makes much of this achievement possible – his language is much closer to that found in Clarissa and Anna's correspondence, it is more passionate and less restrained than Sir Charles's – but both men seem to cherish the closeness of their bond.

Yet when important ruptures in Sir Charles's self-assurance and reserve begin to appear, this very closeness becomes unexpectedly dangerous, affording the reader glimpses beneath the hero's calm, confident exterior into more tumultuous, confused regions of his psyche. One such rupture in his unflappable persona occurs when Sir Charles parts from his beloved Clementina and then from Jeronymo. In this scene, Sir Charles displays more emotion, more believably, than in any other part of the novel. Not surprisingly, he is extremely uncomfortable with this display, as his language reveals: 'I was in too much emotion to wish to be seen'; '[I] bowed upon [her hand], to conceal my sensibility.' He even 'withdrew to Mr. Lowther's apartment; and shut [himself] in for a few moments', hiding his emotion both from the della Porrettas and from his correspondents, only re-emerging 'When [he was] a little recovered' (II, 637–8). Frustrated in his desire for Clementina, and faced with Jeronymo's suffering, our formerly invulnerable hero makes his most profound admission of weakness: 'I would have comforted him', he says, 'but wanted comfort myself.' What occasions this dramatic humbling of the great Sir Charles Grandison is a situation that he seldom experiences and greatly dislikes, one in which Lovelace finds himself when pursuing Clarissa: he is not getting his own way. After having subdued his feelings for Harriet, rekindled his love for Clementina, and overcome her family's opposition, Sir Charles receives his greatest, and ultimately his defeating, setback: Clementina herself refuses him on the grounds of religion. On a scale he has never encountered before, Sir Charles is denied the object of his desires.

Sir Charles loves Clementina and must part with her, yet he cannot do so cleanly and quickly. She keeps calling him back, raising his hopes, exciting his emotions. He wants to embrace her and almost does, 'but restraining [himself] just as [he] had reached her, [he] again hurried to the door' and 'withdrew to Mr. Lowther's apartment; and shut [himself] in for a few moments'. After he regains his composure, one would expect Sir Charles to leave, but he does not.

When a little recovered, I could not but step in to my Jeronymo. He was alone; drying his eyes as he sat: But seeing me enter, he burst out into fresh tears. Once more, my Jeronymo – I would have comforted him; but wanted comfort myself.
O my Grandison! embracing me, as I did him –
CLEMENTINA! The angel CLEMENTINA! Ah, my Jeronymo! – Grief again denied me further speech for a moment. I saw that my emotion increased his – Love, love, said I, the dear – I would have added CLEMENTINA; but my trembling lips refused distinct utterance to the word. – I tore myself from his embrace, and with precipitation left the tenderest of friends.   (II, 637–8)

Why could he 'not but step in to ... Jeronymo'? Why does he put himself through another agonizing parting and compound his grief when he has already bid farewell to Jeronymo earlier? His language – 'I could not but step in to my Jeronymo' – suggests that he is under a strong compulsion from feelings he could not satisfy or release with Clementina. When he enters Jeronymo's room, the two men cry out to one another: 'Once more, my Jeronymo', 'O my Grandison!' – and they embrace. Sir Charles's emotions cannot be contained, and he continues to shout. But as he does so, he begins to confuse Clementina and Jeronymo; they seem to merge in his speech and heart: 'CLEMENTINA! The angel CLEMENTINA! Ah, my Jeronymo!' His feelings are becoming more and more powerful, intensifying his friend's at the same time, and he cries, 'Love, love ... the dear ...' Ostensibly, he 'would have added CLEMENTINA' but grief prevents him naming her. But there is an undercurrent here quickly rising to the surface between the two men. With his feelings keyed to the highest pitch by Clementina, Sir Charles rushes to Jeronymo, whose feminization makes him a sort of substitute woman, in whose arms he is crying, 'Love, love'. He claims he 'would have added CLEMENTINA', as if she were the only object of his grief and desire; but locked in the arms of 'the tenderest of friends', with 'trembling lips', Sir Charles cannot speak her name. Clasping another person 'dear' to him, a man he loves, he finds himself on the verge of losing control – surrendering to his pent-up feelings for Clementina, and perhaps for Jeronymo, too. Whatever the original object[s] of these feelings, they are about to burst their bonds and find release in the arms of another man. Sir Charles takes the only defence possible: 'I tore myself from his embrace, and [left] with precipitation.' Faced with the perils of a supposedly immoral sexuality – homosexuality – Sir Charles flees all the way to England, to the arms of his loving Harriet.

In this climactic – or, more accurately, nearly climactic – scene, in which Sir Charles's superiority momentarily crumbles ('I would have comforted him; but wanted comfort myself'), his relationship with Jeronymo becomes a source of great peril. While on the one hand the feminization of Jeronymo distances the young man from his benefactor, making him even more subordinate, on the other hand, when the men are in such close physical and emotional contact as in this scene, it threatens to overwhelm Sir Charles's precious masculinity. To Sir Charles's dismay, their apparently innocent friendship reveals a dangerously sexual component. Consequently, he must flee from the too ardent love of 'the tenderest of friends', a love which disturbingly resembles a woman's passionate love, especially as it calls up an answering love in Sir Charles himself (whether a transference of feelings originally aroused by Clementina or a genuine response to Jeronymo, or both), a love which makes – or perhaps simply threatens to make – a foray over the blurred boundary separating fraternal from homoerotic love.

Both Sir Charles Grandison and Robert Lovelace eventually put considerable distance between themselves and their closest male friends. In Lovelace's case, however, there has been a corresponding emotional distance between Belford and himself throughout *Clarissa*. The two men follow the rules for a safe, acceptable male friendship, never really taking risks with one another. Their relationship does evolve beyond a mere rakes' companionship, but gives no indication that it could ever approach the fervency of the bond between Sir Charles and Jeronymo in *Grandison*. Because Lovelace and Belford both conform to their society's prescribed masculine role, the fondness they demonstrate for one another remains a 'manly' affection, limited by the necessary restraint that term implies.

Sir Charles and Jeronymo's friendship is fundamentally different. Modelled on a feminine ideal, and with each partner (especially Jeronymo) exhibiting some traditionally feminine traits, their relationship challenges conventional forms of masculine behaviour. In other words, like a fervent friendship between two women, it is subversive. What may have seemed a simple and straightforward extension of female friendship into the male realm proves to be a complicated, dangerous, and even explosive endeavour because it makes visible the inherent erotic element in male friendship. Because Richardson and Sir Charles remain firmly wedded to predominantly traditional conceptions of masculinity, conceptions which are inimical to uninhibited love between men, they have no choice but to reject the discovery they have made. Sir Charles abruptly retreats from his passionate relationship with Jeronymo. Thus the progression of male friendship in Richardson's three novels ends in a final regression. Sir Charles leaves Italy and returns to England to resume his position as the benevolent but unapproachable patriarch. Nevertheless, although Richardson abandons his experiment in Sir Charles, afraid of its forbidden results, he ventures a long way towards introducing a new element to eighteenth-century fiction: the passionate male friendship.

Richardson: original or learned genius?

JOCELYN HARRIS

'Original genius', a term used formerly to praise Samuel Richardson, now serves more often to condemn him. *Orator fit, poeta nascitur*, said Sidney, a tag confirmed for the eighteenth century by that unanswerable example of invention linked to educational deprivation, William Shakespeare. Richardson himself distinguished the true genius, who imitates God's works in nature, from 'the tame imitator of other poets'. Original meant to him innate, unlearned, new, Christian, modern, copious – and English.[1] But as soon as the almost synonymous phrase 'natural genius' was applied to prodigies from the lower class, an enduring condescension entered discussion of Samuel Richardson, this prolific, realistic artisan. The conclusion that Richardson, being unlearned, could only decorate his work with other men's flowers was perhaps inevitable. Alan Dugald McKillop suspected that he did not fully know the plays from which his allusions came, and A. Dwight Culler, believing that he had discovered Richardson using fifty-one quotations from Edward Bysshe's book of 'beauties', attacked the writer for not being 'scrupulous'. Dismissing Erich Poetzsche's argument that Richardson had read all the books to which he referred, Culler implicitly accused Richardson of ignorance and plagiarism. Michael E. Connaughton is even more dismissive in arguing that Richardson resorted to Bysshe 'to compensate for his deficiencies and embellish his characterization with literary allusions often beyond his understanding'. Even Richardson's biographers, T. C. Duncan Eaves and Ben D. Kimpel, assume that he was an 'untutored Natural Genius' rather than 'a learned or even well-read man', and decide, like Culler, that his reading was not extensive, important, or deep.[2] But recent discoveries about his reading and information show Richardson to be allusive on many more occasions than Connaughton's eighty-one.[3] As John Carroll has pointed out, Richardson's obvious awareness of contexts proves that he knew whole works.[4] If, as I shall show, Richardson's references are typically not isolated and ornamental, but organic, connected and controlled, he cannot have been unlearned.

Originality never really meant ignorance, even to the Romantics. When Edward Young addressed his *Conjectures upon Original Composition* to his friend Richardson, he was untroubled, as Johnson saw, that few of its ideas were new.[5] Johnson told Hester Lynch Piozzi that Richardson had 'read little', but Johnson himself was a Modern and a precursor of the Romantics, and actually wanted his friend to be 'original'.[6] Richardson did undoubtedly regret his lack of 'the very great Advantage of an Academical Education' after two years' possible attendance at the Merchant Taylors' School,[7] but his early love of reading, his habit of choosing books to print, his active spiritual life and his youthful attendance at plays made him (as Pope said of Martha Blount) with books well-bred. Such was his admiration for his own language that he recommended the establishment of university professorships for lectures in the mother tongue.[8] Fielding confidently claimed the poet's right to fatten his muse upon the rich common of the Ancients (*Tom Jones*, XII, i), but Richardson's muse was nourished by works translated into English, and by the English Moderns.

As an apprentice, Richardson bought his own candles to read into the night, and, once he prospered, his habit of choosing books to print substantially enlarged his reading.[9] His press produced a range of publications from periodicals, newspapers and the debates of the House of Commons to the works of the greatest Modern, Francis Bacon,[10] whose manifesto *The Advancement of Learning* he calls upon in an early debate of *Sir Charles Grandison*. Glancing allusions such as the distinction between *scientia* and *sapientia*, or to Bacon's important comment that languages are not knowledge itself but only vehicles to knowledge, prove his close familiarity with the work.[11] Richardson printed the proceedings of the Royal Society, whose very existence proclaimed the new ideas of progress and freedom from received opinion that characterize his heroines. James's *Medical Dictionary*, a collaborative work which began his friendship with Samuel Johnson, a part of Ephraim Chambers's *Cyclopaedia*, precursor to the great *Encyclopédie*, and the medical writings of George Cheyne, provided him with humane ideas about the treatment of mental illness for Clarissa and Clementina. By his choice of such works to print, Richardson shows himself progressive and a Modern.

William Merritt Sale's account of five hundred and sixteen books from Richardson's press, meticulous though it is, seriously underestimates what he read by way of business. If we add the manuscripts that Richardson read and rejected, the works for which he wrote prefaces and dedications as a young man, books that he edited, and those he saw through his master's press, the list would greatly swell. If we knew everything he printed it would increase again. Keith Maslen, who adds about a hundred more titles to Sale's list, argues that since Richardson's printing-house was comparable to that of his contemporary William Bowyer, he must have published not five hundred but at least three thousand books.[12] Maslen's identifying of an extra hundred and fifty ornaments in addition to Sale's one hundred and three will assist scholars to come, but for now it is intriguing to know that Richardson printed the works of Virgil in Latin and English (4 volumes, 1753) just in time to expound on the dangers of the martial ancients in *Grandison* (1753–4). He was perhaps remembering the works of Horace in Latin with the Daciers' notes (7th edition, 1727?) when he made Lovelace, about to trap his mistress at Hampstead, recall the Odes, IV, 2 with his '*Io triumphe*! Io Clarissa, sing!' (V, 56; *III, 20*). Richardson's printing of the works of Josephus translated by L'Estrange in 1733 explains likewise why he drew so readily on the story of Mariamne and Herod (III, 163, V 42; *II, 98, III, 10*), or that of Hazael and Benhadad, recalled by Lovelace from that 'half-sacred and half-profane author' (IV, 129; *II, 329*).

Although Richardson recoiled from 'the overflowings of such dirty imaginations' as that of his contemporary, Swift (*Grandison*, I, 348), he printed, in addition to Swift's *A Complete Collection of Genteel and Ingenious Conversations* (1738) and an abridged edition of *Gulliver's Travels* (1727), Volume I of his *Miscellanies* in 1733. In 1760 he printed Volume VII of Pope's works, the very letters which he had once adversely criticized to Lady Bradshaigh. Richardson printed also for John Dennis, whose ideas on sensibility, the Longinian sublime, the superiority of Christian to pagan mythology, and the need for a great author to be a good man he seems to have shared. He published, according to Maslen, not only Dennis's *Remarks on Mr. Pope's Rape of the Lock* (1728) and his *Remarks on Several Passages in the Preliminaries to the Dunciad* (1729),[13] but his *Vice and Luxury Publick Mischiefs; or, Remarks on a Book Intituled The Fable of the Bees* as well (1724). When Richardson attacked Mandeville's doctrine of self-interest by putting it in Lovelace's mouth (V, 222; *III, 145*), he turned professional work to artistic purpose.

Richardson's novels depend upon ancient and modern books, not only locally but structurally. Themes and images from Ovid's immensely popular *Metamorphoses*, which he could have read in any of several contemporary English versions, serve to shape *Clarissa*. As its printer he chose suggestively and deliberately to end the third edition's volume five, the volume containing the rape, with an ornament of Europa and the bull.[14] The visual allusion underlines the fact that sexual pursuit, cruelty, rivalry and change dominate this book with the same ruthlessness as they do Ovid's. Like Volpone wooing Celia in Jonson's play, Lovelace makes Clarissa act out Ovid's tales until they have quite run through and wearied all the fables of the Gods. Lovelace, like

Volpone, thinks thus to keep pleasure alive, but Belford warns that his fate will
be that of Circe's swinish lovers: aged rakes will whine 'thro' squeaking
organs! Their big voices turned into puling pity-begging lamentations! Their
now-offensive paws, how helpless then!'; they will lose strength and shape,
'Each grunting like the swine he had resembled in his life!' (vi, 326; iii,
483–4).

Roles chosen by protaganists reveal them. Lovelace identifies himself with
the shape-changing rapist Jupiter (i, 237; *i, 175*), and with Jupiter's imitators,
Satan, Richard III and Don Giovanni. Such analogies, together with the hints
that he is 'Vice itself' and knows Gad's Hill (v, 307, viii, 185–90; iii, *208, iv,
483–6*), remind us that Lovelace, like Falstaff, is a deceptive misleader of
youth, a *miles gloriosus*, a dangerous pretender to honour, a self-appointed
leader of an amoral gang, and ultimately like Satan a doomed buffoon.
Lovelace casts Clarissa as Arachne, maker and spider-woman (iii, 28; *i,
512*);[15] he also forces her to play Semele destroyed by Jupiter's burning rays
(iii, 163; *ii, 98*). Later she must act Philomela raped, silenced, and turned
into a nightingale, who with 'a thorn in her breast, warbles forth her
melancholy complaints against her barbarous Tereus' (vi, 225–6; *iii, 409*).
Clarissa escapes Ovid's roles only when Lovelace dreams of her assumption
into heaven (vii, 147–8; *iv, 135–6*), when Christianity triumphs over
paganism.

From classical history Richardson calls up allusions to Lucretia's rape and
suicide that set Pamela and Clarissa against a larger background of tyranny
and rebellion,[16] while a reference to Iphigenia's sacrifice controls our
response to Clementina della Porretta, bleeding by command of her cruel
family (ii, 194). Lovelace ludicrously justifies himself by the example of
Aeneas for whom Queen Dido killed herself (vii, 5; *iv, 30*), while the
martyrdom in Carthage of the noble self-sacrificing hostage, Marcus Atilius
Regulus, pierced through in a chest lined with nails, comments by contrast
upon Lovelace's self-pitying vision of himself, rolled down a hill three times
as high as the Monument in a hogshead stuck full of steel-pointed spikes (vi,
281; *iii, 451*). Lovelace plays at being Alexander, Julius Caesar, indeed all the
heroes about whom his classical, martial, masculine education has taught him,
but Richardson, who distrusted the Ancients (*Grandison*, iii, 197–8), proves
that where Lovelace's education destroys him, Clarissa's self-fashioning will
save her soul.

Against such dangerous texts from the ancient world Richardson sets
Christian works in English. He quotes frequently from the King James Bible
together with the sermons, treatises and poetry that shared its language.
Those sacred classics, the books of the Bible, were to him superior to the
pagan ones, as Belford learns in *Clarissa* (vi, 394; *iv, 8*). The oppression of

the Israelites in Babylon deepens our political understanding of Pamela's captivity (pp. 267–71), while numerous references to Job explain the torment of Clarissa, tried simply for being blest. When her false comforters Polly and Sally rejoice at her wretchedness in prison, Clarissa's Bible opens naturally at the Book of Job (vi, 265; *iii, 439*). References to the Song of Solomon similarly underline the pathos of Clementina della Porretta in *Grandison*. Well may Clementina copy out a passage of it (ii, 247), for like her Biblical predecessor she is sick of love, wanders restlessly about to find her lover, suffers persecution and urges her lover to find another woman. To this powerfully allusive representation Richardson adds attributes from several other betrayed women, Iphigenia, Dido, Eloisa, Ophelia (ii, 524), and Henrietta Maria (ii, 219). Characteristically he uses allusive reference to complicate and confirm a type.

The story of Adam and Eve, as told in Genesis and retold by Milton, is important in all three of Richardson's novels. Pamela's recognition that Mr B. only *looks* like Lucifer allows her to hope that they can revert to a happy Golden Age.[17] John Carroll and Gillian Beer[18] perceive how vitalizing *Paradise Lost* is to *Clarissa* when the Satanic Lovelace leads a demonic gang, disguises himself, spies, envies, tempts Clarissa to disobey, or bursts upon her at Hampstead like Satan touched by Ithuriel's spear. He even quotes Milton's lines himself (v, 83; *iii, 41*). Like Satan begetting a spawn of serpents upon his daughter Sin, Lovelace works through the brood of dragon and serpents, Mother Si*n*clair and her daughter-whores, whom he himself seduced (vi, 241; *iii, 421*). At the same time he is Satan's royal son, Death, who in Clarissa's dream stabs her to her heart, tumbling her into 'a deep grave ready dug, among two or three half-dissolved carcasses; throwing in the dirt and earth upon me with his hands, and trampling it down with his feet' (ii, 264; *i, 433*). But with another merging typical of Richardson, Lovelace also plays a kind of Adam when he and Clarissa recriminate 'like the first pair' (iii, 15; *i, 502*). Clarissa, driven out of her garden paradise, looks back like Eve, and a brandished sword prevents her, like our first mother, from ever returning (ii, 333–4; *i, 484–6*). Her father's thundered curse on her 'prohibited correspondence' equates Clarissa's forbidden letters and loveless (Lovelace) rape with Eve's defiance and lust. No wonder that Clarissa feels her father's curse so keenly.

The English Adam, Sir Charles Grandison, offers a happier retelling of Genesis. Signs of Eden at Grandison Hall, where the very fruit trees copy Paradise (iii, 273), promise a pre-lapsarian harmony for Sir Charles and his Harriet Byron. As Harriet, his second Eve, is quick to point out, Sir Charles has dallied with a 'fallen' Eve, Clementina, without sharing in her transgression (ii, 609). When Sir Charles instructed Clementina in the garden, the text was *Paradise Lost*. 'What happy times were those, when I was innocent, and was learning English!', she says (II, 144, 482). Sir Charles himself, who inherits the Divine Right that descends from God to kings to all men, imitates Christ in scenes such as the forgiveness of the woman taken in adultery (I, 365). Here as elsewhere Richardson draws on sacred forms to inform his domestic scenes.

Among more secular English philosophical works, Richardson seems especially familiar with John Locke. He quotes and comments upon lengthy portions of Locke's *Education* in *Pamela II* to develop striking analogies between a swaddled child 'pinn'd and fetter'd down' and a woman, who, once she has broken into notice 'in spite of her narrow Education', finds her genius 'immediately tamed by trifling Imployments' (IV, 320). George Eliot seems to have seized on this image for her own clever woman Dorothea Brooke, 'struggling in the bands of a narrow teaching', who is hemmed in by social life, in *Middlemarch* (ch. 3). To explore the relations between Mr B. and Pamela, and Lovelace and Clarissa, Richardson turned to Locke's political vocabulary of monarch, subject, birthright, usurpation, tyranny and conquest. Concepts about the right to revolt and the supremacy of law even over kings seem to derive from Locke's *Two Treatises of Government*. Mr B., for instance, finally admits law's ultimate rule over kings and queens, using the analogy of the ace's power over court cards (pp. 335–6), and Anna Howe applies the important argument of the *Two Treatises* about the need to separate executive and legislative power (II, ch.xii) to her own domestic sphere (II, 140; *I, 340–1*).

Restoration drama had of course already called upon such political models as Locke's to clarify relations between the sexes. So too had the well-known early feminist, Mary Astell, who, as she lay dying, meditated upon a coffin in her bedchamber after a life of modesty, piety, self-disciplined abstinence and learning very like Clarissa's, as it is described by Anna after her friend's death (VIII, letter 49; *IV, letter 168*). As A. H. Upham suggested long ago, Astell's pioneering essays on women's education and on marriage may well have influenced Richardson. For Astell, as for Clarissa, learning was spiritual and moral, not classical and merely pedantic; Astell corresponded with divines as Clarissa did in youth (VIII, 202–3; *IV, 495*), and her intense intellectual friendship with Lady Elizabeth Hastings was to her as much a forecast of heavenly love as Clarissa's with Anne Howe. Astell's shrewd question, 'If absolute Sovereignty be not necessary in a State, how comes it to be so in a Family?',[19] summarizes an issue central to *Clarissa*, the masculine divine right to power over women that is handed down from God to Adam to kings to all men, whether fathers, brothers, or husbands. Astell proposed a life of mind in an idealized Protestant nunnery such as Richardson praised in

Grandison (III, 9) as an alternative to the marriages in which women were never equal. Clarissa, a learned lady like Astell, also recognizes that a clever and virtuous woman was unlikely to find happiness in marriage (I, 207–8; *I, 153*, for instance), and regrets the loss of such refuges as nunneries (I, 84; *I, 62*). Such parallels to Astell in Richardson's themes and characterization, suggest considerable sympathy with Astell's ideas.

Richardson must have read poetry as well as prose. He develops his image patterns poetically, and Diderot was right to call him 'poète'. Lovelace writes verses to his Stella (III, 282; *II, 188*) as did his courtly predecessor Sir Philip Sidney, whose sonnets Richardson published in 1724. When Lovelace, that other star-loving Astrophil, checks his hat for scorched lace, 'supposing it had brushed down a star' (III, 32; *I, 515*), he remembers the exulting lover's phrase, 'Knock at a Starre with my exalted Head' from Robert Herrick's 'The bad season makes the Poet sad'. This idea of Clarissa as a star knocked down to earth combines with Pope's image of hair-as-star in 'The Rape of the Lock' to recreate Clarissa as a comet with dazzling streaming hair, who bursts fatally, eccentrically, out of her proper sphere (III, 105; *II, 54*). Astronomical imagery controls the scene in which Lovelace dreams of Clarissa's 'azure robe (all stuck thick with stars of embossed silver)' (VII, 148; *IV, 136*), an idea derived from Herrick's 'Azure Robe' like a celestial canopy 'pounc't with Stars' in 'Julia's Petticoat'. The swift merging of secular and religious interpretations reveals that though Lovelace believed Clarissa to be a conventional star-like mistress, her mind was set elsewhere. Lovelace's terrible lament once he has lost Clarissa, his pole-star and the world's microcosm, recalls such poetic visions of apocalyptic darkness as Rochester's triumph of Nothing over Existence, Donne's 'Nocturnall Upon S. Lucies Day', Milton's 'Universal Blanc / Of Natures works to mee expung'd and rais'd' from *Paradise Lost* (III, 48–9), or the ending of *The Dunciad*. 'Having lost her', writes Lovelace, 'my whole Soul is a blank: The whole Creation round me, the Elements above, beneath, and everything I *behold* (for nothing can I *enjoy*), are a blank without her!' (VI, 96; *III, 388*).

Richardson draws upon narratives, works of philosophy and controversy, and a multitude of poets and poems for complex and often openly signalled allusions. Yet the greatest influence upon his writing, upon plot and structure and individual scenes and characters, is always the drama. Richardson's highly dramatic sense has often been remarked upon, and it is noticeable how the novels themselves deploy ideas of play-acting and re-enacting and deceiving. Richardson printed a number of stage plays and refers to a number specifically, but we will never know exactly which plays he saw during his theatre-going years. He had several theatrical friends, and must have known about the players. Miss Betterton, a former mistress of Lovelace, could have been named in memory of Thomas Betterton (1635–1710), the greatest English actor between Burbage and Garrick. It was Betterton who created the part of Don John in Thomas Shadwell's *The Libertine* in 1675, a play from which, as we shall see, a significant part of Lovelace's character seems to have been drawn.

Betterton's leading lady, Anne Bracegirdle, may have contributed similarly to the character of Clarissa. Chaste and charitable, she retired at the height of her powers in 1707, and appeared again only for Betterton's splendid benefit in 1709. Although her virtue was often the subject of scurrilous gossip, she and her mother fought off an abduction by Captain Richard Hill and Lord Mohun, and her resistance to a real Lord Lovelace was rewarded by a purse of eight hundred guineas. Richardson's friend Colley Cibber was still visiting Anne Bracegirdle in 1742, and she died in 1748, the year *Clarissa* was published. Congreve wrote for her, and she played many of the roles 'played' also by Clarissa, including Millamant, Isabella in Gildon's version of *Measure for Measure*, Cordelia in Tate's *Lear*, and Ophelia in Shakespeare's *Hamlet*.[20] When Richardson, himself an apprentice from 1706 to 1713, wrote in the *Apprentice's Vade Mecum*, 'This or that Part of an applauded Actor will perpetually take up [the theatre-goer's] Attention, and he will be desirous of seeing him shine in others, and so will want to trace one Player or other thro' every Scene, and every Season', he may have remembered the brilliant career of Anne Bracegirdle, a woman who in life and on stage often seems to anticipate Clarissa.

Clarissa's world as much as Bracegirdle's is a series of emblematic roles. Just as Lovelace plays Satan, Death *and* fallen Adam all at once, Clarissa's roles too are multiple. They give way each to each, they dissolve into each other to display and explore the character. References to the heroines of Shakespeare cluster around her.[21] Once a family feud precipitates Clarissa's troubles we know that, like Juliet, she will be destroyed by feuds not of her own making; whenever she calls on the law, Portia in *The Merchant of Venice* lends her a sisterly authority; when she, who yearned to be a nun, stands against Lovelace's ugly reinforcement of sex by power, she is Isabella outraged by the world's law in *Measure for Measure*; when in the mad scene she quotes from *Hamlet*, the conscious identification with Ophelia deepens our understanding of her sexual vulnerability, pathos and despair. Oppressed by property and a patriarchal father, she is Cordelia the third child when her words of love are not believed; she is Hermia lost for ever to Anna, who 'loved the dear creature, as never woman loved another' (VIII, 80; *IV, 403*). Like 'absolute Marina', the paragon of a woman in *Pericles*, Clarissa preaches and practises virtue even when placed in a brothel. If Marina's enemies plot there to 'crack the glass of her virginity', the cracked looking-glass in Clarissa's prison room reminds us pointedly of the rape (VI, 273; *III, 445*). Richardson draws especially upon such constant and suffering heroines as Cordelia, Marina and Viola: Harriet Byron explains herself as Patience on a monument, smiling at grief (II, 158). But whenever Richardson's female characters overcome the limitations of their sex by intelligence and wit, whenever they fence as boldly as Rosalind or Beatrice with their suitors, tongues and pens empower them in a world that belongs to men. Richardson's women, that is, tell tales to save their lives.

Lovelace too attempts numerous different roles. When Clarissa calls him 'a perfect Proteus' (III, 141; *II, 82*) she casts about him the mantles of two Proteuses, the changeable water-god in Homer and the reformed villain in *Two Gentlemen of Verona*. If Shakespeare's Proteus first adores a twinkling star, then worships a celestial sun (II, vi), Lovelace falls in love with 'a Sun' among 'faint twinklers' (I, 170; *I, 125*) in an image that enlarges his poetic symbolizing of Clarissa as star, sun and comet. Silvia, called like Clarissa 'sullen', 'peevish', 'froward', 'proud', 'disobedient' and 'stubborn' for not marrying the suitor her father chooses, elopes with Valentine. When the false, perjured Proteus courts her with flattery, she like Clarissa will not believe his oaths, and tears his paper of love in two (IV, iv). The repentance of Shakespeare's villain-hero is too sudden: more realistically, repentance does not last in Lovelace. Again, when Lovelace bends Richard III's words to his own uses, we know he is truly to be feared (VI, 241; *III, 421*); when he cannot sleep he recalls the murderous Macbeth (V, 330; *III, 225*). When he rehearses his players, sets up plays within plays to catch his queen, allows conscience to make a coward of him, confides in his uncomprehending friend or quarrels with Clarissa's brother over the possession of her body, he takes on the very lineaments of Hamlet. Such fatal roles, carelessly and thoughtlessly entered into, pursue him to bitter ends.

Lovelace is Dionysiac, Venerean, Faustian in his boundless wants and energies, a man sold to Satan with his contract about to run out (V, 310; *III, 210*). If Richardson thought here of Marlowe's Faust, he may also have recalled Webster's *Duchess of Malfi*, a play in which another proud woman is tortured by being placed among the mad like the Lady in *Comus*, like Clarissa in the brothel. Bosola's idea that 'we are merely the stars' tennis-balls, struck and bandied / Which way please them' (V, iv), recurs in Pamela's complaint that she is 'a mere Tennis-ball of Fortune!' (p. 212), and in Anna's that Clarissa is made 'the tennis-ball of two violent spirits' (III, 187; *II, 116*). Richardson also calls on Webster's image of the orange-tree to illustrate the difference in women's maturity (*Grandison*, II, 30).[22] On these and other occasions, as when Lady Davers accuses Pamela of wanting to be a fine lady Would-be, from Jonson's *Volpone* (p. 321), or when hints of that Faustian epitome of lust from Jonson's *Alchemist*, Sir Epicure Mammon, exemplify Lovelace's cruelty (IV, 16–18; *II, 248*), Richardson invites us to enlarge our understanding of his novel by recalling knowledge of our own.

Richardson combines the mordant quality of Jacobean drama with the satire of Gay's mock-epic and the sexual knowingness, the power-struggles of Restoratian comedy. Lovelace's cynical underworld with its conflicts and betrayals looks back to Macheath's in *The Beggar's Opera*,[23] and Richardson attacks the sordid avarice of Solmes in words very much like Matt of the Mint's (II, 10; *I, 244*, for instance). Macheath and Lovelace both justify their misdeeds by the examples of great men, and both blame restrictive laws for forcing them into crime. If Macheath boasts of the leadership of his gang, creates all the whores in Drury Lane, and lives under the shadow of the fatal tree, Lovelace the gang-leader and whore-maker imagines himself parading to the gallows amid an admiring multitude, there to be reprieved like Macheath at the last moment. Lovelace's fantastic double vision of himself as malefactor and Lord Mayor seems also to look back to Gay's hint that the procession makes the man, an idea elaborated in the last plates of Hogarth's *The Idle and Industrious Apprentices*. Richardson's black and white street scenes, crowded with caricature and swarming with the movement of 'the pendent, clinging throngs of spectators, with their waving heads rolling to and fro from house-tops to house-bottoms and street-ways', provide precise verbal equivalents for Hogarth's detail. Richardson actually describes the act of 'reading' necessary to comprehend Hogarth in his 'let us look down, look up, look round, which way we will, we shall see all the doors, the shops, the windows, the sign-irons and balconies (garrets, gutters, and chimney-tops included) all white-capt, black-hooded, and periwigg'd, or crop-ear'd up by the *Immobile Vulgus*' (IV, 258–9; *II, 423–4*). He asks us in effect to use Hogarth's scene to enlarge Gay's.

If Lovelace plays numerous dramatic roles, so too does Clarissa, and not only the Belvidera from *Venice Preserv'd* with whom Lovelace wants to identify her. A multiplicity of echoes proves Richardson's familiarity not only with Shakespearian and Jacobean plays, but with lighter plays by Etherege, Congreve and Farquhar. When Clarissa, superior in real knowledge and education to most men, rejects Solmes for his illiteracy and brutish inability to teach her (II, 67; *I, 287*), she sounds like Millamant in Congreve's *The Way of the World*. Congreve's proviso scene provides additional ammunition to Pamela, Anna Howe, Clarissa and Charlotte Grandison in their resistance against dwindling into wives. Farquhar's Mrs Sullen also helps Charlotte. If Mrs Sullen calls herself a mutinous captive under the power of her cruel general of a husband in *The Beaux' Stratagem* (III, iii), Charlotte describes her relationship with her husband Lord G. thus, 'One struggle for my dying liberty, my dear! – The success of one pitched battle will decide which is to be the general, which the subaltern, for the rest of the campaign. To *dare* to be sullen already!' (II, 359–60). But Charlotte Grandison, married like Mrs Sullen to a man she considers foolish, will learn to love him at last.

Richardson is most fascinated by two of the darker comedies of the Restoration stage, Wycherley's *The Country Wife* and Shadwell's *The Libertine. The Country Wife*, mentioned in Richardson's *Apprentice's Vade Mecum*, shadows all three novels. The country girl Pamela who learns quick-wittedness in self-defence often looks like Margery Pinchwife. Mr B. boldly kisses her in the pretence that she is her own pretty sister when she dresses in country clothes (p. 61); Horner had just as swiftly perceived Margery's disguise as her own brother, and kissed the sweet little gentleman, fancying 'he kissed my fine sister'. In *Clarissa*, however, Richardson's use of the play is a meditation on a theme. Lovelace, like Horner, treats all the Hampstead women 'with so much freedom before one another's faces, that in policy they shall keep each other's counsel'. Like Wycherley's pretended prudes, they will share one lover – himself – and so 'knit an indissoluble band of union and friendship between three women' (V, 318; *III, 217*). Lovelace gloats that his ruses are more clever than 'Horner's in the Country Wife' (VII, 20; *IV, 42*), but where Horner's impotence is feigned, Lovelace's will be real. He becomes not a triumphant Horner but an obsessed Pinchwife, insanely seeking out hints of cuckoldry. Just as the inn-signs of 'The Bull's Head, the Ram's Head, and the Stag's Head' become 'every husband's proper sign' to Pinchwife, so too the '*three crooked horns*, smartly top-knotted with ribbands' in the arms of the marriage licence predict deception, cuckoldry and marriage warfare to Lovelace (V, 270; *III, 180*). Belford comments, 'we do but hang out a Sign, in our dress, of what we have in the Shop of our Minds', adding, 'What sort of a Sign must thou hang out, wert thou obliged to give us a clear idea by it of the furniture of *thy* mind?' (VI, 403; *IV, 14*). Lovelace may pride himself on being a Horner, but he is a Pinchwife, cuckolded by Death.

From Shadwell's *The Libertine* (1675), a terrifyingly violent, nihilistic and yet popular version of the story of Don Giovanni, the first in English, Richardson draws some of his darkest scenes.[24] Lovelace derives much of his demonically anarchic defiance of conscience and man's law from Shadwell's Don John, together with his leadership of a criminal gang and his boast of multiple rapes. Don John's father, who provokingly preached 'his sensless Morals' and 'old dull foolish stuff against my pleasure', is put to death at the command of his son, who after murdering the Governor of Seville, kills Maria's lover at the garden gate before seducing her by stratagem and killing her brother. Lovelace, who longs to smother Lord M. (IV, 129; *II, 329*), jeers similarly at his uncle's advice and prudential 'bead-roll of proverbs'. Lovelace duels with Clarissa's brother, and threatens 'two or three murders' at the garden gate when he abducts her (II, 333; *1, 484*). Don John betrays Leonora with a 'solemn Contract' of marriage; Clarissa is deceived by the marriage-licence that Lovelace procures before the rape.

Obsessional sexual pursuit characterizes both Don John and Lovelace. Don John's firing of the nunnery to flush out the nuns and rape them looks forward to Lovelace's firing of the brothel to force out Clarissa and ravish her (IV, letter 59; *II, letter 126*), and in muttering 'something of *ice*' when Clarissa spurns him (IV, 105; *II, 312*), Lovelace seems to refer back to Don John's vow to thaw a woman 'if she were Ice'. But 'What an excellent thing is a Woman before Enjoyment, and how insipid after it', says Don John: Lovelace turns the tag his own way when he acknowledges after the rape, 'Nor did thy Lovelace know what it was to be gloomy, till he had completed his wishes upon the most charming creature in the world' (V, 300; *III, 203*). Although Don John asserts 'there's ne'er a *Lucrece* now a-days, the Sex has learnt Wit since', he is indeed a 'very *Tarquin*'. When the Fourth Woman stabs herself to prevent ravishment, which she calls the 'Unheard of villainy!', the Don is startled into remarking, 'I ne'r thought this had been in thee'. Lovelace may think that Clarissa has 'no Lucretia-like vengeance upon herself in her thought' (V, 323; *III, 220*), but she has already astonished him by threatening to stab herself and stave off what she calls 'a treatment so disgraceful and villainous' (IV, 368; *II, 502*).

Lovelace's desire for variety – he wants to play 'Grand Signor' to Anna Howe and Clarissa (IV, 183; *II, 369*), and allows the whores to cling possessively to him – is prefigured by Shadwell's 'inundation of Strumpets' who pull his '*grand Signior*' of a villain-hero from one to the other and claim him as their husband. Lovelace's scheme to change partners every Valentine's Day like the birds (V, 270–5; *III, 181–4*) is anticipated in the similar appeal of Shadwell's libertine to natural law and liberty:

> Since Liberty, Nature for all has design'd,
> A Pox on the Fool who to one is confin'd.
> All Creatures besides,
> When they please change their Brides ...

In one scene, Shadwell's hero plans to 'hire a Vessel and we'll all to Sea together to seek a refuge, and a new Scene of pleasure': Lovelace plans in a striking parallel fantasy to 'hire a little trim vessel, which shall sail a pleasuring'. Shadwell's blackly comic tale of a man (who cannot swim) threatened with being thrown murderously overboard ends in rape, and so closely resembles Lovelace's extraordinarily detailed plot to kidnap Anna Howe, her mother and the maidservant on the way to the Isle of Wight, rape them, and push Hickman overboard, 'paddling, pawing, and dashing, like a frighted mongrel' because 'he never ventured to learn to swim'. Even if caught for these 'three such enormous Rapes', Lovelace believes he would go free. Richardson restored the passage from the manuscript to the third edition (IV, letter 42; *II, letter 109*) deliberately to underscore the villainy that sends Lovelace to hell just like his predecessor, for all that he distinctly pronounces the words 'LET THIS EXPIATE!' As Don John dies, the ghosts of those he has murdered rise up against him: Lovelace in his delirium seems to see 'some frightful Spectre', and several times cries out 'Take her away! Take her away!' (VIII, 249; *IV, 530*). To understand Richardson's use of Shadwell, indeed of the whole Don Giovanni tradition, is to grasp the scale of his intentions for Lovelace. Romantic readings must be checked if Lovelace, like Don John, represents reason and natural law, and if he too falls defeated by eternal providence.

In *The Libertine* Shadwell deliberately looks back to a real Don John, John Wilmot Earl of Rochester. The poet and playwright Rochester, who in 'To the Postboy' defiantly imagined himself bound for hell after a life of swilling, swearing and swiving, must have acknowledged in *The Libertine* aspects of his own Hobbesian, hedonistic, promiscuous and violent self. The play certainly improved his opinion of Shadwell. But Richardson's characterization of Lovelace seems also to have been inspired by Rochester's own words, as Doody observes.[25] Recurrent animal images of Lovelace as a preying bird and of Clarissa as an 'ensnared Volatile' tamed by confinement (IV, 14; *II, 245–7*) probably develop from Shadwell's image of 'ravenous Bird of prey' for Don John, and birds 'made tame by being cag'd' for women, while the lament in Shadwell's play that no savage beast provoked by hunger and natural rage could be so cruel as Don John seems also to be echoed by Clarissa's discovery that the ravagers of the forest, the kites, hawks and vultures, 'all these beasts and birds of prey were outdone in treacherous cruelty by MAN!', vile man, 'who, infinitely less excusable than those, destroys thro' wantonness and sport what those only destroy through hunger and necessity!' (VIII, 210; *IV, 501*). Clarissa's words are even closer to Rochester's own description of the gratuitous treachery of humans in 'A Satyr against Reason and Mankind', written contemporaneously with Shadwell's *Libertine*:

> Which is the basest *Creature Man*, or *Beast*?
> *Birds*, feed on *Birds*, *Beasts*, on each other prey,
> But Savage *Man* alone, does *Man*, betray;
> Prest by necessity, they Kill for Food,
> *Man*, undoes *Man*, to do himself no good.
> With Teeth, and Claws, by Nature arm'd they hunt,
> Nature's allowance, to supply their want.

But *Man*, with smiles, embraces, Friendships, praise,
Unhumanely his Fellows life betrays;
With voluntary pains, works his distress,
Not through necessity, but wantonness.

It seems likely, therefore, that Richardson worked from both versions of the idea, Shadwell's and Rochester's.

Rochester also inspired Etherege's creation of Dorimant in *The Man of Mode; or, Sir Fopling Flutter* (1676), a play known to Richardson (*Grandison*, I, 99). The half-angelic, half-demonic Dorimant, the most famous stage rake of the time, could in turn have provided Lovelace with his trick of quoting Waller as well as with more conventional rakish attributes. But just as Rochester's own impersonations, self-projections, acting, producing, dramatizing, and training of the actress Mrs Barry prefigure the private theatricals of that exuberant actor, dramatist and producer Lovelace, it is the Rochester of the poems and letters who anticipates Lovelace in his wit, energy, satiric raillery, attractiveness, cruelty and sexual anxieties, above all in his restless longing for a haven in a world of knaves and fools. Richardson, by brooding on Rochester, Shadwell and Etherege all together, may thus have been inspired to draw his most complex and exhilarating character, Robert Lovelace.

Such frequent and resonant allusions are proofs of Richardson's wideranging intertextuality. If modern critical theory encourages readers to interpret texts in the light of their own knowledge and experience, authors should surely enjoy the same licence to work from memories which to some extent constrain our subjective response. Whenever Richardson refers to another work, that work briefly or extensively illuminates his own. Whenever his new work absorbs the implications or emotional charge of the old, his mind may be revealed. Allusion suggests intention, allusion appeals to the reader, allusion deepens the authority of the moment and hints with the doubleness of poetry at other interpretations. Richardson's allusions are not random. They link with one another to accumulate a meaning.

Any theory about Richardson's creativity that depends upon an assumption of his ignorance will not do. It is part of Lovelace's character that he runs through other texts to flex imaginative skills, seeing himself as Shakespearian villains, Miltonic devils, Cavalier poets and Restoration rakes all in turn. Lovelace creates a stage within Richardson's dramatic text on which to strut various roles, only to have other roles forced upon him by the author. Clarissa in a different fashion recollects Biblical and dramatic forerunners to help her comprehend. Richardson's use of Homer to portray Lovelace as Proteus in a winding chase of a desperately altering Clarissa, or his layering of themes of power, change, and deception by interwoven reference to Jupiter, Satan, Faust, Falstaff, Macheath and Don John, all show him thoroughly conversant with contexts. His allusions are rarely casual, but call up entire works to explain and express his meaning. They accumulate significance by expanding reference, they 'reverberate' (in Carroll's word) throughout the whole, they create patterns that are almost metaphorical.

Books, even Richardson's, are made to a significant extent out of other books. Every great new artist is diachronic as well as synchronic, moving easily among other writers' 'languages' in order to make new wholes.[26] Hester Lynch Piozzi knew exactly how Richardson's originality relied upon his reading when she explained in a homely image from Mr Thrale's brewery, 'what he did read never forsook a memory that was not contented with retaining, but fermented all that fell into it, and made a new creation from the fertility of its own rich mind'.[27] Texts fermenting with other texts do indeed give rise to new texts, in receptive minds. Samuel Richardson took his learning from the classics in English and the English classics, but the richness of his fertile invention was his alone.

12

'A Young, a Richardson, or a Johnson': lines of cultural force in the age of Richardson

PAT ROGERS

There is a moment well into the second half of Charlotte Lennox's novel *The Female Quixote* (1752) which repays attention. Hardly any passage in early fiction could be more expressive of alien critical standards, except perhaps to a modern admirer of Young such as the late Barbara Pym.[1] Arabella's suitor Mr Glanville is speaking of the credentials required of a critic:

Nay, then, interrupted Mr *Glanville*, you are qualified for a Critic at the *Bedford* Coffee-house; where, with the rest of your Brothers, Demy-wits, you may sit in Judgment upon the Productions of a *Young*, a *Richardson*, or a *Johnson*. Rail with premeditated Malice at the *Rambler*; and, for a want of Faults, turn even its inimitable Beauties into Ridicule... (VI, ch. 11)

This triumvirate of true wits reads today like a deliberate mismatch; we easily forget that two or three generations ago, Richardson's name would have seemed almost as incongruous as that of Young, linked on such terms of easy quality with Samuel Johnson. Just how remote we are from the standards of the middle of the eighteenth century will be even more apparent if we consider a letter which has recently surfaced, in which Richardson requests Charlotte Lennox to omit his name as 'utterly unworthy of a Rank, or Mention with the two others'.[2] Even if we may suspect a measure of the novelist's habitual false modesty, it is not a wholly ridiculous demurral in the context of 1752. It is well known that Richardson assisted the author of *The Female Quixote*, as did Johnson, and that he did so once more in the case of Young's *Conjectures on Original Composition* (1759). These are not just chance collisions; rather they form part of a large pattern, a shifting procession of convergence and divergence. One way of understanding Richardson more fully is to set him opposite not just Johnson (an exercise that has been briefly attempted on a number of occasions), nor even opposite Young alone – but alongside *both* men, as Lennox would implicitly advise us to proceed.

The remarkable characters who were at Tunbridge Wells with Richardson in 1748, from a drawing in his possession with references in his own writing.

1748 Aug: 4 Mr. Cibber (Colley)   8 Miss Chudley (Maid of Kingston)   12 Dutch: of Norfolk   16 The Baron (A German Gamester)   19 Miss Onslow
1. Dr. Johnson   5 Mr. Garrick   9 Mr. Pitt (First of Chatham)   13 M. de Sordis   17 Anonyma (Mr. Richardson)   20 Mrs. Selwin (his sister)
2. Bp: of Salisbury (Gilbert) 6 Mrs. Frasi (the Singer) 10 Mr. O. Selys (The Speaker)   14 Coll: Lincoln   18 Mr. Onslow   21 Mr. Cibber
3. Ld. Harcourt   7 Mr. Nash   11 Ld. Powis   15 Mr. Lyttelton, afterwards 22 Coppin the Valet
                                                                                              Lord Lyttelton   25 The Woman of the Well

Printed 20th Nov 1814 for Richard Phillips No. 8 New Bridge Street

15 'The remarkable characters who were at Tunbridge Wells with Richardson in 1748, from a drawing in
    his possession with references in his own writing': frontispiece to vol. III of *The Correspondence of Samuel*

In order to carry out this exercise, this essay will be divided into the statutory three parts. First, I shall look at one diagrammatic display of mid-century cultural values, in the shape of a print featuring Richardson and used to illustrate his collected correspondence. Secondly, the relations of Richardson and Young, as gauged principally by their surviving letters, will be explored, with some effort made to trace their interaction within a wider literary field of forces. Finally, it will be necessary to examine more inward aspects of their activity as writers, and in particular to say something of their 'originality', obviously a key notion in the third quarter of the eighteenth century. Throughout the essay Johnson will be intermittently present, as a *tertium quid*, as a control, and as a spectral other: whilst the long-consecrated 'Age of Johnson' evolves, we shall be given more pointers by Richardson and Young than by Johnson concerning the shifts in taste, in authority, and in reputation, which were ushering in a new set of values.

The frontispiece to the third volume of Richardson's correspondence, in the edition by Anna Laetitia Barbauld, has received very little notice, especially in recent scholarship, yet it is a truly remarkable item from several points of view.[3] As figure 15 reveals, it bears an editorial caption, 'The remarkable characters who were at Tunbridge Wells with Richardson in 1748, from a drawing in his possession with references in his own writing'. The hand-writing of the key at the foot does indeed closely resemble that of Richardson at this stage of his career. Since Mrs Barbauld had access to so many genuine items from his hand, it seems unlikely either that she should have been deceived by a forger, or prone to connive in a fabrication. Mrs Barbauld must have then thought it genuine, and so presumably did Richardson, if he went to the trouble of annotating it. In saying 'genuine', I do not mean that the illustration necessarily provides a direct firsthand picture of real events; it is far more likely to represent an imaginative reconstruction, executed by an artist at some distance from the supposed scene. We need not assume that all the individuals were actually in Tunbridge on any given day. But we can reasonably infer that all were, or were expected to be, in Tunbridge during the course of that season. In some cases, we can establish that this was actually the fact: Richardson happens to be one such individual. One of the more puzzling inclusions is the figure on the far left, the first-named on the key as 'Dr. Johnson'. This is very probably not Samuel Johnson, for reasons which will emerge, though he *could* perfectly well have been present in such an imaginary gallery, if we attach weight to one kind of evidence.

But if instead we begin to consider who is not present, rather than who is, then the absence of Edward Young is a notable feature of the print. In sheer literal fact he was probably not there in that year, though this was a break with habit. But more interesting is what can be viewed as the symbolic presence or absence of key cultural figures. Beau Nash, Colley Cibber, David Garrick, George Lyttelton, William Pitt the Elder, the Duchess of Kingston and Speaker Onslow are all present and correct, together with a duchess, a bishop and a 'German Gamester' (the editorial description, not Richardson's). To make sense of these data is to do more than supply a few ticks and crosses in the margin of a social almanac. It is to see mid-century English culture in full display, and if we look for the tracks of Richardson, Johnson and Young we should be able to learn a little more of what linked these men and what separated them: to see them more in the cultural round against a clearer historical background.

Taking these three separate cases in turn, and reserving Richardson until last, we can make some assessment of their eligibility in Tunbridge terms. Young is the simplest to assess.[4] He began his annual visits to Tunbridge Wells in the later 1730s, when he was already well established as rector of Welwyn. This emerges from a letter of 1747, when he writes to the Duchess of Portland, 'My schemes are quite broken, I can not go to Tunbridge tho a ten years Habit, & my Health require it.'[5] The last claim is doubtless seriously made, for Young was a noted valetudinarian, despite the fact that he survived to the age of eighty-one. His first well-documented sojourn in Tunbridge took place in 1740, when he suffered from a prolonged 'fever' which he explicitly linked to the death of 'a friend' (actually his wife) some months earlier. Thereafter Young makes regular reports on his health during his visits to Tunbridge, of which he observed to the Duchess, 'There are but Two Distempers, & Those very different, yt bring People to this place: Either Redundancy, or Want of Spirits.'[6] Young clearly identified with the sufferers from 'Want of Spirits', and he added ironically that 'The virtue of ye Water is yet got no Higher than my Fingers ends, wh[ich] enables me to write.' In 1745 he opened a letter to Richardson himself with the words, 'I bless God I am much better, and am sorry you are not at leisure to be well by coming to these waters. Our disorders are of the same kind.' The reference is obviously to a kind of nervous prostration, and this shared martyrdom to a species of the English malady was one of the factors which brought them together.[7] Young's visits continued until almost the end of his life; in 1763, he told the Duchess, 'My want of Rest, & Appetite, has forced me to this Place, where I propose, God willing, to continue the remainder of the season, tho hitherto I have recd no benefit.'[8]

There is a clear parallel between Young's therapeutic use of poetry in *Night Thoughts* and his trips in search of health to the spa; his most regular attendance at Tunbridge occurred in the period when he was composing his most famous work. In 1742 he went down to Kent soon after the initial success of *The Complaint*, and in a letter to the Duchess describes reading the company there in a protracted metaphor uniting books and human kind. In fact this letter makes explicit the task of reading 'ye general Contents of this Human Folio' as equivalent to that of deciphering a 'Portrait of Human nature.'[9] To attempt to see a like significance in the Barbauld illustration of Tunbridge is thus to embark on an endeavour Young would have fully understood. He speaks in the same letter of his attempts to gain the patronage of the Archbishop of Canterbury and the Duke of Newcastle. This points to the second function of Young's visits. They were designed to facilitate contacts with people whose interest he was seeking in his unsuccessful quest for preferment; as, indeed, in some measure were the successive instalments of *Night Thoughts* with their prominent dedications to persons of consequence – prominent, that is, even by the standards of the age. The two considerations raised in this paragraph indicate that the poet's time spent in Tunbridge served some exactly comparable functions to his literary work itself.

Young, then, may be regarded as a regular visitor to Tunbridge, one who more often than not would have qualified for depiction in the print.[10] Indeed the print puts on display the very company which Young most wished to keep. The entrée he had gained by his literary eminence in the wake of *Night Thoughts* made him a natural subject for inclusion in this particular social register.

The case is totally different with Johnson. His absence would not be inadvertent but, as it were, structural. We must first examine the possibility that the figure labelled Johnson may indeed represent the celebrated Samuel Johnson. The most significant piece of evidence was pointed out by the editors of Boswell: 'There can be no doubt that the figure marked by Richardson as Dr Johnson is not our Samuel Johnson, who did not receive a doctor's degree till more than four years after Richardson's death.'[11] Richardson's gloss clearly reads 'Dr. Johnson', and it is difficult to do anything about that awkward fact. Moreover, the figure does not resemble Johnson in physical appearance, whereas the diminutive Garrick, the pudgy Richardson, and the beanpole Lyttelton are all depicted with enough accuracy to be recognizably themselves. Nor does the woman on the other side of the print, identified by Richardson as 'Mrs. Johnson' (the editor adds, 'The Drs Wife') look much like Tetty, so far as we can get a sharp image of her appearance.[12] The second figure from the left, next to 'Johnson', is Dr John Gilbert, a future Archbishop of York; we might assume that this presence increases the likelihood of an ecclesiastical connection.

It happens that the scene dates from a year where it is difficult to trace the celebrated Samuel Johnson. Not a single letter survives from 1748, and Boswell has no separate entry in his narrative. What we do know is that his

wife's health had begun to deteriorate, and that (as Boswell unkindly put it)
Tetty now 'indulged herself in country air and nice living, at an unsuitable
expence, while her husband was drudging in the smoke of London'.[13] Her
favourite resort was Hampstead, 'whose fine air and chalybeate springs were
thought to have health-giving properties'. Johnson's biographer adds,
'According to one account [the couple] had visited the place as early as 1746;
they were certainly there in the autumn of 1748.'[14] Tunbridge was also a
chalybeate spring noted as a health resort, but one of higher tone. It would not
be altogether misleading to describe Hampstead as a poor man's Tunbridge
and if the Johnsons were literally there in 1748 it can be taken as a measure of
their social distance from the world of opulence and distinction at Tunbridge.

At this time Johnson was working on the *Dictionary*; *Irene* was still
unproduced, and *The Vanity of Human Wishes* lay just ahead. He had not
consolidated his position in the previous decade, after some early success in
the purlieu of Grub Street. Unlike Young, he had not achieved a settled
career, had made no powerful impact at Oxford, and had enjoyed no success
remotely comparable to *Night Thoughts*. A still more striking contrast could be
drawn in respect of Richardson. Both men had a book-trade background, but
the elder had dramatically advanced his position in the world. Richardson had
moved an immense degree above the provincial bookseller's shop and
market-stalls such as Johnson had known in his youth, and had reached the
pinnacle of his profession. After the sudden explosion of *Pamela* at the start of
the decade, Richardson the novelist had consolidated his reputation in the last
few months with the first two instalments of *Clarissa*; the final volumes were
just about to appear, in December 1748. Richardson, in short, was at the
apogee of his career. His admirers extended through all ranges of society, and
he was increasingly an habitué of political society. We usually think of this rise
to fame in connection with Fielding's parallel achievement at this time, but it
may be more useful to draw a comparison between *Clarissa* and *Night
Thoughts*. Both works were to attain a huge international reputation; both
were, as we shall see, specially favoured among women readers. Allies and
almost contemporaries, Richardson and Young had both established their
place in the cultural scheme of things by their middle-aged 'expressive'
compositions.

Johnson was as yet only on the fringe of middle age; his great work in
progress was, on the face of things, embodied in one of the least expressive
literary forms imaginable – the dictionary. He was still poor and socially
unconnected. If Tetty's health and other circumstances had drawn him
(implausibly, but not impossibly) to Tunbridge, he would not have felt nearly
as much at home in that confident society as Richardson or Young. That his
friend David Garrick was already at the head of *his* profession would not have

eased matters. Others in the print (Beau Nash, Colley Cibber; the Duchess of Kingston, not to mention the German Gamester) would not have been among Johnson's natural companions at this stage of his life, in any case. We may reasonably conclude that Samuel Johnson was neither literally nor symbolically present in the Tunbridge gallery that year.

Richardson himself is certainly represented towards the right-hand side of the print, though the label is coyly evasive ('Anonym.'). Trudging along by himself, a walking stick in one hand whilst the other is planted in his coat bosom, the personage depicted immediately recalls a self-description which Richardson sent to Susanna Highmore at this precise juncture. The letter bears the dateline, 'Tunbridge Wells, 2 August 1748', and provides the closest literary analogue to the graphic view under consideration.

Lord, Lord! Miss Highmore! What figures do Mr. Nash and Mr. Cibber make, hunting after new beauties, and with faces of high importance traversing the walks! God bless you, come and see them! – And if you do, I will shew you a still more grotesque figure than either. A sly sinner, creeping along the very edges of the walks, getting behind benches: one hand in his bosom, the other held up to his chin, as if to keep it in its place: afraid of being seen, as a thief of detection. The people of fashion, if he happen to cross a walk (which he always does with precipitation) *unsmiling* their faces, as if they thought him in their way; and he as sensible of so being, stealing in and out of the bookseller's shop, as if he had one of their glass-cases under his coat. Come and see this odd figure! You never *will* see him, unless *I* shew him to you: and who knows when an opportunity for that may happen again at Tunbridge?

Another letter refers in a scornful way to the two aged luminaries: 'To see Mr. [Nash] at eighty (Mr. Cibber calls him papa), and Mr. Cibber at seventy-seven, hunting after new faces; and thinking themselves happy if they can obtain the notice and familiarity of a fine woman! – How ridiculous!'[15] The same letter goes on to describe Cibber's pursuit of Miss Chudleigh, shortly to achieve notoriety as the bigamous Duchess of Kingston. Cibber had much admired the sentiment of *Pamela*, and 'the two men became fast friends in spite of the differences between them'. The friendship, which may originally have owed something to a common hostility towards Henry Fielding, survived for many more years, though it was tried somewhat in 1749 when Cibber proposed that Richardson's new hero might be provided with a mistress when *Sir Charles Grandison*, then in the early stages of composition, was under discussion.[16]

In addition Richardson's new friend Cibber had been acquainted at Tunbridge with Edward Young. We are told that 'the gay blooming Colley' arrived from London in 1742 to spend a pleasant evening with Benjamin Victor. 'The very next morning who should kind fortune add to the party but my worthy, valuable, reverend friend Dr. Young?' As one of Cibber's biographers remarks, 'The fop and the author of the *Night Thoughts* were, one suspects, equally pleased, for they too had much in common.'[17] This similitude provides one more sign of the parallelism which we have already observed in the careers of Richardson and Young; and it is further confirmation that Young symbolically belongs in the Tunbridge group.

The visit of 1748 is the only documented period which Richardson ever spent in Tunbridge, though there are hints he may possibly have made occasional trips at other times. He entrusted the entry for the waters at Tunbridge to Dr George Cheyne when Defoe's *Tour* was re-edited in 1742, although this decision was simply a matter of reliance on a specialist (Bath, Bristol and Cheltenham were treated by the same hand). Obviously Richardson had more direct connections through the Leake family with Bath, but this does not preclude acquaintance with the Tunbridge scene. It is relevant to note that the revised *Tour* contains tributes to a number of Richardson's friends, including one to 'the Reverend and learned Dr. Edward *Young*, so famed for his excellent Compositions' at Welwyn; and one on the 'inimitable Performances' of Colley Cibber. The standard biography of Richardson adds that he did not 'seize every possible occasion to compliment his friends', which seems a rather faint praise.[18] Among those *not* so honoured were Aaron Hill and Speaker Onslow, who is prominent in the centre of the Tunbridge print.

Richardson's truly remarkable success in achieving social recognition has not often been fully appreciated, perhaps because he did not consort with many members of the aristocracy on terms of near-equality, as Young did. (After all Young had married a woman whose parents were the Earl of Lichfield and a natural daughter of Charles II.) By contrast, Richardson may have felt more at home with the gentry and lower echelons of high society; notoriously, Horace Walpole thought Richardson unconvincing whenever he sought to portray the manners of upper-class characters. Significantly, it was in the very year of the print, as the final instalment of *Clarissa* was about to appear, that Lady Bradshaigh began to write to him as Mrs Belfour. This was not merely an appropriation of a fictional name: it was also a kind of social dressing-downwards, in so far as the lady's husband had succeeded to a baronetcy the previous year. Richardson wrote to Aaron Hill in May 1748 of a class of readers whom he designated 'the greater Vulgar'; possibly Lady Bradshaigh might qualify for this description.[19] His dealings with a man like Arthur Onslow, Speaker of the Commons, were more intimate, but even here a certain stiffness is apparent, compared to the natural flow to be found in the correspondence and commerce with the great carried on by Young (or much later, by Johnson).

Richardson was a man of humble birth who had made his way through trade – albeit a trade at the heart of high culture. Unlike even the licensed buffoons depicted at Tunbridge, Nash and Cibber, he had enjoyed little formal education. Of those depicted in the print, he resembles David Garrick most closely in his social situation. Each man had attained respect by his artistic achievements, and had come to stand for a new kind of broader popular appeal, a new kind of creative autonomy, a new kind of meritocratic ranking order. But there is an important difference. Garrick worked in a public arena and was adept at using people. Richardson pursued an intensely private mode of art, and he was shy with strangers. Once more, the print tells us the essential facts. Garrick is shown amid close-knit groups, engaged in animated conversation – admittedly with a singer where he might just as well have been caught hobnobbing with the Earl and Countess of Burlington.[20]

Across the other side of the walk, Richardson is heading out of the frame, head down, seemingly oblivious of his surroundings, driven by some inner urge which makes his thoughts a secret even in the very company he has dazzled and impressed with his remarkable books. Garrick has become intimate with the social group he has entered, since his mode of expression as an artist permits easy access to his audience on an everyday level. Meanwhile Richardson skulks on the edge of the same group that he has conquered intellectually. Garrick's cultural stance may be termed Augustan; as much as Nash, Cibber, or for that matter Pope, and Handel, he subsumes the personal within a wider range of humane and communal values. It is just Richardson's distinction that he uses the novel to explore states of being that are psychological before they are moral, personal before they are public. As is *not* the case with his great rival, Fielding, his vision extends beyond that of the orderly worldview accepted by commonsensical men and women of the time; it is formed around secrets, guilt, repression and the disallowed feelings of men and, especially, women. His art thus brings him social recognition but not complete social acceptance. He is permitted entrée to Tunbridge, but he is reduced to a caricatured posture of hiding in the undergrowth – marginalized not by his birth, but by his dangerous insights into hidden areas of life.

The more one examines the evidence, the less it seems a coincidence that Richardson should have been drawn in friendship to Young at the period when each made his sudden advance into the highest literary eminence. One body of information which demonstrates the concrete form which their alliance took around 1751 is to be found in the subscription campaign mounted on behalf of Aaron Hill's posthumous *Works*, to which I shall return presently. But the acquaintance of the two men began much earlier. As Richardson's biographers, Eaves and Kimpel, note, 'by the middle of 1744 the two men were writing to each other informally, with a freedom that already indicates some intimacy'. Further, by 1745, 'Young had visited

Richardson and was intimate enough to ask to be allowed to stay at North End'.[21]

The same authorities tell us that 'the intimacy between the two men is not fully reflected in the letters they exchanged', and in broad terms this is true. Nevertheless, the close literary relations they maintained at the time when *Clarissa* was in composition do emerge from the correspondence of the later 1740s. The letters are kept up throughout the next decade, and major publications by either man are regularly discussed. Richardson's last surviving letter to Young dates from May 1759, and mentions amongst other things Samuel Johnson's interest in Young's new work. Richardson says: 'Your subject of original composition is new, and nobly spirited.'[22] There is a mere handful of further letters on Young's side, initially concerned with the publication of the *Conjectures on Original Composition*. The final message from Young belongs to September 1760, when his eyesight was failing. For the sake of completeness in our running comparison, it should be noted that the few surviving letters exchanged by Richardson and Johnson cluster around the early 1750s, though their acquaintance may well have gone back to 1745 or even earlier. By this later date, Johnson was one of the eager group reading *Sir Charles Grandison* in manuscript, a sign that he had already made up some of the ground on Young before the *Dictionary* confirmed his stature.

Young's culminating tribute to the friendship occurs in his late poem, *Resignation*. In the first part of this work the author addresses Mrs Boscawen on the loss of a dear friend, unnamed but immediately identifiable:

> Perhaps your settled grief to sooth
> I should not vainly strive,
> But with soft balm your pain assuage,
> Had he been still alive;
>
> Whose frequent aid brought kind relief
> In my distress of thought,
> Ting'd with his beams my cloudy page,
> And beautified a fault.
>
> To touch our passions' secret springs
> Was his peculiar care;
> And deep his happy genius div'd
> In bosoms of the fair.
>
> Nature, which favours to the few
> All art beyond imparts,
> To him presented, at his birth,
> The key of human hearts.

But not to me by him bequeath'd
His gentle smooth address;
His tender hand to touch the wound
In throbbings of distress.[23]

Personal benevolence and literary insight are merged in this passage; Young lays stress on Richardson's psychological penetration and especially on his insight into women. It is also noteworthy that these gifts were presented to Richardson 'at birth', a matter of heaven-born instinct rather than learning or education. In this respect, the novelist matches up to the standards set for the creator of 'original composition' as defined in the *Conjectures*.[24]

The letters between Richardson and Young contain a good deal of mutual admiration, and it would be an unreliable mode of analysis to take such compliments altogether literally. In some respects it is more revealing to note that Young wrote in warm praise of *Clarissa* to socially prominent correspondents such as the Duchess of Portland and Mary Delany. To the former he exclaimed, 'Has your Grace read ... Clarissa? What a beautiful Brat of ye Brain is there? I wish your Grace would stand God-mother, & give it its Name; – *Clarissa ye Divine.* That Romance will probably do more good than a Body of Divinity. If all Printers could turn such Authors, I would turn Printer in order to be Instrumental in promoting such Benefit to Mankind.'[25] This is a remarkable tribute from a distinguished clergyman, even if we may suspect that Young's anxiety to name Richardson as 'my Friend' owes something to a desire to be connected in the Duchess's mind with this rising star in the literary firmament. Ten days later Young addressed Delany in similar terms, describing *Clarissa* as 'a Work of true, & uncommon Genius', and once more associating himself with 'my Friend (pardon ye Vanity) my *Friend* Mr. Richardson'.[26] There is indeed some vanity on Young's part, but also a kind of disguised condescension. By the end of this same year, Young was speculating on the effects of attaching his renown even more closely to that of his friend: 'Suppose in the title-page of the *Night Thoughts* [which Richardson had just printed in a new collected edition], you should say – *published by the author of Clarissa.* This is a trick to put it into more hands; I know it would have that effect.'[27]

For his part Richardson was a little more guarded, though he awarded Young flattering references in *Grandison* and the *Tour of Great Britain.* Richardson was proud enough of his association with *Night Thoughts*, as a printer, but it is possible to wonder whether he may not initially have shared the doubts of some readers. In 1742 Elizabeth Montagu had told the Duchess of Portland that she found 'a great deal of absurdity' in the poem, and Aaron Hill had written to Richardson in 1744 that Young did not know when to stop.[28] Even in later years, when Young's eminence was unquestioned, especially among the bluestocking set, Montagu saw that all the ladies courted Dr Young, the poet, 'more because they heard he is a genius, than that they know him to be such'. However, as time went on, and Young's international fame spread, there are no signs of reservation on Richardson's part. At the start of 1751 he returned a compliment by observing, 'It is true, when I have a mind to give myself reputation, and consequence, I talk of being acquainted with Dr. Young. But, that I may not be thought too vain, I tell, that you do not acquaint me either with what you are doing, or with what you design to do.' A few years later, Richardson was expostulating that the 'favours' which Young claimed to have received from him were 'more than balanced' by Young's favours to him.[29] Soon afterwards Richardson told Frau Meta Klopstock that it was not Edward Young but Philip Yonge who had been made Bishop of Bristol: 'We who are his Friends, think he has not had Justice done to his merits.' She had thought it impossible that the king should only award such a man the see of Bristol, when Canterbury itself was vacant.[30] The Klopstock circle had adopted Richardson and Young as their favourite authors, and the significant parallelism of this German cult confirms their receptability and, if the word may be permitted, translatability.[31] So it was at the time of their closest literary collaboration, on the *Conjectures*: Richardson's share in this work has long been on record, and indeed the surviving letters document the point. Each was celebrated as a literary innovator, and although from our present vantage-point the claim seems far more amply substantiated in the case of Richardson, we need to reconsider Young's claim too if we are to live within the cultural space his friend inhabited.

At this point we need to take account of the highly successful subscription on behalf of the posthumous *Works* of Aaron Hill, which appeared in 1753. It is evident that Richardson took a leading share in mounting this enterprise. Two other promotional centres can be located, first in Garrick and his theatrical circle; and secondly in a cluster which includes Young but may have radiated from Mary Delany. Naturally it is impossible to keep such groupings watertight, since many people were on close terms alike with Richardson, Garrick and Young, not to mention the Delany family or the Duchess of Portland. In this promotion, Richardson appears to have been the key figure (after all, he had more experience of marketing books than anyone else). The venture was mounted for the benefit of Hill's daughters and Richardson had more direct interest in the family than the other promoters. The subscription list, which shows an above average proportion of women, reveals in a more extended fashion some of the lines of cultural force we have traced in the Tunbridge print from five years earlier. Johnson is present on the list but without many obvious contacts or supporting figures, whilst the Young faction is more pervasive and more influential than we should expect today.

The Hill subscription project prompts a number of conclusions with regard to the cultural dynamics of England at the high point of Richardson's career. It appears that the opposition who had clustered around the Prince of Wales, before his death in 1751, used this venture, possibly with others, to reassert their cohesive and surviving sense of purpose. Subscriptions were one way of showing a flag and a way of demarcating boundaries. For the friends of Richardson, Garrick and Young to identify themselves in this grouping was partly a tribute to Aaron Hill, the deceased; partly a matter of disinterested charity extended towards his daughters. But in obscure ways, with which we have not yet fully come to terms, it was a statement about present affinities and enduring loyalties. Essentially Johnson is present as an individual subscriber, even though he was already intimate with Richardson and Garrick; the large block of his friends and allies we could detect in lists of the 1770s is just not apparent. He has yet to find a role in the main cultural narrative of his time, just as he awaits a natural right of admission to the Tunbridge scene. The dynamics which were to shape literary politics in his years of dominant influence were, nevertheless, already in the process of formation.

In very broad terms, the simplest way of describing these dynamics is to draw a rough line dividing the literary world into two opposing camps. One is that of Johnson, and includes Goldsmith, Burke, Reynolds, Boswell and others at one remove from the Club. The other could be most naturally grouped around Horace Walpole and includes Gray, Mason (more central than he now appears), Hurd and, again at one remove, figures such as Beattie and Cowper. The former group is ostensibly the more conservative, and despite the personal beliefs of Burke and Reynolds, owes much to the traditions of Tory satire – though this is a matter of rhetoric rather than ideology. Smollett, odd as it may seem, broadly belongs in this camp. On the other side we can trace dynastic Whig loyalties, for example a surviving attachment to Lyttelton. These groupings are of course not watertight, and they do not necessarily correspond with personal friendships; whilst some figures, notably Sterne, are difficult to fit into the scheme. Nevertheless, as an overall pattern the classification makes more sense of the period than any other, since it is possible to move beyond loose intellectual denominations such as 'sensibility' by taking account of a wider range of factors.

To understand the forces which helped to set this pattern, it is essential to bring Richardson and Young into play. For the period between the death of Pope and Swift, and that of Johnson forty years later, is the age of Richardson

– equally the age of Young, bizarre as that sounds until we remember the triumvirate inscribed by Charlotte Lennox in 1752, as the pattern began to take shape. All three men celebrated for their 'inimitable Beauties' were in many respects *traditional* moralists who yet seemed novel to their contemporaries. It is relatively easy for us to see this in the case of *Clarissa*; much less obvious in the case of *Night Thoughts*. We should hardly think of *The Rambler* at all in this context, yet that is the work which must have been central in the mind of Charlotte Lennox.[32] Johnson's role as an advocate of Richardson is important here; indeed, his critical influence at this juncture probably concerned the novel, about which he had written so powerfully in *Rambler* 4, as much as it did poetry. We tend to think of Johnson as unwelcoming in his attitude towards the significant literary innovations of his time, and we suppose that his enthusiasm for the radically new art of Richardson was something of an aberration. When we observe that he quoted *Clarissa* almost one hundred times in the *Dictionary* – far more than any other text by a living author – we assume that Richardson had become an honorary ancient. (Incidentally, the three living authors next in frequency of citation are Johnson himself, Lennox and Young.)

But this line of reasoning is fundamentally flawed. Johnson's tributes to Richardson's power as an imaginative artist are numerous and unambiguous. They celebrate not an eccentric or maverick talent, such as Sterne's; they assert a centrality and depth which belongs to the mainstream of writing. Hester Thrale tells us that Johnson used to say that in fiction 'no combination [i.e. of plot or situation] could be found and few sentiments that might not be traced up to Homer, Shakespeare & Richardson'.[33] Johnson *understood* Richardson from the start. It has been suggested recently that he may even have assisted Richardson in making revisions for the third edition of *Clarissa* in 1751.[34] Whether or not this is true, we need to be clear, as Jocelyn Harris is, that Richardson satisfied many of Johnson's most pervasive demands of literature; above all, his preference for 'natural to educated genius' and 'creativity to bookish allusion'. Many of the positions Johnson took in the literary debates of his later life make more sense if we hold on to this recognition: for example, even James Macpherson in these terms belongs to the Walpolian party of fancy, archaeological reconstruction, and ultimately frivolous artifice. In the quarrels of authors, Johnson naturally clings to Richardson; their affinities had been securely forged by 1750, when Johnson reached a belated adulthood as a writer, and *Clarissa* spoke for the present moment. It is always hard to remind ourselves that things in the past might have been different, and we tend to lose the shock of recognition which attended the appearance of sudden surprising masterpieces such as *Clarissa* – or, the age would have said, *Night Thoughts*. It is even harder, with two centuries of encrusted dogma to dislodge, to see that it was Johnson's impressionability, that is his search for new literary effects, which accounts for his readiness to hail Richardson as a modern master.

It is, once more, no accident that Richardson, Young and Johnson came together most directly in the case of *Conjectures on Original Composition*, which can be regarded almost as a joint production of the two former with significant contributions by the last. A reference in Richardson's letter to Young of 24 May 1759 has been taken to confirm these facts: 'Mr. Johnson is much pleased with it: he made a few observations on some passages, which I encouraged him to commit to paper, and which he promised to do, and send to you.'[35] It may be added that Richardson's previous paragraph alludes to the approval of 'the Speaker', that is Arthur Onslow, a prominent figure in the Tunbridge print.[36] In addition we should recall that the *Conjectures* are addressed to 'the Author of *Sir Charles Grandison*'. The currency of this novel is illustrated by the fact that it had already been translated into German, and a first printing of 2500 copies shows the scale of that enterprise. 'In Germany', Richardson told his friend in the letter just quoted, 'they revere Dr. Young in his works more than they do those of any other British genius.' For Richardson, Young was an important model and inspiration, and his pleasure in the international success of *Grandison* owes much to his sense of emulating Young's triumph with *Night Thoughts*. This was a renown Johnson was never fully to equal, though *Rasselas* (like *Night Thoughts*), was much reprinted in cheap editions and the *Rambler* papers were widely circulated via the provincial press.[37]

It appears certain that Richardson saw the emphasis which Young laid on originality as a validation of his own literary procedures. In many ways he could be viewed in his own time as standing in much the same relation to Fielding as Young stood to Pope, that is in his rejection of inherited forms of language in favour of a more personal, expressive and openly emotional idiom. This is not the way in which readers today are inclined to view the matter, and our continuing surprise at Johnson's hostility towards Fielding would be mitigated if we were able to read literary history in this spirit. For Johnson, Fielding's moral inferiority was accompanied by a lack of human penetration and a failure to uncover the true springs of human passion. Though he admired Young, there is less evidence that he was prepared to realign the history of poetry to dethrone Pope in favour of Young. But others, such as Joseph Warton, were less inhibited; and of course Samuel Richardson never expressed very much full-hearted praise of Pope – often quite the contrary. Richardson's biographers attribute this distaste for Pope to the influence of Aaron Hill and Thomas Edwards.[38]

In another sense, this was part of the process of revaluation in which Young was to be given primacy. It is symptomatic that Richardson should have explicitly urged his friend to tone down some praise of Pope in the *Conjectures*: 'The tame imitator of other poets is a copier of portraits, the true genius a noble painter of originals, to whom nature delights to sit in every variety of attitude ... I cannot imagine that Pope would have shone in blank verse; and do you really think he had invention enough to make him a great poet? Did he not want the assistance of rhyme, of jingle? What originality is there in the works for which he is most famed? Shall I say, that I wish you would be pleased to reconsider all you say of the creative power of Pope?'[39] It must be suspected that Richardson's own self-definition as an artist was bound up in such judgements. To impugn Pope in implied opposition to Milton (or, in a different context, Young) is not simply to express a preference for blank verse, or divine subjects. It is equally to stress the need for 'creative power', and to endorse all Richardson's procedures as a novelist.

Whilst the concept of 'originality' is not highlighted in the *Conjectures*, the adjective 'original' (some fifteen occurrences) and the noun 'original' (some thirty) are extremely prominent. Both counts fall well below that for 'genius', which figures over eighty times. The entry on Young in the *Biographia Dramatica* (1782) attributes to his verse 'much originality but little judgment', which (along with examples in Gray, Reynolds and others) advances the appearance of this crucial term some years before *The Oxford English Dictionary* traced it. Johnson's own verdict on *Night Thoughts* in his *Lives* is close to that of *Biographia Dramatica*: 'he has exhibited a very wide display of original poetry ... a wilderness of thought in which the fertility of fancy scatters flowers of every hue and of every odour ... The wild diffusion of the sentiments and the digressive sallies of the imagination would have been compressed and restrained by confinement to rhyme. The excellence of this work is not exactness but copiousness.'[40] Johnson's well-known remark that *Night Thoughts* was one of the few poems 'in which blank verse could not be exchanged for rhyme but with disadvantage' represents one major disagreement with the *Conjectures*, where in an equally celebrated phrase Young wrote of blank verse as 'verse unfallen, uncurst'.[41]

A less considered but possibly more frank version of Johnson's attitude appears in a conversation on Skye in September 1773, which Boswell reports in his *Tour to the Hebrides*:

He told us, the first time he saw Dr. Young was at the house of Mr. Richardson, the author of *Clarissa*. He was sent for, that the doctor might read to him his *Conjectures on Original Composition*, which he did, and Dr. Johnson made his remarks; and he was surprised to find Young receive as novelties, what he thought very common maxims.

He said, he believed Young was not a great scholar, nor had studied regularly the art of writing; that there were very fine things in his *Night Thoughts*, though you could not find twenty lines together without some extravagance.[42]

This is an important passage for any assessment of the critical climate in the middle of the century. Especially noteworthy is Johnson's belief that Young received as 'novelties' ideas which Johnson took to be 'very common maxims'. It seems likely that Johnson had in mind particularly Young's local judgements on Shakespeare, as well as his general position on matters of taste and genius. Certain phrases bear comparison with the great *Preface* which Johnson was to publish in 1765: for example, the view that Shakespeare is the equal of great classic writers 'and that, in spite of all his faults'. The reasoning implicit in Young's assertion, 'Perhaps he was as learned as his dramatic province required', reaches a broadly Johnsonian conclusion: 'whatever learning he wanted, he was master of two books ... the book of Nature, and that of man'.[43]

In fact, though there is a forward-looking quality in the *Conjectures* at times – as in some Hazlitt-like passages concerning imitation and emulation – the main drift of its argument was not drastically new by 1759. Anyone whose formative years had been passed in the literary climate of the 1740s and early 1750s would have recognized many of the key ideas. And Johnson, though entering middle age, only truly emerged as a critic in that period. The critical endeavour which Young was codifying and summarizing was a dominant movement of ideas. Young's account ends with Addison, as the consummation of one stream of English literature: 'He has a more refined, decent, judicious and extensive genius, than Pope or Swift.'[44] As early as 1776, 'Courtney Melmoth' was essaying a comparison between Johnson and Young on the basis of a common 'nerve' in their writings. According to Melmoth, Johnson lacks the ease of Addison, whilst Young wants the smoothness of Pope; but in compensation they possess a certain strength. Along this line of thinking, Johnson is the natural successor to Addison, one who exhibits the purity of style and outlook found in his predecessor together with a higher emotional temperature. For Young, *Cato* was weakened by 'a philosophic reserve and a sort of moral prudery' which inhibited any strong dramatic effect. Again we come on an unsuspected truth: Johnson could be seen by contemporaries as exemplifying, along with Young himself, the qualities which had been praised in the *Conjectures*. Not for nothing did his friends regard Johnson as the true heir of Addison in his *Rambler* papers.[45]

But Richardson is the true off-stage hero of this text. The fact that the work is addressed to Richardson means that this cannot be avowed openly. But at one point there is a transparent admission of the truth. Young has been speaking of the need 'to grasp at all which is laudable within [our] reach', that is for writers to 'embark in the ... bold bottom of new enterprise'. He proceeds:

A friend of mine has obeyed that injunction; he has relied on himself, and with a genius, as well moral as original (to speak in bold terms), has cast out evil spirits; has made a convert to virtue of a species of composition, once most its foe. As the first Christian emperors expelled demons, and dedicated their temple to the living god.
But you, I know, are sparing in your praise of this author.[46]

Unmistakably, the author is Richardson himself; the new 'species of composition' is the novel; and among the evil spirits one must perceive a prominent role allocated to Henry Fielding. So, twenty years later, Johnson would berate Hannah More for quoting 'from so vicious a book' as *Tom Jones*, and would break out in a panegyric on Fielding's 'competitor', Richardson, as 'superior to him in talents as in virtue'.[47] The preferences expressed here, which have occasioned so much puzzlement, require less in the way of gloss when we appreciate that the *Conjectures* underwrite a scale of values identical to Johnson's. It was obviously Young's belief that *Clarissa* and *Grandison* had opened up a new epoch in letters, and he might well have hoped that this age would be one propitious to the reputation of *Night Thoughts*, too. Contemporaries would have understood that works such as *The Rambler* were likewise harbingers of the new outlook. Richardson would certainly have been well pleased with this assessment of his achievement, and would have relished the company it allowed him to keep.[48]

A final point of congruence may be mentioned. All three of the leading figures in this story evidently needed the approval of women and appear to have sublimated sexual drives in the search for esteem in the salon. This may seem least obvious in the case of Johnson, but even at the end of his life William Mason could write to Walpole of 'founding a literary coalition' with his near enemy Johnson. 'Our object is no less than the complete administration of the Blue-Stocking Club – which we mean to govern in a purely constitutional way without any concurrence from Madam Montagu.'[49] Though the tone is joking, the association between Johnson and various learned ladies is a real and lasting one. It would be otiose here to itemize the members of Richardson's female set, or to rehearse the evidence which demonstrates the immense renown which Richardson enjoyed among the Bluestockings. What is less well known is the extent of Young's repute in the same circle.

It was not just at the slightly comic Batheaston *cénacle* of Lady Miller that 'solemn Young' was a name to conjure with.[50] Anna Seward was a member of the Batheaston circle, but her tastes were formed at other times and places, and she acknowledged that 'the mournful and angry Night thoughts' were among her especial favourites – an admission provoked, it would seem, by reading the account of Young in Johnson's *Lives* in 1781, as she went on to describe Johnson's 'tolerably civil' treatment of the poet, and to depict the character of 'that being [Johnson], so heterogeneously constructed'.[51] Elizabeth Montagu was a friend of Young, and amongst her allies was the learned Elizabeth Carter, who combined with her friend to urge Young to fresh literary endeavours.[52] A representative comment is one made by Carter in June 1759: 'By your account of them both, I find myself much more tempted to look out for Dr. Young's harmless bouquet, than the infernal composition of deadly weeds, made up by Voltaire.'[53] The works in question seem to be the *Conjectures*, just on the point of publication, and *Candide*. Two years later Montagu told Carter à propos of Young's *Resignation*, 'You will be pleased I think with what he says of Voltaire, you know we exhorted him to attack a character whose authority is so pernicious.'[54] In the same year Richardson's friend Miss Talbot reported one of her last conversations with the novelist, and once more Young's 'charitable Endeavour' in attempting to show Voltaire the light was discussed.[55] Johnson's name does not occur in this exchange, but again we can be sure that the campaign against Voltaire mounted by Richardson, Young and the Bluestocking ladies would have had his support. It is true that when Montagu prolonged the campaign in her *Essay on Shakespear* (1769), Johnson was not able to summon up much enthusiasm for the book; but this is most unlikely to have been caused by the treatment which Voltaire receives as a critic of Shakespeare. By this stage shifting alliances had made Johnson in some sense a member of an opposing camp, in that Mrs Montagu had formed an independent circle of patronage. In later years her somewhat uncritical admiration of James Beattie, not to mention Lord Lyttelton, was to put her at a distance from Johnson. But this is essentially a circumstance of Johnson's final period, the one we know best, and we should not extrapolate attitudes too blithely from the 1770s and 1780s to the preceding decades.

It is a fallacy to suppose that only women admired Young, any more than this was the case with Richardson. And beyond this we must recall that some female admirers belonged to quite a different world; Mary Wollstonecraft, surely a buff rather than a blue, frequently cited Young, especially in *Mary: A Fiction* (1788). And Charlotte Lennox, from whom we started, was closer in background to Richardson and Johnson than to the well-born society ladies. Nevertheless, it is undeniable that Richardson and Young both enjoyed a cult, rather than simply the kind of intellectual influence which Johnson came to know. (By the word 'cult', I mean an active programme of support and promotion rather than passive admiration.) As late as 1814 Hester Piozzi was quoting with approval Young's views on originality. Women took a large share in sponsoring these promotional campaigns, perhaps in part because women had few opportunities to direct the course of literature in more direct modes of creativity. To this extent we can fairly conclude that female suffrage moulded taste more successfully in the middle of the eighteenth century than in any previous period of English literature.[56] Richardson and Young were the prime beneficiaries. Later efforts by Montagu were in general doomed to failure. By that time Johnson had achieved his own independent authority. He had done so without any fundamental transformation in his literary values, but it is hard for us today to perceive the intellectual roots of these values, in so far as they are bound up with the cult of 'originality' in Richardson and Young.

The definitive expression of this moment in creative literature survives in *Clarissa*, *Grandison* and *Night Thoughts*. Quite apart from their similarities in outlook, personality and moral conviction, Richardson and Young seemed to contemporaries parallel because of their common exploitation of 'original composition', that is their supersession of Augustan norms and their union of virtue with sensibility. Both had made death a central concern in their greatest works; both produced an exemplary literature which provides guidance, sustenance and models of existential self-direction. Both wrote books with a special appeal to women readers, and enjoyed special esteem among women prominent in literary circles. By this time we are well aware that these things are true of Richardson. If we can come to appreciate that they were also true of Young, and could have been true of Johnson (though it did not quite work out that way), we shall be able to define Richardson's appeal more closely. To rephrase an earlier contention – the age of Johnson had its roots in the age of Richardson, and could not have taken the same form without those origins.[57]

However we look at the matter, Richardson is at the centre of eighteenth-century writing. As soon as people begin to think in terms of 'original composition', they invoke his name above all – as we must still.

13

'A novel in a series of letters by a lady': Richardson and some Richardsonian novels

ISOBEL GRUNDY

Richardson inherited the epistolary novel from writers such as Aphra Behn, Catharine Trotter, Mary Davys, and Elizabeth (Singer) Rowe. The nature and the immense reputation of his three works stamped the form indelibly with his image, without diminishing its concentration on women characters and the issues affecting their lives. The intimate, chiefly female circle which attended the birth of his later works fluctuated between, or sometimes combined, devout admiration and vigorously-argued resistance. These attitudes persisted through the following generations. Those women, especially, who chose to write fiction in letters, found it congenial to work from his ingredients: authorial invisibility; foregrounded female characters; plots of courtship, seduction (threatened or actual), or married relationships; debate on women's education and the roles of daughters, sisters and wives; a morally educative aim; and naked appeal to the reader's emotional susceptibilities. Here was one serious literary tradition which excluded neither woman as reader nor woman as writer. Richardson served simultaneously as a teacher to be imitated and a father to be challenged.[1]

Women took a leading role in the contemporary debate swirling round Richardson's work. Eliza Haywood got in early with her attack on *Pamela*; Hester Mulso argued with him in the style of one of his own characters taking another to task; Lady Echlin literally re-wrote him. Sarah Fielding and Jane Collier found him an enabling factor in their own careers, but chose deliberately un-Richardsonian structures for their fiction. In succeeding generations writers such as Maria Susanna Cooper claimed him as precedent for novels so didactic as hardly to qualify as imaginative fiction at all, while others made him godfather to melodramatic intensities. Some, like the Scots novelist Jean Marishall, hailed him as practical champion of their sex, working for improved marital equality in 'such publications as would tend to improve the minds of the women'. Others again, with views as widely different as the conservative Laetitia-Matilda Hawkins and the radical Catharine Macaulay, agreed in classing him, because of the sexual element in his work, as a harmful rather than a beneficial influence.[2]

Richardson's professed disciples signalled allegiance through choice of form, themes, and even names. Sophia Briscoe's heroine in *Miss Melmoth; or, The New Clarissa* (1771) endures incarceration in an 'odious house', but in other respects resembles Richardson's exemplar no more and no less than the protagonist of her other novel, *The Fine Lady* (1772), which draws its names mostly from *Sir Charles Grandison*. Susannah (Minifie) Gunning's Clarissa in *Fashionable Involvements* (Dublin, 1800), a third-person narrative of broad satirical cast, and Sarah Green's in *Parents and Wives; or, Inconsistency and Mistakes* (1825) also pay tribute to Richardson, long after the *Quarterly Review* had implied that his influence was extinct. Neither of these writers learned as much from him as Briscoe did, especially of epistolary technique; but both allude to him in incidents and borrowed phrases. Green's elderly rake explicitly calls Lovelace his prototype.[3] Their heroines, superior in sensibility and virtue to those around them, suffer like Clarissa (the later ones also vindicate middle-class against noble values); but they arrive at earthly happiness like that of Harriet Byron.

Richardson's whole *œuvre* had much to offer in the techniques of letters for retrospection, self-expression, self-analysis, and variety of narrative tone, and for the special uses of mad letters, posthumous letters, letters copied, circulated, forged, or intercepted. Pamela's elevation was too bold for authors of either sex to follow (heroines might come from reduced circumstances but not from the actual lower classes), but her combination of formal humility with inner assertiveness was one which women writers were not slow to appropriate. *Pamela II*, as a novel about marriage, had a powerful but generally non-specific influence. *Clarissa* offered the immensely attractive central myths of female near-perfection, sensibility, suffering and redemption, and the particular motifs of paired heroines, elopement/abduction, rakes either reforming or unreformable, undeserved loss of reputation, and carefully composed deathbeds both pious and impious. While Clarissa, with her serious aspirations to autonomy, significance, influence, and sanctity, appealed more than any other Richardson character to women writers, many of them preferred to set their fictions in the complex, interactive social world of *Grandison* rather than in the introspective, myth-ridden isolation of *Clarissa*. *Grandison* was, in Joyce Tompkins's words, 'more practicable'. Most later writers bypassed the central issue of the hero who loves two women, but turned eagerly to the paragon/mentor, the family of love, and the heroine's moral battle to accept what she cannot understand, to conquer jealousy and endure the pangs of love which may be unrequited. Even more than the earlier novels, *Grandison*'s expansive framework provided a myriad of sub-ordinate plot-elements, a whole vocabulary and syntax of domestic fiction.[4]

Richardson shared many views and interests with even the least submissive women writers who followed. Yet more practicably, his various characters provided models for every shade of opinion about the nature and status of women: from obsessive, exploitative interest to unthinking, dismissive chau-vinism, from condescension to idealization, from Christian submissiveness to proto-feminist anger. His usefulness was largely independent of agreement or disagreement. Those of his followers who have attracted critical attention are now perceived as debaters rather than echoes. Frances Sheridan, Frances (Moore) Brooke, Frances Burney, Elizabeth Inchbald, and Jane Austen have all been detected using him as both trainer and sparring partner. (Evidence mounts against the view that women writers *wholly* 'accepted myths of feminine destiny as created by men'.)[5] I hope to show how useful his teaching proved, and also how energetically his practising female disciples pursued the debate begun by his non-professional female correspondents, composing rejoinders, especially, to his authoritative pronouncements about or on behalf of their sex. Richardson provided a starting-point for the treatment not only of beleaguered female excellence (as the name Clarissa invariably signals), but also of marriage, of female and of male sexuality, and of women's claims to increased autonomy.

Modern critics, mostly unsympathetic to the novel of sensibility, have often blamed Richardson for encouraging identification of the feminine with the delicate and the vulnerable, for cultivating readers' taste for distress (especially female distress), and for teaching a school of sentimental novelists to wallow in excessive emotion, superhuman distress and impossible rem-edies.[6] This, however, simplifies and falsifies the effect of even *Clarissa* alone. Richardson's example was a check rather than a spur to sentimental self-indulgence, as can be seen by tracing his influence among writers of that school. Reference to him, either explicit or submerged, often signals a note of toughness and moral rigour amid the torrents of feeling. His characters, even when most distressed, continue to use the language of common life, and to be judged not by the quality of their sensations but by Christian moral precept. Epistolary technique, too, offers a means of containing emotion. A character writing letters has both opportunity and motive to combine self-analysis with outpourings of pain and grief, as Richardson's heroines unfailingly do. 'Thus foolishly dialogu'd I with my Heart', writes the first of them, 'and yet all the Time this Heart is *Pamela*' (p. 217).

The epistolary form militates against a technique of objectifying and prettifying distress by pictorial presentation. Such a narrative as that in which 'Nature beheld the graceful weakness of these her favourite children through tears of delight', and the heroine becomes 'the most interesting object grief had ever made', which 'the eye of sensibility ... never tired of gazing on',[7] presupposes an authorial voice rather than one engaged in the action. Letters must employ some character to hold up such a lens for the reader's gazing; and a human character, pen in hand – like Belford reporting the dying Clarissa (VII, 412; *IV, 332*) as 'in a charming attitude' – is more open to the reader's question than is Nature or the eye of sensibility.

The women writers who followed Richardson into emotional intensity often achieve a power which belies critical dismissal of the sentimental novel. Richardson's influence is not least crucial where it is most diffuse and hard to pinpoint. In the unalluringly titled but surprisingly effective *Delia, A Pathetic and Interesting Tale*, 1790, the exceptionally obscure Miss or Mrs Pilkington (neither Mary nor Laetitia of that name) creates a heroine possessed of satirical wit and resilience worthy of Anna Howe or Charlotte Grandison. She gives her Delia notable warmth and generosity in female friendship, interest in women's potential and role in society, a first love-affair destroyed by malicious interception of letters – and a saintly and heart-rending death after fearful emotional pressure from the men in her life. The successful fusion of such apparently disparate elements owes more to the quality of writing than to reliance on Richardson; yet no single element in it could have existed without the model he provided. In particular, the pathetic force and moral intensity of the conclusion, which could so easily have slid into mawkishness or melo-drama, is preserved through Richardsonian close attention to particular circumstances and particular epistolary styles.

Women's plots of distress turn less often on seduction or rape than on elements which must have been more frequently met with in women's actual experience. The gravely wronged but invincibly self-sacrificing wife, who appears in Richardson only in peripheral stories like that of the elder Grandisons, was the favourite motif in the novels of Elizabeth Griffith (who, although she refers sometimes to Sterne, enjoys a much more considerable legacy from Richardson). All his three novels come together in Griffith's first novel, *The Delicate Distress* (1769), which not only deals, in several plots and sub-plots, with 'the perfidy of man', but does so in a public moral arena among characters debating the validity and integrity of each others' actions. The two sexes are compared for their capacities both in friendship and in letter-writing;[8] Lord Woodville voices 'a fear that women are our superiors, in every thing' (II, 140). One sub-plot discusses marriage between Catholic and 'heretic' (I, 145 ff.), in terms directly borrowed from *Grandison.*

Griffith boldly foregrounds the issue of marital infidelity – of competing, conflicting, mutually destructive loves and loyalties – which Richardson had merely touched. Richardson pointed the way in Pamela's jealousy of the

Countess, and in Harriet's doubts and fears. Griffith explores the subjectivity of the passion which drives Lord Woodville to betray the wife he also genuinely loves, as well as the anguish of Lady Woodville, which suggests an unacknowledged depth of sexual feeling. Griffith builds on and transforms hints from Richardson's plots; she renders Richardsonian consciousness in all its complexity and self-deception. When Woodville writes, 'Rejoice with me, my friend; the conflict is past!' the reader suspects, accurately, that it is not; yet, battling vainly with his obsession, Woodville takes a justifiable hold of the reader's sympathy.[9]

Griffith's later and less wholly forgotten novels, *The History of Lady Barton* (1771) and *The Story of Lady Juliana Harley* (1776), further established the unhappy-marriage plot, which is rare in masculine fiction but a staple of later women novelists. The heroines have married, dutifully though reluctantly, husbands who are not inadvertently unfaithful but systematically tyrannical, developing the potential not of a Mr B. but rather of a Solmes. Griffith's plots enquire what may happen to a woman who carries Clarissa's pursuit of perfection into such a marriage as that which menaces Clarissa in Richardson's first two volumes. It is under threat of a father's curse (one of Clarissa's deepest terrors) that Juliana Harley consents to marry a man she detests. Lady Barton's approaching death renders her husband finally penitent: a resolution which Richardson stoutly resisted but which Lady Echlin wrote for him (see note 2). But the marriage which Griffith has depicted is not that of a Clarissa and a Lovelace. Where Clarissa was intransigent, Lady Barton is pliable; where Lovelace was obsessed with women, and especially with their writing (and Lord Woodville obsessed with one woman), Sir William Barton is brusquely, almost perfunctorily dismissive of women, in the manner of Lovelace's rakish friends on one hand and James Harlowe on the other, rather than Lovelace himself. Close as she is to Richardson at every point, Griffith is telling an untold tale of women's lives, which turns on the institutionalization of misogyny as well as the workings of marriage and the intensities of feeling: the problems she presents are, accordingly, less extreme than those of *Clarissa* but less soluble than those of *Pamela* or *Grandison*.

The heroine of *Emma; or, The Unfortunate Attachment* (1773) by Georgiana Spencer, later Duchess of Devonshire, actually transfers her affections, as Clarissa could not, at the command of her father. (Both the father and the suitor he favours are incomparably more sympathetic than Clarissa's.) Dutifulness, it seems, pays off: Emma duly grows to love her husband. Letters addressed to Emma's father then bring news of the death in battle of her early, first-chosen suitor, Algernon Sidney. The news, however, is withheld from the reader, who, with that rising suspense so often provoked by Richardson himself, can only guess at the implications of a friend's frightened and baffled account of Emma's sudden raving delirium and her Clarissa-like vision of her husband 'covered with the blood of Sidney', whom he has just killed, coming to stab her with the same sword. Reading, we confront the psychological consequences before the event which produced them, which is then revealed in the text of the letters Emma has read. Not only is her old lover dead: he has left her, with a harrowing posthumous message, his 'small fortune', concrete evidence of that emotional past she has undone. Her violent reaction suggests that, like Sir Charles, she has room in her heart for more than one love. Her feelings, related to the past, are blameless (unlike Lord Woodville's consummated extramarital passion). Yet, through techniques learned from Richardson – the posthumous letter, the 'fatal legacy' which rivals Clarissa's dairy house in power to awake resentment – the author approaches a new and dangerous possibility of unlicensed desire in a heroine.[10]

Emma's story is developed on lines clearly suggested by *Clarissa*. Her husband rejects her (with that refusal to acknowledge her integrity which Richardson's heroine meets at every turn). Her friends, like Anna Howe, are prevented by circumstances from providing help or even company. Like Anna too, one friend has lent readers some relief by strongminded feminist critique of wifehood; another offers Emma money – 'are not our hearts cemented by the strongest bonds, and shall our fortunes be divided?' – only to have her bank-bill returned as Anna's were.[11] Developing a Clarissa-like weariness of life, Emma retires to a desolate country house which fulfils several functions of the bailiff's where Clarissa was imprisoned. Each provides for visual description, at the heroine's nadir, not of her own appearance but of surroundings used for explicitly emblematic purposes. Emma calls her chosen lodging the complete 'emblem of a dungeon'; Belford deliberately describes Clarissa's unchosen prison room in an effort to make Lovelace recognize the iniquity of his usage of her. Despite some gothic touches by Georgiana Spencer, each setting is essentially one of domesticity laid waste: each has defective doors, broken and darkened windows, worm-eaten furniture and accumulated dirt. Rather as Clarissa is to call her coffin her house, Emma uncomplainingly chooses a little room to 'call my parlour'.

The novels are none the less set on different courses. Richardson's Belford, spurred towards sentiment and repentance, demands of the bailiff: 'is this an apartment for such a Lady?' (VI, 274; *III, 446*). His similar outburst to Lovelace receives no response. In Spencer's novel it is the husband (arriving hot-foot just in time to forestall the exit of his 'dying saint') who sees and is softened. 'Gods', he cries, 'what a dwelling is this for *my wife!*' Clarissa's shadow moves away; the final letter, written by the husband while his wife lies in, and signed by both, symbolizes the marriage tie.[12] Unlike many happy endings, however, this one does not negate the sense of precariousness which the story has produced: for this fact, as for the precariousness itself, intelligent response to Richardson is largely responsible.

Another woman writer who selected Richardson as model for the serious handling of sexuality was Anna Maria Bennett, a best-selling author of the Minerva press. She changed course to do so, having previously established herself as a follower, albeit a revisionist follower, of Fielding. Her first novel, *Anna; or, Memoirs of a Welch Heiress* (1785), exploits its heroine's vicissitudes for smiles as well as tears, and can on occasion portray a rake as a joke instead of as a threat; her second, *Juvenile Indiscretions* (1786), draws a woman's-eye-view of a scapegrace youth, driven to distraction by unsought conquests, a man who might well envy the insouciance of Tom Jones.

In *Agnes De-Courci* (1789) Bennett drops her narrative form for letters and the sentimental mode.[13] She still favours a blend of comedy with intense feeling, and two distinct streams mingle here, each of which owes something to Richardson. The doomed love between Agnes and Edward Harley, who turns out to be her half-brother, involves anguished renunciation, rescues from fire and water, and finally suicide and madness. Such consistently extreme situations are remote from any Richardson chose to write about, although Clarissa's story is an influence, and Agnes's mother (a British Jacobite exile who broke her convent vows to love and marry, and died penitent leaving Agnes well provided with Catholic mentors) owes something to Clementina in *Grandison*. Yet this stream of melodrama probably originates in one significant detail in Richardson: Lovelace's fantasy about fathering, on Clarissa and Anna, children who will grow up to 'intermarry' in ignorance of '*consanguinity*' (VI, 13; III, 251). The source of each stream of the *Agnes* plot is the now-dead rake James Neville. His sacrilegious marriage under an assumed name produced Agnes; his seduction of a woman who later killed herself produced Harley; his socially acceptable but actually bigamous marriage produced Julia, who becomes a friend of Agnes; his death has left his unhappy (second) wife free to marry her early love, who (unknown to any but himself) is Agnes's uncle. Richardson's closely-encountered rake has here receded into the past, but his exploits (kept secret as a measure of their shamefulness as well as in order that the plot may function) cast a pervasive blight over the present.

The novel's other stream owes more to *Grandison* than to *Clarissa*. Bennett understands the saving grace of comedy: even as a homeless wanderer, Agnes herself can perceive the humour in her encounter with a once-jilted but now resilient countrywoman who befriends her, who is grimly dismissive of the whole male sex and of any hint of a love-story (II, 203). Though it proves finally necessary to read Agnes's history of pathos (parentage, convent upbringing, doomed love, and later solitary wanderings) in terms of purely fictional, not social norms, society's efforts to deal with her are made a source of penetrating and comic analysis, and of a pathos more convincing and delicately painted than that of the heroine herself.

Early in the novel, while Agnes suffers because people suppose her to be the kept mistress of her impeccable benefactor (and uncle) General Moncrass, the reader's sympathy is less closely engaged with her than with suffering at an altogether more credible level: that of the General himself and his wife Lady Mary. To the latter's simple jealousy of her husband's supposed infidelity are added two extra humiliations: she is a noblewoman who, in middle age, has taken the bold step of proposing herself to her long-loved social inferior and now fears it was a foolish move, and she is one-time wife of the rake Neville, who now finds herself re-immersed in a pain she had thought forever past.

These intense personal emotions, like those depicted in *Grandison* and unlike those in many sentimental novels, are firmly grounded in social situations. Lady Mary Moncrass differs widely from the married Pamela in class and from Harriet, Clementina, Emily, or Olivia in experience and character. But, though Bennett has learned much from the suffering wives of Elizabeth Griffith, she has learned more from Richardson's various women characters who struggle to preserve some dignity while painfully caught between social imperatives and avowed love. She has learned from Harriet, who so often expresses the fear that the 'ignoble passion' of love will make her behave meanly (e.g. II, 2, 19), to let her essentially admirable Lady Mary behave meanly under pressure of circumstances, in a manner that few of the novelist's contemporaries were prepared to risk. When first Lady Mary instructs the servants to pry into her husband's doings, she feels ashamed of her own action and tries – too late – to countermand her order; next time she is unvisited by doubt (I, 21–3). She admits *past* self-censure for a step which she has now begun to justify; she unwittingly reveals how she is fabricating interpretations of her husband's doings (I, 41–2, 52–3).

Though a novice in the epistolary form, Bennett is sensitive to its potential. Lady Mary chafes under the restraint of correspondence: 'my God! – How have I patience to give you this detail?' The answer – 'my unalterable friendship, my respect to your opinion' (I, 26) – in turn glosses the significance of her refusal of this means of communication with her husband: 'I have now made up my mind, and do not open any letters from him' (I, 31). Bennett uses letters of first-person narrative in which central characters explore their inner turmoil, and letters of third-person narrative to dramatize the conflict of social pressure and counter-pressure. Her rich and varied ensembles derive from such scenes in *Grandison* as that where Sir Charles confronts the various open and hidden agendas of the Porretta family (III, 229 ff.).

Major Melrose, a one-time rake and friend of the General, writes a brilliantly revealing account of a meeting with Lady Mary, her father (who embodies her own outraged pride of lineage) and daughter (not only a reminder of her first, unhappy, marriage but also a critic of her mother and partisan of her stepfather). The Major himself represents another viewpoint: that of society at large, expressing concern but blind to nuances of feeling, vainly hoping to keep up a public façade, privately recognizing something wrong, but in the crassest terms. He admires Lady Mary, in a conventionally gallant and trivializing fashion: 'Bating her pride, Lady Mary is, and bating her *age too*, the finest woman in England; her features glowed with indignation, she grew an inch taller' (I, 90). He supposes that her suspicions are correct, but not that a husband's keeping a mistress is any great matter: he begs his friend to 'act a little like other men; marry the girl to your Chaplain, and go back to your wife' (I, 107). Indeed, his incomprehension faintly echoes such inadequacies as Anna's advice to Clarissa to marry after the rape (VI, 234–5; *III, 416*), or Lovelace's 'Who the devil could have expected such strange effects from a cause so common and so slight?' (V, 301; *III, 203*). But here the comic mode prevails: the Major's inadequate comprehension causes pain to Lady Mary, indeed; but it is a pain she brings on herself, to the reader's amusement as well as sympathy.

Lady Mary and her husband are complex characters seeking to conduct emotional and moral lives within the confines of society, at odds with themselves, unwilling to admit all their motives, well aware how already-shaped personality limits freedom of action. This is a novel full of Richardsonian detail even in its more melodramatic aspects: the corpse of the fallen innocent 'Patty of the mill', going to burial attended by maidens, and that of Agnes making a ceremonial entry to the home of her childhood, recall Clarissa's last journey and funeral; Harley's 'small white obelisk ... sacred to friendship' alludes to Sir Charles's 'little temple' dedicated to the same cult.[14] But the most valuable lesson learned from Richardson is the unmelodramatic art of locating moral and emotional significance in the domestic and the quotidian as well as in the exceptional and the extreme.

Not only disciples of Richardson found him a useful resource: direct critique, rather than even revisionist imitation, informed some interesting works. Some who were provoked, like Lady Echlin, by Lovelace's outsmarting of the abducted Clarissa, went beyond Echlin and staged a re-play of that game of wits to give their heroines victory. Maria Harcourt in Mrs Mathews's *Simple Facts* (1793) is abducted by a rake whose name, Sir Richard Harlow,

points to *Clarissa*, though he recalls Mr B. rather than Lovelace: he confines
Maria in 'a genteel house in the middle of a park' (II, 99), attended by an old
woman who sings his praises; he demands sometimes marriage, sometimes
possession without marriage.[15] Maria, fluctuating between plotting escape
and sinking into despair, has a dream which seems designed to mystify,
though readers of *Clarissa* would recognize it as allusive. She dreams that her
dead brother appears and promises her 'great happiness', which she can
attain only by 'first going to church with Sir Richard Harlow'. Still dreaming,
'she went trembling to church, and just as the Minister was going to
pronounce them one, an Angel caught her up and carried her off' (II,
116–17). The last sentence recalls Lovelace's dream of Clarissa ascending to
heaven, which he misinterpreted to mean marriage (VII, 147–8; *IV, 135–6*).
Maria's whole experience recalls Clarissa's riddling letter to Lovelace, which
by giving him hopes of seeing her 'at my Father's' buys her undisturbed time
to prepare for death (VII, 175–6; *IV, 157*). Maria cannot understand her own
dream, but she uses the prescribed form of words to Sir Richard, and this
buys her an end of isolation, as her friends are summoned to the wedding. At
'any . . . impediment' she boldly interrupts, thus freeing herself from persecution and enabling her to marry her chosen love after rumours about her
having 'gone off with' Harlow are scotched. Both Richardson's abduction plot
and his forced-marriage plot are thoroughly, though sympathetically and
respectfully, rewritten and answered.

As well as offering her heroine an escape-route which Richardson's
imprisoned heroines lack, Mathews slightly softens her ordeal in other
respects. Sir Richard eagerly accepts the coming marriage as 'the last trial of
your fortitude', whereas Lovelace always had another trial planned *before* any
possible marriage. Clarissa invented and carried out her own ruse (which did
not, however, save her), while Maria only carries out a plan uncomprehend-
ingly taken from a male supernatural helper. A sermon is preached on her
case as proving that God will raise up friends to protect the innocent, in
contradiction of Clarissa's famous 'GOD ALMIGHTY WOULD NOT LET
ME DEPEND FOR COMFORT UPON ANY BUT HIMSELF' (VII, 421; *IV,
339*).[16]

Softening plays no part in the response to Richardson of Ann (Masterman)
Skinn. Emily Ravensworth, heroine of *The Old Maid* (1771), is part autobiographical, part formed in the mould of Anna Howe and Charlotte
Grandison. She writes flippantly and cynically of marriage, offers to 'turn
Knight-errant' in a female friend's defence (I, 126), and never modifies her
biting irreverence about the older generation. She briefly becomes 'this sweet
angel' when thought to be dying, but she recovers to imagine the recipient of a
letter saying 'Bless me, I thought the girl had been dead a week ago!' (II, 57–8,

71). But, as Susan Staves notes, she acts as a contradiction of *Clarissa*, when she fights off a friend's husband by stabbing him through the hand with pointed scissors, turning her rage not inwards but outwards. She remains impenitent, and later her ridicule of and escape from Lord Wilton 'play[s] itself off against' Clarissa's non-escape from Lovelace.[17] Successful, un-reproved, she is more interesting as a comment on Clarissa than as a copy of Anna or Charlotte, especially since she finally picks a husband willing to 'deliver the pen into her hands' (III, 131).

The century's end produced another respondent: Eliza Fenwick, whose *Secresy; or, The Ruin on the Rock* (1795) is a sexual-revolution novel like those of Mary Wollstonecraft and Mary Hays, but richer, more acute, and more assured than theirs, and linked to the Richardson tradition as theirs are not. Although his works had contributed towards this revolution, Richardson would hardly have approved of Fenwick's title-page assertion 'By a Woman' (instead of 'Lady'), nor the way her dedication, aspiring to immortality, dismisses the familiar letter as 'a sort of corruptible substance'. Nor would Richardson have approved of her two heroines. These are Caroline Ashburn, who has survived spoiling by wealthy parents and Indian servants to make herself an intellectual and a feminist, and Sibella Valmont, a child of nature who passionately loves both Caroline and (a childhood sweetheart) Clement Montgomery. The plot is positively anti-Richardsonian. Clement, at first merely weak and passive, unequal to Sibella's love, descends first to casual infidelity, then to sponging on a rich doting woman (Caroline's mother). Possessing no revolutionary principles of his own, he is willing to take advantage of Sibella's conviction that a private, personal contract is the equivalent of marriage. Once she is pregnant he drops her (not knowing she will have money) to marry his wealthy admirer. Her baby dies in Caroline's arms; so do Sibella herself and Sibella's more worthy suitor Arthur Murden; Caroline thus loses both the woman and the man whom she loves.

Everything here subverts the moral code promulgated in Richardson's works. Sibella's unusually secluded upbringing is presented as an actual moral wrong done to her, as Clementina's, for instance, is not. Her sexual actions do not embarrass the estimable characters, nor is penitence ever suggested to her; Christian hope is equally lacking. Caroline not only, like Clarissa, asserts her moral responsibility for her own actions; she requires responsibility from men and women alike not to their families but to the human race. Where Clarissa shrinks from taking possession of her legal inheritance for fear of upsetting her male relatives, Caroline proposes to investigate the sources of hers, since if it comes from the 'depredating practices' of 'those who perfidiously call themselves the protectors' of India she will want to renounce it (I, 65–6, 165–6). To Arthur, wild with despairing love, she writes, 'You are but two beings in the great brotherhood of mankind, and what right have you to separate your benevolence from your fellow-creatures and make a world between you, when you cannot separate your wants also?' (This is hardly unprecedented advice, since it echoes Samuel Johnson, but from a woman to her friend's suitor it is unprecedented indeed.)[18] Having lamented Sibella's self-deception (so like that of other characters in Richardson and his followers) Caroline comments, 'Oh, a laborious horse deserves to be canonized in preference to the woman whose sole industry consists in the active destruction of her understanding' (III, 120, 141). Sibella's not only loving but bedding Clement, error of judgement though it is, challenges the cautious and scrupulous self-examination of Richardson's heroines for 'preference'. The moral enforced is not avoidance of rash passion, but avoidance of corroding secrecy about discreditable facts.

Despite all this, Richardson is mighty yet. The promptness, vividness, and variety with which Fenwick establishes her various epistolary voices come from him. So do innumerable minor devices, such as female attempts to assess a male blend of rakishness and benevolence; rumours of a village seduction; male epistolary use of the intimate *thou* for *you* (I, 72–5, 172–7). So does Fenwick's sense of the contingency and inadequacy of people's emotional response to each other – which letters can sometimes circumvent. Caroline has to explain later in writing why when face to face she did *not* say, '*I love you: – I love you, Sibella, with all my soul*' (I, 18). Fenwick pushes beyond Richardson's limits, but in the same path. Where Clarissa and Anna indignantly assert that female friendship is as true and strong as that of men, Caroline writes 'Men, my dear Sibella, have not that enthusiasm and vigour in their friendships that we possess' (I, 176). Beside the instant, ardent rapport between these two, the devotion of Richardson's female friends may look pallid; yet the basis of their friendship – firm commitment, letters sharing confidences, discoveries, and reciprocal criticism – is the same.

Relations between the sexes have altered more, except for that between the would-be rake and his prey. It is here that Fenwick moves closest to Richardson. Lord Filmar, who wants Sibella before he meets her, because of her reputed beauty, money, and exceptionally obedient principles, expects to 'be the least noosed of any married man in England. She will want no more than a cage, and a closet, and one smile a month from her sovereign Lord and master': no doubt he has in mind the Lovelace who expected on marrying Clarissa not to 'be *much at home with her, perhaps, after the first fortnight, or so*'.[19] But when he attempts midnight abduction, he finds himself struck dumb by his first sight of Sibella. Confronted with 'my will is free. I tell you, Sir, I am beyond your reach', Filmar resembles that Lovelace who was left without 'any thought but what reverence inspired' by Clarissa's 'My soul is above thee, man!' Like Lovelace, he recovers more than once: he calls Sibella 'goddess', 'sweet saint', and – he suspects – 'lovely lunatic'. He also writes that after gagging her he will 'heal those lips with kisses! My lines stagger – No wonder! – I am on the summit!' So Lovelace had imagined both inflicting bruising kisses and swelling to 'snuff the moon with my proboscis'.[20]

Filmar fails to emulate Lovelace; but as he grows in moral stature while Clement Montgomery declines, he comes to emulate Belford, aspiring to higher things under the heroine's moral influence. Like Clarissa's Mr Wyerley, too, he renews his offer of marriage once he has heard Sibella's whole story (by means of letters), including her sexual experience. Like Mowbray but more winningly, he provides some relief for the reader, by his crudity of style, from other people's fine-spun sensibilities.[21]

The narrative measures first one character and then another for the role of Lovelace; but none of them fits. The heroinism which Richardson depicted in a struggle to the death with rapacious male individuals (both bourgeois and rakish) is seen by Fenwick as engaged on the one hand against self-destructive forces within (love misplaced or unrequited) and on the other against a more extensive complex of social and political repressive forces. Women are still trained to guard themselves against the rake, and the rake still goes through the motions of seduction; but the real danger lies elsewhere. Richardson's plot in *Clarissa* has become a sub-plot. Sibella's destroyer is not a strong but a weak man, acting not against society but in collusion with its sinister forces: isolation, secrecy, enforced ignorance, and greed for wealth ravished from India.

Of the lesser-known writers discussed here, Eliza Fenwick stands furthest from Richardson in spirit but closest in achievement; apart from Austen, she has perhaps made more various and ingenious uses of Richardson than any other woman writer. Her themes are his: moral excellence, its exercise, and its dangers; the workings of power in individuals and in society; the roots of evil; women's nature and women's role, with their potential for change. The characters' minds and hearts obey the same inner laws in *Clarissa* and in *Secresy*; but their emotional goals, social relationships, and political ideology are immeasurably different (as Richardson's are from those of Griffith, Green, or Austen). Fenwick exemplifies the anxiety of influence, female style: her 'willful and purposeful misprision'[22] must wring from her literary father not an inherited share of his myths or his fame, but a right apparently vested in his gender, the right to tell her story in a version significantly distinct from his. She can stand as culmination, though not as conclusion, of a line of remarkable women writers who learned from Richardson the means of articulating their related but radically different texts. Richardson might have found it dubious praise to say he has enabled some daughters to challenge that teaching which so many daughters eagerly accepted; I see it as praise of the highest kind.

14

Publishing Richardson's correspondence: 'the necessary office of selection'

PETER SABOR

Shortly before the publication of the first two volumes of *Clarissa*, Richardson complained to Edward Young: 'What contentions, what disputes, have I involved myself in with my poor Clarissa, through my own diffidence, and for want of a will! I wish I had never consulted any body but Dr. Young.'[1] Had Richardson consulted only Young about *Clarissa* and his other novels, his correspondence would not be filled with literary arguments, with conflicting views on every aspect of novel writing – and we would be poorer for the loss. As a protracted debate on the art of fiction, Richardson's correspondence is without parallel in the eighteenth century. His correspondents themselves were amazed by his compulsive desire to engage in debate on his own works: Joseph Spence, for example, urged him to 'take up a resolution (which perhaps may be new to you) of neither trusting others, nor distrusting yourself, too much'.[2] But Richardson took up no such resolution, and from the publication of *Pamela* in 1740 until his death in 1761, the central topic of his correspondence is the composition, correction, publication and interpretation of his novels. This essay will examine the disjointed publication history of Richardson's correspondence and its disappointing critical reception, using one set of letters, the exchanges with Aaron Hill, to illustrate Richardson's predominant epistolary concern and to show why a collected edition of his correspondence is badly needed.

The survival of any author's letters depends partly upon his own endeavours, partly upon those of his correspondents, partly upon subsequent collectors and editors. Few of Richardson's letters written before the publication of *Pamela* are extant; his correspondents began to keep his letters only after he acquired sudden fame with his first novel. Our knowledge of Richardson's earliest letters depends upon his recollections in later correspondence: in 1753, for example, he describes to Johannes Stinstra an intriguing letter written over half a century earlier when, 'not Eleven Years old', he assumed 'the Style and Address of a Person in Years' in a reproachful missive to a widow of about fifty, a notorious scandalmonger. Other information on Richardson's early correspondence derives from the same letter to Stinstra. He describes a series of love letters that he composed at the age of thirteen on behalf of three young women, who helped develop his rhetorical skills as they alternately instructed him to 'chide, and even repulse' or to return 'Vows of everlasting Love'. He also mentions an extensive correspondence that began after his apprenticeship to the printer John Wilde in 1706, with a 'Gentleman greatly my Superior in Degree':

Multitudes of Letters passed between this Gentleman and me. He wrote well: was a Master of the Epistolary Style: Our Subjects were various: But his Letters were mostly narrative ... I could from them, had I been at Liberty and had I at that time thought of writing as I have since done, have drawn great Helps: But many Years ago, all the Letters that passed between us, by a particular Desire of his, (lest they should ever be published) were committed to the Flames.[3]

The parenthetical phrase, 'lest they should ever be published', is revealing: even in his early youth, Richardson was involved in a correspondence that had the potential, at least, to appear in print.

Much the earliest of Richardson's letters to be published was one that he wrote to his nephew and printing apprentice Thomas Verren Richardson in 1732. This lengthy epistle of advice and instruction was, as A. D. McKillop notes, 'destined to have a long and curious history'.[4] After his young nephew's death in November 1732, Richardson revised the letter considerably, expanding it and making it less personal in tone, for publication as the second part of his first known work, *The Apprentice's Vade Mecum: or Young Man's Companion* (1733). The published letter was praised by two writers in the *Weekly Miscellany*, with their compliments reprinted in the *Gentleman's Magazine* and *London Magazine*. Much later, in 1804, the original letter was printed in the *Imperial Review*, and then, as McKillop states, with further alterations was 'regularly reprinted by the Stationers' Company down to our own day and presented by them to the youths bound at their hall'.[5]

Although few of Richardson's subsequent letters achieved such circulation, the possibility of publishing parts of his correspondence continued to interest him. From 1734 onwards he kept the engagingly choleric letters of the Bath physician and author, George Cheyne; after Cheyne's death in 1743 he had the file of eighty-two letters, together with obituary accounts and other related material, copied into a notebook, prefaced by an admonition dated 11 August 1744: 'This Book, and the Letters in it, on no Terms, or Consideration, whatever, to be put, (or lent) into such hands, as that it may be printed, or published.'[6] In preserving Cheyne's letters, however, Richardson had already transgressed his correspondent's warning to 'Besure you destroy all my Letters when perused',[7] and the mere act of preservation, despite the prefatory injunction, greatly increased the prospect of their eventual publication – ultimately fulfilled in 1943 on the bicentenary of Cheyne's death. Cheyne's letters are of considerable literary, as well as medical, interest, revealing much about eighteenth-century publishing practices and containing some pungent criticism of *Pamela* and its sequel. His objections to the novel's physical appearance, in which Richardson as printer, as well as author, took some pride, is characteristically forthright: 'I wonder you make your modern Books in so small a Type and so bad Paper. It must certainly disgust it to many, the tender and old who only read Books, and it gives an ill Impression of a Book before its Character is established.'[8] Subsequent letters by Cheyne continue to find fault with numerous aspects of the novel, including its overt displays of physical affection, low language, lack of action and excessive length – eliciting in turn some of the fullest commentaries by Richardson on his first novel.[9] It is significant that Richardson took care to preserve Cheyne's letters; that he did so suggests that he was not merely seeking praise from his correspondents, but was genuinely interested (as he repeatedly claimed) in critical discussions of his novels. An author seeking flattery would hardly have sustained a friendship with Cheyne, the most acerbic and uncompromising of correspondents, or preserved such abrasive criticism.

Another early correspondent whose letters were preserved by Richardson himself was Aaron Hill, the poet, dramatist and critic, whose surviving correspondence with Richardson begins in 1736. Six of Hill's letters were first printed, in abridged form, as an Introduction to the second edition of *Pamela*, together with brief interlinking comments by Richardson, and a concluding poem, also by Hill. In subsequent editions of *Pamela*, Richardson made extensive alterations to the already heavily edited letters, evidently regarding them no longer as Hill's but as part of the text of his novel.[10] After Hill's death in 1750, some of his letters to Richardson were included in the *Works of the Late Aaron Hill* (1753), 'Printed for the Benefit of the Family'. Not surprisingly, in this collection intended to dignify Hill's memory and to provide much-needed financial support for his three surviving daughters, the letters chosen for publication were all harmonious and uncontroversial. As Pat Rogers has shown, Richardson actively promoted the edition, which attracted an impressive list of 1,800 subscribers.[11] No further letters to or from Richardson were to be published in his lifetime, but his own file of correspondence continued to swell, and nothing, however hostile, seems to have been discarded.

After the publication of *Sir Charles Grandison* (1753–4), Richardson began a systematic organization of his correspondence with the possibility of future publication in mind; he arranged it in volumes, indexing it, revising and deleting passages, and sometimes altering or obliterating names. As well as assembling voluminous collections of letters relating to his three novels, he also arranged the exchanges with his principal correspondents: Aaron Hill and his daughters, Edward Young, Thomas Edwards, Sarah Chapone, Sarah Westcomb, Lady Bradshaigh (his favourite and most prolific correspondent), and the remarkable confidence trickster Eusebius Silvester (labelling the latter's exchange of forty-five letters 'a *Warning Piece* to Posterity').[12] In 1757 the German bookseller Erasmus Reich hoped to publish a selection of Richardson's correspondence: 'Vos Lettres ... avec celles de vos amis choisis, feroient beaucoup du bien au monde!' Richardson's reply, however, was hedged with restrictions: the selection must be printed anonymously, in German '& in *that only*', and the correspondents must apply for permission to Richardson, rather than he to them.[13] Like Pope, his contemporary, Richardson was well aware of the charges of vanity that would be levelled against a writer publishing an edition of his own correspondence without sufficient pretext. But unlike Pope, an edition of whose *Letters* was among the last works to be issued at Richardson's press,[14] Richardson failed to create such a pretext; and after Reich pointed out the impossibility of his demand – 'Mais comment faire pour faire consentir vos amis au projet que je vous ai propose?' [*sic*] – the project was abandoned. Equally unfruitful was a proposal by William Richardson in 1780 to issue a collection of his uncle's letters 'on moral and entertaining subjects, never before published'.[15] Only after the death of his last surviving daughter, Anne Richardson, and of all but one of his principal correspondents, Susanna Highmore, was a selection of Richardson's correspondence finally published, edited, in 1804, by the poet and essayist Anna Laetitia Barbauld.

Although Barbauld points out in a prefatory Advertisement that she has performed 'the necessary office of selection' (I, vi), and later remarks that Richardson's complete correspondence with Lady Bradshaigh would alone be as extensive as her entire edition – 'a proof, by the way, that the bookseller and the editor have had some mercy on the public' (I, ccviii) – the *Correspondence of Samuel Richardson*, with its six volumes totalling over 2,000 pages, is often regarded as virtually complete. It contains, however, only some 400 letters, one third by Richardson; whereas about 560 letters by and 1060 letters to Richardson are known to be extant today. The 130 letters chosen by Barbauld in her 'necessary office of selection' have become canonical, while most of Richardson's other 430 surviving letters remain unpublished and largely unread. In the collection of critical essays *The Familiar Letter in the Eighteenth Century* (1966), for example, containing pieces on most of the major letter-writers of the century, Malvin Zirker's study of Richardson's corres-

pondence is based almost exclusively on Barbauld's edition: since she has
determined for Zirker which letters will be quoted, she assumes an important
though invisible role.[16]

While establishing the canon of Richardson's correspondence, Barbauld
wielded her editorial powers with a licence characteristic of her age. Since the
originals of many of the letters that she prints are no longer extant, it is
uncertain to what extent she was responsible for the garbled state of their
texts; Eaves and Kimpel point out that she might well have inherited files of
letters already altered by Richardson and some of his correspondents.[17] The
Young correspondence is especially chaotic, with as many as four letters
covering a period of ten years conflated into a single composite fabrication.[18]
Parts of the correspondence with Lady Bradshaigh are similarly mangled;
Eaves and Kimpel note grimly that 'most of Barbauld's letters of 1751 are in
utter confusion', and it takes John August Wood ten pages of patient
explication to untangle the chaotic texts of the Bradshaigh–Richardson letters
of that year.[19] No letter printed by Barbauld should be assumed to be reliably
presented. The earliest letter in her edition, from Aaron Hill, is dated 1730; it
was actually written in 1738. The latest letter she includes, from Bishop
Hildesley, is dated 24 September 1761, nearly three months after Richardson's death; the correct date is March of that year. At times Barbauld ascribes
the letters of one correspondent to another, confusing, for example, the
Reverend Samuel Lobb with his son William.[20] And throughout she revised
the correspondents' style, often for the worse: changing, for example, Colley
Cibber's wish to 'nibble upon' a slice of Harriet Byron to a desire to 'piddle
upon' (i.e. pick at) her – although the correct reading is found in a facsimile of
the letter in her own edition.[21]

For all its shortcomings, however, Barbauld's edition remains standard,
supplemented but not superseded by other collections and rightly made
available in a modern reprint for want of any alternative.[22] The supplemen-
tary collections, of varying degrees of accessibility, add primarily to the store
of letters by Richardson's correspondents. The earliest, the selection of Hill's
letters to Richardson in Hill's collected works (1753), contains many letters
printed by Barbauld in radically different versions, as well as some letters
omitted from her edition. Shortly after the *Correspondence* was published in
1804, selections from Richardson's correspondence with Sarah Westcomb,
Elizabeth Carter, Tobias Smollett and Edward Young appeared in the
European Magazine and the *Monthly Magazine*.[23] The Young correspondence
is of especial importance: 111 letters were printed, with reasonably accurate
texts,[24] as against the twenty-one fabrications in Barbauld's edition. After
these early nineteenth-century publications, no substantial new collection
appeared until C. F. Mullett's fully documented edition of George Cheyne's

letters to Richardson – none of which are in Barbauld – in 1943. William Slattery's 1969 edition of Richardson's correspondence with the Dutch clergyman Johannes Stinstra, translator of *Clarissa*, contains twelve letters by Richardson and eleven by Stinstra, apparently the complete file of their extant correspondence, as against the three extracts printed by Barbauld. This collection prints in its entirety, for the first time, Richardson's famous autobiographical letter, giving much the fullest account of his shadowy childhood and youth.

Many other letters to and from Richardson have appeared sporadically in a variety of forms, including Henry Fielding's remarkably generous response to the middle volumes of *Clarissa* and a useful gathering of Richardson's letters to Charlotte Lennox.[25] But the only modern general edition of Richardson's letters is one edited by John Carroll in 1964, providing 128 letters written to thirty-three individuals. Carroll's *Selected Letters* differs radically from Barbauld's *Correspondence*. While it contains almost as many letters by Richardson as Barbauld's edition, only about a third of their selections overlap. Carroll complains that Barbauld 'gives excessive space to trivial communications from Richardson's friends' (p. 7); his edition, in contrast, contains no letters to Richardson at all. Barbauld organizes erratically by correspondent – printing, for example, half of the Richardson–Bradshaigh correspondence in volume four, with the remainder in volume six – while Carroll favours strict chronological order. Barbauld's annotations are perfunctory and her index incomplete, omitting hundreds of important references to individuals and literary works scattered throughout her six volumes; Carroll's annotations are exhaustive and his indexing meticulous. Most important, his transcriptions are admirably accurate, on the whole, and based on manuscript sources wherever they are available.

Despite these advantages, Carroll's *Selected Letters* is a deeply unsatisfactory edition. In order to cram over a fifth of Richardson's ample letters into 350 pages, Carroll provides merely selections from his selections; many letters begin and end *in medias res*, sometimes in the midst of the discussion of a significant issue, with no indication of what or how much is being omitted. Extensive material is also deleted within the letters, so that the entire emphasis of a letter is often changed by Carroll's editing. The effect is oddly similar to that of the now discredited abridged editions of *Clarissa*, until recently popular as classroom aids, in which the protracted, journal-like letters exchanged by the protagonists become terse, almost telegraphic communications. While *Selected Letters* can be read as an anthology of Richardson's views on literary matters, as an anthology it cannot reveal the characteristic shape and rhetorical art of Richardson's correspondence. In some cases, it is still preferable (when possible) to read a letter in the version furnished by Barbauld, with a garbled but more complete text.

Furthermore, the elaborate system of shaped brackets, daggers, square brackets and asterisks by which Carroll signals insertions, deletions, and conjectural readings in his text is so rebarbative that some passages are scarcely comprehensible without repeated reference to the explanatory note on symbols. Even so, confusion can result. In a letter to Aaron Hill of 26 January 1747, Richardson writes of designing in Clarissa 'no *Voluntary* Fault, but that of meeting [Lovelace], tho' resolved to go back'; in revising the letter he changed the last phrase to 'tho' resolved not to go off with him'. In Carroll's text, the passage reads 'tho' resolved +not+ to go +off with him+ <back>' (p. 83); not surprisingly, a recent critic has been misled by the plethora of symbols to suppose that 'what Richardson first wrote was a revealing slip: "tho' resolved to go"'.[26] A plain text with variant readings in the form of notes would obviate such disastrous misreadings.

Both Barbauld's early-nineteenth- and Carroll's mid-twentieth-century editions of Richardson's letters were extensively reviewed; in neither case, however, was much regret expressed that the 'necessary office of selection' had been so stringently exercised. The reception of Barbauld's edition was mixed. Almost all reviewers justly admired her 200-page biographical and critical introduction to Richardson prefixed to the first volume – an essay still of considerable value today – and there was some applause too for the letters themselves. The *Anti-Jacobin Review* found in them 'a great portion of entertaining and useful matter ... the whole correspondence is interesting'; the *Imperial Review* pronounced 'the greater part [of the letters] interesting', although 'in the perusal of some of them the attention flags'. In America a review in the *Literary Magazine*, possibly by its editor Charles Brockden Brown, was positive.[27] Such commendation, however, was balanced by diatribes in the *Critical Review* ('So much panegyric, praise so profuse, swallowed with a little affected coyness, but still swallowed with manifest gratification, must at times excite disgust'); in the *Eclectic Review* (the letters, primarily to and from young ladies, 'mostly are too trifling for notice'): and in the *Edinburgh Review* by Francis Jeffrey, who terms the correspondence a 'melancholy farrago', 'so loaded with gross and reciprocal flattery, as to be ridiculous at the outset, and disgusting in the repetition'.[28]

Jeffrey's fulminations against Richardson's correspondence can be matched by similarly strident objections from reviewers of Carroll's *Selected Letters*. Although Carroll himself regards the letters merely as 'helpful but incomplete guides to an understanding of the novels' (p. 35), even this modest claim seemed presumptuous in the early 1960s. The anonymous *Times*

Literary Supplement reviewer termed Richardson almost 'the world's dullest letter-writer' and rejoiced that 'mercifully Mr. Carroll has made a selection from among the hundreds of letters extant'.[29] Morris Golden called the letters 'singularly dull – full of the avuncular coyness which faintly mars even his best work', and noted about Carroll's editing that 'though, unlike Johnson's woman preaching, this is done well, we may still wonder why it was done at all'.[30] Ian Watt declared that 'Richardson's letters lack variety; the subjects, the personality, the style, and the general purport – all are rather uniform', while S. E. Read proclaimed, 'not only does he lack the brilliance, charm, wit, and incisiveness of Walpole or Gray; he is also, all too often, pompous, dull, repulsively pious, and boringly self-centred'.[31] A remarkable exception to this litany of abuse was Rachel Trickett's suggestion that Carroll had been 'too cautious in estimating the value of the letters' that 'betray the intensive conviction, the deep absorption in his own imaginings which enabled Richardson, however unexpectedly, to produce the finest tragic novel in English'.[32] Here, for once, was a suggestion that Richardson's are a novelist's letters, as well as letters about novels, and that as such they possess literary interest comparable to that of the epistolary novels themselves.

The most recent collection of Richardson's letters to be published, William Slattery's edition of the Stinstra correspondence, appeared in 1969, two years before Eaves and Kimpel's massive biography and the critical revaluation of Richardson that followed in its wake. The timing was unfortunate, and the reviews of the collection predictably negative. Robert Kelly asserted flatly, 'It is well known that Richardson's letters are dull and prosaic, and those included in this edition are no exception.'[33] The *Times Literary Supplement* reviewer, similarly, declared that the letters 'only serve to deepen the impression of Richardson's pomposity and simpering vanity'.[34] And John Carroll regretted that there were 'no resurrected treasures in these letters, no further revelations of great moment. A few mild flurries do occur, but exchanges of admiration and esteem are the rule.'[35]

This charge of vanity on Richardson's part and of excessive admiration on that of his correspondents, a charge reiterated here by Carroll, editor of the standard selection of Richardson's letters, is clearly central to any discussion of the correspondence. It is, of course, true that Richardson's taste for praise was highly developed, as is true of the majority of writers and artists. And it is true that Richardson used some sycophantic parts of Hill's letters in the Introduction to *Pamela* – passages that Fielding was quick to parody through the prefatory exchanges of Parson Tickletext and Parson Oliver in *Shamela*. In thus publicizing his novel, however, Richardson was merely following a time-honoured tradition that continues to the present in the convention of the dust-jacket accolade: readers of William Beatty Warner's *Reading Clarissa*

(1979), for example, are informed on the authority of J. Hillis Miller that this 'brilliant analysis of Richardson's book' is 'sure to establish itself as a major book on Richardson as well as an admirable model for the interpretation of fiction'.[36] What has long been considered standard practice among other authors, however, is regarded in Richardson as a peculiar quirk; their quest for fame is his egregious vanity.

The various editors of Richardson's correspondence, regrettably, have done much to reinforce the idea that the letters are largely a giving and receiving of flattery. Thus the excerpts from Richardson's correspondence with Hill published in Hill's *Works* and in Barbauld's *Correspondence* portray the relationship as one of mutual admiration, each author vying to excel the other in the generosity of his praise. In Carroll's *Selected Letters*, for the first time, another side to this correspondence can be glimpsed: here we find letters revealing part of a long-simmering dispute between two strong-minded writers over questions of plot, structure, characterization and morality in *Clarissa*. But Carroll's selected edition necessarily omits some of Richardson's fullest, most cogent letters to Hill, and all of Hill's replies: one of the most intriguing literary disputes of the century thus remains largely unpublished.

Hill's first remarks on Richardson's as yet untitled work in progress were made in a letter of 24 July 1744. Five years later, in July 1749, the two correspondents were still discussing *Clarissa*; in the intervening years Hill's initial outbursts of enthusiasm had gradually given way to persistent, stringent criticism that forced Richardson into a detailed explanation and justification of his novel. The turning point came in a letter (still unpublished) from Hill to Richardson, written on 23 October 1746. Up to this point, the only substantial issue being debated was the length of the work, which both Hill and Richardson regarded as excessive, but difficult to curtail. Here, for the first time, Hill proposes changes in the characterization of both Lovelace and Clarissa. Lovelace's character requires some 'Softening': 'I wish you would incline to change the Arrogance and Insult he affects to triumph with, for something of a generous Reluctance to exert his conscious Superiority, against the Brother of his Mistress, so beloved.' There follows the suggestion that Clarissa should have been 'in downright Love' with Lovelace from the outset: 'For then, how irresistibly must she be hurried, by a new Increase of Passion, on her Lover's being forced into such Hazard of his Life, for her Sake only.'[37] As Eaves and Kimpel note, this proposal was particularly likely to meet resistance, since 'Richardson never wanted Clarissa clearly to acknowledge her love for her future ravisher.'[38] But Hill went a good deal further. An 'absolute Love', he declares, 'sees nothing that it would not see'. For Clarissa to remain blameless she must experience such blind love for Lovelace, and thus lose responsibility for her actions:

And, as such unsuspicious and full Confidence will give a better Face to her Desertion with him, so it will increase her Horror and Surprize, to find him, after it, so full of Perfidy. Besides this, it will double the Pity to her undeserved Distress, when a mistaking Faith betrayed her to it. As it is now, the Family's Resentment, may be thought more just, than *her Affection* for a Man who openly avows his hatred of, and triumphs over, her Relations, with a Vein of Scorn, that ought to shake her Inclination to converse with him.[39]

These and other proposals in Hill's letter galvanized Richardson into analysing at length his own novel in progress. First, he found a putative friend who took issue with Hill's remarks, and copied the friend's response at the foot of Hill's letter. This anonymous justification of *Clarissa*, which has never been published, contains many observations that Richardson subsequently reiterated to several of his correspondents and critics. Lovelace, the friend urges, must remain thoroughly base: '*Your* Lovelace delights in Cruelty, and enjoys the Tears of distressed Beauty; *His* is actuated by Generosity and true Love.' Hill, similarly, has 'given us also a New Clarissa, but such a one as might be easily adopted by any giddy Wench that ever ran away with her Father's Footman'. And the advice, at the end of Hill's letter, that Richardson 'ought not to be sparing in abridging', is likewise rejected: Richardson has, the friend complains, already removed large parts of the text, and 'What Descriptions, what animated Conversations, have we lost by it!'[40]

Since Richardson's voluminous reply to Hill of 29 October 1746, as well as several later letters on *Clarissa*, are included in Carroll's edition, while Hill's copious responses are represented only through fragments in footnotes, *Selected Letters* gives the impression that Hill's objections were soon silenced. But Hill's letter of 5 November again expressed the view of the heroine most likely to exasperate Richardson. Clarissa, Hill argued, should not give her name to the title since, unlike Pamela, she was not 'an Example to be imitated'. Instead, Hill proposes 'The Lady's Remembrancer: Or, the Way of a Young Man, with a Maid'. This would be followed by an ample subtitle, describing 'the Life and Ruin of a lately Celebrated Beauty Miss Clarissa Harlowe' which will 'furnish a Warning to Unguarded, Vain, or Credulous Innocence'. Richardson's indignation is suggested by the three large exclamation marks he inserted beside the phrase 'the Way of a Young Man, with a Maid': his heroine was being diminished by Hill's insistence on her credulity and her 'Ruin'. An alternative title supplied by Hill, 'The Lady's Legacy', also avoided mention of the heroine's name, but at least it did not focus attention on Lovelace's 'Way'.[41]

At the end of 1746, Hill sent Richardson a twenty-four page abridgement of the first seven letters of *Clarissa*, eliciting a courteous but clearly aggrieved reply. Hill had deleted some two-thirds of the text, thus making an excessively long novel excessively brief: 'all that I design'd by it, I doubt cannot be answer'd in so short a Compass'.[42] Eaves and Kimpel's description of Hill's vigorous unpublished response as 'not ... entirely submissive'[43] is a considerable understatement. Richardson's letter, Hill begins, 'has thrown me under such a Perplexity and Concern, as I neither know how to describe, or to act in it'. As well as defending his own abridgement, Hill makes some further wounding remarks about *Clarissa*, suggesting that it might be overshadowed by the brilliant success of *Pamela*: readers will bring 'high and justly founded Expectation ... from Effect of that inimitable Excellence that lies before them for Comparison'. Lovelace, he insists, is being blackened 'beyond Necessity', and 'no young Woman, who shall read him, will suppose *her* Lover such a base and wicked one as *he* (by choice) will seem to her to be'. Far from being exemplary, Clarissa has merely chosen to 'go off with a suspected Rake'; yet, Hill reiterates, 'no Inducement weaker than resistless Love, will justify Clarissa's rash Elopement with a Man. To be sure, the Fear of being forced to marry Solmes can never be enough to justify it.' Clarissa's duty, then, was to remain at Harlowe Place, defying her father's demands that she marry Solmes, rather than 'running away from his House, with a worse, if possible, of her own choosing – at least of her own trusting to'.[44]

In his very full reply to these criticisms, printed in *Selected Letters*, Richardson takes pains to counter Hill's unfavourable comparison of *Clarissa* to *Pamela*, of which the 'strange Success at Publication is still my Surprize'. In Clarissa's 'Preparation for Death, and in her Death, I had proposed to make this a much nobler and more useful Story than that of Pamela; *As all must die*'. Quoting Hill's offending phrases, 'a rash Elopement with a Man' and 'running away from her Father's House', Richardson insists that Clarissa has been 'tricked off' rather than departing voluntarily, and laments: 'I am very unfortunate, good Sir, let me say, to be so ill-understood.' Clearly aware that this must seem insulting, Richardson deleted the last five words, and added 'to have *given Reason*, to be so little understood'.[45] Hill's unpublished reply, however, shows that he was not mollified by this judicious addition: in his charge that Hill has read 'without due *Attention*', Richardson has 'not done [Hill's] Application Justice'. Once again Hill stresses that Clarissa should not be permitted to leave Harlowe Place with Lovelace, and again he asks that Lovelace's character be made less profligate and 'ungentlemanlike', since ''tis a *Clarissa*, to whose Heart he has found Entrance'. The tone is adamant and unrepentant, especially at the end of the letter. Here Hill declares that the changes he proposes to Clarissa's conduct are an 'indispensable Necessity – A Point essential – And not merely Ornamental, and Embellishing'. Should Richardson ignore this advice, the novel will fail in its aim: 'For where Example and Instruction are in View, too Wrong an Error in the *Moral*

Content of the Party the Instruction is to be derived from absolutely cuts off the Effect expected from it.'[46]

At this tense point, the extant correspondence between Richardson and Hill breaks off for about nine months. Eaves and Kimpel speculate that 'perhaps letters have been lost, and there was no real quarrel',[47] but when Hill next writes to Richardson he has clearly lost touch with the progress of *Clarissa*, and now at last desists from further criticism. In their remaining correspondence on the novel there is a preponderance of flowery encomiums, exemplified by Hill's unctuous letter of 5 May 1748:

Your moral hints are sudden, like short lightning; and they strike with the same force and subtility! – You sow benevolence in every soil you travel over; and it must be *rock*, indeed, that does not let it *spring* to a proportion'd harvest! ... The fabled *Circe* only turned men into beasts; you (truly) turn beasts into men.[48]

This and similar letters represent the Richardson–Hill correspondence both in Hill's *Works* and in Barbauld's *Correspondence*, and the editors, intent on suppressing any signs of dissent, have unwittingly done great harm to Richardson's reputation. It is patently unjust to judge an author's correspondence on the basis of a highly restricted selection, yet this is what the great majority of Richardson's critics have done. When William Henry Irving, for example, declares that Richardson's letters are 'straightforward in style and a bit dull', or when Malvin Zirker proclaims that 'his letters generally are informal, rambling ... relatively uninteresting as examples of the letter form',[49] the letters in question are merely a fraction of the entire correspondence: the fraction sanctioned by Anna Laetitia Barbauld.

Few critics, in fact, have chosen to write on Richardson's letters; Zirker's essay, surprisingly, remains the only substantial published discussion. Bruce Redford's recent book on eighteenth-century letter writers opens promisingly with a quotation from one of Richardson's letters to Sarah Westcomb, and the statement that 'Samuel Richardson takes us to the heart of the matter – to the *cor* of correspondence',[50] but thereafter, oddly, this supposed heart of the matter disappears from sight. Some fruitful criticism is appearing in doctoral theses such as that by Daphne Swabey, who compares Richardson's personal, model, and fictive letters, urging that the correspondence be studied for more than its biographical interest, and by Tom Keymer, whose analysis of Richardson's 'epistolary rhetoric' is based on an extensive examination of the manuscript letters.[51] But while much of the correspondence remains unpublished, such readings will necessarily be uncommon.

Some seven hundred letters to and from Richardson remain in manuscript, the bulk in the Victoria and Albert Museum, with others dispersed among over forty libraries and private collections. Single correspondences too are scattered. Of the thirty letters that Richardson exchanged with Lady Barbara Montagu between 1753 and 1760, not one has been printed; and although most of the correspondence is at Cornell, the remainder is divided among the Hyde Collection, the Wisbech and Fenland Museum, and libraries at Harvard and Yale. During the same period Richardson exchanged over forty letters with Lady Elizabeth Echlin, the most prolific and intimate of his later correspondents after her sister, Lady Bradshaigh. Some of this correspondence is in Barbauld, a few further excerpts are in Carroll, and more recently Dimiter Daphinoff has given Lady Echlin posthumous fame by printing her hitherto unpublished alternative ending to *Clarissa*, as well as a fine, ironic response from Richardson, suggesting that, since in Lady Echlin's version no rape takes place, both Clarissa's and Lovelace's lives might have been spared:

I know not, if I had persued your Ladyship's Plan, whether I would not have spared the Mother, and made the gloomy Father repent and die. Clarissa recovered to good Health, and Mrs. Norton, both living with the mother, what Happiness might they have known! what Good have done! what an exemplary Widowhood!

Lovelace, by his own Interest, and that of his Uncle, might have been made a Governor of one of the American Colonies; and there shone, as a Man you had reformed, by giving an example of Piety, and enacting, or causing to be enacted, Laws promotive of Religion and good Manners.[52]

The passage, written with the same caustic irony that many of the letter-writers in *Clarissa* wield to good effect, is splendidly energetic, and one of many such lively pieces in the Richardson–Echlin letters. To follow the correspondence in its entirety, however, readers must consult no fewer than twelve manuscript collections, as well as diverse printed sources.

To exercise, as both Barbauld and Carroll have done, the 'necessary office of selection' is to create an arbitrary canon of Richardson's letters. The tercentenary of his birth is surely not too early to recover all that remains of his correspondence and to publish it in its entirety. It would, of course, be essential to print both sides of the correspondence. Some parts of such an edition would, inevitably, find more favour than others, as is true of any collected edition of a body of writings. But a *Collected Letters* would give readers the immeasurable benefit of being able to read Richardson without editors having decided on their behalf what is or is not of interest. A *Collected Letters* would print each letter whole, showing how discussions of the novels grow out of the particular relationship that Richardson sustained with each of his correspondents. It would reveal the striking amount of criticism made of the novels, and show Richardson's willingness to debate critical issues; it would dispel the persistent idea of Richardson's seeking only praise. Such an edition would make Richardson's personal letters as accessible as the famous letters that constitute his novels: it would perform the really 'necessary office' of collection.

15

The rise of Richardson criticism

SIOBHÁN KILFEATHER

In the last four decades Samuel Richardson's novels have been the object of greater study and the site of greater controversy than at any time since the eighteenth century.[1] Most of that attention has focused on *Clarissa*, where ethical and political issues of the greatest current concern interweave so as to be almost indistinguishable from issues of writing and interpretation. Recently there have also been significant developments in theoretical writings surrounding Richardson's other novels, which for many years seemed less relevant to contemporary critical concerns. If one looks at the rise of Richardson criticism since the powerful and influential readings offered by Dorothy Van Ghent and Ian Watt[2] certain trends emerge. The first of these is a revolution in attitudes to the representation of women, and particularly of violence against women. A second trend is a reversal of the tendency to seek archetypal patterns which would codify and unify Richardson's unwieldy texts, into a tendency to celebrate their diversity and disjunction. These two lines of development may be attributed respectively to concurrent developments in feminism and in other kinds of literary and political theory. In contradistinction, I detect as a third strand of Richardson criticism the consolidation of biographical readings of the novels, and of the relation between the novels and an idea of the author, which tend towards a particularly class-conscious interpretation of Richardson's life. The feminist, Marxist, and post-structuralist readings which have dominated Richardson criticism in the 1980s have been largely uninterested in revising the biographical interpretations, and the most radical new readings often rely on some very dated historical research and class perceptions.

Many of the most interesting critical discussions of *Pamela* have taken place in the context of arguments about the 'rise' or development of the novel in the eighteenth century, rather than in book-length studies of Richardson's corpus, where *Clarissa* tends to be the central locus of debate. Its comparative brevity makes *Pamela* the most popular of Richardson's novels for the college curriculum, and it is well served by two good paperback editions.[3] Margaret Anne Doody, in her introduction to the Penguin edition, points out that '*Pamela* has never ceased being a controversial work' (p. 7), and the controversy has centred on issues of class and sexuality first raised in Fielding's famous parody. Jina Politi begins her chapter on *Pamela* in *The Novel and its Presuppositions* by stating that 'the Pamela controversy does not originate in a concern over the truth or falsity of the fact as such, but in a culture's prepossessions as to what it is desirable to consider probable and possible, and what as improbable and impossible'.[4] Politi's 'dualistic' reading of *Pamela* favours a structural rather than allegorical approach to the religious themes of the novel, and looks for meaning in its series of linguistic oppositions. Richardson's own linguistic strategies are in an oppositional relation to those of Fielding because each writer is invested in a notion of probability dependent on class-prepossessions.

Morris Golden, in his study of *Richardson's Characters*, tries among other things to analyse Richardson's bourgeois fantasy of aristocracy.[5] Golden makes some very suggestive comments on the exchanges negotiated in the novels between the manners of the aristocracy and the ethics of the bourgeoisie. Golden's early attempt to sort Richardson's characters into 'a few staple types' (p. 1) no longer seems completely satisfactory, however. Richardson's characters are more divided and incoherent than they appear here. Golden has recently returned to examine the effects of the macro-political world on the construction of self in the novels, an aspect of Richardsonian studies relatively little pursued outside the socio-historic analysis of class conflict and ideological change.[6] The major biographical studies of Richardson by William Sale, and by T. C. Duncan Eaves and Ben D. Kimpel, with their particular emphasis on Richardson's printing activities, and his wide business and social acquaintance, offer material for much more extended accounts of his party political interests, and their possible influence on the novels, than we have yet seen.[7]

Cynthia Griffin Wolff approaches the issue of characterization in Richardson from a somewhat different angle, one which describes 'the agonized psychological probing of *Pamela* and *Clarissa*' as 'an appropriate way to depict identity in crisis', while 'the confident social articulation of personality in *Grandison* is appropriate to the assertion of a unified, coherent sense of self'.[8] Wolff assumes that 'Puritan' character models (such as saints' lives, or stock sinners like Bunyan's Mr Badman) were familiar to Richardson and his audience, and that the novel may be understood as a placing of those models under stress. That emphasis on stress is the most interesting feature of Wolff's argument, which resembles other attempts to account for Richardson's development of the novel in terms of source studies, in that it often seems to pass over what is most interesting about the fiction in favour of the formulaic.

A number of commentators on Richardson have dealt with the question of how epistolary fictions, and particularly 'writing to the moment' have figured in the creation of the self.[9] Roy Roussel discusses *Pamela* in terms of the sexual and seductive aspects of correspondence, especially of the ways the hiding and disclosure of letters, as well as their exchange, mediates distance and presence.[10] Terry Castle criticizes Roussel for giving 'a rather sentimental existential reading' to Pamela and B.'s relationship, in an essay where she argues that critics have been reluctant to talk about sex in *Pamela*, and have redescribed the heroine's behaviour in terms of other kinds of experience.[11] Castle's reading is primarily psychoanalytic and feminist, revealing a myth of female sexual development operative within the novel. In a concluding note Castle acknowledges that the psychosexual economy she has outlined in the text relates to the sociological and religious themes noted by other critics.[12]

Ian Watt suggests that Richardson's 'concern with that most private aspect of experience, the sexual life' drove him to develop new, intimate forms of writing, and made him not only the spokesman for his class but also the central precursor for the English novel, which Watt and others have seen as the conscience of that class. It is in debates over sexual ethics in Richardson, and in class assumptions, that one may most clearly monitor the history of anxiety and disturbance which makes these novels an important site of ideological controversy. Those who, in the 1980s, are angry and concerned about sexual violence, may look back with astonishment on some of the critical remarks on the rape of Clarissa made in the 1950s. But it is possible to discern the traces of certain psychoanalytic interests and historical assumptions from earlier readings surviving unexamined through the decades. The very length of *Clarissa* and *Sir Charles Grandison*, and the fact that they are organized into small epistolary units which overlap in patterns of slight variety in repetition, creates particular critical problems. Even a book-length study of a single Richardson novel can colonize only a small proportion of the text. To discuss the plots – which are always in dispute within the novels – is deceptively simple, but does not take one very far. The letters are the action.

Samuel Johnson, who asked Richardson for an index to the novels,[13] was one of the first readers to acknowledge that recollection would be a particular problem for these texts. The reader's memory operates very differently on Richardson's novels than on other texts nearly as long. To remember the plot of a Fielding novel, *Tom Jones* for example, may not be all one wants to say about it, but plot covers a great part of one's relation to the text, and chapter divisions make the plot easily remembered. The implied reader is in a position of control similar to that of the implied author. In Richardson, as many commentators have observed, the reader's role is more analogous to the partial, prejudiced activities of interpretation in which the characters are engaged. Where so many acts of reading are taking place simultaneously, not even the interpretation of the 'editor' occupies a privileged place of authority.[14] These issues of memory and interpretation have had a particular effect on Richardson's critics. It is more convenient for them, even than for other critics, to rely on the readings of their predecessors. One critic will cite another as a shorthand reference to a whole area of historical background, formal analysis, thematics, or iconography within the novels. Such readings are taken for granted in developing new areas for critical attention within the novels. The danger is that certain 'truisms', which developed in a particular context, underpin subsequent readings. This has happened to a great extent with Richardson biography. The figure of the prurient printer and 'unconscious' genius pops into the most formal, theoretical analyses of the novels.

One consequence of this reliance on other readers has been the increasing frequency of essays such as this one. Kinkead-Weekes, Warner, Castle, Goldberg, and, most notably, Eagleton, have found that writing about Richardson is such a gripping and partisan activity that one is provoked into battle with other critics.[15] It seems to help one maintain a sense of the coherence of the issues at stake, to feel that one is addressing some other partial, passionate interpreter in a novelistic debate. It is not only academic critics who continue to find Richardson's stories interesting and polemic. *Pamela* and *Clarissa* have recently been seen in theatrical adaptations, and Merchant Ivory have produced a film based on the dramatic adaptation of *Sir Charles Grandison* by Jane Austen and/or a member of her family.[16]

Until very recently another unchallenged survivor of earlier critical endeavours was mid-twentieth-century historiography. For a long time the admittedly exemplary historical analyses of Watt and Christopher Hill[17] were hardly modified or supplemented by more recent thinking on ideology, nor significantly altered by thirty years of subsequent research into economic history and the history of the family. The addition of Lawrence Stone as an authority on the history of the family in the eighteenth century did not significantly alter the terms set by Watt and Hill, and readers debating political and textual interpretations cited without apparent qualm thirty-year-old thinking on the rise of the Puritan middle-classes.[18] In the last few years however, a renaissance of political criticism on the left has produced new work, including three series of books from British publishers – *New Accents* from Methuen, *Re-reading Literature* from Basil Blackwell, and *Questions for*

Feminism from Verso – which have offered historical contextualizations of the institutionalization of literary criticism in this century, as well as revisions of major theorists on the left such as Watt and Hill.

Critical practice has always been interwoven with other social, political and ethical concerns. Ian Watt's identification of Richardson's fiction with the rise of the bourgeoisie provides his explanation for the fact that 'the great tradition' developed out of bourgeois realism, rather than from the 'class fixity' characteristic of Fielding's plots.[19] Frank Kermode's 1950 essay on Richardson and Fielding reinscribes the contrast between two fictional projects which literary critics since Samuel Johnson have discerned as being in profound opposition to one another.[20] Dorothy Van Ghent and Leslie Fiddler are more interested in the archetypal patterns of seduction and betrayal, the drama of sexual warfare, which turn Clarissa and Lovelace into major cultural symbols with a resonance familiar to many people who have never read the novel in which they appear.

The Rise of the Novel is the critical text which did most to re-introduce Richardson as a central figure in the eighteenth-century canon. Watt brings together social, economic, and geographical historical details, as well as a wide survey of eighteenth-century political, fictional, and aesthetic writings into an eloquent account of the changing form and content of fiction. In choosing to identify 'formal realism' as the distinguishing feature of the novel, Watt seems to indicate that Richardson is the most quintessentially novelistic of eighteenth-century writers. Richardson's editorial framing fictions, his epistolary form and his 'writing to the moment', his use of dialects and slang, his detailed descriptions of households and occupations, as well as his concern with close psychological monitoring of his characters, almost exhaust what we understand English realism to be. Watt describes changes in the English novel as participating in, and reflecting, a change in self-consciousness – 'the rise of individualism'.[21] Influenced by Q. D. Leavis, Watt offers an account of how readers participate in the creation of a climate for certain fictions. He consistently emphasizes a gendered reader – as in so much else he here prefigures recent trends in Richardson scholarship. Unfortunately he writes about Richardson's appeal to women readers in terms of the novelist's feminine sensibility. Although Watt tries to keep these comments placed in the context of his argument about the feminization of English culture in the latter half of the eighteenth century, they tend to slide into psychoanalytic remarks on Richardson's attitude to sexual relations. It is more accurate to observe that Richardson's novels make statements about the exchange of masculine and feminine characteristics, and about personal freedoms, which are politically and imaginatively interesting to women, than either to credit or damn the novelist with a peculiarly female temperament. Watt's comments on

Richardson's sexuality serve his overall programme of showing how individual experience feeds into the 'formal realism', reproducing middle-class 'individualism' in the novel. Watt has a tendency to psychoanalyse, while he historically describes, a whole class. His misreadings of Richardson arise from a too complete identification of the printer and novelist with a consistent set of conscious and unconscious political, social, sexual, and religious beliefs.

Watt is very good at describing how social changes, from door numbering and urbanization to the development of print culture, and changes in gender roles affect the texture as well as the content of writing. Part of his project is canon formation – he frequently reiterates a line of development from Richardson through Austen and Eliot to Forster and Lawrence – but he knows and gives credit to (what he considers) the minor fiction of the eighteenth century. A recent essay by Margaret Anne Doody challenges Watt's description of Richardson and his heroines as hostile to urban life, and it is likely that our current interest in new historicism will see other details of his comprehensive argument re-visited.[22]

Michael McKeon's recent rethinking of the origins of the novel begins by asking what problems are 'thrown into high relief' by the shortcomings of Watt's theories.[23] McKeon points out that 'romance' and the 'novel' are not the absolutely discrete categories implied by Watt, and he also questions Watt's evidence for the dominance of the middle class in the early eighteenth century (pp. 2–3). His choice of *Pamela* rather than *Clarissa* as the exemplary text from Richardson's *œuvre* is notable, considering how far the latter novel has been central to recent critical debate; but McKeon does discuss Richardson's first novel in terms of the textuality, and struggles over interpretation, that are familiar from *Clarissa* criticism, as well as in terms of the oppression of the heroine on grounds of class and gender. McKeon's description of Mr B. could just as well be applied to Lovelace: 'B. reveals that his dominant motives are not strictly sexual but political, and that he takes power to consist in the ability to make others accept one's version of events as authoritative' (p. 359). The parallel struggles over the control of textual production and over the class and gendered definitions of honour and virtue within the novel are discussed by McKeon through his paradigmatic 'questions of truth' and 'questions of virtue'. McKeon concludes his chapter with a direct comparison of *Pamela* and *Clarissa*, classifying the former as a fantasy of 'material and social empowerment', while the latter is concerned with 'discursive and imaginative empowerment'; according to McKeon, '*Pamela* is not an inferior first attempt to achieve what is fulfilled only in *Clarissa*; it successfully achieves an authentic species of fulfilment which *Clarissa*, ambitious of other ends, does not even attempt' (p. 380).

Christopher Hill's 1955 essay on 'Clarissa Harlowe and her Times' glosses the novel in terms of a consolidation of patriarchal power within the family, and an increased investment of family wealth in the hands of the male heir, rather than in the *paterfamilias*, with an accessory degrading of the rights of female children. Hill and Watt both presume implied definitions of the terms 'Puritan' and 'middle class' that not only equate easily with one another, but that also carry a whole baggage of social and sexual codes of conduct. Into this network of beliefs and practices they cast Richardson's writings as fairly unambiguous documents, reflections of class conflict rather than the sites of struggles over cultural meaning. Terry Lovell is one recent critic who asks us to reconsider the novel as one of the earliest cultural commodities.[24] Lovell suggests that rather than simply looking for a bourgeois realist reflection of capitalism's ideal self-characterization in fiction, we might analyse these novels in terms of fantasy and surplus. Lovell is also one of many writers to point out how different the terrain of eighteenth-century fiction looks when women novelists are included in discussion.[25]

Critical debates over *Clarissa* generally centre on issues of gender and sexuality, whether they choose to define 'woman' as an object of exchange in society, as a silenced subject, as a myth, or as a metaphor for linguistic indeterminancy. Those hostages offered to fortune by previous commentators on the rape of Clarissa have been documented and satirized by Terry Castle and Terry Eagleton, whose angry indictments of critical misogyny are useful and necessary.[26] It may now be time to follow them up by historicizing those readings of rape, and asking what, in addition to misogyny, the readings reveal about critical practice in earlier decades, and how they colour even current readings of some other aspects of the novels. V. S. Pritchett's 1947 essay on *Clarissa* in *The Living Novel* tells us that 'those who put up their price by the device of reluctance invite the violence of the robber. By setting such a price upon herself, Clarissa represents that extreme of Puritanism which desires to be raped.'[27] Dorothy Van Ghent, who cites Pritchett on the rape, probes further into what her own era, apparently unconcerned with an idea of chastity, finds of archetypal significance in a novel about rape. Van Ghent saw in *Clarissa* a mythology of the feminine as appropriate to the 1940s and early fifties as to the 1740s. The nervous excess of Van Ghent's argument is revealed when she describes *Clarissa's* plot as 'a singularly thin and unrewarding piece of action – the deflowering of a young lady – and one which scarcely seems to deserve the universal uproar which it provokes in the book' (p. 47). Van Ghent is able to identify for the 1950s the oppression of women in the symbolic, but she is unsure of the significance of rape. Her hesitation reminds us that rape has only recently begun to be widely defined as a crime of violence. The number of critics who use the terms seduction and rape interchangeably when discussing *Clarissa* indicates the dilemma of Van Ghent. Her fantasy of Clarissa as the victim of a psychopathic 'ripper' alerts us to her perception of a violence she cannot articulate in the conventional vocabulary of 'deflowering' available to her. Van Ghent's inability to look directly at the rape forces her to throw the emphasis of her interpretation elsewhere, which she does by describing the novel as an archetypal battle of the sexes. In this reading, Clarissa becomes a man-hater, as unreasonable and malevolent in her own way as Lovelace. Van Ghent, like Pritchett, is repelled by values she understands as 'Puritan' and 'bourgeois' and which she assumes that Richardson endorses through his heroine. Neither critic appreciates the crimes involved either in the Harlowes' persecution of their daughter, or in Lovelace's attack on her, and so both miss the radical features of the novel.

Van Ghent is a particularly skilful image-tracer and supports her view of the novel by investigating Clarissa's use of the word 'man'. Janet Todd, in a chapter largely devoted to the women in *Clarissa*, and particularly to the friendship between Anna and Clarissa, adopts Van Ghent's reading of Clarissa the man-hater.[28] Those parts of Todd's feminist reading of *Clarissa* which suggest that Clarissa is complicit in patriarchal structures have been coloured by Van Ghent's hostility to the heroine. For Todd the hatred of men would be an appropriate response to Clarissa's oppression, while for Van Ghent it is partly the expression of a repressed sexuality. There are such elements in the text, but as Florian Stuber has pointed out, Clarissa encounters a cast of male characters much more various and complicated than the mere villainy of James Harlowe, Jr. and Solmes, or the complex villainy of Lovelace.[29]

Some feminists are anxious to read *Clarissa* against the grain of a construction of the feminine within patriarchy as self-silencing, anorexic, ultimately suicidal. The earliest modern example of this trend seems to come in Leslie Fiedler's eccentric but enthusiastic comments on Richardson in *Love and Death in The American Novel*.[30] Fiedler prematurely announces the victory of feminism, musing that 'to seem if not to be Clarissa ... was a burden not cast off till the battles of the feminists had been fought and won. The imposition of the Clarissa-image on the young girl represents an insidious form of enslavement' (p. 36). Sue Warrick Doederlin regards 'the tragic feminine paragon' as a crucial element 'for determining those changes in sexual behavior and individual feeling' that brought about the closed domestic nuclear family.[31] There is, however, a contrary, and more per-suasive body of criticism, which reads *Clarissa* as a major feminist text precisely because it argues that women's rights to self-determination begin with rights over the body, and with economic rights. Among Richardson's most ardent feminist champions have been Terry Castle, Margaret Anne Doody, Terry Eagleton, Carol Houlihan Flynn, Mark Kinkead-Weekes, and Katharine M. Rogers.

Margaret Anne Doody has been the most passionate recuperative critic of Richardson. *A Natural Passion* attacks many of the prejudices which infect Richardson criticism and produces a sketch of the novelist, from his letters and fictions, as a more self-conscious and successful artist than had been previously acknowledged. Doody discusses the dramatic and fictional contexts in which the novels appeared, and produces careful thematic readings of the whole corpus which have become a standard resource for subsequent critics. Like Kinkead-Weekes, Doody is interested in the dramatic qualities of Richardson's fiction, and shows how dramatic parallels and allusions operate in the pastoral comic world of *Pamela* and the tragic theatre of *Clarissa*. She describes in great detail the courtship novels (mostly by women) published before Richardson, explains what he learned from these and where he departed from and expanded upon them. Doody is one of the people who have made the early novel much better known today than it was in 1974. Like Ian Watt, Doody is interested in establishing Richardson as a 'great' writer, which means that she emphasizes the ways in which he is better than earlier novelists. However, Doody, like Richardson, was reading these novelists and taking them seriously at a time when they were being completely trivialized by the majority of the critical establishment. Features of Richardson's writing which previous critics had attacked as freakish or perverse are placed within conventions. The obscurity of some of the imagery, particularly in *Clarissa*, is partially clarified in Doody's account of (and reproductions from) contemporary iconography. Her conviction that *Sir Charles Grandison* is Richardson's second great achievement helped, along with Jocelyn Harris's 1972 edition,[32] to reinstate *Grandison* in critical debate.

Although widely acknowledged, Doody has not been unchallenged, particularly by those critics who attack the theoretical status of intentionalism.[33] However, one should remember that Doody has defined intentionalism as a political issue in the campaign for good authoritative texts of Richardson. While there was no *Clarissa* in print, and the mangled Sherburn abbreviation was still widely read, it was important to point out that Richardson, in common with the major women novelists of the eighteenth century, was censored for the modern reader. Although Penguin have recently given us the first edition of *Clarissa*, there is still a need for an authoritative third edition;[34] and for a new edition of the letters.

The other major critical work on Richardson from the early 1970s was Mark Kinkead-Weekes's *Samuel Richardson: Dramatic Novelist*. Kinkead-Weekes presents Richardson as the founder of the 'psychological' novel, and

– as his title implies – accounts for the innovativeness of Richardson's style in its debt to dramatic structures.[35] This is a subtle reading of the dramatic influence – one which appreciates how Richardson learned from drama the significance of the silence between words, and how, as a printer, he realized the potential of punctuation and notation to characterize such gaps. Kinkead-Weekes shifts psychological analysis away from an idea of the author and refocuses that analysis on detailed readings of the characters' psychic insurrections and role-playing. He pays attention to nightmares and daydreams. In B., Lovelace, and Grandison he recognizes very similar strategies of self-presentation that involve 'acting' and ambition. At the same time he urges something that increasingly seems theoretically undesirable as well as impossible, that is an attempt to think oneself into Richardson's language, particularly into the language of his religious faith.

Rosemary Bechler, John Dussinger, Margaret Anne Doody, and Carol Houlihan Flynn are just a few of the critics who have pointed out that the religious discourse of Richardson's novels is complicated, and open to contradictory interpretations.[36] Alan Wendt's meditation on 'Clarissa's Coffin' influenced the careful explicators of Richardson's iconography, and those critics who are concerned to understand the very particular religious convictions most explicitly articulated in the discourse surrounding Clarissa's death.[37] To talk of Richardson's indebtedness to 'Puritan' character-types or ideas now seems too crude a categorization. At the same time we can still appreciate careful analyses of his literary allusions to religious discourse, such as we find in Gillian Beer's excellent essay on 'Richardson, Milton, and the Status of Evil' (1968), which draws out and expounds upon the parallels – intimated by the text and felt by many previous readers – between Lovelace and Milton's Satan.[38]

In the late 1970s and early 1980s sexual politics and deconstruction (and what one might have to say to the other) occupied the central place in the debate over Richardson, a debate which became as heated and novelistic in discourse as it had been in the 1740s or 1950s. John Preston's *The Created Self* – a study of the reader's response to eighteenth-century fiction – posits that we value a novel in proportion to what it demands of us as readers. Preston analyses the frustration of the reader's empathy with Belford and Anna Howe, and suggests how the process of reading becomes at once compulsive and alienating – 'a reflection of the existential crisis generated within the novel itself' (p. 61). Preston's examination of the interpretive struggles in *Clarissa* influenced William Beatty Warner and Terry Castle in their respective deconstructive studies of that novel.

An influential essay by Leo Braudy suggests the possibility of reading deconstructively the extraordinary sexual/textual metaphors in *Clarissa*.[39]

Warner cites Nietzsche and Derrida as major influences on his 1979 study, *Reading Clarissa: The Struggles of Interpretation*.[40] He finds in *Clarissa* a struggle between two ideas of the self, one single, unified, full of light, and the other given to rhetoric, surface, and a free play of signifiers. These are respectively Clarissa and Lovelace. To suppose that this theory eschews the old arguments would be mistaken. The pleasure of Warner's book comes not simply from its theoretical analysis but also from its novelistic passion for the character of Lovelace, whom Warner aims to rescue from the 'slanderous characteristics' of 'Clarissa's party' (p. 268). Warner has been repeatedly attacked for his provocative comments on the rape. He is among other things a self-conscious deployer of psychoanalytic theory, so when he tells us that Clarissa is not a *common* slut (p. 50), asks 'is she hiding something unsavory beneath her garments?' (p. 26), and argues that 'rape is the most cogent response to Clarissa's fictional projection of herself' (p. 49) one is bound to read these as studied acts of aggression. One then wants to enquire, against what is that aggression directed? Warner's identification of Clarissa with a rigid logocentrism denies the political aspects of her oppression, and his refusal to take her suffering seriously denies that those who represent rape and other forms of violence have a responsibility for that representation. Feminists decode Warner's book as revealing an attack on their own critical practice, which becomes associated with Clarissa's 'antitheoretical style' (p. 7) – that is to say, her demands for self-representation and self-control, and her at least provisional commitment to the theoretical possibility of communication, which is an issue with very different stakes for a subject in a non-dominant position than for an aristocrat like Lovelace. In the late 1970s, when Warner's book appeared, feminist criticism was often perceived as 'antitheoretical'. Terry Castle's *Clarissa's Ciphers* offers an example of how far a deconstructive methodology can serve political and feminist ends.

Terry Castle's book on *Clarissa* might be described, Castle herself acknowledges, as a gloss for a single utterance from the heroine of that massive text: 'I am but a *cypher*, to give *him* significance, and *myself* pain.'[41] As her title indicates, Castle is as interested as Warner in the novel's textuality, and in the struggles for interpretation that occur within and around the text, but, unlike Warner, Castle insists on a political context for her readings. Her counter-argument to Warner states that 'the excruciating situation *Clarissa* dramatizes is that a rhetorical system is *not* "powerful" unless grounded in political power'.[42] Castle draws aptly and succinctly on Derrida's *Of Grammatology* (particularly 'Writing Before the Letter') and Tzvetan Todorov's *The Poetics of Prose* for her theoretical argument. Her brief, elegant chapters describe Clarissa's attempts to engage in 'natural' expression and 'natural' interpretation, and show how she is thwarted and misconstrued by her family, by Lovelace, and even by Anna Howe. Castle's semiotic analysis is at its best when describing the language and gestures of Clarissa's encounters with the Harlowe family in the fourth chapter, 'Interrupting "Miss Clary"'. No one has better placed Richardson in the context of recent theoretical discussion. There are, however, some problems with Castle's argument. Although her 'real reader' is deliberately gendered, thus introducing an idea of difference, her readings are surprisingly monolithic. Castle's profession that she is engaged in 'the thematicization of interpretation', while Richardson imagined that he was writing a 'transparent' history, is merely a reverse of the intentionalism she criticizes in others. Her theoretical argument, that rape is an act of silencing, is politically very appealing, particularly in its linking of the textual representation of violence, and the physical brutality of sexual violence in the world. Her quotations from Simone Weil in particular are telling. However, somewhere this argument seems not to do justice to Clarissa, who is not cut off and silenced by rape in quite the ways that Castle describes. Richardson's argument is politically powerful in that it reveals how far the desire to silence someone is an impulse behind all levels of sexual violence, but the novel also has features which are enabling to survivors of violence, like Clarissa, because it suggests ways in which she retains some kind of control over self-representation.

In *The Rape of Clarissa*, Terry Eagleton examines how 'the feminization of discourse prolongs the fetishizing of women at the same time as it lends them a more authoritative voice' (p. 13). Eagleton's lively polemic does not so much propound Richardson as a feminist writer, as discuss his writing in terms of a feminization of values in the eighteenth century. Theoretically Eagleton's argument, like those of Lovell and Armstrong, seems to owe something to Ann Douglas's work on *The Feminization of American Culture*, while the historical tracing of a 'shift in the ideology of gender' (p. 14) is indebted to Jean H. Hagstrum.[43] Eagleton devotes almost as much space to a reading of *Clarissa*'s critics as to his analysis of sexual politics and class politics in the eighteenth century. In discussing 'Clarissa' – woman and text – as commodities, Eagleton revives the framework of analysis provided by Watt and Hill, now informed by theories of language and of literary reproduction chiefly indebted to Pierre Machery, V. N. Voloshinov, and Raymond Williams.

In 1975, when J. Paul Hunter observed of Richardson and Fielding that 'England's two best writers at mid-century failed in their last and least characteristic novels', he was indulging in a critical commonplace which has only very recently undergone substantial revision in new readings of both *Amelia* and *Sir Charles Grandison*.[44] Peter Sabor, for example, has argued that the novels are bound to disappoint if they are matched against the templates of their authors' better known fictions, and that *Amelia* and *Grandison* should be read as experimental fictions in which Richardson and Fielding each have learned from the other's writings as well as from his own earlier novels.[45]

Sylvia Kasey Marks's book-length study of *Sir Charles Grandison* considers Richardson's last novel as 'the compleat conduct book'.[46] Marks, responding to what she describes as modern critics' neglect, even slighting of *Grandison*, writes a defensive account of the novel. Marks seeks to place *Grandison* historically in the context of Richardson's intentions as expressed in his correspondence about the novel, and to place the novel aesthetically in the context of some suggested generic origins, including drama, fable, and (primarily) the conduct book. Marks detects a coherence in Richardson's whole literary career, and she suggests ways in which *Grandison* may be related to books Richardson printed, including Defoe's *A New Family Instructor* and *Religious Courtship*, and to early projects such as the revision of L'Estrange's *Aesop's Fables*, *The Apprentice's Vade Mecum*, and *Letters Written to and for Particular Friends, on the Most Important Occasions*, as well as to the other novels. She is interested in showing how a reading of *Grandison* which accepts the novel as an exhaustive conduct manual will illuminate tedious or lengthy arguments, and bring disparate elements of the plot together. In making this argument so successfully, Marks neglects the case that there are reasons more than sociological why we might wish to read *Grandison* today.

The problem with emphasizing the indubitable influence of conduct books upon the novel's structure is that doing so seems to promote both those formulaic features of the plot and those exemplary aspects of Sir Charles's character that are least appealing to novel readers. Jocelyn Harris's introduction to the 1972 edition of *Sir Charles Grandison*, which narrates the story of the novel's composition through Richardson's correspondence, is more successful in suggesting the tensions and contradictions of the narrative, as Richardson swings his attention back and forth between Harriet and Clementina, and is pressured and teased by interested friends to send the story in various directions. Like Marks and Doody, Harris discusses the influence of the drama on the characterization as well as the dialogues in the novel, and she also makes an argument for the influence of romance on the English as well as the Italian scenes – again emphasizing the novel's most entertaining qualities. Harris draws out those aspects of *Grandison* which appealed to nineteenth-century novelists, and sketches its influence on Jane Austen, George Eliot, and George Meredith.

The influence of *Grandison* on subsequent eighteenth-century fiction is the subject of a book by Gerard Barker, *Grandison's Heirs*.[47] Barker's genealogy of Grandison's exemplary character through *The Spectator* and the sentimental drama, and through earlier fiction by Jane Barker, Mary Davys, and Penelope Aubin is a familiar one; his tracing of the Grandisonian influence on later

novels such as Frances Sheridan's *Memoirs of Miss Sidney Bidulph*, Thomas
Holcroft's *Anna St Ives*, and Elizabeth Inchbald's *A Simple Story*, which have
received comparatively little critical attention, is a promising project, particularly in so far as it brings out the political interest of the Grandisonian
character for the so-called Jacobin novelists. Although he is by no means the
first critic to make these points, Barker is very effective in tracing Grandison's
manipulations of other characters, and the psychological constraints that his
exemplarity forces upon Harriet. Barker shows us what Godwin in particular
is able to make of the anxious self-deprecation which other characters feel in
the face of Grandison's relentless public perfection. Barker's choice of novels
is excellent but his readings are disappointing, particularly when he treats
women writers whom he often seriously misjudges as slight and derivative,
and he fails to make much of this promising project.

In *Adultery in the Novel* Tony Tanner glances at one feature of *Grandison*
which has fascinated critics – the development of a non-consanguinous
extended family. The 'affective intensification' of kinship bonds is characteristic of pre-Romantic fiction, and has been a concern of those critics who
bring Richardson into comparison with contemporary European literatures.[48] Tanner's major interest, however, is in another form of 'contract' and
most of his discussion of Richardson relates to the various manifestations of
the word 'will' in *Clarissa* (pp. 100–12). The importance of will in the novel,
including the ways in which the metaphor is made literal when Clarissa makes
her will, was previously discussed by Doody in *A Natural Passion*. Tanner
looks for a Nietzschean formulation of this concern. Tanner examines not
only textual interpretations of the law, but the metaphors of legalism and
contract in his book.

Janet Todd's introduction to 'sensibility' covers some of the same ground
as Barker in looking at *Grandison* and its successors.[49] Todd's account of the
'gendering of sensibility' (p. 78) explains why it is the watching women and
not the active hero who not only display feelings, but are able to write and
comment on them at length. In Clementina, according to Todd, 'Richardson
shows female sensibility pushed to the extreme of hysteria, and he charts the
progress and cure of this disease as outlined in the medical books of Robert
James and Dr George Cheyne which he printed' (p. 79). Todd refreshes
one's sense of the extraordinary nature of the Richardsonian equations of the
woman's body with sensibility: 'because of their greater physical susceptibility
and because of the social constraints on their verbal expressiveness, women
are more sincere in gesture than in words in a social situation, and language
frequently exists only to censor a truth expressed by the body' (p. 86). The
difficulty of rendering such body language is partially met by Richardson's
creation of the private letter as a figure analogous to the female body. Todd's

observations on the expressive bodies of Harriet and Clementina suggest one way in which Richardson was to prove a resource for Burney and Inchbald.

Todd's investigation of how the metaphoric readings of the woman's body and the body of the text are both exchanged and made literal is characteristic of current modes of critical inquiry in eighteenth-century studies. John Bender's study of prisons is exemplary of recent work.[50] Bender analyses the prison as a figurative device in the eighteenth-century novel, by concurrently offering a new historical investigation of prisons in the eighteenth century, by considering the penitentiary and the novel as analogous cultural systems, and by offering a reading of the various metaphors of imprisonment and sentencing in a number of texts from the period. Robert Erickson not only employs a history of fictional mid-wives, but examines the use of metaphors of midwifery and giving birth, in his discussion of Defoe, Richardson, and Sterne.[51] Christina Gillis's elegant monograph on the relationships between space, privacy, and epistolary form in *Clarissa* is informed by a sensitive reading of architectural spaces.[52] Among the most virtuosi displays of new historical and metaphorical analyses is Terry Castle's discussion of *Pamela II* in her study of the carnivalesque in eighteenth-century culture.[53] Castle examines the paradox of the sequel in which Richardson both wants and does not want to repeat his original story. She analyses the stasis of the plot in the sequel as an act of repression – Pamela's history of social mobility is what the plot seeks to repress – and accounts for the reader's pleasure at the return of plot in the masquerade scenes.

Every writer on Richardson, including those discussed above, is indebted to the ordering of Richardson studies made by his biographers and bibliographers. William Merrit Sale's 1936 bibliography has been supplemented by two recent secondary bibliographies by Richard Gordon Hannaford and Sarah W. R. Smith.[54] T. C. Duncan Eaves and Ben D. Kimpel scrupulously tracked down the details of the Richardson biography, assembling invaluable information from archives and teasing out the biographical hints and obscurities of an extensive correspondence. *Samuel Richardson: A Biography* has been an invaluable resource for subsequent critics. Critically the biography may be associated with the spate of revisionist studies of the life and work, which set out to recuperate Richardson's reputation as a conscious literary artist.[55] Eaves and Kimpel complement the account of Richardson's printing career provided by William Sale, and the earlier literary biography of A. D. McKillop, with a detailed investigation of Richardson's life, and their *Biography* is particularly informative about his friends and correspondents during the period when he was composing the novels. Eaves and Kimpel have also supplemented the *Biography*'s enormous contribution to Richardson scholarship with additional notes and articles on the life. Many valuable critical observations now follow on hints thrown out in Sale or Eaves and Kimpel. However, many facts about Richardson's life are still not known, and in particular one must regret the paucity of information about the novelist's early years. It may be the absence of commentary on Richardson's formative adult years which diminishes the psychological persuasiveness of the biography. Eaves and Kimpel seem to have brought to their research into Richardson's life an already-conceived critical prejudice that the novels are exotic fruits of a dull, almost offensively dull, experience. So, while the biography is an excellent reference work, it fails to evoke imaginatively the temperament which could have written the novels. Carol Houlihan Flynn's *Samuel Richardson: A Man of Letters* (1982) is the most useful and interesting subsequent blend of criticism and biographical commentary published to date. Although her study is primarily critical, Flynn tries to integrate Richardson's writing practice with his experience, and to trace the effects of some previously unexplored historical and literary contexts for the novels – the legal treatment of 'fallen' women, literature on rakes, crime, and the use of fairy tales. Among its other virtues Flynn's book supplies a valuable bibliography of these fields. In these aspects Flynn's study prefigures some of the diversity of recent Richardson studies, which have been influenced by feminist readings of sexual politics on the one hand, and by new historical investigations on the other. While such concerns remain central to eighteenth-century studies the extraordinary details of Richardson's novels are unlikely to be neglected; but it seems both probable and desirable that there will be less intent to rescue his literary reputation and monumentalize his works than in previous criticism, and more interest in placing the novels in conjunction with the wealth of eighteenth-century texts that are presently being rediscovered.

Notes

Introduction

1 Eaves and Kimpel's *Biography* provides the source for much of the biographical information here.

2 We are grateful to Tom Keymer, who supplied the copies of works printed by Richardson from which these ornaments (reproduced on our jacket, title-page, introduction-page, and p. 266) were photographed. Sale, in *Master Printer*, discusses the provenance and identifiability of these marks and their use by Richardson; see pp. 266, 271, 307.

3 John Carroll, ed., *Samuel Richardson: A Collection of Critical Essays* (Englewood Cliffs, NJ: Prentice-Hall, 1969), p. 19; Rosemary Cowler, ed., *Twentieth-Century Interpretations of Pamela: A Collection of Critical Essays* (Englewood Cliffs, NJ: Prentice-Hall, 1969), p. 13.

4 Margaret Collier to Richardson, 3 October 1755, *Correspondence*, II, 78.

5 *Pamela*, ed. T. C. Duncan Eaves and Ben D. Kimpel (Boston: Houghton Mifflin, 1971); *Pamela*, ed. Peter Sabor with an Introduction by Margaret Anne Doody (Harmondsworth: Penguin, 1980).

6 *Clarissa*, ed. Angus Ross (Harmondsworth: Penguin, 1985); *Clarissa*, ed. George Sherburn (Boston: Houghton Mifflin, 1962). The baneful influence of Sherburn's abridgement is discussed in Margaret Anne Doody and Florian Stuber, '*Clarissa* Censored', *Modern Language Review*, 18 (1988), 74–88.

7 *Sir Charles Grandison*, ed. Jocelyn Harris (London: Oxford University Press, 1972; paperback reprint, 1986).

1 Florian Stuber: Teaching *Pamela*

I write this essay for Hugh Amory who, at Columbia College, first taught me how to read the novels of Samuel Richardson.

1 Following the example set by the villagers of Slough (see Alan D. McKillop, 'Wedding Bells for Pamela', *Philological Quarterly*, 28 (1949), 323–5), classes went on holiday when Pamela married Mr B. One class recreated their celebration,

complete with authentically designed eighteenth-century costumes, for the video film *Pamela's Wedding Day at FIT* (Stuber–Doody Productions, 1985).

2 For one interesting study of Pamela as a writer, see Patricia Meyer Spacks's chapter on Richardson in *Imagining a Self: Autobiography and Novel in Eighteenth-Century England* (Cambridge, Mass.: Harvard University Press, 1976), pp. 193–226.

3 R. F. Brissenden, 'Samuel Richardson', in *British Writers*, ed. Ian Scott-Kilvert (New York: Charles Scribner's Sons, 1980), III, 80. This handsomely printed, seven-volume set brings together the *Writers and Their Work* series initiated in 1950 by the British Council 'as part of its worldwide program to support the teaching of English language and literature, an activity carried on both in the English-speaking world and in many countries in which English is not the mother tongue' (III, vii). Perhaps because the publisher claims the essays were 'completely revised, brought up to date, and re-edited for publication' in 1980, original dates of publication are not given. A reader of the 1980 edition thus has no way of knowing that Brissenden's article in the third volume first appeared as a pamphlet in the series in 1958. The thoughts seem current – are current, in Brissenden's view, for despite the almost twenty-five years of intervening criticism noted in his bibliography, Brissenden saw no need to revise his essay in any substantial way. So long may critical notions prevail, and pass into the future. *British Writers* is 'intended to appeal to a wide readership, including students in secondary and advanced education, teachers, librarians, scholars, editors, and critics, as well as the general public' (III, vii).

4 *Ibid.* As recorded in encyclopaedias and reference works, such opinions about *Pamela*'s faults have remained surprisingly consistent throughout the twentieth century: writing on Richardson for the eleventh edition of the *Encyclopaedia Britannica* (1910–11), Austin Dobson noted *Pamela*'s 'rather sickly morality', its 'unpleasant pruriency', its 'shuffling, loose-shod style', and its heroine's 'keen eye for the main chance' (XXIII, 301). Indeed, seventy years later, the twentieth century's essential view of Richardson had changed so little that in his *Samuel Richardson: An Annotated Bibliography of Critical Studies* (New York: Garland, 1980), Richard Gordon Hannaford could still praise Dobson's article as a 'careful review' and 'good summary' of Richardson's achievement. Reading the articles written for such standard sources, I found only one that discussed Richardson and *Pamela* without condescension, with real respect, and that was Margaret Anne Doody's essay for the *Dictionary of Literary Biography* (1985), XXXIX, 377–409.

5 Watt, *The Rise of the Novel*, p. 173.

6 Apparently thinking of Watt, Maximillian Novak approvingly cites this phrase of 'one critic' in his entry on Samuel Richardson for the new International Edition of the *Encyclopedia Americana* (1984), XXIII, 508.

7 Rosemary Cowler, 'Introduction', *Twentieth-Century Interpretations of Pamela* (Englewood Cliffs, NJ: Prentice-Hall, 1969), p. 7.

8 *Ibid.*, pp. 7, 13.

9 F. R. Leavis, *The Great Tradition* (1948; rpt. New York: New York University Press, 1969), p. 4.

10 Kinkead-Weekes, *Dramatic Novelist*, p. 502.

11 'Calculating she must inevitably seem', says William M. Sale, Jr, in his entry on Richardson for *Collier's Encyclopedia* (1987), XX, 72.

12 The twelve sections of *Pamela* are as follows.

In Volume I (1) Letters 1–13 cover events of a year, ending with reactions to the scene in the summer-house; (2) Letters 14–26 begin with Mr B.'s return home after an absence of two weeks and end with the first bedroom scene; (3) Letters 27–31 end with the Editor's explanation of Pamela's abduction; (4) 'Letter 32', the first section of Pamela's journal (pp. 94–134), is sent to Pamela's parents with Parson Williams's help (Mr Andrews eventually brings the packet to Lincolnshire, pp. 251–2); (5) pp. 134–50 are hidden under the rosebush when Pamela vainly tries to escape; they are later seized by Mrs Jewkes and given to Mr B. (p. 197); (6) pp. 150–89 are eventually divided into two packets (p. 205), both of which are later given to Mr B. (p. 207).

In Volume II (7) pp. 193–223 are given to Mr B. to read (p. 239), and later to Mr Andrews, who takes them home with him (p. 273); (8) pp. 223–74 end with Mr Andrews's departure for home with section 7; (9) pp. 274–301 end with Pamela's signature, Pamela B., and are sent to her parents with section 8; (10) pp. 301–44 concern Lady Davers's confrontation with Pamela; (11) pp. 344–88, together with section 10, are signed and sent to Pamela's parents after her return to Bedfordshire; (12) pp. 388–401, ending with Pamela's signature, are sent to her parents to read on their way to the Bedfordshire estate.

13 In Letter 4, Mrs Jervis tells Lady Davers that Pamela 'was Fifteen last *February*' (p. 29). Since the first thirteen letters cover a 'Twelve-month' (p. 35), Pamela is sixteen during most of the novel.

14 In a letter to Lady Bradshaigh, 14 February 1754, *Selected Letters*, p. 289.

15 William M. Sale, Jr, 'Richardson, Samuel', *New Encyclopaedia Britannica* (1985), X, 49. In *Samuel Richardson: Dramatic Novelist*, Mark Kinkead-Weekes argues that Pamela's text actually presents B.'s fully complex personality, but he concludes: 'The fact that Pamela is the only source of narrative makes it too easy to confer the reliability of her reportage on to her interpretation also; and hence to assume that she herself, her parents, and her view of B., are meant to represent Richardson's own vision' (p. 24).

16 Eagleton, *The Rape of Clarissa*, pp. 33–5.

17 John J. Richetti, 'Richardson, Samuel', in *Great Writers of the English Language: Novelists and Prose Writers*, ed. James Vinson (New York: St Martin's Press, 1979), III, 1027.

18 Mark Kinkead-Weekes, 'Introduction', *Pamela* (New York: Dutton, 1966), p. x.

19 T. C. Duncan Eaves and Ben D. Kimpel, 'Introduction', *Pamela* (Boston: Houghton Mifflin, 1971), p. xi. Cf. Brissenden, 'Samuel Richardson', p. 84: 'Once the marriage has occurred, the tension disappears; and apart from one or two scenes the rest of the book ... is dull, worthless stuff.'

20 In a letter to Lady Echlin, 10 October 1754, *Selected Letters*, p. 315.

21 The requirements of the Composition course prevented me from teaching the sequel also. Yet at the end of each semester, some students went on to read *Pamela*

II on their own. They came back to tell me they enjoyed it, and I believe them. After living with *Pamela* in this way, I too read its sequel with increased pleasure. The connections between the two parts are more sophisticated, more playful, and more genuinely interesting than is generally perceived. But that is the subject of another essay.

22 See Abraham H. Maslow's hierarchy of human needs in *Motivation and Personality* (New York: Harper & Row, 1954).

23 Martin Battestin, 'Introduction' to *Joseph Andrews and Shamela* (Boston: Houghton Mifflin, 1961), p. xi.

24 *Ibid.*, p. xvi. The intervening pages are filled with enthusiastic anti-*Pamelist* praise.

25 Lionel Trilling, 'On the Teaching of Modern Literature', *Beyond Culture* (New York: Viking, 1968), pp. 10–11.

2 Gillian Beer: *Pamela*: rethinking *Arcadia*

1 William Merritt Sale argues on the basis of the printer's ornaments used that Richardson printed the introductory matter for the first volume of Sidney's *Works* (books I and II of the *Arcadia*); none of Volume II (books III, IV and V of the *Arcadia*); the whole of Volume III (the 'sixth book' of *Arcadia* by R.B.), and the rest of Sidney's works. Sale gives the printing dates as 1725, 1724, 1724, the first volume thus being printed later than the other two. See Sale, *Master Printer*, p. 204. Eaves and Kimpel simply remark that 'the output of his [Richardson's] press during the rest of the 1720s ... is not especially distinguished. The most literary items are the works of Sir Philip Sidney (1724 and 1725)', *Biography*, p. 47.

2 *The Works of the Honourable Sir Philip Sidney, Kt. in Prose and Verse*, 14th edn, 3 vols. (London: E. Taylor *et al.*, 1725), III, 6. Further reference will be given parenthetically in the text.

3 See Maurice Evans, ed., 'Introduction' to Sir Philip Sidney's *The Countess of Pembroke's Arcadia* (Harmondsworth: Penguin, 1979), pp. 10–13.

4 Jacob Leed, 'Richardson's Pamela and Sidney's', *Journal of the Australasian Universities Language and Literature Association*, 40 (1973), 240–5.

5 Henry Fielding, *The Adventures of Joseph Andrews*, ed. Martin C. Battestin (Oxford: Clarendon Press, 1967), p. 325.

6 See *The Oxford Dictionary of English Christian Names*, ed. E. G. Withycombe (Oxford: Oxford University Press, 1977), and Eaves and Kimpel, *Biography*, pp. 116–17.

7 Richard Steele, *The Tender Husband: or, The Accomplish'd Fools*, in *The Plays of Richard Steele*, ed. Shirley S. Kenny (Oxford: Clarendon Press, 1971), pp. 233–4, 238. Pamela writes her own commentary on *The Tender Husband* in *Pamela II*; see IV, 79–88.

8 'While I was writing the two volumes, my worthy-hearted wife, and the young lady ... used to come in to my little closet every night, with – "Have you any more of Pamela, Mr R.? We are come to hear a little more of Pamela", &c. This encouraged me to prosecute it' (*Correspondence*, I, lxxiv–lxxv).

9 See *OED*, s.v. 'linsey-woolsey'. The statement that the fabric is 'a signe of inconstancie' and thus forbidden by God is taken from a homily on preparation for marriage.

10 Guillaume de Salluste du Bartas, *Du Bartas, His Devine Weekes and Workes Translated ... by Joshua Sylvester*, 4th edn (London: H. Lownes, 1613), p. 552.

11 'The Wife of Bath's Tale', ll. 1162–4, in *The Works of Geoffrey Chaucer*, ed. F. N. Robinson (London: Oxford University Press, 1957), p. 87.

3 John A. Dussinger: Truth and storytelling in *Clarissa*

1 See Fielding's emotional response to *Clarissa* in a letter to Richardson; E. L. McAdam, Jr, 'A New Letter from Fielding', *Yale Review*, 35 (1948), 300–10.

2 Hester Lynch Piozzi, *Anecdotes of the late Samuel Johnson* (London, 1786), p. 221.

3 [Samuel Richardson], *A Collection of the Moral and Instructive Sentiments, Maxims, Cautions, and Reflexions, Contained in the Histories of* PAMELA, CLARISSA, *and Sir* CHARLES GRANDISON. *Digested under Proper* HEADS, *With References to the Volume, and Page, both in Octavo and Twelves, in the respective Histories* (London, 1755). See pp. iii–v.

4 Alan Dugald McKillop, *Samuel Richardson: Printer and Novelist* (Chapel Hill: University of North Carolina Press, 1936), p. 217.

5 See Bruce Robbins, *The Servant's Hand: English Fiction From Below* (New York: Columbia University Press, 1986), pp. 53–90.

6 *Emma*, in *The Novels of Jane Austen*, ed. R. W. Chapman (London: Oxford University Press, 1933, rpt. 1960), IV, 431.

4 Edward Copeland: Remapping London: *Clarissa* and the woman in the window

1 *The Dialogic Imagination: Four Essays by M. M. Bakhtin*, ed. Michael Holquist, trans. Caryl Emerson and Michael Holquist (Austin: University of Texas Press, 1981), p. 302.

2 Two other well-known contemporary paintings of Covent Garden on view in recent exhibitions ('Londoners' at the Museum of London, and 'The Image of London: Views by Travellers and Emigrés, 1550–1920' at the Barbican) show gentry occupying the piazza as a pleasure ground for the display of fine clothes and elegant courtship: Josef Van Aken's 'Covent Garden Market' of about 1730, and Balthasar Nebot's 'Covent Garden Market' of about 1737. These are both reproduced in the catalogue *The Image of London: An Exhibition at the Barbican Art Gallery from August 6th to October 18th 1987*, intro. and catalogue by Malcolm Warner (London: Trefoil Publications, 1987), Plate XIX, and Figure 66.

3 'The best hiding place in the world', wrote Miss Howe (II, 242; *I, 416*).

4 See John Barrell, 'The Public Prospect and the Private View: The Politics of Taste in Eighteenth-Century Britain', in *Projecting the Landscape* (Humanities Research Center: Australian National University, 1987) for a discussion of the ideological implications of the horizon in eighteenth-century painting (pp. 15–35).

5 'I remember she was once', Lovelace says of the heroine, 'very inquisitive about the Stages, and their prices; praising the conveniency to passengers in their going off every hour' (v, 25; *II, 524*).

6 'The post, general and peny, will be strictly watched', Lovelace promises after Clarissa's first escape from Mrs Sinclair's (v 166; *III, 103*).

7 See Northrop Frye, *Anatomy of Criticism* (New York: Atheneum, 1969) for a description of *romance* that offers a revealing insight into Richardson's faith in the punctuality of municipal services: 'a world in which the ordinary laws of nature are slightly suspended' (p. 33).

8 Richardson himself periodically edited and revised Defoe's account: first in 1738; again in 1742; and for extensive revisions in 1748 (the year the last volumes of *Clarissa* appeared); another revision appeared in 1753; and a final one in 1761–2. William M. Sale, Jr, *Samuel Richardson: A Bibliographical Record of his Literary Career with Historical Notes* (New Haven: Yale University Press, 1936), assumes that Richardson contributed to all these editions (pp. 39–40). Eaves and Kimpel, *Biography*, write that 'It seems to us almost certain that Richardson's connection with the *Tour* began in 1738' (pp. 72–3, fn. 56). For a study of the influence of roads, monuments, and service systems on our images of cities, see Kevin Lynch, *The Image of the City* (Cambridge, Mass.: MIT Press, 1960).

9 Nicholas Shakespeare, *Londoners* (London: Sidgwick & Jackson, 1986), p. 3.

10 Mrs Townsend commutes regularly from Deptford for 'her days of being in town', says Miss Howe, 'and then is at a chamber she rents at an Inn in Southwark, where she keeps patterns of all her Silks, and much of her portable goods, for the convenience of her London customers' (IV, 152–3; *II, 346*).

11 The recommendation of the Heath for an 'Airing' is found in editions of the *Tour* for 1725 (III, 5); 1738 (II, 194); and 1742 (II, 156–7).

12 See John Thomas Smith, *Nollekens and his Times*, 2nd edn, 2 vols. (1829), I, 68, cited by Doody, *A Natural Passion*, p. 200.

13 *A Copy of the Poll for a Citizen for the City and Liberty of Westminster; Begun to be Taken at Covent-Garden, Upon Wednesday the Twenty-second Day of November, and Ending on Friday the Eighth Day of December 1749* (London: Printed for J. Osborne, 1749). Osborn, incidentally, is Richardson's publisher.

14 See *The A to Z of Georgian London*, introductory notes by Ralph Hyde (London: Harry Margary, Lympne Castle Kent in association with Guildhall Library, London, 1981), p. 24.

15 Defoe's *Tour* divides London into its two historical orientations of east and west: the '*Court-end* of the Town' in the west, and 'the *City*' in the east.

16 The separation is consistent except for a tavern Lovelace visits near Lincoln's Inn Fields while he waits for a wedding licence at Doctors' Commons.

17 She reclaims the northern suburbs for herself through another round of church going: services at the old church in Hampstead during her stay with the Widow Bevis; services in Highgate later on a Sunday 'Airing' with Mrs Lovick and Mrs Smith, 'a little repast' in Highgate, and a stop in Islington for the afternoon service.

18 The truth is, debtors' prison was an extremely effective agent for recovering bad debts. A recent study of imprisonment in the eighteenth century shows that in

1791 a committee of the House of Commons found that 'of 12,000 writs issued against defaulters in Middlesex and London the year before, only 1,200 committals to prison resulted ... The majority must have paid up', Christopher Harding, Bill Hines, Richard Ireland, and Philip Rawlings, *Imprisonment in England and Wales: A Concise History* (London: Croom Helm, 1985), p. 79. For Clarissa's particular plight, see Jay Cohen, 'The History of Imprisonment for Debt and its Relation to the Development of Discharge in Bankruptcy', *The Journal of Legal History*, 3 (Sept. 1982), 153–71.

19 'The Man-made World of Clarissa Harlowe and Robert Lovelace', in *Passion and Prudence*, ed., Myer, p. 74.

20 Eaves and Kimpel, *Biography*, pp. 8, 18, 64.

21 Eagleton, *The Rape of Clarissa*, pp. 75–7, 84. Christopher Hill, *Puritanism and Revolution* (London: Panther, 1968), p. 364. See also, R. F. Brissenden, *Samuel Richardson* (London: British Book Council, 1958), p. 27; and Brissenden, *Virtue in Distress* (London: Macmillan, 1974), p. 186.

5 James Grantham Turner: Lovelace and the paradoxes of libertinism

1 IV, 139; *II, 337*; cf. William Congreve, *The Old Batchelour*, Song in II, ii.

2 Ovid, *Ars Amatoria* I, 673–80; Marguerite of Navarre, *Heptameron*, discussion after tale 10; Alexander Pope, *Of the Characters of Women* (*Moral Essays* II), l. 216.

3 IV, 311; *II, 460*; Lovelace is particularly tormented here by the feeling that 'my invention is my curse'. Cf. Anthony Winner, 'Richardson's Lovelace: Character and Prediction', *Texas Studies in Literature and Language*, 14:1 (Spring, 1972), p. 61.

4 Bernard Mandeville, *A Treatise of the Hypochondriack and Hysterick Passions* (London, 1711), p. 103.

5 Cf. Aphra Behn, *Love-Letters Between a Nobleman and His Sister*, ed. Maureen Duffy (London: Virago, 1987), p. 3.

6 Antoine, Comte de Hamilton, *Mémoires de la Vie du Comte de Grammont* (Cologne, 1713), pp. 1–3, 114, 143. Hamilton's account of Grammont's adventures is particularly interesting because they took place for the most part at the English (not the French) court, and thus bridge both cultures – as does Lovelace himself, who lived for a long time 'at the French Court' (II, 106; *I, 315*). Clarissa cites an episode from these memoirs in her posthumous letter to Morden (VIII, 158; *IV, 462*).

7 Jane Barker, 'On the Follies of Human-Life' and prose meditation [after the death of Charles II], in *A Patch-Work Screen for the Ladies* (London, 1723), pp. 112–14.

8 Rochester, *Letters*, ed. Jeremy Treglown (Oxford: Basil Blackwell, 1980), p. 228. The importance of Rochester's letters in the formation of Lovelace has been recognized by Doody in *A Natural Passion*, p. 130.

9 See David Farley-Hills, ed., *Rochester: The Critical Heritage* (London: Routledge, 1972), pp. 46, 49 (Gilbert Burnet: 'His Wit had a Subtilty and Sublimity both, that were scarce imitable.')

10 Claude Reichler, *L'Age libertin* (Paris: Minuit, 1987), chs. 1 and 2. I discuss Reichler's book in 'The Culture of Priapism', *Review*, 10 (1988), 37–70.

11 Rochester, *Satyr [Timon]*, ll. 21–2; John Sheffield, Earl of Mulgrave, 'The Appointment', in *The Gyldenstolpe Manuscript Miscellany*, ed. Bror Danielsson and David M. Vieth (Stockholm: Almqvist and Wiksell, 1967), p. 234. Lovelace himself despises obscene discourse and *double entendre* because 'In *Love* . . . it has always been my maxim, to *act*, rather than *talk*' (VII, 12; *IV, 36*).

12 Author unknown, 'The Last Night's Ramble (1687)', ed. Harold Love, in his *Restoration Literature: Critical Approaches* (London: Methuen, 1972), p. 310; Chorier, *Aloisiae Sigeae Toletanae Satyra Sotadica de Arcanis Amoris et Veneris* (1660–1668), ed. Bruno Lavagnini (Catania: Romeo Prampolini, 1935), p. 214. La Mettrie's erotic philosophy is discussed in my ' "Illustrious Depravity" and the Libertine Sublime', *The Age of Johnson*, II (forthcoming).

13 John Dryden, *Essays*, ed. W. P. Ker (Oxford: Clarendon Press, 1929), I, 239 (a hostile reference perhaps intended to disparage Rochester, whose *Allusion to Horace* launched the Augustan imitation). For Oldham, see *OED*, 'Libertine' B.3.b.

14 'L'Examen du *Veuve*'.

15 Richardson, *Selected Letters*, p. 293n; de Sévigné, letters of 26 July 1679, 5 and 7 January 1689.

16 This account of Clarissa is heavily influenced by Peter Brooks, *The Novel of Worldliness: Crébillon, Marivaux, Laclos, Stendhal* (Princeton: Princeton University Press, 1969), esp. ch. 1.

17 See Flynn, *Man of Letters*, pp. 208–9. The 'dog' (man or beast?) appears at III, 30; *I, 513*.

18 IV, *362*; *II, 498*; in the same letter, Lovelace attempts a moral justification of his libertinism on precisely the grounds that it is controlled by his volition: those who *do* all the wickedness they *can*, who do not exercise choice (as he has apparently chosen to delay his conquest of Clarissa), are far worse than he (IV, 354; *II, 492*). Cf. Doody, *A Natural Passion*, pp. 104–5.

19 Alexander Pope, *Correspondence*, ed. George Sherburn (Oxford: Clarendon Press, 1956), I, 48.

20 *L'Age libertin*, pp. 37–9, 45–55.

21 Cf. III, 88; *II, 32*: once she has 'Love *within*, and I *without*, she will be *more* than woman, as the poet says, or I *less* than man, if I succeed not'. Richardson may have seen this phrase in a pseudo-Rochesterian obscene burlesque, in which Swivanthe, rejoicing in the 'eager Thrusts' of Tarsander, declares that 'She that alone her Lover can withstand, / Is more than *Woman*, or he less than Man' (*Miscellany Poems*, in *The Works of the Earls of Rochester, Roscommon, [and] Dorset* [London, 1721], II, 196).

22 Eagleton, *The Rape of Clarissa*, p. 52.

23 III, 79; *II, 30*. This example is particularly rich because, in confessing that he could *not* produce tears on command, he suggests two different topoi; in misogynist literature women are supposed to be able to cry at will, but in Ovid's *Ars Amatoria* it is the male seducer who must produce tears, if necessary using saliva on the back of his hand (I, 659–62).

24 It is this passivity that leads Judith Wilt to suggest, with Swiftian exaggeration, that

Lovelace is one of the few characters *not* to rape Clarissa in the novel; 'He could Go No Farther: A Modest Proposal about Lovelace and Clarissa', *PMLA*, 42 (1977), pp. 19–32.

25 III, 30; *II, 35*. The same point ('I was ever nice in my loves') ushers in a gruesome passage, worthy of Swift, in which Lovelace airily explains to Leman his rules for the childbirths and deaths of his ex-mistresses (III, 229; *II, 148*).

26 III, 30; *I, 513*; cf. Pope: 'Ladies, like variegated Tulips, show / 'Tis to their Changes that their charms we owe' (*Characters of Women*, ll. 41–2); 'Woman's at best a Contradiction still' (l. 270).

27 'De umiddelbare erotiske Stadier, eller det Musicalsk-Erotiske' ('The Immediate Stages of the Erotic, or the Musical-Erotic'), in *Enten-Eller (Either/Or)*, Part One.

6 Tom Keymer: Richardson's *Meditations*: Clarissa's *Clarissa*

1 22 December 1746, Forster Collection, Victoria and Albert Museum, XIII, 3, fos. 68, 66.

2 See Christopher Hill, 'Clarissa Harlowe and her Times', *Essays in Criticism*, 5 (1955), 318; Janet Todd, *Women's Friendship in Literature* (New York: Columbia University Press, 1980), p. 9.

3 5 January 1746/7, *Selected Letters*, p. 77.

4 The phrase is Eliza Haywood's, from *Anti-Pamela: or, Feign'd Innocence Detected* (1741).

5 William M. Sale, *Samuel Richardson: A Bibliographical Record* (New Haven: Yale University Press, 1936), p. 64. Other copies are now in the Houghton Library, Harvard, and the Beinecke Rare Book Room, Yale; and the Beinecke copy has been reproduced as vol. XV of Garland Publishing's facsimile series *Richardsoniana* (New York, 1976).

6 Castle, *Clarissa's Ciphers*, p. 121.

7 See Castle's account of the hermeneutic implications of the mad papers, pp. 117–21. Mark Kinkead-Weekes notes Blake's approval of Richardson, and suggests that 'The Sick Rose' may derive from his reading of Clarissa's fragments, *Dramatic Novelist*, p. 237.

8 George Eliot, *Daniel Deronda*, ed. Graham Handley (Oxford: Clarendon Press, 1984), p. 173. Closer to Richardson's day, Adam Smith, whose chapter on conscience in *The Theory of Moral Sentiments* applauds his novels for their exemplary extension of the reader's sympathies beyond self, stresses the same need for conscience to aspire to objectivity: 'It is only by consulting this judge within, that we can ever see what relates to ourselves in its proper shape and dimensions; or that we can ever make any proper comparison between our own interests and those of other people.' 'Before we can make any proper comparison of those opposite interests, we must change our position. We must view them, neither from our own place nor yet from his, but from the place and with the eyes of a third person, who has no particular connexion with either, and who judges with impartiality between us' (*The Theory of Moral Sentiments*, ed. D. D. Raphael and A. L. Macfie (Oxford: Clarendon Press, 1976), pp. 134–5.

9 See Rita Goldberg's subtle reading of the parable, *Sex and Enlightenment: Women*

in Richardson and Diderot (Cambridge: Cambridge University Press, 1984), pp. 120–2.

10 For an account of the relation between Clarissa's deathbed preparations and the writings of Jeremy Taylor, see Doody, *A Natural Passion*, pp. 168–79.

11 Patrick Delany, *Fifteen Sermons upon Social Duties* (1744), pp. 125–6; William Worthington, *An Essay on the Scheme and the Conduct, Procedure and Extent of Man's Redemption* (1743), p. 496.

12 John Garnett, *A Dissertation on the Book of Job* (1749), p. 129.

13 Garnett, *Dissertation*, p. 91.

14 Garnett, *Dissertation*, p. 168.

15 Richard Grey, *An Answer to Mr. Warburton's Remarks on several Occasional Reflections, so far as they concern the Preface to a late Edition of the Book of Job* (1744), p. 50.

16 Grey, *An Answer to Mr. Warburton's Remarks*, p. 87.

17 [Early December 1748], *Correspondence*, IV, 216.

18 15 December 1748, Forster Collection, XI, fo.7.

19 16 December 1749, *Correspondence*, IV, 307.

20 1 January 1749/50, *The Correspondence of Edward Young*, ed. Henry Pettit (Oxford: Clarendon Press, 1971), p. 341.

21 7 January 1749/50, Pettit, *Correspondence of Young*, p. 342.

22 1 January 1749/50, Pettit, *Correspondence of Young*, p. 341.

23 Quoted by Harold Forster, *Edward Young: The Poet of the Night Thoughts, 1683–1765* (Harleston: Erskine Press, 1986), p. 233. Richardson seems at the same time to have sent a copy to Mary Delany herself: since the writing of this essay a copy inscribed by her as 'given me by the author, 12 January 1749/50' has been offered for sale by Ken Spelman. See H. R. Woudhuysen, 'Sales of Books and Manuscripts', *Times Literary Supplement*, 17–23 June 1988, 689–90 (p. 690).

24 7 January 1749/50, Pettit, *Correspondence of Young*, p. 342.

25 9 July 1750, Forster Collection, XIII, 3, fos.132–3.

26 14 July 1750, *Correspondence*, IV, 7–8.

27 24 September 1750, *Correspondence*, IV, 27–8.

28 12 October 1750, Forster Collection, XII, 2, fo.4; 19 October, fo.6; 24 November, fo.16.

29 6 December 1752, *The Richardson–Stinstra Correspondence and Stinstra's Prefaces to Clarissa*, ed. William C. Slattery (Carbondale: Southern Illinois University Press, 1969), p. 6; 2 April 1753, p. 10.

30 Quoted by Eaves and Kimpel, *Biography*, p. 311.

31 See Melvyn New, 'Sterne, Warburton, and the Burden of Exuberant Wit', *Eighteenth-Century Studies*, 15 (1982), 245–74 (p. 259). Whether Richardson followed the controversy is unknown. He appears, however, to have discussed it in a partially extant correspondence with Thomas Edwards in 1753 (the year of his break with Warburton), when he forwarded to Edwards as a gift from Speaker Onslow an attack on the *Divine Legation*, Charles Peters's *Critical Dissertation on the Book of Job* (1751). Edwards replied that he had never seen 'a more visionary

hypothesis than that of Mr Warburton on the book of Job' (6 July 1753, Forster Collection, XII, 1, fo.79).

32 25 April 1748, *Correspondence*, VI, facsimile page. The reference is to the divine intervention from the whirlwind (Job 38), of which, in the *Divine Legation*, Warburton takes a more cynical view: God's speech 'clears up no difficulties', he argues, thus providing 'a plain proof that the Interposition was no more than a piece of poetical Machinery' (*Divine Legation*, 4th edn, 5 vols. (1764–5), V, 22–3).

33 7 January 1749/50, Pettit, *Correspondence of Young*, p. 342.

34 See Mark Kinkead-Weekes, '*Clarissa* Restored?', *Review of English Studies*, n.s. 10, no. 38 (1959), 158–71. Kinkead-Weekes's influential thesis has recently been questioned by Florian Stuber, 'On Original and Final Intentions, or Can There Be an Authoritative *Clarissa*?', *TEXT*, 2 (1985), 229–44. Nevertheless, Kinkead-Weekes's central point that Richardson 'was driven to tinker with *Clarissa* to drive its message home in terms the crudest reader could understand' (p. 169) remains intact.

35 See Sale, *Samuel Richardson: A Bibliographical Record*, p. 63; Eaves and Kimpel, *Biography*, pp. 317, 594–5.

36 See *Remarks on Clarissa*, ed. Peter Sabor (Los Angeles: Augustan Reprint Society, 1985), p. 41.

7 Margaret Anne Doody: Identity and character in *Sir Charles Grandison*

1 David Hume, *A Treatise of Human Nature*, ed. L. A. Selby-Bigge (1888) (Oxford: Clarendon Press, rpt., 1965), Book I, 'Of the Understanding', Part IV, Section vi, 'Of personal identity', p. 252.

2 *Ibid.*, p. 253. John Sitter points out resemblances between Hume and Richardson in their valuation of 'momentary intensities', in *Literary Loneliness in Mid-Eighteenth Century England* (Ithaca and London: Cornell University Press, 1982), p. 26.

3 John Locke, *Essay Concerning Human Understanding*, ed. Peter H. Nidditch (Oxford: Clarendon Press, 1975), Book II, chapter 27, 'Of Identity and Diversity', p. 346.

4 [Edmund Law], *A Defence of Mr. Locke's Opinion concerning Personal Identity; in Answer to the First Part of a Late Essay on That Subject* (Cambridge: J. Archdeacon, 1769), 'Appendix', pp. 39–40. Law's *Defence* was reprinted after Locke's *Essay* in the 1777 edition of Locke's *Works* produced by Law, and in subsequent editions of Locke's *Works*; see Jean S. Yolton and John W. Yolton, *John Locke: A Reference Guide* (Boston: G. K. Hall, 1985), p. 29.

5 Hume, *Treatise*, I, IV, Section vi, p. 259.

6 Henry Fielding, 'An Essay on the Knowledge of the Characters of Men' in *Miscellanies*, Volume I, ed. Henry Knight Miller (Oxford: Clarendon Press; Middletown, Conn: Wesleyan University Press, 1972), p. 155.

7 *Ibid.*, p. 156.

8 *Ibid.*, pp. 156–7.

9 Dickens may have been recollecting this passage in his own elaborated fantasia of persons as houses in chapter 21 of *Little Dorrit*:

> The house so drearily out of repair ... the house with the blinds always down ... the house where the collector has called for one quarter of an Idea, and found nobody at home – who has not dined with these? The house that nobody will take, and is to be had a bargain – who does not know her? The showy house that was taken for life by the disappointed gentleman, and which does not suit him at all – who is unacquainted with that haunted habitation?

(*Little Dorrit*, ed. John Holloway (Harmondsworth: Penguin, 1967), p. 292.)

10 Adam Smith, *The Theory of Moral Sentiments*, ed. D. D. Raphael and A. L. Macfie (Oxford: Clarendon Press, 1976), Part I, 'Of the Propriety of Action'; Section I, 'Of the Sense of Propriety'; chapter I, 'Of sympathy', p. 10.

11 *Ibid.*, chapter 5, 'Of the amiable and respectable virtues', p. 25.

12 *Ibid.*, chapter 4, 'The manner in which we judge of the propriety or impropriety of the affections of other men ... continued', p. 22; chapter 5, p. 24.

13 Lady Dorothy Bradshaigh to Samuel Richardson, Oct.–27 Nov. 1753, Forster Collection, fos. XI, 45r–47r.

14 Richardson to Lady Bradshaigh, 8 December 1753, *Selected Letters*, p. 255.

15 Richardson to Lady Bradshaigh, 8 February 1754, Forster Collection, XI, fo. 66r; cf. *Selected Letters*, pp. 276–7.

16 Lady Bradshaigh to Richardson, 22 February 1754, Forster Collection, XI, fo. 83r–v.

17 Richardson, *Copy of a Letter to a Lady, who was solicitous for an additional volume to the History of Sir Charles Grandison*, reprinted in Harris, *Sir Charles Grandison*, III Appendix, pp. 467–70; see p. 470.

18 Richardson to Lady Bradshaigh, 8 December 1753, Forster Collection, XI, fo. 49r.

19 Lady Bradshaigh to Richardson, 23 December 1753–14 January 1754, Forster Collection, XI, fos. 62r–v.

20 *Ibid.*, fo. 64v.

21 Richardson to Lady Bradshaigh, 8 December 1753, *Selected Letters*, p. 252.

22 Sarah Chapone to Richardson, 10 December 1753, Forster Collection, XIII, fo. 95r.

23 *Ibid.*

24 Lady Bradshaigh to Richardson, 23 December 1753–14 January 1754; Forster Collection, fo. XI, 62v. The reference to Mary Blandy is to a contemporary murderess who poisoned her father with arsenic powder that her lover had given her; Mary Blandy protested that she had been told that the powder was 'love powder' that would make Mr Blandy fond of her lover. She was not believed, and was hanged in 1752.

25 Sarah Chapone to Richardson, as above, Forster Collection, XIII, fo. 94r.

26 Richardson to Lady Bradshaigh, 14 February 1754, *Selected Letters*, p. 286.

27 Richardson to Lady Bradshaigh, 25 February 1754, Forster Collection, XI, fo. 87r; cf. *Selected Letters*, p. 296.

28 John Keats to Richard Woodhouse, 27 October 1818, in *The Letters of John Keats 1814–1821*, ed. Hyder Edward Rollins (Cambridge, Mass.: Harvard University Press, 1958), I, 387.

8 Carol Houlihan Flynn: The pains of compliance in *Sir Charles Grandison*

1 Letter to Lady Bradshaigh, 22 April 1752, *Correspondence*, VI, 165.

2 In *The History of Manners: The Civilizing Process* (New York, 1978), Norbert Elias considers the pains of becoming civilized, the ways 'ought' became internalized while sexuality became 'increasingly removed behind the scenes of social life and enclosed in a particular enclave, the nuclear family', p. 180.

3 Peter Sabor, '*Amelia* and *Sir Charles Grandison*: The Convergence of Fielding and Richardson', *Wascana Review*, 17 (1982), 14.

4 Randolph Trumbach, 'Modern Prostitution and Gender in *Fanny Hill*: Libertine and Domesticated Fantasy', in *Sexual Underworlds of the Enlightenment*, ed. G. S. Rousseau and Roy Porter (Chapel Hill: University of North Carolina Press, 1988), p. 73.

5 Daniel Defoe, *Conjugal Lewdness; or Matrimonial Whoredom, a Treatise Concerning the Use and Abuse of the Marriage Bed* (1727), ed. Maximillian Novak (Gainesville, Florida: Scholar Press, 1967), p. 46.

6 *Correspondence*, VI, 116–217. Typically, Richardson exults, 'I knew that I should provoke my dear correspondent by what I wrote of men's setting out right in the marriage warfare; or governing by fear; of prerogative early exerted; and such like strange assertions' (VI, 146). Richardson's self-conscious, almost parodic awareness of the 'strange' nature of his provocative assertions does not keep him from making them.

7 Daniel Defoe, *The Family Instructor: in Two Parts relating 1. To Family Breaches, and their Obstructing Religious Duties. 2. To the Great Mistake of Mixing the Passions in the Managing and Correcting of Children* (London, 1809), pp. 41, 33, 58.

8 Eaves and Kimpel, *Biography*, p. 345.

9 See Eaves and Kimpel, *Biography* on her history, pp. 198–9. The correspondence here cited took place according to Barbauld from 1747 to 1754, chiefly in 1750–51.

10 More schematically, Richardson's friend and admirer, Jane Collier, discusses the art of tormenting in her *Essay on the Art of Ingeniously Tormenting*, which Richardson printed in 1753.

11 Doody, *A Natural Passion*, p. 322.

12 Richardson wrote to Thomas Edwards that he 'designed [Harriet] to have a livelier Turn than Clarissa, and something to be Defective in, in the way of Vivacity, in order, were I to proceed, to rein her in, when the good Man appeared'. Cited in Sylvia Kasey Marks's recent work, *Sir Charles Grandison: The Compleat Conduct Book* (Lewisburg, London and Toronto: Associated University Presses, 1986), p. 98.

9 Janet E. Aikins: Richardson's 'speaking pictures'

1 Alexander Pope, 'Epistle II: To a Lady', in *Epistles to Several Persons*, ed. F. W. Bateson (London: Methuen and New Haven: Yale University Press, 1951), l.216, ll. 1–20.

2 His choice of Hubert François Gravelot as the artist for *Pamela* may have resulted from his work on *Aesop's Fables*, since he is likely in the process to have studied the engravings Gravelot had recently contributed to the second volume of John Gay's *Fables*. For a discussion of Gravelot's importance, see Robert Halsband in 'The Rococo in England: Book Illustrators, mainly Gravelot and Bentley', *Burlington Magazine*, 127, n. 993 (December 1985), 875.

3 *Selected Letters*, pp. 120–2, 65, and 315–16. In letters to Susanna Highmore he praised her skill in 'painting' with words and that of Edmund Spenser, whom she had admired. See *Correspondence*, II, 207 and 245.

4 Jonathan Richardson, *An Essay on the Theory of Painting* (London, 1715), pp. 16, 24 and 12.

5 Joseph Highmore, *Essays, Moral, Religious, and Miscellaneous*, 2 vols. (London, 1766), II, 88–9.

6 'Remarks on some Passages in Mr. Webb's "Enquiry into the Beauties of Painting" ', *Gentleman's Magazine*, 36 (1766), 356. See also *The Practice of Perspective, On the Principles of Dr. Brook Taylor* (London, 1763) and *A Critical Examination of those Two Paintings On the Cieling* [*sic*] *of the Banqueting-house at Whitehall in which Architecture is introduced, as far as it relates to the Perspective* (London, 1754), p. ii. The latter was printed by Richardson.

7 'A Discourse on the Dignity, Certainty, Pleasure, and Advantage of The Science of a Connoisseur', in *Works* (London, 1792), pp. 211–12. This essay was first published in 1719.

8 Terry Castle, 'P/B: *Pamela* as Sexual Fiction', *Studies in English Literature, 1500–1900*, 22 (1982), 469–89; Robert Folkenflik, 'A Room of Pamela's Own', *English Literary History*, 39 (1972), 585–96; Carey McIntosh, 'Pamela's Clothes', *English Literary History*, 35 (1968), 75–83; and Roy Roussel, 'Reflections on the Letter: The Reconciliation of Distance and Presence in *Pamela*', *English Literary History*, 41 (1974), 375–99.

9 Richardson printed Sir Philip Sidney's *Defence of Poesy*, from which the term comes, in 1724–5. See Sale, *Master Printer*, p. 230.

10 Peter Sabor, ed., *Pamela; or, Virtue Rewarded* (Harmondsworth: Penguin, 1980), pp. 82–3. Richardson's final revisions were not published during his lifetime but were used as the copy text for the 1801 edition of *Pamela*. See Sabor, *Pamela*, p. 21.

11 For discussion of *ekphrasis*, see Jean H. Hagstrum, *The Sister Arts: The Tradition of Literary Pictorialism and English Poetry from Dryden to Gray* (Chicago: University of Chicago Press, 1958), p. 18; Joseph Kestner, 'Secondary Illusion: The Novel and the Spatial Arts', in Jeffrey R. Smitten and Ann Daghistany, *Spatial Form in Narrative* (Ithaca and London: Cornell University Press, 1981), pp. 100–28; and Joel Snyder, 'Picturing Vision', *Critical Inquiry*, 6 (1980), 499–526.

12 Sabor, ed., *Pamela*, p. 206. In 1746, Richardson printed Anthony Blackwall's *An Introduction to the Classics*, 6th edn, which defines the very effect he would later achieve by changing Pamela's imitation of Colbrand from the third to the first person. 'Change of Time *is*', writes Blackwall, '*when Things done and past are describ'd as now doing and present.* This Form of Expression places the Thing to be

represented in a strong and prevalent *Light* before us, and makes us *Spectators* rather than *Hearers*' (p. 254).

13 *Correspondence*, I, 56 and *Pamela: or, Virtue Rewarded*, 2 vols., 2nd edn (London, 1741), I, xxxvi.

14 T. C. Duncan Eaves, 'Graphic Illustration of the Novels of Samuel Richardson, 1740–1810', *Huntington Library Quarterly*, 14 (1950–1), 353 and Marcia Epstein Allentuck, 'Narration and Illustration: the Problem of Richardson's *Pamela*', *Philological Quarterly*, 51 (1972), 886.

15 Eaves, 'Graphic Illustration', 353.

16 *Pamela*, 2nd edn, I, xxxvii and Aaron Hill, *Works*, 4 vols. (London, 1754), II, 165. Eaves points out the great expense of these illustrations in 'Graphic Illustration', p. 357, and in *Aesop's Fables*, Richardson himself commented on the cost of the 'cuts' which he took trouble to include in that edition.

17 *Pamela: or, Virtue Rewarded*, 4 vols., 6th edn, Corr. (London, 1742), I, 214. Subsequent references will be listed in parentheses in the text.

18 Eaves, 'Graphic Illustration', 358–9.

19 Eaves, 'Graphic Illustration', 372.

20 *Correspondence*, IV, 255–6. See T. C. Duncan Eaves, ' "The Harlowe Family", by Joseph Highmore: A Note on the Illustration of Richardson's *Clarissa*', *Huntington Library Quarterly*, 7 (1943–4), 89–96.

21 See, for example, IV, 67; *II, 284*; V, 24; *II, 525*; and VI, 249–51; *III, 427–8*.

22 Joseph Spence, *An Essay on Pope's Odyssey*, 2 vols. (London, 1726), II, 126. Richardson had printed the second edition of the work in 1737.

23 Richardson himself wrote an eleven-page pamphlet defending the fire scene in which he speaks of the importance of 'description' and 'painting' in words. See T. C. Duncan Eaves and Ben D. Kimpel, 'An Unpublished Pamphlet by Samuel Richardson', *Philological Quarterly*, 63 (1984), 401–9.

24 For a discussion of these objects as 'man-made', see Margaret Anne Doody, 'The Man-made World of Clarissa Harlowe and Robert Lovelace', in *Passion and Prudence*, ed. Myer, pp. 52–77.

25 The footnote mentioning Clarissa's portrait by Highmore is in Volume III, p. 260 of the first edition. For information about Highmore's knowledge of Van Dyck and his collection of pictures, see Elizabeth Johnston, 'Joseph Highmore's Paris Journal, 1734', *The Walpole Society*, 42 (1968–70), 65–7.

26 I rely upon Brian Allen, *Francis Hayman* (New Haven and London: Yale University Press, 1987); David Bindman, *Hogarth* (London: Thames and Hudson, 1981); Ronald Paulson, *Emblem and Expression: Meaning in English Art of the Eighteenth Century* (London: Thames and Hudson, 1975); and Paulson, *Hogarth: His Life, Art, and Times*, 2 vols. (New Haven and London: Yale University Press, 1971).

10 David Robinson: Unravelling the 'cord which ties good men to good men': male friendship in Richardson's novels

1 Janet Todd, *Women's Friendship in Literature* (New York: Columbia University Press, 1980), p. 1.

2 *Ibid.*, p. 68.
3 *Ibid.*, p. 62; Morris Golden, *Richardson's Characters* (Ann Arbor: The University of Michigan Press, 1963), p. 43.
4 Golden, *Richardson's Characters*, pp. 18, 18–20.
5 *Ibid.*, pp. 1–28.
6 Doody, *A Natural Passion*, pp. 398–9.
7 Eagleton, *The Rape of Clarissa*, pp. 95–6.
8 Aristotle, *The Nicomachean Ethics* (New York: Penguin, 1976), p. 284.
9 *Ibid.*, p. 272; material enclosed in brackets is by Hugh Tredennick, who wrote the notes for the Penguin edition.
10 *Ibid.*
11 Todd, *Women's Friendship in Literature*, p. 3.

11 Jocelyn Harris: Richardson: original or learned genius?

1 *Selected Letters*, p. 333. For a fuller discussion of Richardson's own attitude to creativity see my 'Learning and Genius in *Sir Charles Grandison*', in *Studies in the Eighteenth Century* IV, ed. R. F. Brissenden and J. C. Eade (Canberra: Australian National University Press, 1979), pp. 167–91.
2 Alan Dugald McKillop, *Samuel Richardson, Printer and Novelist* (Chapel Hill: University of North Carolina Press, 1936, rpt. 1960), p. 141; A. Dwight Culler, 'Edward Bysshe and the Poet's Handbook', *PMLA*, 63 (1948), 858–85; Erich Poetzsche, *Samuel Richardsons Belesenheit* (Kieler Studien zur englischen Philologie, Kiel, 1908) new series, vol. 4; Michael E. Connaughton, 'Richardson's Familiar Quotations: *Clarissa* and Bysshe's *Art of English Poetry*', *Philological Quarterly*, 60 (1981), 183–95; Eaves and Kimpel, *Biography*, pp. 11, 117, and chapter 23, 'Richardson's Reading and Criticism'.
3 For a comprehensive survey of Richardson's reading, see McKillop, Eaves and Kimpel, Kinkead-Weekes, *Dramatic Novelist*, Doody, *A Natural Passion* and Jocelyn Harris, *Samuel Richardson* (Cambridge: Cambridge University Press, 1987). Two articles by Doody, one on Richardson for the *Dictionary of Literary Biography*, 39 (Detroit: Gale, 1985) 377–409, and her 'The Man-made World of Clarissa Harlowe and Robert Lovelace', in *Passion and Prudence*, ed. Myer, pp. 52–77, provide further hints. See also Helen Sard Hughes, 'Characterization in *Clarissa Harlowe*', *Journal of English and Germanic Philology*, 13 (1914), 110–23; Ira Konigsberg, 'The Dramatic Background of Richardson's Plots and Characters', *PMLA*, 83 (1968), 42–53, and *Samuel Richardson and the Dramatic Novel* (Lexington: University of Kentucky Press, 1968); John Dussinger, 'Richardson's Christian Vocation', *Papers in Language and Literature*, 3 (1967), 3–19, 'Conscience and the Pattern of Christian Perfection in *Clarissa*', *PMLA*, 81 (1966), 236–45, and 'Richardson's Tragic Muse', *Philological Quarterly*, 46 (1967), 18–33. Janet E. Aikins traces the effects of one play alone in 'A Plot Discover'd; or, The Uses of *Venice Preserv'd* within *Clarissa*', *University of Toronto Quarterly*, 55 (Spring 1986), 219–34. Richard Cohen's *Literary References and Their Effect upon Characterization in the Novels of Samuel Richardson* (Bangor, Maine: Hudson College

Press, 1970), and Richard Gordon Hannaford's *Samuel Richardson: An Annotated Bibliography of Critical Studies* (New York and London: Garland, 1980) are helpful. Sale, *Master Printer*, lists works from Richardson's press.

4 John Carroll, 'Richardson at Work: Revisions, Allusions, and Quotations in *Clarissa*', *Studies in the Eighteenth Century II*, ed. R. F. Brissenden (Canberra: Australian National University Press, 1973), pp. 53–71.

5 James Boswell, *Journal of a Tour to the Hebrides with Samuel Johnson*, ed. George Birkbeck Hill and L. F. Powell (London: Oxford University Press, 1950), p. 234.

6 See my 'Samuel Johnson, Samuel Richardson, and the Dial-Plate', *British Journal for Eighteenth-Century Studies*, 9 (1986), 157–63.

7 *Selected Letters*, p. 158; Eaves and Kimpel, *Biography*, pp. 9–11.

8 *Correspondence*, III, 237.

9 *Selected Letters*, pp. 229, 59.

10 Sale, *Master Printer*, p. 101.

11 See my 'Learning and Genius in *Sir Charles Grandison*'.

12 Personal communication. Maslen's study of Bowyer is now in press.

13 Eaves and Kimpel usefully gather up Richardson's references to Swift and Pope, *Biography*, pp. 574–80. For Dennis, see Sale, *Master Printer*, pp. 166–7.

14 See John Carroll, 'Lovelace as Tragic Hero', *University of Toronto Quarterly*, 42 (1972), 14–25. A revision to *Pamela* made in the 1801 edition comparing bulls to wicked libertine men (ed. Sabor, pp. 187–8) suggests that Pamela's fear of bulls may derive from Jove's rape of Europa in Ovid.

15 See Doody's 'The Man-made World of Clarissa Harlowe and Robert Lovelace' for a discussion of Clarissa as Arachne.

16 See Ian Donaldson, *The Rapes of Lucretia: A Myth and its Transformations* (Oxford: Clarendon Press, 1982), pp. 75–6.

17 See Dustin Griffin, *Regaining Paradise: Milton and the Eighteenth Century* (Cambridge: Cambridge University Press, 1986), p. 192. The effect of Milton on fiction in the eighteenth and nineteenth centuries must surely have been as powerful as it was on poetry. The odd notion of over-leaping the Fall is central to James Thomson's *The Seasons*, a work which Richardson printed. See Sale, *Master Printer*, pp. 209–11.

18 Details may be found in Carroll's 'Lovelace as Tragic Hero', Beer's 'Richardson, Milton, and the Status of Evil', *Review of English Studies*, new series 19 (1968), 261–70, and my *Samuel Richardson*. See also Carroll's 'Richardson at Work', and his 'Annotating *Clarissa*', in *Editing Eighteenth-Century Novels: Papers on Fielding, Le Sage, Richardson . . . given at the Conference on Editorial Problems, University of Toronto, November, 1973*, ed. Gerald E. Bentley, Jr (Toronto: Hakkert, 1975). He argues as I do that Richardson uses quotation to characterize his personae, for instance Ariosto, Swift, Montaigne, and Prior at his bawdiest for Lovelace. For Carroll too, Richardson's awareness of contexts proves his familiarity with sources.

19 'Mary Astell as a Parallel for Richardson's Clarissa', *Modern Language Notes*, 28 (1913), 103–5, and Astell's *Some Reflections upon Marriage*, 4th edn (1730, rpt. New York: Source Book Press, 1970), p. 106.

20 For Betterton and Bracegirdle see Philip H. Highfill Jr, Kalman A. Burnim, and Edward A. Langhans, *A Biographical Dictionary of Actors, Actresses, Musicians, Dancers, Managers, and Other Stage Personnel in London, 1660–1800* (Carbondale and Edwardsville: Illinois University Press, 1973–).

21 See *Selected Letters*, p. 250, for Richardson's knowledge of Shakespeare. Valerie Grosvenor Myer explores links with *Measure for Measure, Twelfth Night, Romeo and Juliet, Hamlet, Othello*, and *The Tempest*, in 'Well Read in Shakespeare', in *Passion and Prudence*, pp. 126–32. Lady Betty Lawrence also takes her surname from *Romeo and Juliet*.

22 *Selected Leters*, p. 259.

23 The actress Mrs Egleton, a name Richardson used for a minor character in *Grandison*, played Lucy Lockit when Gay's *The Beggar's Opera* was first performed in 1728.

24 See *The Complete Works of Thomas Shadwell*, ed. Montague Summers (London: The Fortune Press, 1927), III.

25 *A Natural Passion*, pp. 373–4, n. 1. Doody also notes possible parallels in *Clarissa* to the 'Satyr', to Rochester's play *Valentinian*, and to his published letters. Dustin H. Griffin's *Satires Against Man: The Poems of Rochester* (Berkeley, Los Angeles and London: University of California Press, 1973) describes a personality and philosophy remarkably like Lovelace's. Raman Selden's 'Rochester and Shadwell', in *Spirit of Wit: Reconsiderations of Rochester*, ed. Jeremy Treglown (Oxford: Basil Blackwell, 1982), pp. 177–90, explores that connection. The quotation is from *The Poems of John Wilmot Earl of Rochester*, ed. Keith Walker (Oxford: Basil Blackwell, 1984), p. 95.

26 Robert Scholes, *Structuralism in Literature: An Introduction* (New Haven: Yale University Press, 1984), p. 30.

27 'Piozziana', *Gentleman's Magazine*, n.s. 34 (1850), 267.

12 Pat Rogers: 'A Young, a Richardson, or a Johnson': lines of cultural force in the age of Richardson

1 For Pym's fond attitude towards *Night Thoughts*, see *A Very Private Eye*, ed. Hazel Holt and Hilary Pym (New York: Vintage, 1985), p. 61. It is also surely significant that at this period Barbara Pym gave her first great love, Henry Harvey, the nickname 'Lorenzo' (pp. 18–37).

2 Charlotte Lennox, *The Female Quixote*, ed. Margaret Dalziel (London: Oxford University Press, 1970) pp. 253–4; quotation from Appendix, 'Johnson, Richardson, and *The Female Quixote*', by Duncan Isles, p. 422.

3 Among the few references are these: Willard Connely, *Beau Nash: Monarch of Bath and Tunbridge Wells* (London: Laurie, 1955), p. 140, where a coloured print made by the artist 'Loggan the dwarf' is described; and Elizabeth Mavor, *The Virgin Mistress* (London: Chatto, 1964), p. 51. A byline tells us that the print was executed for Richard Philips in 1804, the year in which the Barbauld edition appeared.

4 Information on Young is drawn from Henry C. Shelley, *The Life and Letters of Edward Young* (London: Pitman, 1914); Harold Forster, *Edward Young: The Poet of the Night Thoughts* (Harleston, Norfolk: Erskine Press, 1986); and *The Correspondence of Edward Young 1683–1765*, ed. Henry Pettit (Oxford: Clarendon Press, 1971).

5 *Correspondence of Young*, p. 279.

6 *Ibid.*, p. 122.

7 *Ibid.*, p. 207. 'Richardson is a lowspirited man, not only deserves, but wants satisfactions' (Young to Duchess of Portland, 24 October 1749: *ibid.*, p. 333).

8 *Ibid.*, p. 577. Compare Richardson's statement to Young in January 1758, 'I have been often at Bath; but remember not that I received benefit from the waters' (*ibid.*, p. 468). On this occasion Young had improved in health as a result of his stay in Bath and had invited Richardson to join him (p. 467).

9 *Ibid.*, p. 142.

10 For his visit in 1745, see Shelley, *Life and Letters of Edward Young*, pp. 187–94.

11 James Boswell, *The Life of Samuel Johnson*, ed. G. B. Hill and L. F. Powell (Oxford: Clarendon, 1934–64), I, 190.

12 The best known description is that of Garrick cited by James L. Clifford, *Young Samuel Johnson*, (London: Heinemann, 1955), p. 146.

13 Boswell, *Life*, I, 238.

14 Clifford, *Young Samuel Johnson*, pp. 300–1.

15 *Correspondence*, II, 206; III, 316.

16 Eaves and Kimpel, *Biography*, pp. 180–2; Helene Koon, *Colley Cibber: A Biography* (Lexington: University Press of Kentucky, 1986), pp. 168–72. For Johnson's view of Cibber, see Eaves and Kimpel, *Biography*, p. 182.

17 R. H. Barker, *Mr Cibber of Drury Lane* (New York: Columbia University Press, 1939), p. 239.

18 Eaves and Kimpel, *Biography*, p. 74.

19 *Selected Letters*, p. 87.

20 For Richardson's relations with Garrick, which became more intimate around this very year of 1748, see Eaves and Kimpel, *Biography*, pp. 460–1; Garrick to Richardson, 12 December 1748, *The Letters of David Garrick*, ed. D. M. Little and G. M. Kahrl (London: Oxford University Press, 1963), I, 95; and Richardson to Aaron Hill, 27 October 1748, in *Correspondence*, I, 123.

21 Eaves and Kimpel, *Biography*, pp. 183–4.

22 *Correspondence of Young*, pp. 501–2.

23 *The Poetical Works of Edward Young*, ed. Thomas Park (London: Sharpe, 1806), IV, 133.

24 For Richardson and Young, see Eaves and Kimpel, *Biography*, pp. 182–7; Forster, *Edward Young*, pp. 215–33. The biographers do not perhaps fully bring out the intimacy of the two men, reflected in phrases such as 'I love you, and delight in your conversation, which permits me to think of something more than what I see' (Young to Richardson, 17 July 1746: *Correspondence of Young*, p. 235). Young offered to supply Joseph Spence with biographical details after Richardson's death

(p. 544). For Richardson and Johnson, see Eaves and Kimpel, *Biography*, pp. 332–9; James L. Clifford, *Dictionary Johnson* (London: Heinemann, 1980), pp. 119–21.

25 *Correspondence of Young*, p. 311.
26 *Ibid.*, p. 314.
27 *Ibid.*, p. 338.
28 *Correspondence*, I, 102.
29 *Correspondence of Young*, pp. 354, 445; Shelley, *Life and Letters of Edward Young*, p. 190.
30 *Correspondence of Young*, p. 473; Shelley, *Life and Letters of Edward Young*, p. 247.
31 See *Correspondence of Young*, pp. 535–6.
32 Richardson's connection with *The Rambler* is documented by Eaves and Kimpel, *Biography*, p. 333. Both Richardson and Young considered that *The Rambler* equalled or even excelled *The Spectator*: see Forster, *Edward Young*, p. 257.
33 Boswell, *Life*, IV, 524.
34 Jocelyn Harris, 'Samuel Johnson, Samuel Richardson, and the Dial-Plate', *British Journal for Eighteenth-Century Studies*, 9 (1986), 157–63.
35 *Correspondence of Young*, p. 498: but see also pp. 550–1, 503.
36 Also in the print is the speaker's only daughter Anne Onslow, whose death in 1751 Young deplored in a letter to Richardson, asking his friend to pass on 'my duty and love' to Onslow: Young, *Correspondence*, p. 378.
37 See two essays in *The Widening Circle: Essays on the Circulation of Literature in Eighteenth-Century Europe*, ed. Paul Korshin (Philadelphia: University of Pennsylvania Press, 1976): R. M. Wiles, 'The Relish for Reading in Provincial England Two Centuries Ago', pp. 87–115; and Bernhard Fabian, 'English Books and their Eighteenth Century German Readers', pp. 119–96.
38 Eaves and Kimpel, *Biography*, pp. 574–8. Margaret Anne Doody has pointed out to me that Richardson's parallel feelings of admiration for Milton and Dryden should not be overlooked in this context.
39 *Correspondence of Young*, p. 449.
40 Samuel Johnson, *Lives of the Poets*, ed. G. B. Hill (Oxford: Clarendon Press, 1905), III, 395–6.
41 *English Critical Essays: XVIth–XVIIIth Centuries*, ed. Edmund D. Jones (London: Oxford University Press, 1922), p. 291.
42 Boswell, *Life*, V, 269–70.
43 *English Critical Essays*, pp. 298–99.
44 *Ibid.*, p. 305.
45 *Ibid.*, p. 301; 'Courtney Melmoth' (S. J. Pratt), *Observations on the Night Thoughts of Dr Young* (London: Richardson, 1776), p. 4; Forster, *Edward Young*, p. 257. Johnson had already written in 1751 (*Rambler* 121) of the perils of facile 'imitation', and had celebrated there 'that power of giving pleasure which novelty supplies'. It is worth mentioning that long before he actually met Young, Johnson is likely to have heard something of the poet from his own great friend Richard Savage. Young and Savage met in 1724 and were on terms of some intimacy thereafter: the latter's *Authors of the Town* (1725) is dedicated to the former. See

Clarence Tracy, *The Artificial Bastard: A Biography of Richard Savage* (Cambridge, Mass.: Harvard University Press, 1953), pp. 78–9.

46 *English Critical Essays*, p. 298.

47 William Roberts, *Memoirs of the Life and Correspondence of Mrs Hannah More* (London: Seeley, 1834), I, 169.

48 For an exchange between Richardson and Young on the nature of originality (i.e. whether it could inhere in both 'subject' and 'manner'), see *Correspondence of Young*, pp. 502–3.

49 *The Yale Edition of Horace Walpole's Correspondence* (New Haven: Yale University Press, 1937–83), XXIX, ed. W. S. Lewis, Grover Cronin, Jr, and Charles H. Bennett, p. 287.

50 Ruth Avaline Hesselgrave, *Lady Miller and the Batheaston Literary Circle* (New Haven: Yale University Press, 1927), p. 50.

51 Hesketh Pearson, *The Swan of Lichfield: A Selection of the Correspondence of Anna Seward* (London: H. Hamilton, 1936), p. 65.

52 For example, the impulse for *Resignation*, addressed to Frances Boscawen, came from a request the ladies made *en route* to Tunbridge in 1761: *Correspondence of Young*, p. 529.

53 *Letters from Mrs Elizabeth Carter to Mrs Montagu*, ed. Rev. Montagu Pennington (London: Rivington, 1817), I, 44.

54 Cited in *Correspondence of Young*, p. 541.

55 *Correspondence of Young*, p. 546. For Talbot and Carter in relation to Richardson, see Eaves and Kimpel, *Biography*, pp. 354–64; for their shared admiration for *Night Thoughts*, see *A Series of Letters between Mrs Elizabeth Carter and Miss Catherine Talbot*, ed. Montagu Pennington (London: Rivington, 1809), I, 68, 74–5. In the very same letter (9 October 1744) Carter refers to Johnson's *Life of Savage*: later, of course, she was to become a close friend of Johnson, to contribute papers to *The Rambler* and (unwittingly) to furnish a poem for the text of *Clarissa*.

56 For the views of Hester Piozzi, see William McCarthy, *Hester Thrale Piozzi: Portrait of a Literary Woman* (Chapel Hill: University of North Carolina Press, 1985), p. 68. Young was echoing the feelings expressed by many women readers when he asserted in a letter to Mary Delany that 'tho All may find their Advantage in [*Clarissa*], yet they that have daughters will find themselves, more particularly, indebted to Mr Richardson' (*Correspondence of Young*, p. 314). He went on to add: 'For, I conceive that *Clarissa*, may not improperly be calld – *The Whole Duty of* WOMAN.'

57 It is worth noting that just after Richardson's death, in December 1761, Hugh Kelly gave a list of contemporary writers in which Young was placed first and Johnson second (Goldsmith ranked sixteenth). See Samuel H. Woods Jr, 'Boswell's Presentation of Goldsmith: A Reconsideration', *Boswell's Life of Johnson: New Questions, New Answers*, ed. J. A. Vance (Athens, Georgia: University of Georgia Press, 1985), p. 246.

13 Isobel Grundy: 'A novel in a series of letters by a lady': Richardson
      and some Richardsonian novels

1 For influence of women both on and by Richardson see Jane Spencer, *The Rise of the Woman Novelist: Aphra Behn to Jane Austen* (Oxford: Blackwell, 1986), p. 89. For a suggestive and useful, though not complete or wholly accurate, list of 'Richardsonian' novels see Sarah W. R. Smith, *Samuel Richardson: A Reference Guide* (Boston: G. K. Hall, 1984), Appendix 1. Most of the research for this essay has been done for Virginia Blain, Patricia Clements, and Isobel Grundy, *A Feminist Companion to Literature in English* (Batsford and Yale University Press) forthcoming.

2 Eliza Haywood, *Anti-Pamela, or Feign'd Innocence Detected* (June 1741); Elizabeth, Lady Echlin, *An Alternative Ending to Richardson's Clarissa*, ed. Dimiter Daphinoff (Bern: Francke, 1982); Maria Susanna Cooper, *The Exemplary Mother* (1769) and *The Daughter* (1775); Jean Marishall, *A Series of Letters* (Edinburgh, 1788); Catharine (Macaulay) Graham, *Letters on Education, With Observations on Religious and Metaphysical Subjects* (London, 1790), p. 142–8; Laetitia-Matilda Hawkins, *Memoirs, Anecdotes, Facts and Opinions* (London, 1824), I, 195–9.

3 E.g. Gunning, *Fashionable Involvements*, I, 228, 231, II, 104; Green, *Parents and Wives*, I, 218, 220; *Quarterly Review*, III, 1807, p. 340, quoted in Patricia Voss-Clesly, *Tendencies of Character Depiction in the Domestic Novels of Burney, Edgeworth and Austen: A Consideration of Subjective and Objective World* (Salzburg: Institut für Anglistik und Amerikanistik, Universität Salzburg, 1979), p. 12.

4 Robert Palfrey Utter and Gwendolyn Bridges Needham, *Pamela's Daughters* (London: Lovat Dickson, 1937), despite its title, concentrates on fashions in (mostly lower-brow) fictional heroines, not on any specific influence. J. M. S. Tompkins, *The Popular Novel in England 1770–1800* (London: Constable, 1932), p. 339. Gerard A. Barker deals with revisions of Sir Charles himself by Burney, Frances Sheridan, Inchbald, Austen, and male writers: *Grandison's Heirs: The Paragon's Progress in the Late Eighteenth-Century English Novel* (Newark: University of Delaware Press, 1985).

5 See Barker, *Grandison's Heirs*; Margaret Anne Doody, 'Frances Sheridan: Morality and Annihilated Time', in *Fetter'd or Free? British Women Novelists, 1670–1815*, ed. Mary Anne Schofield and Cecilia Macheski (Athens: Ohio University Press, 1986), pp. 327, 339, 343; Lorraine McMullen, *An Odd Attempt in a Woman: The Literary Life of Frances Brooke* (Vancouver: University of British Columbia Press, 1983), pp. 60–1; Ralph W. Rader, 'From Richardson to Austen: "Johnson's Rule" and the Development of the Eighteenth-Century Novel of Moral Action', in *Johnson and His Age*, ed. James Engell (Cambridge, Mass.: Harvard University Press, 1984); Park Honan, 'Richardson's Influence on Jane Austen (Some Notes on the Biographical and Critical Problems of an "Influence")', in *Passion and Prudence*, ed. Myer, pp. 166, 168, 170, 174, 175–6; Nancy K. Miller, *The Heroine's Text: Readings in the French and English Novel, 1722–1782* (New York: Columbia University Press, 1980), pp. 153–4.

6　See Godfrey Frank Singer, *The Epistolary Novel: Its Origin, Development, Decline, and Residuary Influence* (Philadelphia: University of Pennsylvania Press, 1933).

7　Elizabeth Blower (who, after one fairly Richardsonian novel, switched from letters to narrative and became steadily less sharp and more sentimental), *Features from Life; or, A Summer Visit* (London [1788]), I, 12; II, 191, 192.

8　Elizabeth Griffith, *The Delicate Distress* in *Two Novels*, with Richard Griffith (London, 1769), I, 99, 137, 107–8, 120. Janet Todd treats the debate over women's friendship, and notes Richardson's key position in it, in *Women's Friendship in Literature* (New York: Columbia University Press, 1980).

9　*Delicate Distress*, II, 40; Joyce Tompkins observed in 1932 that this is a far better novel than R. B. Sheridan suggests in *The Rivals* (*Popular Novel*, p. 159). Yet Elizabeth R. Napier grants it merely 'a certain pathos' (*Dictionary of Literary Biography*, XXXIX: *British Novelists, 1660–1800*, ed. Martin C. Battestin (Detroit: Gale Research Company, 1985), I, 249).

10　Georgiana Spencer, later Duchess of Devonshire, *Emma; or, The Unfortunate Attachment. A Sentimental Novel* (London, 1773), I, 205–6; II, 145, 217ff., 223–4, 238ff., 245; III, 82.

11　*Emma; or, The Unfortunate Attachment*, II, 211, 124–5, III, 187, 189; *Clarissa*, III, 265–6; *II, 175–6*.

12　*Emma; or, The Unfortunate Attachment*, III, 46, 86–7, 201, 203.

13　Anna Maria Bennett, *Agnes De-Courci. A Domestic Tale* (Bath, 1789), 4 vols. I have sometimes altered punctuation in quoting. A Dublin edition, 2 vols., appeared the same year. The fact that Bennett is often wrongly called 'Agnes Maria' perhaps attests to this novel's popularity.

14　*Agnes*, I, 184ff., IV, 268ff.; *Clarissa*, VIII, 64–90; *IV, 390–410*; *Grandison*, III, 455.

15　*Simple Facts; or, The History of an Orphan* (1793). The Mrs Mathews of its title-page cannot be, as usually said, Eliza Kirkham (Strong) Mathews, who married in 1797 and had published under her maiden name in 1796.

16　*Simple Facts*, II, 127, 130, 148ff., 206, 212. Clarissa foresees 'common fame' reporting her as 'gone off with a man' (II, 316; *I, 471*).

17　Susan Staves, 'Matrimonial Discord in Fiction and in Court, The Case of Ann Masterman', in *Fetter'd or Free?*, ed. Schofield and Macheski, p. 173; Ann (Masterman) Skinn, *The Old Maid; or, The History of Miss Ravensworth* (London, [1771]), I, 86. Olivia's 'poniard' attack (*Grandison*, II, 380) is not relevant here: Emily seeks not revenge for coldness but an end to harrassment. It is not Emily but her favoured suitor who shoots at Lord Wilton.

18　*Secresy*, III, 117–18. Humanity 'is one vast republick', where every individual must labour to repay the benefits received from others; this labour 'none have a right to withdraw' (*Idler* no. 19, ed. W. J. Bate, John M. Bullitt, and L. F. Powell (New Haven and London: Yale University Press, 1963), I, 59).

19　*Secresy*, II, 84–5; *Clarissa*, III, 281; *II, 187*.

20　*Secresy*, II, 211–13, 216; *Clarissa*, IV, 202–3, 22, III, 185; *II, 382–3, 251, 114*.

21　*Secresy*, III, 249–50; *Clarissa*, VII, 236–9; *IV, 201–4*; VII, 425–8; *IV, 342–4*.

22　Annette Kolodny, 'A Map for Rereading: Gender and the Interpretation of

Literary Texts', in *The New Feminist Criticism: Essays on Women, Literature and Theory*, ed. Elaine Showalter (New York: Pantheon, 1985; London: Virago, 1986), p. 51.

14 Peter Sabor: Publishing Richardson's correspondence: the 'necessary office of selection'

1 Letter of 19 November 1747, *The Correspondence of Edward Young 1683–1765*, ed. Henry Pettit (Oxford: Clarendon Press, 1971), p. 289.
2 *Correspondence*, I, 320. Eaves and Kimpel provide an invaluable appendix in their *Biography*, listing the dates and present locations of Richardson's extant correspondence.
3 Letter of 2 June 1753, *The Richardson–Stinstra Correspondence and Stinstra's Prefaces to Clarissa*, ed. William C. Slattery (Carbondale and Edwardsville: Southern Illinois University Press, 1969), pp. 26, 27, 25.
4 *The Apprentice's Vade Mecum*, ed. Alan Dugald McKillop (Los Angeles: William Andrews Clark Memorial Library, 1975), p. i.
5 McKillop, *The Apprentice's Vade Mecum*, pp. i–ii.
6 *The Letters of Doctor George Cheyne to Samuel Richardson (1733–43)*, ed. Charles F. Mullett (Columbia, Missouri: University of Missouri Studies, vol. XVIII, 1943), p. 19.
7 Letter of 2 May 1742, Mullett, *Letters*, p. 96.
8 Letter of 13 December 1740, Mullett, *Letters*, p. 63.
9 The three surviving letters from Richardson to Cheyne are all included in John Carroll's *Selected Letters*.
10 The various forms of the Introduction are provided in *Samuel Richardson's Introduction to Pamela*, ed. Sheridan W. Baker, Jr (Los Angeles: William Andrews Clark Memorial Library, 1954).
11 Rogers, 'Richardson and the Bluestockings', in *Passion and Prudence*, ed. Myer, p. 152. Rogers also cites here his forthcoming article, 'Richardson, Garrick, Young, and the Pattern of Subscriptions: A Case Study'.
12 John Douglas to Silvester, 21 August 1759, quoted in Eaves and Kimpel, *Biography*, p. 470. Tom Keymer, whose Cambridge University Ph.D. dissertation, '"Mock Encounters": The Reader in Richardson's *Clarissa*' (1988), includes a stimulating discussion of the Silvester correspondence, notes that at some point Richardson scratched out the phrase 'to Posterity' and replaced it with 'to his Friends and Family'.
13 Although neither Reich's letters of 11 June and 7 September 1757 nor Richardson's replies are extant, they are quoted in Richardson's letter to Lady Bradshaigh of 2 January 1758, *Selected Letters*, p. 338.
14 The edition was printed in 1760; see Jocelyn Harris's chapter, p. 190.
15 John Nichols, *Literary Anecdotes of the Eighteenth Century* (London, 1812–15), IV, 581.
16 Malvin R. Zirker, Jr, 'Richardson's Correspondence: The Personal Letter as

Private Experience', in *The Familiar Letter in the Eighteenth Century*, ed. Howard Anderson, Philip B. Daghlian and Irvin Ehrenpreis (Lawrence, Kansas: University of Kansas Press, 1966), pp. 71–91.

17 Eaves and Kimpel, *Biography*, pp. 183–4, n.52. Henry Pettit, however, blames Barbauld entirely for this work of 'forgery' (*Correspondence of Edward Young*, p. xxxiv).

18 See Pettit, 'The Text of Edward Young's Letters to Samuel Richardson', *Modern Language Notes*, 57 (1942), 668–70.

19 Eaves and Kimpel, *Biography*, p. 657; Wood, 'The Chronology of the Richardson–Bradshaigh Correspondence of 1751', *Studies in Bibliography*, 33 (1980), 182–91.

20 *Correspondence*, I, 1–3, V, 145–9, I, 186–9; the corrections are made in Eaves and Kimpel's Appendix, 'Richardson's Correspondence'.

21 Letter of 6 June 1753, *Correspondence*, II, 176 and facsimile, VI, following p. 288.

22 New York: AMS Press, 1966.

23 *European Magazine*, 53–5 (1808–9), correspondence with Westcomb; *Monthly Magazine*, 33 (1812), with Carter; 36–47 (1813–19), with Young; 48 (1819), with Smollett.

24 See Pettit, *Correspondence of Young*, p. xxxiv.

25 E. L. McAdam, Jr, 'A New Letter from Fielding', *Yale Review*, 38 (1948), 300–10; Duncan E. Isles, 'The Lennox Collection', *Harvard Library Bulletin*, 18 (1970), 317–45.

26 Janet Butler, 'The Garden: Early Symbol of Clarissa's Complicity', *Studies in English Literature 1500–1900*, 24 (1984), 543. Two reviews of Carroll's edition criticize its byzantine typography: Robert Halsband, *New York Times Book Review*, 4 April 1965, p. 19; John Preston, *Modern Language Review*, 61 (1966), 500.

27 *Anti-Jacobin Review*, 19 (1804), 171; *Imperial Review*, 2 (1804), 419; *Literary Magazine*, 2 (1804), 522–33. These reviews are listed by Sarah W. R. Smith, *Samuel Richardson: A Reference Guide* (Boston: G. K. Hall, 1984), which also notes the attribution to Charles Brockden Brown (p. 109). Other reviews are listed by Richard Gordon Hannaford, *Samuel Richardson: An Annotated Bibliography of Critical Studies* (New York: Garland, 1980).

28 *Critical Review*, 3rd series 3 (1804), 282; *Eclectic Review*, 1 (1805), 127; *Edinburgh Review*, 5 (1804), 44, 33–34.

29 *Times Literary Supplement*, 18 February 1965, p. 128.

30 Golden, *Journal of English and Germanic Philology*, 64 (1965), 741.

31 Watt, *University of Toronto Quarterly*, 35 (1966), 211; Read, *Canadian Literature*, 27 (1966), 77.

32 Trickett, *Review of English Studies*, 17 (1966), 326.

33 Kelly, *Philological Quarterly*, 49 (1970), 376.

34 *Times Literary Supplement*, 25 September 1969, p. 1106.

35 Carroll, *Review of English Studies*, 22 (1971), 219.

36 Miller, dust-jacket comment on Warner's *Reading Clarissa: The Struggles of Interpretation*.

37 Forster Collection, XIII, 3, fos. 59, 60.

38 'The Composition of *Clarissa* and its Revision before Publication', *PMLA*, 83 (1968), 420.

39 Forster Collection, XIII, 3, fo. 60.

40 Forster Collection, XIII, 3, fos. 61, 62.

41 Forster Collection, XIII, 3, fos. 65, 66.

42 Letter of 5 January 1747; *Selected Letters*, p. 75.

43 'The Composition of *Clarissa*', p. 424.

44 Letter of 23 January 1747, Forster Collection, XIII, 3, fos. 82–4.

45 Letter of 26 January 1747, *Selected Letters*, pp. 78–83.

46 Letter of 9 February 1747, Forster Collection, XIII, 3, fos. 89, 91–2.

47 'The Composition of *Clarissa*', p. 425.

48 *The Works of the Late Aaron Hill* (London, 1753), II, 269–70.

49 *The Providence of Wit in the English Letter Writers* (Durham, North Carolina: Duke University Press, 1955), p. 271; Zirker, 'Richardson's Correspondence', p. 81.

50 Redford, *The Converse of the Pen: Acts of Intimacy in the Eighteenth-Century Familiar Letter* (Chicago: University of Chicago Press, 1986), p. 1.

51 Swabey, 'Conventions of Characterization in Samuel Richardson's Personal, Model, and Fictive Letters', Ph.D. thesis, University of Michigan, 1984; Keymer, 'Mock Encounters'.

52 Letter of 14 February 1755; *An Alternative Ending to Richardson's Clarissa*, ed. Dimiter Daphinoff (Bern: Francke, 1982), p. 178.

15 Siobhán Kilfeather: The rise of Richardson criticism

1 It is impossible to discuss more than a fraction of the mass of recent criticism on Richardson, and in attempting to indicate the variety of that criticism I have inevitably passed over some fine essays and books of great service to Richardson scholars. Where limitations have made themselves felt, I have attempted to introduce as many of the more recent books and essays as space permits.

2 Dorothy Van Ghent, *The English Novel: Form and Function* (New York: Rinehart, 1953); Watt, *The Rise of the Novel*.

3 *Pamela; or, Virtue Rewarded*, ed. T. C. Duncan Eaves and Ben D. Kimpel (Boston: Houghton Mifflin, 1971); and *Pamela*, ed. Peter Sabor, with an introduction by Margaret A. Doody (Harmondsworth: Penguin, 1980). It is perhaps owing to its place in the curriculum that *Pamela* is the only one of Richardson's novels to have been distinguished by a collection of critical essays: *Twentieth-Century Interpretations of 'Pamela': A Collection of Critical Essays*, ed. Rosemary Cowler (Englewood Cliffs, NJ: Prentice-Hall, 1969). Monographs on *Pamela* include James Louis Fortuna, *'The Unsearchable Wisdom of God': A Study of Providence in Richardson's 'Pamela'* (Gainesville: University Presses of Florida, 1980); Bernard Kreissman, *Pamela–Shamela* (Lincoln: University of Nebraska Press, 1960); and Christian Pons, *Pamela* (Paris: A. Colin, 1970).

4 Jina Politi, *The Novel and its Presuppositions: Changes in the Conceptual Structure of Novels in the 18th and 19th Centuries* (Amsterdam: Adolf M. Hakkert, 1976), p. 91.

5 Morris Golden, *Richardson's Characters* (Ann Arbor: University of Michigan Press, 1963).

6 Morris Golden, 'Public Context and Imagining Self in *Clarissa*', *Studies in English Literature*, 25 (1985), 575–98; 'Public Context and Imagining Self in *Sir Charles Grandison*', *The Eighteenth Century: Theory and Interpretation*, 29 (1988), 3–18.

7 Sale, *Master Printer*; Eaves and Kimpel, *Biography*; see also the still influential study by Alan Dugald McKillop, *Samuel Richardson: Printer and Novelist* (Chapel Hill: University of North Carolina Press, 1936).

8 Cynthia Griffin Wolff, *Samuel Richardson and the Eighteenth-Century Puritan Character* (Hamden, Connecticut: Archon Books, 1972), p. 4.

9 John Preston, *The Created Self: The Reader's Role in Eighteenth-Century Fiction* (London: Heinemann, 1970) remains one of the most impressive attempts to define the self in terms of the construction of the reader's contribution to interpretation; Stephen Cox, *'The Stranger Within Thee': Concepts of the Self in Late Eighteenth-Century Literature* (Pittsburgh: University of Pittsburgh Press, 1980) has a chapter on *Clarissa*; Nancy Armstrong, *Desire and Domestic Fiction: A Political History of the Novel* (Oxford: Oxford University Press, 1987), a recent Marxist–feminist revision of the rise of the novel, has a chapter on strategies of self-production in *Pamela*.

10 Roy Roussel, *The Conversation of the Sexes: Seduction and Equality in Selected Seventeenth- and Eighteenth-Century Texts* (Oxford: Oxford University Press, 1986).

11 Terry J. Castle, 'P/B: *Pamela* as Sexual Fiction', *Studies in English Literature*, 22 (1982), pp. 469–89.

12 For a more masculinist perspective on the Oedipal conflict in *Pamela* see John Dussinger, 'What Pamela Knew: An Interpretation', *Journal of English and Germanic Philology*, 377–93.

13 *The Letters of Samuel Johnson*, ed. R. W. Chapman (Oxford: Clarendon Press, 1952), Letter 31, p. 30; Letter 49, p. 49.

14 The reader's memory of Richardson's novels is even more confounded by the lack of authoritative texts. With *Clarissa* in particular, each rereading may be of a text literally different.

15 Castle, *Clarissa's Ciphers*; Eagleton, *The Rape of Clarissa*; Rita Goldberg, *Sex and Enlightenment: Women in Richardson and Diderot* (Cambridge: Cambridge University Press, 1984); Kinkead-Weekes, *Dramatic Novelist*; Warner, *Reading Clarissa*.

16 Florian Stuber and Margaret Doody, *Clarissa: A Theater Work, Part 1* appeared Off Off Broadway at the West Side Theater in October–November 1984; James Ivory directed *Jane Austen in Manhattan* (Merchant Ivory Productions, 1980), based on *Jane Austen's 'Sir Charles Grandison'*, ed. Brian Southam (Oxford: Clarendon Press, 1980).

17 Christopher Hill, 'Clarissa Harlowe and her Times', *Essays in Criticism*, 5 (1955), 315–40.

18 Lawrence Stone, *The Family, Sex and Marriage in England 1500–1800* (London: Weidenfeld and Nicolson, 1977).

19 Watt, *The Rise of the Novel*, p. 270.

20 Frank Kermode, 'Richardson and Fielding', *Cambridge Journal*, 4 (1950), 106–14.

21 Watt, *The Rise of the Novel*, p. 187.
22 Margaret Anne Doody, 'The Man-made World of Clarissa Harlowe and Robert Lovelace', in *Passion and Prudence*, ed. Myer, 52–77. Watt reviews the limitations of his own work in *Novel*, 1 (1968), 205–218; Diana Spearman is one commentator who rejects the importation of nineteenth-century class-analysis into discussion of the eighteenth century – see Spearman, *The Novel and Society* (London: Routledge and Kegan Paul, 1966). Other major revisions of Watt include feminist works by Nancy Armstrong, and by Jane Spencer, *The Rise of the Woman Novelist: From Aphra Behn to Jane Austen* (Oxford: Basil Blackwell, 1986).
23 Michael McKeon, *The Origins of the English Novel, 1600–1740* (Baltimore: The Johns Hopkins University Press, 1987), p. 1.
24 Terry Lovell, *Consuming Fiction*, in the *Questions for Feminism* series (London: Verso, 1987).
25 Lovell, like Nancy Armstrong, does not engage in any extended discussion of eighteenth-century women writers. Spencer, *The Rise of the Woman Novelist* and Dale Spender, *Mothers of the Novel: 100 Good Women Writers Before Jane Austen* (London: Pandora Press, 1987) are two of the most frequently cited book-length accounts of a female tradition in eighteenth-century fiction.
26 Eagleton's study, of course, in its title, in Blackwell's original cover picture (a detail from Fragonard's *Le Verrou*), and in its liberal dose of prurient quotation, participates in the general critical tendency to make discussion of female sexuality sensational.
27 V. S. Pritchett, *The Living Novel* (New York: Reynal and Hitchcock, 1947), p. 28.
28 Janet Todd, *Women's Friendship in Literature* (New York: Columbia University Press, 1980), pp. 9–68.
29 Florian Stuber, 'On Fathers and Authority in *Clarissa*', *Studies in English Literature*, 25 (1985), 557–74. Stuber's account of male authority in the novel is a useful supplement and corrective to Todd.
30 Leslie Fiedler, *Love and Death in the American Novel* (New York: Stein and Day, 1960).
31 Sue Warrick Doederlin, 'Forum: Clarissa in the Hands of the Critics', *Eighteenth-Century Studies*, 16 (1983), 402–3.
32 Samuel Richardson, *Sir Charles Grandison*, ed. Jocelyn Harris (Oxford: Oxford University Press, 1972; reprinted by Oxford in The World's Classics, 1986).
33 See Warner, *Reading Clarissa*, p. 267; and Castle, *Clarissa's Ciphers*, pp. 189–90.
34 Florian Stuber persuasively suggest 'if an editor followed Richardson in printing the text with "Dots, or inserted Full-points" before the lines of "revised" or "restored" passages, the reader could himself analyse and judge the wisdom of Richardson's later additions': Florian Stuber, 'On Original and Final Intentions, or Can There Be an Authoritative *Clarissa?*', *TEXT: Transactions of the Society for Textual Scholarship*, 2 (1985), 241. Doody and Stuber's recent analysis should convince anyone still in any doubt that the Sherburn abbreviation is a serious misrepresentation of Richardson's novel: Margaret Anne Doody and Florian Stuber, '*Clarissa* Censored', *Modern Language Studies*, 18 (1988), 74–88.

35 Ira Konigsberg approaches the same issue from a different perspective, arguing that the modern English novel grew out of a fusion of drama and fiction, and seeking to locate this fusion in Richardson: *Samuel Richardson and the Dramatic Novel* (Lexington: University of Kentucky Press, 1968).

36 Rosemary Bechler, ' "Trial by what is contrary": Samuel Richardson and Christian Dialectic', in *Passion and Prudence*, ed. Myer, pp. 93–113; John Dussinger, 'Conscience and the Pattern of Christian Perfection in *Clarissa*', *PMLA*, 81 (1966), 236–45; Margaret Anne Doody, *A Natural Passion*, pp. 178–82; Carol Houlihan Flynn, *Man of Letters*, pp. 3–49.

37 Alan Wendt, 'Clarissa's Coffin', *Philological Quarterly*, 39 (1960), 481–95.

38 Gillian Beer, 'Richardson, Milton, and the Status of Evil', *Review of English Studies*, new series 19 (1968), 261–70.

39 Leo Braudy, 'Penetration and Impenetrability in *Clarissa*', *New Aspects of the Eighteenth Century. Essays from the English Institute*, ed. Philip Harth (New York: Columbia University Press, 1974).

40 See also William Beatty Warner, 'Proposal and Habitation: The Temporality and Authority of Interpretation in and about a Scene of Richardson's *Clarissa*', *boundary 2, 7 (1979), 169–99.*

41 Castle, *Clarissa's Ciphers*, p. 15.

42 Castle, *Clarissa's Ciphers*, pp. 24–5.

43 Ann Douglas, *The Feminization of American Culture* (New York: Avon Books, 1978); Jean H. Hagstrum, *Sex and Sensibility: Ideal and Erotic Love from Milton to Mozart* (Chicago: University of Chicago Press, 1980).

44 J. Paul Hunter, *Occasional Form: Henry Fielding and the Chain of Circumstance* (Baltimore: Johns Hopkins University Press, 1975), p. 214.

45 Peter Sabor, '*Amelia* and *Sir Charles Grandison*: The Convergence of Fielding and Richardson', *Wascana Review*, 17 (1982), 3–18.

46 Sylvia Kasey Marks, *Sir Charles Grandison: The Compleat Conduct Book* (Lewisburg, Pa.: Bucknell University Press, 1986).

47 Gerard A. Barker, *Grandison's Heirs: The Paragon's Progress in the Late Eighteenth-Century English Novel* (Newark: University of Delaware Press, 1985).

48 Tony Tanner, *Adultery in the Novel: Contract and Transgression* (Baltimore: Johns Hopkins University Press, 1979), p. 178. Other comparative discussions of Richardson in the context of eighteenth-century French writing include Rita Goldberg; Marie-Paule Laden, *Self-Imitation in the Eighteenth-Century Novel* (Princeton: Princeton University Press, 1987); and Nancy K. Miller, *The Heroine's Text: Readings in the French and English Novel, 1722–1782* (New York: Columbia University Press, 1980).

49 Janet Todd, *Sensibility. An Introduction* (London: Methuen, 1986).

50 John Bender, *Imagining the Penitentiary: Fiction and the Architecture of Mind in Eighteenth-Century England* (Chicago: University of Chicago Press, 1987).

51 Robert A. Erickson, *Mother Midnight: Birth, Sex, and Fate in Eighteenth-Century Fiction (Defoe, Richardson, and Sterne)* (New York: AMS Press, 1986).

52 Christina Marsden Gillis, *The Paradox of Privacy: Epistolary Form in Clarissa* (Gainesville: University Presses of Florida, 1983).

53 Terry Castle, *Masquerade and Civilization: The Carnivalesque in Eighteenth-Century Culture and Fiction* (Stanford: Stanford University Press, 1986).

54 William M. Sale Jr, *Samuel Richardson, A Bibliographical Record of His Literary Career* (New Haven: Yale University Press, 1936); Richard Gordon Hannaford, *Samuel Richardson: An Annotated Bibliography of Critical Studies* (New York: Garland, 1980); Sarah W. R. Smith, *Samuel Richardson: A Reference Guide* (Boston: G. K. Hall, 1984); there is also a short annotated bibliography by John Carroll in *The English Novel: Select Bibliographic Guides*, ed. A. E. Dyson (Oxford: Oxford University Press, 1974).

55 For example, Doody, Kinkead-Weekes, and Elizabeth Bergen Brophy, *Samuel Richardson: The Triumph of Craft* (Knoxville: University of Tennessee Press, 1974).

Index